Economic
Policy-Making

Economic Policy-Making

Rosalind Levačić

Lecturer in Economics
The Open University

WHEATSHEAF BOOKS · SUSSEX
BARNES & NOBLE BOOKS · NEW JERSEY

First published in Great Britain in 1987 by
WHEATSHEAF BOOKS LTD
A MEMBER OF THE HARVESTER PRESS PUBLISHING GROUP
Publisher: John Spiers
16 Ship Street, Brighton, Sussex
and in the USA by
BARNES & NOBLE BOOKS
81 Adams Drive, Totowa, New Jersey 07512

© Rosalind Levačić, 1987

British Library Cataloguing in Publication Data
Levačić, Rosalind
    Economic policy-making: its theory and
    practice.
    1. Economic policy
    I. Title
    330.9   HD87

    ISBN 0-7108-0291-9
    ISBN 0-7108-0218-8 Pbk

Library of Congress Cataloging-in-Publication Data
Levačić, Rosalind.
    Economic policy-making.

    Includes bibliographies.
    1. Economic policy. 2. Great Britain—Economic
    policy. I. Title.
    HD75.L48   1987   338.941   87-11543
    ISBN 0-389-20741-1

Typeset in 10pt Times by Woodfield Graphics, Fontwell,
Arundel, West Sussex

Printed in Great Britain by Biddles Ltd, Guildford and King's Lynn

To
Anna

Contents

Preface

The idea of writing this book originated while I was working on an interdisciplinary Open University course, Decision Making in Britain. This was the first time I had strayed from the straight and narrow path of teaching economics on economics courses. It made me realise that economists have traditionally ignored how economic policy is actually made, sticking instead to their particular speciality—offering policy advice on the presumption that policy makers are rational decision takers who have clearly defined objectives and trade-offs between these objectives which they seek to attain to the best of their ability given the economic constraints they face.

This rational approach to economic policy-making largely ignores or assumes away the distributional conflicts that the political system resolves in a different way than the market does; it also neglects the institutional context in which economic policy is made and how this affects policy outcomes. Once these factors are taken into account it becomes evident that economic policies are the outcome of a political bargaining process in which the rational policy-making approach that distinguishes the economist's contribution is but one element.

Economists who have worked as policy advisers are usually conscious of the significance of political bargaining in the making of economic policy, as was made clear by David Henderson in his 1985 Reith Lectures. A common concern has now developed across a number of fields of economics with how economic agents respond to the sanctions and incentives operated by different kinds of institutions and systems of allocating resources. Economists are now more interested in what goes on inside firms and state bureaucracies, focusing in particular on the ways in which internal and external incentives and sanctions determine how resources are allocated and distributed. Industrial economics and public choice economics are examples of two fields where these issues are of central concern. It is notable that under the Thatcher government the notions of managerial efficiency have been given pride of place rather than those of optimal resource allocation, applied via such techniques as marginal cost pricing or cost-benefit analysis, which flowered in the days of greater certainty and consensus.

However the teaching of economic policy by economics teachers has not been sufficiently informed by these considerations and developments. Much of it is still firmly rooted in the rational approach to economic policy, as if students were being trained as mini economic advisers for an ideal world of rational collective decision makers. This approach fails to educate students as citizens who can understand how economic policy is actually made. This book is largely aimed at those readers who are not going to be specialist economic advisers applying the tools peculiar to the trade, but who do want a better understanding of how economic policy is made and how it can be appraised. Because of the importance given to political decision-making within institutions the general principles are developed in the context of actual institutions and policies. So this is a book about economic policy-making in Britain, though the basic analysis is applicable to all representative democracies. The rationale of the book and its structure are explained in the Introduction. This may, however, not be fully comprehensible to those new to economics, for whom the book is intended to be accessible; such readers may prefer to start at chapter 1 and read the Introduction later. The concepts needed to understand the issues discussed in the book are developed as the book unfolds; the exposition is mainly verbal and geometry is only used when I have judged it to be essential in explaining a concept.

Both the ideas in this book and the way in which they are presented are the product of many influences, including my Open University colleagues and others who over the years have commented on my efforts to understand and communicate economics. I would like to thank them all, especially Alan Gillie and Alex Rebmann, for reading the book thoroughly and giving detailed advice, and John Black, Wheatsheaf's assessor, for his detailed comments. I remain responsible for the final structure and content, errors and omissions. Thanks also to Sasha Rebmann for helping with computer graphics, to Betty Atkinson for secretarial assistance and to Doreen Warwick and Debbie Coast for helping with the typing. I am also grateful to the developers of cheap personal computers and word processors who have freed unskilled typists like me from pen, paper and tippex. Finally a special thank you to Alex, Sasha and Anna for their practical support and tolerance over the two years this book has taken from the first hesitant word to this final one.

Introduction

This book is about economic policy and the making of economic policy. The word *making* in the title is significant because it indicates the book's synthesis of the approaches of the disciplines of economics and politics to the study of economic policy, and so draws on the relevant strengths of each to counterbalance their particular weaknesses. The strength of economics lies in its analysis of the economic impact of policy measures. However, economics is relatively weak at explaining how economic policy is actually made because of its assumption that it is the outcome of rational decision-making procedures. The prerequisite for a rational policy-making procedure is that all those involved in making the decision can agree on a collective set of objectives. Having done that they can then seek and implement the policy measures which best achieve those objectives. The distinctive approach of economics is its presumption that economic behaviour can be analysed and hence explained as if it were based on rational action.

However this premise runs into much greater problems when collective, rather than individual, decisions are analysed. The problem is not necessarily that individuals are non-rational; it is that a group consisting of rational individuals pursuing different preferences has to solve the problem of whose preferences to satisfy and to what extent. There is no readily available mechanism for ensuring that a consistent set of priorities for policy can be agreed. Majority voting is one way of choosing what to do but it does not necessarily produce consistent policy choices. Economists have spent much effort in exploring the problem of developing decision rules for rational collective decision-making in a branch of the discipline known as welfare economics. But the practical decision rule they have produced—cost-benefit analysis—has only been accorded very limited application in government (notably to trunk road investment in the UK). The reason for this is that politicians and interest groups have been unwilling to accept its solution for adjudicating between conflicting

1

preferences, such as those between road users and environmentalists over motorways.

The strength of the politics discipline for explaining how policy is actually made is its full recognition that collective decision-making is undertaken by individuals and groups with conflicts of interest, within specific organisations and institutions, and in the context of existing rules and procedures. The discipline provides empirical, detailed explanations of how political systems and government bureaucracies take policy decisions and implement them. It has no methodological presumption that collective behaviour is rational, and many of its practitioners go further and reject the assumption that individuals behave rationally. However the weakness of the discipline in studying economic policy is its focus on policy-making to the exclusion of much interest in the content of policy and its ultimate impact on the economy. The latter is the province of economists.

So I have drawn on the analytical strengths of economics to provide criteria for assessing the impact of economic policy. In particular two criteria are singled out and used extensively throughout the book. These are *allocative efficiency* and *distribution*; or, less formally, the effects of a policy on the total size of the kitty available for distribution, and the way the kitty is shared out amongst the individuals who make up society. The various meanings of the terms *efficiency* and *distribution* are explained and explored in the context of specific policies, concerning taxation, the welfare state, agriculture and the nationalised industries, to name a few.

The criteria of *efficiency* and *distribution* are interwoven with another central theme of the book; this is, that economic policy in a mixed economy is fundamentally about the respective roles of market forces and government in the provision and production of goods and services. The distinctive contribution of economics is to demonstrate how the criteria of efficiency and distribution can be used to assess whether market or government provision is the better mechanism for providing a particular good or service. Controversy over the relative merits and failures of the two systems has remained a fundamental issue in economics since it emerged as a discrete area of human knowledge some 200 years ago. This controversy remains at the heart of political disagreement, and has become more acute in the last ten years when the postwar consensus over the managed mixed economy broke down.

The market and political systems are different ways in which individuals can signal their preferences for goods and services. In a market this is done by exchanging goods and services for money. In the political market it is done by citizens exchanging votes with politicians in return for policy promises. Exchange is fundamental to both systems. The basis of government is that citizens agree to give up the freedom to do as they like and accept the constraints and obligations of government in return for its collective benefits. Citizens agree to compulsory taxation in order to finance the collective provision of goods and services by government.

In a liberal democracy the powers of government are limited by a constitution and by its accountability to its citizens in regular, free elections. Voting, whether for representatives or directly in referenda for policies, is one important way in which citizens register their preferences. But there is also continual agitation by a wide range of political interests, many of whom are organised into pressure groups. Some have direct access to government, others campaign stridently outside government; some do both to various degrees. Policy-making by government is the result of responding to these various pressures and producing some workable resolution of conflicting interests. The process is essentially one of bargaining between the various political interests, some of whom are represented by different organs of government. A particular interest group, such as teachers, offers its continued cooperation, or threatens disruption, in return for favourable legislation or state finance. The government is itself a sprawling web of interests, some of whom form coalitions, while others are antagonistic. Any policy outcome is the consequence of pressures exerted by various political interests in the context of particular rules and procedures which constrain what can be done. This book argues strongly that economic policy-making is best understood as the outcome of political bargaining, in which rational decision-making procedures may provide a subsidiary input.

Hence the criterion of *distribution* is directly linked to the important role of political interests in policy-making. Each one argues the case for redistribution in its favour. Their presence also explains why the economists' criterion of *efficiency* has not taken root as a depoliticised method of taking collective decisions. This is because the efficiency criterion does have distributional implications and these are not generally acceptable. The economists' models of policy-making and rational decision rules are primarily an aid to the essentially political process of policy-making. The weakness of the traditional economics approach to policy-making, with its concentration on relating the instruments of policy to predetermined objectives, is that it ignores the political and institutional context in which policy is made and the consequent difficulty of determining objectives. However the influence of the public choice economists has been slowly percolating down over the last thirty years.[1] Economists are now beginning to look into the black box of governmental and political institutions, in order to provide explanations and predictions of how policy is made and with what consequences. In this book I attempt to do this in order to examine the implications for the formulation and implementation of economic policy of the political and institutional contexts in which it is made.

But once an economist does this he or she is no longer on home ground but has crossed into territory occupied by other disciplines. In particular the methodology of economics, which is to analyse agents as if they were utility-maximisers, is no longer the obvious one to use. However the public choice school of economists has, over the last thirty years, developed a strong body of theory, together with some empirical support, based on the premise that individuals behave with respect to political decisions and within governmental organisations with the same self-interested motivations as they do in the marketplace. The chief actors in the policy-making process—the voters, the politicians and the public sector bureaucrats—are assumed to behave so as to maximise their own utility. On the basis of this assumption, deductions are made as to how the different preferences of the three sets of actors are reflected in economic policy outcomes.

The public choice perspective can be married with the approaches to policy-making of other disciplines, such as politics and organisation studies. There is nothing inconsistent in assuming that the individuals involved in the various stages of policy-making are rational in the pursuit of their personal ends, while collective decision-making itself is a non-rational activity which is best explained as a bargaining process between political interests, each attempting to further their objectives to the best of their ability.

In developing this analysis and description of economic policy-making within the confines of a manageable book, there is a lot that I have left out. In particular I have not followed the standard economists' approach to economic policy, which concentrates on the relationship between economic policy objectives and policy instruments, with little attention, except at a very abstract level, to the political processes through which economic policy emerges. As this book focuses on economic policy-making, I have paid little attention to models of how the economy itself works, which describe relationships between those variables that are the objectives of economic policy and the instrumental variables that the government can operate upon. To do this would be to cover the whole of positive economics and to reproduce what is readily available elsewhere. I have instead deliberately concentrated on the use of policy instruments, assessed against the criteria of efficiency and distribution—constructs which typify the economist's approach to the analysis of policy. But I have brought in much more of the political and institutional processes which determine how economic policy is formulated and implemented. However, this book is not a detailed examination of the stages and processes of the formulation and implementation of particular economic policies, which would be an entirely political or public administration perspective on policy-making; for combined with an economics perspective, this would result in an impossibly long book. The book aims to convey general insights into the political and institutional processes through which economic policy is formulated and implemented, and the impact of these upon economic policy outcomes. I therefore fleshed out the more abstract contributions of the economic analysis of policy, in particular those of welfare economics and the public choice school, with illustrative details of the institutional and procedural aspects of actual policy-making in Britain.

The advantages of a clearly analytical approach, which is characteristic of economics, is that it provides a general framework for organising one's understanding of the world. In developing analytical constructs, such as the concept of *efficiency*, I have tried to avoid the excessive, and often empty, formalism of economics, which so often repels people who are interested in the subject matter of economics but who perceive that, unless they want to gain entry to the community of professional economists, the mathematicisation of economics is not necessary to understand economic policy issues. Such people quite sensibly do not want to invest considerable effort in acquiring the technical apparatus without which so many academic economists feel naked and ashamed. So I have deliberately made this book non-technical. There are no equations and only a few diagrams. All the concepts are explained verbally. Often they are introduced and then amplified and illustrated in later sections of the book. Nevertheless some difficult ideas are discussed, but they are not cloaked in mathematics.

PLAN OF THE BOOK

The book is divided into three parts. The core of the book is Part II, which concentrates on the analysis of policy-making by examining the roles of the chief actors—voters, politicians and public sector bureaucrats. In part, their impact on economic policy is analysed from the public choice perspective, but this is amplified by supporting descriptive and empirical material. A simple model underlies my exposition of policy-making. It is that policy-making is a process into which the major sets of actors feed inputs in the form of actions and decisions. They do this in the context of existing institutions, rules and procedures, which themselves help to determine the policy outcomes that emerge from politcal bargaining between the various interests.

But as the central concerns of Part II are somewhat abstract—albeit illustrated with practical examples—I have postponed it until the scene has been set, by introducing the basic themes and concepts in the context of descriptive material on specific economic policies. Many of the points emphasised in Part II, such as the importance of political interests and political bargaining in the making of economic policy, first occur in the opening chapters of Part I.

The book proper begins in Chapter 1 by defining economic policy as the use of government as an allocative and distributive mechanism in contradistinction to the market or to non-market private sector institutions, such as families and charities. Economic policy is thus defined in the context of the mixed economy. Chapter 2 provides a parallel treatment of the political system of liberal representative democracy in the context of UK and foreign governmental institutions through which economic policy affecting the UK is made.

Chapter 3 uses a case-study of the 1984–85 miners' strike to demonstrate how government and the market allocative systems interact in a mixed economy. It also provides a vehicle for introducing the key concepts of *efficiency* and *distribution*. Chapters 4 and 5 together describe and analyse two basic instruments of economic policy—government expenditure and taxation—using in a preliminary way the concepts of efficiency and distribution. They also illustrate the roles of political interests and institutional procedures in the formulation and implementation of policy. It is shown how these factors account for the non-rational aspects of public expenditure determination and tax-setting. Part I concludes with an analytical chapter on government and the market as allocative and distributive mechanisms. It presents the arguments for and against market and government allocation, subdivided into three main considerations: *efficiency, distribution* and the *ethical attributes* of an allocative mechanism. This brings in Austrian school and socialist ideas, in contrast to the technically pragmatic stance of neoclassical welfare economics.

The analytical core of the book is Part II. It is here that I have developed the case that economists' preoccupation with devising decision rules for collective rationality has led them to neglect the study of how economic policy is actually made. However, my approach to the investigation of policy-making is essentially that of an economist. I have imported from economics a central concern with how the preferences of all the individuals in a society are combined or aggregated into the expression of collective preference that is government policy. In examining this central issue I make considerable use of the methodology of public choice economics, which relies on the assumption that voters, politicians and bureaucrats aim to maximise their personal utility.

The sequence of the material presented in Part II starts from a simple ideal model of the policy process, which is then modified to reflect reality. In an ideal representative democracy, voters elect politicians to a legislative assembly on the basis of the policies the politicians advocate. Thus the elected representatives choose policy options which have the backing of the majority of the electorate. These policies are then implemented by neutral and dispassionate public service officials. So the first link in this policy-making sequence is that between electors and politicians, investigated in Chapter 7. To what extent do voters' preferences count? Or are they ill-informed and gullible so that politicians can gain power to pursue their own preferences? The next link in the chain, examined in Chapter 8, is that between politicians and state sector bureaucrats. Do the latter use their powers over the implementation of policy and the provision of information to further their own interests rather than to attend to the voters' preferences as expressed through their elected representatives? Chapter 9 considers the role of political interests and pressure groups, both within and outside government. These channels of pressure supplement, and probably dominate, voting as a method of registering preferences and are used by citizens, politicians and bureaucrats. The all-pervasive presence of political interests makes political bargaining rather than rational decision-making the primary form of economic policy-making.

The final chapter in Part II considers the position of economists as policy advisers. Their specialist contribution is devising schemes for rational policy-making, by providing information on which measures will best achieve the objectives sought from economic policy. In some scenarios the economists leave the political process to determine the objectives, in others the economist offers his own solution to the problem of aggregating society's preferences by providing decision rules to implement the criterion of social efficiency. Both approaches are used in government departments which employ economists. I have deliberately placed the economist's role last. In order to appreciate its significance—or lack of it—in the policy-making process one must see it in the context of the overall picture. Because of their particular specialism, economists are apt not to perceive that the contribution of rational policy-making techniques is a relatively subsidiary one.

The influence of economic ideas in policy-making is probably much more significant. Here they contribute both to the general climate of opinion that impinges upon policy-makers and to the cases argued by political interests. Pressure groups stating a case to government, or seeking the aura of intellectual respectability, will use economic argument and employ sympathetic economists to undertake such argument on their behalf. I can no longer entirely agree with Keynes' well-known passage;

I am sure the power of vested interests is vastly exaggerated compared to the gradual encroachment of ideas. Not, indeed, immediately, but after a certain interval; for in the field of economic and political philosophy there are not many who are influenced by new theories after they are twenty-five or thirty years of age, so the ideas which civil servants and politicians and even agitators apply to current events are not likely to be the newest. But, soon or late, it is ideas, not vested interests, which are dangerous for good or evil.[2]

I am not so dismissive of the influence of interests relative to ideas. The lifetime of some economic nostrums is short nowadays and the activities of political interests and pressure groups more intense than in the 1930s. Economic arguments and ideas are often the bedfellows of particular interests. I had originally intended a separate chapter on the influence of economic thinkers, but time, space and prudence prevented its inclusion. Instead, I have referred to economic schools, such as Keynesians, monetarists, supply-siders, Austrians, libertarians and socialists.

Finally, Part III presents some important areas of economic policy, all characterised by a significant extent of government intervention in the workings of the economy. I have made no attempt to be comprehensive. My aim is to demonstrate the usefulness of the ideas developed in Parts I and II for understanding how economic policies are arrived at, what can be said about their implications for efficiency and distribution, and why, in some instances, reform on rational lines is so difficult to achieve. Some major areas of policy are covered—public corporations, the welfare state and agricultural policy. I have not written a separate chapter on macroeconomic policy because it is discussed in the chapters on government expenditure and taxation, and in the chapter on economists as rational optimisers. Given space limitations I decided it would be better to concentrate on micro-level policies than to attempt a short piece on monetary policy which, given the complexity of the subject, would be either unsatisfactory or incomprehensible. I have made several references to the place of the Bank of England in the scheme of things; it is of course a political interest too.

It should be evident from this account of the organisation of the book that its structure is not a simple linear one but a spiral. This has been done to avoid the dryness of presenting theory independently of its applications. I have interwoven the two, so that ideas are introduced and used in a policy context, to be amplified and used again at some later stage. I hope that this will enhance the accessibility of the book for those relatively new to economics. As an additional aid to the reader, concepts and terms are italicised when first defined, or when the definition is later extended. The terms can be cross-referenced from the index where the page numbers on which definitions appear are indicated in bold.

NOTES

1. In 1986 public choice economics received its seal of respectability with the award of the Nobel prize for economics to its leader, James Buchanan.
2. J.M. Keynes, *The General Theory of Employment, Interest and Money* (Macmillan, London, 1936), pp. 383–4.

Part I

1 Economic Policy and the Mixed Economy

> Our policy to be effective,
> Must choose a suitable objective,
> So, our economy should be
> Both Growing, Stable, Just and Free.
> The Dog would surely be a Dunce
> Who tried to chase four things at once,
> Yet this is just the way we plan
> The task of Economic Man.
> (Kenneth Boulding, economist)[1]

The standing of a government and its ability to hold the confidence of the electorate at a General Election depends on the success of its economic policy. (Harold Wilson, Labour Prime Minister, 1964–70, 1974–6)[2]

Opinion polls record that voters consider unemployment and inflation to be important issues and economic policies feature strongly in political party election manifestos. Economic policy is regarded as important because it concerns the measures governments can take that affect people's material well-being. Though economic policies undoubtedly can have significant impacts on people's livelihoods, this does not mean that governments or economists can accurately predict these effects. The speculative nature of economic knowledge, combined with conflicts of interest over the possible effects of economic policy, contribute to the crescendo of disagreement that accompanies the making of economic policy.

So what is economic policy? The popular conception is that it is government actions which affect things like unemployment, inflation, economic growth and the balance of payments, and that it involves changes in taxation, interest rates, the money supply and exchange rates. Economists see economic policy in the context of a more general framework: it concerns all sorts of measures government organisations can take which affect how well-off people think they are. Economic policy is about government actions in the form of spending money, raising money and legislation, which affect the allocation and distribution of resources.

Any economic system, be it a primitive tribal community or a large, technically advanced country, has to resolve the problem of what goods and services to produce, how to produce them, and to whom to distribute them. In economists' jargon, the what and how questions are about *allocating economic resources*, and the for whom question concerns *distribution*[3]. Decisions which bring about the allocation and distribution of resources in the economy are taken by a wide range of individuals and institutions. When individuals make buying and selling decisions as consumers or as workers they are acting through markets. But they can also influence economic allocation by voting or campaigning for specific government actions. Thus there are two main mechanisms for deciding the allocation and distribution of resources: leaving it to markets or to government. Economic policy is about which mechanism to use in specific instances and about how to use it. Associated with this is the question of whether activities should be undertaken by private sector institutions, such as firms, households or voluntary organisations, or by public sector institutions. For instance, should health care be provided by the state? If so, which services should patients pay for? Should private health provision be banned? These are all questions concerning the economic roles of the market and the state. This central issue is by no means a recent concern. Edmund Burke, the eighteenth-century politician, saw it as 'one of the finest problems of legislation, namely to determine what the State ought to take upon itself to direct by public wisdom and what it ought to leave with as little interference as possible to individual exertion'.

THE MIXED ECONOMY

The mixed economy is a familiar term for describing an economy in which both government institutions and markets are important in allocating and distributing resources. Economies can be categorised according to the extent to which markets or government prevail. At the market extreme can be placed Victorian Britain as an approximation to the *laissez-faire* model in which most economic activity, including the provision of welfare services, is undertaken by the private sector. The government has a minimal role in maintaining the framework of law, order and external security required for the operation of private sector institutions. At the other extreme is a centrally planned economy, such as the USSR, where most goods and services are produced and distributed by the state. However, neither of these economies corresponds entirely to its theoretical extreme. There is some private sector activity in USSR—in agricultural goods and personal services. At the other end of the spectrum, Victorian governments went beyond their minimal role in various ways—by passing factory Acts to regulate working conditions, enacting public health legislation, and enabling local authorities to supply gas and electricity, for instance.

The Rise of the Mixed Economy
The main configurations of today's mixed economy were laid down in Britain by the Labour government that won power after World War II. Prior to that there had been, since the mid-nineteenth century, a gradual extension of the economic role of the state. The welfare state slowly evolved with the government extending its provision of education, social services and social benefits, albeit in a piecemeal fashion. The state began to run businesses, such as the Forestry Commission (1919), the British Broadcasting Corporation (1927), the London Passenger Transport Board (1933) and British Overseas Airways Corporation (1939). The 1930s depression encouraged other forms of government intervention: import tariffs to protect British firms from foreign competition; reorganisation of the ailing cotton industry; assistance to declining regions, to name just a few. The high tide of government control of the economy occurred during World War II. While most firms remained in private hands, they were linked to sponsoring government departments and directed by them as to what to produce and in what quantities. Government control of the supply of raw materials helped it to enforce its directives. The economy was planned through a network of detailed regulations, embracing almost all goods from toilet rolls to pigeon food. To prevent shortages pushing up prices, these were regulated by the government and many goods could only be acquired legally by using ration cards as well as money.

In 1945 the first Labour government was elected with a sufficiently large parliamentary majority to carry out a wide-ranging programme of socialist reforms, some of which had already been embarked upon by the wartime coalition government. They created the postwar welfare state by setting up the National Health Service and the social security system which pays cash benefits to the unemployed, to families with children, the old and the poor. The welfare state provides free or means-tested medical care, in contrast to market-based provision where people have to pay for treatment or for private medical insurance. Schooling is provided free by the state, while housing and public transport are subsidised.

The 1945 Labour government's other major contribution to the mixed economy was the creation of the nationalised industries: railways, coal, gas, electricity, steel, docks and road haulage were taken into public ownership. Road haulage was subsequently denationalised, as was steel, until embraced by a further spate of nationalisation by Labour in the 1970s which took in shipbuilding and aerospace. In the 1970s public ownership of business expanded by the government acquiring shares or complete control of individual firms rather than nationalising whole industries. It was then that British Leyland, Rolls-Royce and numerous smaller firms, which have since been either liquidated or returned to the private sector, became state-owned.

Although in the thirty years following the end of World War II there were skirmishes between the Labour and Conservative Parties over the boundaries of the mixed economy, a large measure of consensus reigned over the nature of the welfare state and the extent of the nationalised sector. The postwar consensus included a commitment to Keynesian economic policy. Keynes' famous book, *The General Theory of Interest, Employment and Money*, was born out of the experience of high unemployment in the 1930s. It set out the Keynesian theory that unemployment is due to an insufficient aggregate demand for goods and services in the economy. This can be remedied by the government itself spending more or taxing people less, in order to stimulate more private sector spending. In the 1944 White Paper *Employment Policy*,[4] the government committed itself to the achievement of this objective. It was generally believed that Keynesian economics provided the means to prevent mass unemployment. Up to the mid-1970s successive Conservative and Labour governments adjusted taxes and interest rates and, to a lesser extent, government spending, in order to regulate the level of aggregate demand. This was done in an attempt to stabilise the economy so that neither inflation nor unemployment rose too high.

The End of Consensus on the Mixed Economy

By the end of the 1970s the consensus over the mixed economy was breaking down, increasing the heat with which economic policy is debated. The economic performance of the western economies had deteriorated in the 1970s, particularly with the quadrupling of oil prices in 1974. Growth rates slowed down, inflation rose, as did unemployment. Britain's economic performance remained poor, relative to other developed economies. Keynesian policies seemed no longer to work, and inflation, rather than unemployment, became the overriding concern.

The election in 1979 of a Conservative government, under Margaret Thatcher, marked the final collapse of the postwar consensus on the mixed economy. Her government's avowed aim has been to reduce the economic role of the state by diminishing the size of the public sector. A new word—privatisation—has been coined to denote such policies. Keynesian economic policy, which had ceased to operate by 1976, was officially abandoned, being held responsible for higher inflation in the longer term and for contributing to the general inefficiency of the economy. Instead, the aim has been to reduce inflation by controlling the money supply and to reinvigorate the private sector by reducing taxation and enlarging its activities.

This brief dash through history illustrates that economic policy is about what mixture of market and government the mixed economy should consist of. While economic policy determines the boundaries of the mixed economy, it is itself conditioned by the existing institutions of the public and private sectors and the interactions between them.

THE PUBLIC SECTOR

As economic policy is about the actions government takes in the economic sphere, it is important to be clear that in this book I am including all the institutions of the public sector in the term *government*. The institutions which make up the public sector are officially classified into three main categories: central government, local authorities and public corporations. So my definition of government is somewhat broader than that sometimes employed which restricts it to central and local government, together, termed *general government*.

Central government consists of all bodies which are accountable to Parliament. These are mainly the government departments. The chief departments whose activities involve economic policy are the Departments of Trade and Industry, Employment, Health and Social Security, Education and Science, Environment, Defence, Transport, and the Ministry of Agriculture, Fisheries and Food. All these are spending departments: their work concerns the provision of goods and services, like health, education, museums, defence, and so on. The Treasury is responsible for the overall control of the other departments' spending, for the financing of that spending, and for the overall management of the economy. Other organisations, such as the National Health Service and Atomic Energy Authority, are classified as part of central government, though they are not government departments.

The *local authority sector* consists of authorities which can raise funds by means of rates and other levies. They provide services such as education, buses, housing, personal social services and refuse collection. About half of local authority expenditure is financed by central government. Thus, although 60 per cent of education expenditure is financed centrally, schools and colleges are part of the local authority sector. Universities, however, are officially allocated to the private sector because they have royal charters, even though 90 per cent of their funds come from central government. Thus official classification has more to do with legal and constitutional considerations than with economic criteria.

The third set of public sector institutions are the *public corporations*. These are business enterprises with a considerable degree of financial independence from central government, but whose assets are publicly-owned and which are publicly-controlled in that their management boards are wholly or partly appointed by the government. Bodies as diverse as the Regional Water Authorities, Her Majesty's Stationery Office, the Bank of England, the Royal Mint, the New Towns Development Corporations, the Forestry Commission, the Independent Broadcasting Authority and British Leyland (BL) were all public corporations in 1986.

THE SIZE OF GOVERNMENT

The growth of government economic activity since the mid-nineteenth century, and recent attempts to rein it back, have already been noted but without much precision. There are various measures which can give us some idea of how big government has become in relation to the rest of the economy. Defining government economic activity in terms of the amount of output produced by the public sector and number of people employed in it give two such measures.

Table 1.1 shows the size of the public sector in terms of employment. Between 1958 and 1968 the numbers employed in the public sector rose, all the growth being concentrated in the local authorities. Central government employment fell, due to cuts in the armed forces. Public sector employment as a proportion of total employment in the economy stayed around 24.5 per cent over the decade 1958−68 but took off at the end of the 1960s. By 1978 it had reached 29.3 per cent. Growth was rapid in general (central plus local) government but non-existent in the public corporations. General government employment continued to rise until 1982. Over seven years of Conservative rule the numbers employed in the public sector fell by nearly 11 per cent, while the proportion of the labour force in the public sector has declined to around 27 per cent. The main brunt of this decline has fallen on the public corporations, due mainly to declining markets in certain sectors, such as coal, motor cars, ships, steel and railways. Technical and organisational improvements which have increased labour productivity have also contributed. Latterly, privatisation of large concerns such as British Telecom have taken their toll. Measuring the size of the public sector in terms of the percentage of gross domestic product it produces gives a very similar impression of its size, as can be seen from Table 1.2. In 1985 it produced around 26.5 per cent of gross domestic product. The relative size of the constituent parts of the public sector varies with the measure used. The public corporations are larger than the local authority sector if measured in terms of output, but the local authorities employ nearly twice as many people, because they produce labour-intensive services.

Table 1.1: Size of public sector: employment

Year	Public sector total '000s	Public sector % of labour force	Central government total '000s	Central government % of total labour force	Local government total '000s	Local government % of total labour force	Public corporations total '000s	Public corporations % of labour force
1958	5926	24.4	2232	9.2	1656	6.8	2028	8.4
1968	6275	24.8	1888	7.5	2310	9.1	2077	8.2
1978	7326	29.3	2333	9.3	2932	11.7	2061	8.2
1985	6513	26.9	2360	9.7	2890	11.9	1260	5.2
% change 1968–78	16.8	18.2	23.6	25.1	26.9	28.5	−0.8	0.4
% change 1978–85	−11.1	−8.2	1.2	4.3	−1.4	1.2	−39.0	−37.0

Source: Economic Trends.

Table 1.2: Size of public sector: % GDP produced

Year	Total public sector	Central government	Local authorities	Public corporations
1958	23.6	8.5	6.5	8.6
1968	26.4	6.7	8.9	10.8
1978	27.8	7.3	9.3	11.2
1984	26.5	7.7	9.5	9.3

Source: National Income and Expenditure.
Note: GDP is at factor cost.

Using either output or employment measures, the size of the public sector is around 27 per cent of the economy. However, in terms of the proportion of the nation's capital stock it owns, the public sector was 39 per cent of the economy in 1984 compared to 44.5 per cent twelve years earlier. The larger size of the public sector when measured in terms of the ownership of fixed assets is due to the concentration of public corporations in capital-intensive industries such as electricity, gas, steel and water supply, and the local authorities' large-scale ownership of houses, schools and infrastructure.

The three measures discussed so far relate to public sector organisations as producers of goods and services. But, as already mentioned, this is just one dimension of the economic role of the state. There are many ways in which government can affect the economy which do not involve producing goods and services. The three main instruments of economic policy available to government—spending money, raising money and passing laws—need involve no production, apart from administration. So further indicators of the extent of government economic activity can be obtained from data on government expenditure and taxation.

In the UK, government expenditure in the official statistics is defined to be spending of central and local government, and central government grants and loans to the public corporations.[5] The operating expenditure of public corporations on wages and goods and on investment financed out of their own resources is not included. Neither is general government expenditure financed by user charges.

Table 1.3: UK government expenditure as percentage of GDP, 1890–1985

1890	1910	1925	1938	1946	1955	1965	1975	1985
8.4	11.3	23.4	27.5	45.4	33.5	37.2	48.9	44.8

Sources: C.H. Feinstein, *Statistical Tables of National Income Expenditure and Output of the UK 1855–1965* (Cambridge University Press, Cambridge, 1972); A.T. Peacock and J. Wiseman, *The Growth of Public Expenditure in the UK* (George Allen & Unwin, 1967); *Economic Trends*.

Note: GDP is at market prices.

The availability of statistics on government expenditure since the nineteenth century, makes it possible to estimate the growth of government economic activity over the last century. The rise of the economic role of government from its small beginnings to its present-day size is shown in Table 1.3. This shows that government expenditure as a proportion of GDP rose steadily over time. It leapt upwards during World War II then declined to a low of 33.5 per cent by 1955. It then crept steadily upwards to 41.6 per cent by 1973, and took a sudden leap in 1974–75 as a consequence of fiscal laxity and the acceleration of world inflation following the quadrupling of oil prices in 1973. In 1975 government expenditure in the UK attained its highest share of GDP at 48.9 per cent. In 1976 the then Labour government took firm steps to control the growth of government expenditure and brought it down to around 43 per cent of GDP. Despite the Conservative government's desire to reduce government expenditure it was 44.8 per cent of GDP in 1985—down from a peak of 46 per cent in 1981.

A steadily rising share of GDP going into public expenditure has been experienced throughout the developed world, as Figure 1.1 shows. (The difference in definitions accounts for discrepancies between the OECD data and the Central Statistical Office statistics used in the other tables.) Government expenditure as a proportion of GDP in the UK is not excessively high by international standards. While considerably higher than either Japan, the USA or Switzerland, it was less in 1983 than in West Germany, France or Italy, and considerably below that of Sweden at 67 per cent or the Netherlands at 64 per cent. Other countries have also, to varying degrees, been concerned with containing the growth of government spending.

As UK government spending has risen, so has the proportion of national income that the government takes in tax. Between 1954 and 1964, around 28–29 per cent of national income was accounted for by taxes and National Insurance contributions. By 1975 it was 38 per cent, fell to 34 per cent by 1977, then rose again to over 38 per cent in the early 1980s.

The size of government, especially in terms of the proportion of national output it spends, takes in tax and borrows, gave rise to increasing disquiet by the late 1970s. Governments pledged to cut back on the size of the state sector were elected in the UK, the USA and West Germany. Governments in Belgium, the Netherlands and even in socialist France, after an initial foray into extending state ownership became concerned to curtail the growth of public spending. International bodies, like the Organisation for Economic Cooperation and Development (OECD) and the International Monetary Fund (IMF) echoed these concerns. The IMF required most countries borrowing from it to curb their spending. However, these policies have not won general acceptance: issues concerning the appropriate size and economic role of government remain central to arguments over the conduct of economic policy.

MARKET AND NON-MARKET ALLOCATION

The previous section has described government as a set of institutions, with identifiable outputs, employment, assets and expenditures. At the beginning of the chapter I also distinguished between market and

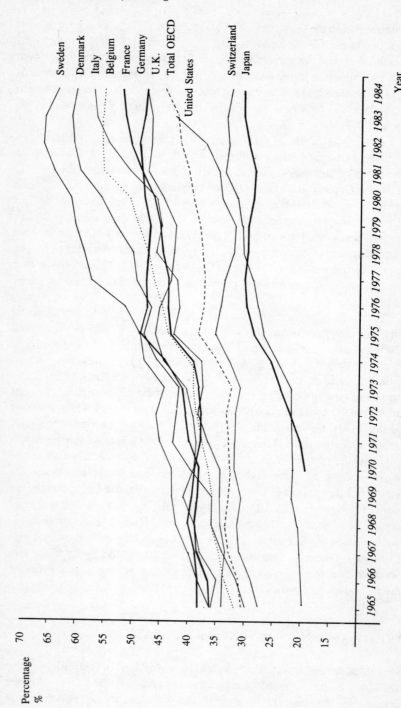

Figure 1.1: Total outlays of government as a percentage of GDP

government as *allocative mechanisms*. Government as an *allocative mechanism* is quite distinct from the institutions of government, in that it is a way of taking decisions about what, how and for whom to produce, which contrasts with the market way of making allocative decisions. But as well as government, there are other non-market ways of allocating resources, notably the family and voluntary organisations. The remainder of this chapter outlines briefly the main distinctive features of both markets and government as allocative mechanisms. This is done in order to introduce the key idea, developed throughout the book, that economic policy is about the role of government in *allocating* and *distributing* resources in relation to the parts played by market and non-market institutions in the private sector.

Non-Market Private Sector Allocation

Many services are produced and exchanged within families and the broader network of relatives and friends. Most of these services can be bought for money on the market. Housework, childcare, home maintenance, gardening, can be bought for money, but most of these tasks are shared within the family, with traditional patterns of sexual specialisation prevailing. Alternatively, the state provides welfare services, such as care of the elderly and sick, pre-school education and childcare and home help, that are also extensively provided by family and friends. An important aspect of the rise of the welfare state is the increasing state provision of personal welfare services that once were the sole domain of kinship networks. Private voluntary organisations and charities are another source of welfare services—Dr Barnardo's, the Royal Women's Voluntary Service, the Royal Lifeboat Institution, the British Heart Foundation, are just a few of the collective private sector organisations which produce goods or services for non-profit motives. Family and voluntary organisations differ from markets as allocative mechanisms, in that they do not involve a direct exchange of goods and services for money. Even in the traditional marriage where the wife receives housekeeping money for her services, the exchange aspect of the relationship is dominated by personal elements.

The Market as an Allocative Mechanism

The market is the setting in which buyers and sellers voluntarily exchange goods and services with each other, with money usually changing hands. The two basic participants in the market are households and firms. A firm is a very general term for any individual or group that produces goods and services which are sold to others for money. Firms come in many forms— shops, banks, farms, self-employed plumbers, private sector schools and hospitals, as well as industrial companies. Households interact with the market as consumers of goods and services and as sellers of labour and capital. A good or service exchanged on a market is characterised by having a price, and is termed a *marketed good*.

Prices serve a crucial function in markets as they signal information to buyers and sellers. Consumers indicate to suppliers, by the amount they are willing to buy at various prices, what their *demand* for particular products is. For most goods the quantity demanded increases as price falls. So if there is more supplied to a market than consumers wish to buy at the current price, sellers can respond by cutting prices and/or reducing supply in order to eliminate excess supply. Similarly, excess demand can be removed by raising the price and choking off excess demand as well as by increasing the amount supplied. A market is said to *clear* when *demand* and *supply* are equal. Prices, therefore, serve to change the quantities demanded and supplied so as to bring about market clearing.

Buyers and sellers on markets are considered to be motivated by self-interest. A consumer will only buy a product if its price does not exceed its value to him/her. Similarly a worker will only accept a job if the wages and conditions are better than the alternative of no work or another job. Firms are motivated by the desire to make profits. Private sector firms are constrained to earn revenues that cover their costs, otherwise they will become insolvent and have to go out of business. Economists often assume that firms aim to maximise profits. Profits are another important signal in markets. If existing firms in a market charge prices in excess of production costs then the resulting profits provide an incentive for new firms to enter that market. As supply increases, prices fall in order to induce consumers to buy more. A *competitive market* is one in which firms can enter and exit freely so that prices are kept in line with production costs. The significance of competitive markets is that prices convey to consumers correct information about firms' production costs. Advocates of the market way of allocating resources see its virtue as harnessing the inevitable self-interest of individuals so as to promote the general interest. The basis of this argument and criticisms of it will be examined at greater length in the course of the book, particularly in Chapter 6.

Government as an Allocative Mechanism

Government as an *allocative mechanism* contrasts with the market mechanism in several respects. First it represents collective decision-making by the state in contrast to individual decisions to buy and sell on markets. Not all market transactions are made by individuals. Many are undertaken by private sector organisations, in particular by firms. However, these are usually analysed as individual economic agents. Individuals also form collective private sector organisations such as trade unions, workers' cooperatives and golf clubs. What distinguishes government collective action is that it is ultimately backed by the coercive power of the state. In a liberal democracy it is held that citizens have consented to this coercive power because it is in the general interest to curtail the freedom of individuals to do as they like, provided that these restrictions are established in laws enacted by elected assemblies and enforced by an impartial judiciary. Without a framework of law and order the market could not operate, as there would be no means of ensuring that exchanges are undertaken voluntarily and not by extortion, and that contracts can be enforced.

The second way in which government allocation differs from market allocation is in the way that individuals signal their preferences. In the marketplace an individual must either have money or something somebody else is willing to buy. In a liberal democracy individuals record their preferences as to how the government allocative mechanism should be used by voting. Although political activity is ultimately about winning elections in order to gain control of the power to legislate, spend and tax, it takes many other forms which also determine how the government allocative mechanism is used. For example, pressure groups try to gain a leverage on government by threatening to withdraw support: teachers, farmers, miners and lawyers are just a few recent examples.

The third way in which government as an allocative mechanism differs from the market is that it uses different criteria for allocating and distributing resources. In particular, government institutions need pay no regard to the profit motive. Government can redistribute income through taxes and transfer payments or produce goods and distribute them free of charge to consumers. Goods and services, like education, defence and medical care, which the government provides at zero prices, are termed *non-marketed goods*. Other goods, like dental care, rural public transport or local authority housing, are partially subsidised, and so are neither pure marketed nor non-marketed goods. There are many other aspects of the government allocative mechanism. Indirect taxes and subsidies alter the relative prices of goods and so affect the amounts consumers want to buy and hence the quantities firms produce. Regulations affect the relative costs of goods. For instance, European Community legislation to reduce nitrogen oxide, hydrocarbon and carbon monoxide emissions from car exhausts will raise the production cost of cars.

Thus government as an *allocative mechanism* is quite distinct from government as a set of public sector institutions. As an allocative mechanism, government permeates the private sector, in the form of laws and regulations, taxes, subsidies, government purchasing and the provision of goods and services to the private sector. Goods can be produced in the private sector but still be greatly influenced by government. One way is through government purchases, which account for about 10 per cent of private sector output: NHS drugs and defence equipment are two prime examples. Another part of the private sector highly dependent on government is agriculture, examined in Chapter 14. Under the European Community's Common Agricultural Policy, the government keeps farm prices way above the levels that competitive markets would attain.

The three main instruments available to government, which enable it to alter the way markets allocate and distribute resources, are the power to spend money, the power to raise money by taxation, borrowing with unlimited credit and by creating money and, finally, the power to make and enforce laws. All these imply various costs and benefits to individuals and institutions in the private sector and so give rise to continuous political activity by economic agents anxious to reduce the costs and increase the benefits to them of government actions.

Another way of seeing how government as an allocative mechanism is distinct from government as a set of public sector institutions is to observe that the public sector is itself affected by market forces. By and large, public corporations produce marketed goods and services and are required to earn sufficient revenue to cover their costs. Several nationalised industries—shipbuilding, steel, coal and railways—have been unprofitable for a number of years due to declining demand for their products as well as low efficiency. Market forces have prevailed, and output and employment in these industries have contracted over the years, though at a slower rate than if government had not intervened. In some cases firms owned by the state can operate just like private sector firms in that they pursue purely commercial goals and are profitable. The most significant factor for the performance of public sector enterprises is not so much their ownership as the nature of the competitive environment within which they operate.

Market forces impinge on central and local government as well. One area where this occurs is public sector wage determination. Although pay is determined by bargaining between government and public sector trade unions, private sector wages exert some influence, either as a benchmark for public sector wages or in determining whether there is a shortage of requisite skills in the public sector which needs to be diminished by offering higher pay. Recently the market element in the provision of public sector services has been slightly increased by government requirements that private sector contractors should be asked to tender for cleaning, catering, laundry services, refuse collection and maintenance work in competition with each other and with existing direct labour forces.

CONCLUSION

This chapter has described in broad terms what economic policy is about in the context of the mixed economy. I have defined economic policy as measures which concern the use of government as an *allocative mechanism*. This involves determining the extent to which market and non-market private sector institutions, such as families and charities, are left to allocate resources, and setting the institutional and legal framework within which markets operate. Government, as a set of public sector institutions, has been distinguished from government as an allocative mechanism, and the public sector described and quantified.

While the role of family and voluntary organisations is significant in relation to policies which concern the welfare state, the main focus for economic policy is the distinction between markets and government as allocative mechanisms. Government is the manifestation of *collective action* by society, which is ultimately backed by the coercive power of the state. It can, if it chooses, use non-market criteria for allocating resources. The distinction between market and government as allocative mechanisms provides an analytical core for the book. How they appear to work, how they interact, what are their advantages and disadvantages, and how they relate to particular areas of economic policy, are questions addressed in the rest of the book. Since economic policy is about what governments do to affect the allocation and distribution of resources, it is inevitably the outcome of political processes, which in turn depend on the interaction of various types of decision-makers and the institutions within which they operate. Chapter 2 considers who is involved in the making of economic policy.

NOTES

1. K. Boulding, *Principles of Economic Policy* (Staples Press, London 1959).
2. Excerpt from speech to the Parliamentary Labour Party, reported in *Financial Times*, 8 March 1968.
3. Terms and concepts are italicised in order to indicate their importance. The page numbers where they are defined are indicated in bold print in the index.
4. HMSO *Employment Policy*, Cmnd. 6527 (London, 1944).
5. See P. Stibbard 'Measuring public expenditure', *Economic Trends*, August 1985 (HMSO, London).

2 Who Makes Economic Policy?

Conservative voter Abe Blieden failed in a High Court bid for damages against Premier Margaret Thatcher and Hampstead MP Sir Geoffrey Finsberg for alleged breaches of election promises to provide him with employment and cut his rates and taxes. He was ordered to pay costs. (*Financial Times*, 19 September 1985)

In Chapter 1 economic policy was defined as the use of government as a mechanism for allocating and distributing resources. As such it involves setting the legal framework within which markets operate, as well as redirecting or replacing market forces. It would seem from this definition that economic policy is made by governments, and hence by the politicians and officials who operate the machinery of government. But in a liberal democracy government is answerable to the electorate, both through elections and, during its term of office, via accountability to Parliament. So to answer the question 'Who makes economic policy?' we need to examine the roles of the chief actors—voters, politicians and bureaucrats.

Policy-making is usefully seen as a process occurring over time, into which are fed inputs in the form of decisions and actions by individuals and groups. These operate within institutions and are constrained by rules and procedures. The inputs combine to produce policy outcomes with discernible effects. Crucial questions are whose preferences influence policy outcomes, to what extent, and with what effect. A *representative democracy* is a system in which citizens elect representatives from a set of contending politicians who advocate a range of different policy options. Those which are supported by the majority of elected representatives are then implemented by them with the assistance of civil servants and other public sector bureaucrats. Thus voters, politicians and bureaucrats all provide inputs into the policy-making process, but in an 'ideal' representative democracy it is the voters' preferences alone which determine policy.

However actual representative democracies diverge from the ideal model in that the preferences of politicians and public sector bureaucrats, which may well differ from each other and from those of the voters, also determine policy outcomes and may even predominate. Policy-making is also influenced by the laws, institutions and culture that have evolved over time in each country. In any given period these constrain what policy-makers can do, though they are also modified in order to effect policy changes.

In Part II we shall discuss how the preferences of the main types of policy-making actors are fed into the policy-making process and with what consequences. First, this chapter undertakes a preliminary review of the role of the main actors and institutions involved in British economic policy-making and outlines the political context in which economic policy is conducted.

The nature and extent of the influence of voters, politicians and bureaucrats varies both with the type of policy and with the stage of the policy-making process. There are two distinct stages—the formulation of policy and its implementation. The former involves campaigning for a policy to be adopted, securing the necessary power to carry it through and determining the precise measures which make up the policy. It is this stage where the voters can be influential and where politicians find their *raison d'être*. The implementation stage is dominated by the bureaucrats—a term which to save words I shall use in a wide sense to embrace all public sector employees. The term will include doctors, miners, BBC producers, local authority refuse collectors, as well as civil servants, judges, chairmen of nationalised industries and the Governor of the Bank of England. However, there is no watertight division of labour. Bureaucrats influence the formulation of policy for a number of reasons: politicians require their advice and expertise, and bureaucrats are concerned to see policy operates in their own interests.

THE VOTERS

The influence of voters on economic policy is to some extent determined by the constitutional framework. In the UK the direct link between what the majority of voters want and what governments do is very tenuous and uncertain. Unlike Switzerland or Italy, for instance, referenda on individual items of policy, such as nuclear power or wage indexation are not held. The British referendum in 1975 on staying in the EC was an exception. The political parties set out their policies in their election manifestos: these may be couched in vague terms. A voter has to choose between about three main policy packages and cannot indicate preferences or strengths of preferences for individual policies. There is no guarantee that the winning party will carry out all the policies in its manifesto and it can add new ones once in power. Nor is it necessarily the case that voters choose which party to vote for by weighing up the relative merits of their policies. The image and style of politicians, as conveyed to the electorate by the media, are also influential, although how much relative to policy issues is still an unresolved issue amongst academics. Even if people vote for policies rather than images, the current first-past-the-post voting system in the UK has so far led to governments' obtaining parliamentary majorities without securing the support of the majority of voters. (The extent to which voters' preferences influence policy is the subject matter of Chapter 10.)

PARLIAMENT

The British constitution gives considerable power to an elected government. A government with a comfortable majority in the House of Commons can usually get what legislation it wants onto the statute book and has considerable discretion in using existing statutes. The system of party whips ensures that in the normal course of events few Members of Parliament act as independent representatives, rather than as party lobby fodder. Some details of policy are amended on their way through Parliament, but unless a government has a very small majority, it will usually succeed in getting its legislative programme passed. The failure of the government in 1986 to win the vote on the second reading of the Shops Bill to legalise Sunday trading was exceptional.

Although Parliament's rise to power during the seventeenth century was based on the Crown's need to secure parliamentary votes for money, its role nowadays in economic policy-making is limited. The tradition that Parliament has to vote approval for the government's expenditure of money still holds good, but these 'supply votes' only cover around 60 per cent of government expenditure and are normally a rubber-stamping operation. In any case, Parliament can only refuse to vote an item of expenditure and cannot pass a measure to increase expenditure. The main decisions about public expenditure, as we shall see in Chapter 5, are taken by the executive arm of government. Similarly Parliament has little independent control of taxation. Each year the Chancellor of the Exchequer presents his Budget to Parliament and the tax changes then announced are contained in the annual Finance Bill, which is normally passed by Parliament with little significant amendment. The relative impotence of the legislature in economic affairs in Britain contrasts with the much greater powers of Congress in the USA. There the President has to negotiate his Budget proposals with both Republican and Democratic representatives, and often fails to secure support for his initial proposals.

Parliament's main role *vis-à-vis* economic policy is to act as a debating chamber where government and opposition score points off each other to impress the media and thereby the electorate. Parliament puts some constraint on the government's actions via backbench opinion in the government's own party. The ultimate backbench sanction is to refuse to vote for the government. However backbench disquiet and reports of dissatisfaction in the constituency parties are often sufficient to restrain the government. For example, in 1984 the Secretary of State for Education withdrew his proposal that well-off parents should pay their children's university fees, following an outcry in the Conservative Party.

Parliament's other role is to monitor policy. This is largely done through its select committees which are empowered to call on ministers, civil servants and other bureaucrats to give evidence. While select committees do succeed in obtaining information and in making government departments and public corporations respond to criticism, they have no direct power to obtain information the Executive wishes to withhold nor to enforce their recommendations. Through its Public Accounts Committee Parliament monitors public expenditure, but its main function is an accounting one, ensuring that money is spent on the items voted for, rather than assessing whether the objectives of economic policy have been adequately secured.

CENTRAL GOVERNMENT

In Britain the focus of power for formulating economic policy is central government. This embraces government ministers and the civil servants in the government departments and other bodies attached to them, such as the Manpower Services Commission and the NHS. In addition there is the Bank of England, a public corporation with considerable independence, which formulates and implements monetary policy—that is, policy with respect to interest rates, credit, the money supply and exchange rates. It also regulates the financial system with the aim of protecting investors and preserving stability.

The powers of local authorities in formulating and even in implementing economic policy are considerably circumscribed by central government in the UK. This is an almost inevitable consequence of the financial dependence of local authorities, which obtain about half their finance from central government and whose total expenditure counts officially as public expenditure, which it is the Treasury's remit to control. As the central government's concern with controlling the overall level of public expenditure has grown, so have its powers over local authority spending and revenue-raising. Some local authorities—mainly Labour-controlled—have tried to pursue a more vigorous local economic policy by investing public money in selected local firms. These policies have clashed with those of the Thatcher government, which has been particularly keen to prevent local authorities from spending money as they see fit.

Economists distinguish between *macroeconomic* and *microeconomic* policies. The former are policies concerned with the economy as a whole and so focus on aggregate level variables such as inflation, unemployment, the growth of national output and the balance of payments, which are seen as the ultimate objectives of macroeconomic policy. Microeconomic policies concern parts of the economy, such as selling public corporations to the private sector, reforming the social security system or regional assistance. The economic variables that a government can change in attempting to achieve its objectives are called *policy instruments* or *instrumental variables*. The chief instruments of macroeconomic policy are the overall level of government spending and taxation and the money supply. In addition macroeconomic policy is concerned with interest rates and the exchange rate, but these are even less under government control than the other three.

The formulation and implementation of macroeconomic policy is very much the province of central government, with the Treasury and the Bank of England taking the leading roles. Although macroeconomic policy may be operated within a longer-term framework, like the Conservatives' medium-term financial strategy, which set year-by-year targets for the money supply and the public sector borrowing requirement (the difference between the government's spending and its tax revenues), it is still a reactive policy. It responds to short-term economic disturbances, such as a rapid depreciation in the sterling exchange rate or an unexpected increase in the public sector borrowing requirement. The nature of these responses is largely determined by a few decision-makers in the Treasury and the Bank of England, rather than by the government as a whole.

Microeconomic policy is by no means totally divorced from macroeconomic policy. It may be used to support macroeconomic policy, as in the case of Manpower Services Commission schemes to train people and create employment for them or the efforts of the Price Commission (1974–79) to reduce inflation by price controls. Microeconomic policies are also often constrained by macroeconomic policy. A policy to keep down the overall level of public spending puts pressure on wide areas of the public, and even private, sector to cut costs or reduce output, as we shall see in the case of the coal industry in Chapter 3. Given the level of taxation required to achieve the Government's target for the public sector borrowing requirement, decisions regarding what to tax and by how much have microeconomic effects on the allocation and distribution of resources.

The responsibility for microeconomic policy is much more diffused and this is particularly true of its implementation, which involves a wide range of public sector employees in the local authorities and public corporations, as well as central goverment. Although I have painted a picture of a relatively powerful central government this does not imply that a single minister will find it easy to initiate changes. For one thing government is a coalition of interests, some of them conflicting, and each represented somewhere in the system by a minister and group of civil servants or bureaucrats. It will be difficult to secure the political will for change if vested interests within government oppose it.

POLITICAL INTERESTS OUTSIDE GOVERNMENT

The formulation of policy by government usually involves consultation of those outside government whose interests are affected. These interests can supply government with specialist information and this, together with minimising their objections to the policy, will help to ensure its effective implementation. To this end government departments maintain permanent relations with organised political interests and may consult or listen to other outside political interests. Political interests is a term used to denote any group of people with a common interest, who may be organised as an explicit pressure group or may be much more loosely connected. The links between the Ministry of Agriculture, Food and Fisheries and the National Union of Farmers and those between the Ministry of Transport and the British Road Federation are just two examples of the symbiosis between government and organised political interests.

This two-way channel of communication between the government and outside interests and the permanent representation of political interests within the organs of government, provide an alternative means of representation for the clients of economic policy to those provided by voting in local and general elections. This network of consultation and pressure is considered by many to predominate over the institutions of parliamentary democracy. However it is difficult to separate the two channels of representation, as underlying the government's desire to consult and to appear to pay heed to clamouring political interests, is the need to secure its parliamentary majority.

Functional Interests and Corporatism
The evident weakness of Parliament with respect to economic policy, relative to the ascendent influence of political interests, has focused attention on functional *interests* as separate nuclei of economic power which are quite independent of government. By *functional interests* is meant political interests defined in terms of their role in production. The two major functional interests are labour and employers. The latter mainly consist of the management side of industry plus the interests of those who

provide finance, and so are sometimes subsumed under the category 'capital'. Each of the two major functional categories is made up of a hierarchy of constituent organisations. In the UK the Confederation of British Industry (CBI) and the Trades Union Congress (TUC) are the apex of the organised functional interests. The third element in this trichotomy of economic power is government.

The division of economic and political power between the three major representatives of functional interests—labour, management and government, each hierarchically organised—is referred to as *corporatism*. It offers an alternative way of representing interests within society to parliamentary democracy. In a *corporatist* system government makes economic policy by bargaining with management and labour organisations to secure their agreement. This process of consultation and agreement bypasses the legislative assembly. Corporatism is advocated by some on the grounds that it acknowledges the reality of where economic power is located and makes use of it to forge a consensus which ensures that economic policy is accepted, is widely implemented and is thereby successful. It is criticised on two counts: for suppressing competition and thus encouraging inefficiency, and for diminishing the political rights of individuals by enhancing the power of organisations, to which individuals must then belong to further their interests.

There is an element of corporatism in British economic policy-making. It is enshrined in certain institutions, which have tripartite representation of the TUC, the CBI and central government on their governing boards. One example is the Manpower Services Commission. Another is the National Development Council, set up in 1962, together with its secretariat, the National Economic Development Office. It was charged with the task of promoting economic growth and improved economic performance by providing a forum where government, labour and management can discuss economic policy. The NEDC has come to represent a distinct brand of economic policy, one that lobbies for protection from foreign competition and for intervention on the behalf of industry by government. It has been distinctly out of tune with the Thatcher government's economic policy and has had little influence, apart from detailed work to improve the performance of individual sectors. Even when given a more central role in economic policy, masterminding the Labour government's 1975–79 'Industrial Strategy', the tangible results of its efforts were hard to detect.

Under the Thatcher government, corporatism has been out of fashion, in contrast to earlier Labour and Conservative administrations. The Labour Party, with its close affiliation to the trade union movement, is much more attached to functional representation, while certain Conservatives, who subscribe to consensual politics, have a lingering fondness for it. In the 1960s and 1970s, attempts by Conservative and Labour governments to reduce inflation by various forms of prices and incomes policy, extended the corporatist element. Prices and wages controls require the acquiescence, or even better, the active cooperation of unions and management. Though corporatism is currently in eclipse it remains latent, ready to be reawakened by a more sympathetic government.

FOREIGN AGENTS

So far this discussion of the chief actors in the process of economic policy-making has ignored a key role—that of foreign agents. As an open economy, Britain is inextricably linked to the world economy and, as a member of the European Community, is increasingly subject to policies which strive for economic and political integration. This influences economic policy-making in Britain in two ways. First there are agents outside the UK who make policies which affect the British economy. Second, economic policy-making within Britain is constrained by its interlinkages with other economies. In general, the more closely an economy is linked to others and so the less autonomous it is, the more difficult it is for government to plan the economy while at the same time encouraging efficiency. As the complexity of international linkages increases so the number of potential sources of economic change multiplies. Consequently the information and policy instruments required for efficient planning expand and it becomes increasingly difficult to plan the economy effectively. The move away from central planning in Hungary and from mixed economy planning in France since the mid-1960s, as these economies became more open, bears this out.

Britain's integration into the world economy takes the form both of trade in goods and services and capital transactions, where London functions as an important international financial centre. It is most manifest in the behaviour of the balance of payments and the exchange rate. The exchange rate is determined by the demand for and supply of sterling by both domestic residents and foreigners, and can quickly reflect changes in their expectations. These reactions constrain government policy, particularly when the foreign exchange operators expect such policies to increase domestic inflation and so sell sterling, causing the exchange rate to depreciate. Both Labour and Conservative governments have been constrained to cut planned public expenditure or refrain from tax reductions in order to prevent the exchange rate from further depreciation, which would raise import prices and so fuel inflation. As a consequence of the 1976 sterling crisis, the Labour government was forced to seek a loan from the International Monetary Fund, which insisted on public expenditure cuts. A sudden depreciation of the pound in 1985 forced the Conservative government to raise interest rates and delay promised tax cuts.

The European Community

Governments and governmental agencies outside the UK make policies which affect the British economy. The most important of these is the European Community which Britain joined in 1973. The European Community aims to create a common market in goods and services, including labour and capital. This involves removing all barriers to trade between members, while maintaining common external barriers in the form of tariffs, quotas and regulations. This process has now been going on for nearly thirty years and has by no means been completed. Britain is thus subject to policies negotiated with other EC governments in the Council of Ministers, implemented by the EC's executive—the European Commission—and adjudicated by the European Court. An important aspect of EC economic policy is the Common Agricultural Policy, which aims to protect farm incomes by keeping the prices of farm produce above market-clearing levels. Government funds are spent on buying in and stocking surplus output. Farm support accounts for 70 per cent of the EC budget, while most of the rest is spent by the EC Social Fund on regional aid. Britain, with a relatively small farm sector, has complained about the size of its net contribution and secured some reduction.

Another way the EC affects the allocation and distribution of resources in the UK is by regulations which alter the relative prices of goods and the conditions under which they are supplied. Since the main economic aim is the creation of a common market, the EC is working towards the elimination practices which discriminate between members' markets. Thus British firms have to comply with EC competition policy which bans uncompetitive practices, such as colluding on prices or restricting retail outlets. But at the same time other industries, like coal, steel, shipbuilding and air transport, have protected markets. The European Commission attempts to control and eventually eliminate the subsidies member state governments pay to their own industries and to stop governments favouring their own firms when purchasing goods.

So from the point of view of individual firms and industries, as well as consumers, the way the government allocative mechanism is used by the EC can be extremely important. This is illustrated by the clash of interests between car buyers and British motor car manufacturers and dealers, who object to the European Commission's attempts to reduce the differential in car prices between member states. EC policies now pervade the details of economic life. The price of food, the technical standards of goods, the number of video cassette recorders imported from Japan, subsidies to industry, pollution controls on car exhaust fumes, the recognition of professional qualifications, the relative taxes on beer and wine, and myriads more, are all affected by EC policies.

Apart from the EC there are other international governmental institutions, to which Britain subscribes, which make economic policies that directly affect the UK. The two most important are the General Agreement on Tariffs and Trade (GATT) and the International Monetary Fund (IMF).

GATT

GATT consists of a series of international agreements, negotiated since the 1950s, to liberalise international trade by reducing tariffs and eliminating discrimination in trade in manufactures between countries. The agreement is monitored by a small secretariat in Geneva. Under GATT, Britain has undertaken a series of mutual tariff reductions. The GATT agreement also bans export subsidies and import quotas on most manufactured goods. Import quotas can be imposed provided that the domestic industry can be shown to be suffering undue harm and the quota is placed on all countries. Textiles have enjoyed separate treatment. The Multifibre Arrangement, established in 1974 in response to demands from textile manufacturers in the developed economies for protection against imports from newly industrialised countries, sets out separate quotas for trade in specified items between countries. The GATT agreement limits the type of protective trade policy available to governments, though breaches of GATT may bring little in the way of retaliation and less visible methods, such as subsidies, technical standards and safety regulations, can serve the same purpose as tariffs and quotas.

The IMF

The IMF was set up in 1944 to operate the postwar system of fixed exchange rates between countries. Its prime role was to lend to countries with balance of payments deficits, so that they could maintain their exchange rate while measures to correct the deficit were put in hand. Britain has borrowed from the IMF on several occasions to maintain the sterling exchange rate. The importance of the IMF to British policy has waned somewhat since the system of fixed exchange rates broke down in 1972 and was replaced by flexible rates, under which members of the IMF are no longer committed to maintaining their exchange rate. The IMF is still a forum for annual discussions by Finance Ministers, at which broad policy stances are debated with a view to establishing some general agreement as to the thrust of macroeconomic policy. The possibility of discussions reaching a more binding agreement on international monetary arrangements has been mooted. Such an agreement would constrain individual governments' policy reactions.

THE ROLE OF ECONOMISTS AND ECONOMICS

So finally, what is the role of economists in the making of economic policy? Economists primarily see themselves as advisers to the policy-makers, either as bureaucrats within government employed to give policy advice, or outside government, in universities, research institutes, firms or the media, commenting on policies and advocating their own solutions to policy problems. To justify their existence many academic economists see their endeavours as advancing knowledge of how economies work in order to inform and thereby improve economic policy-making.

The economist's idealised model of policy-making is one in which objectives are clearly established and then the means which best achieve these ends are discovered and employed. The role of the economist, as an expert, is to discover and advise on the means which will achieve the objectives desired by the political policy-makers. His role is not to make value judgements about what objectives the policy-makers should pursue. An economist is quite entitled to make such value judgements, but this is in his role as a citizen, not as an expert on economics. The knowledge of what means will achieve the objectives—given that they are feasible—is the domain of *positive economics*. This is the area of economics where, in principle at least, value judgements do not count. *Positive economics* consists of a body of theories or hypotheses which can be refuted by testing them against empirical evidence. Whilst a theory remains unrefuted and so is consistent with the evidence, it forms the basis for offering policy advice on whether the objectives are feasible and if so, how they may be attained and at what cost. That area of economics which is concerned with value judgements is called *normative economics*.

Whether this idealised model of economic policy-making and the role of economics and economists in it actually applies is extremely doubtful. (Here, of course, a strong element of personal judgement enters.) One problem is that the objectives of policies are not clearly stated. One reason for this is that policies are made by groups of decision-makers with divergent, and often conflicting, objectives. Therefore no single set of objectives emerges clearly as the one that is being pursued. Even when government organisations state their objectives, there are often several such objectives which are to some extent mutually inconsistent, so that some choice or trade-off has to be made between them. It is extremely rare for government to reveal what its trade-off is, say, between inflation and unemployment over the next two years. And for good reason. Apart from internal disagreements as to what the trade-off should be, which are better kept private, the factual knowledge as to how much extra inflation might be generated by reducing unemployment next year by one per cent is extremely imprecise.

This consideration points to another major problem with the economist's idealised view of policy-making. The knowledge of what means will achieve particular objectives is highly conjectural. Even if a high degree of probability can be attached to the direction in which an economic relationship is expected to work—say we know that reducing the rate of growth of the money supply will bring down inflation—there is greater uncertainty about the magnitude of the relationship: how much the rate of growth of the money supply needs to be contracted to reduce inflation by one per cent still has to be determined. So even if one were attempting a truly objective assessment of the state of economic knowledge on a particular relationship, there would be room for a considerable degree of doubt about its magnitude, if not its direction.

But economists have not dispassionately proposed their theories and gathered and assessed the evidence, with their value judgements set aside in cold storage. Their value judgements about what constitutes a good society and about which interests in society should be favoured, have permeated and informed their work. The methodology of positive economics has not proved robust enough to select a body of accepted economic relationships with demonstrable predictive power. Instead, the sieve of testing hypotheses to see if they are refuted by empirical evidence has a fairly wide mesh and very few theories have failed to get through. What empirical economics has provided is a set of elaborate rules which economists of different political persuasions use to argue about whether a particular policy measure will achieve the intended result. Economics provides some of the ammunition which political interests use to further their ends. One example of this is the issue of whether to abolish minimum wage laws and the Wage Councils which agree minimum pay levels. Research by economists at the Department of Employment showed that minimum wage laws reduce employment, while the Low Pay Unit, a pressure group, produced research to show that repealing them would not bring down unemployment. It would be much easier to decide on this issue if one knew how much extra employment would be created for those currently unemployed by abolishing minimum wage laws and what the cost in lower earnings would be for those currently employed in these industries.

But the idealised model of economic policy-making should not be dismissed out of hand. To some extent it does inform policy-making. Whatever a policy-maker's value judgements, it is still important to know what the effects of operating on a particular set of policy instruments are likely to be. Faith and ideology are not sufficient guides to achieving economic policy objectives. Some assessment of how economic agents react to policy changes, and so some idea of how the instruments of policy relate to the desired ends is required. What has to be borne in mind is that a lot of so-called 'economic evidence' paraded by governments and their critics is biased by the perspectives of those who produced it. The fact that the Treasury and the TUC can use the Treasury's economic forecasting model to predict quite different consequences for unemployment of increasing government spending, is just one instance of the games played with 'economic evidence'. So the role of economic knowledge in the making of economic policy is a dual one. It does offer some objective guidance on what aims are feasible and what means need to be employed to achieve them. Because economic evidence has this role, it is an important tactic for political interests to mould the evidence to suit their ends.

CONCLUSION

This chapter has sketched the political context in which economic policy is made in the UK. This country belongs to the type of political-economic system characterised by a *mixed economy* and *liberal democracy*. The latter refers to a system of elected government whose powers are clearly circumscribed by law, which is administered by an independent judiciary. There is therefore considerable scope for individual freedom. The other main characteristic of the political system is *pluralism*. This refers to a political decision-making process in which a wide range of political interests have some influence. This is brought to bear not only through periodic elections but, more importantly, throughout the continual process of policy formulation and implementation, by means of lobbying government, influencing public opinion and being consulted and appeased by government.

A preliminary indication of the significance of the political system in the UK was given in this chapter by discussing who makes economic policy. Three primary groups of actors—voters, politicians and bureaucrats—were considered and their roles related to the main institutions involved in the making of economic policy. The role of these actors and of governments and governmental institutions outside the UK was emphasised.

Chapters 1 and 2 have presented the two major mechanisms in a pluralist mixed economy for representing the interests of individuals—the market and the political system. The way the political system registers the preferences of individuals, through voting and through the activities of political interests, contrasts with the way markets convey individuals' preferences through casting money votes and so registering willingness to exchange goods, services and money. The distinction between markets and government as allocative devices parallels the distinction between the market and the political system as mechanisms for representing individual and collective interests. Chapter 3 examines how government and markets interact to determine the allocation and distribution of resources, using the coal industry as a case-study.

3   Markets or Planning?
The Case of Coal

The key aims are for the coal industry to earn a satisfactory return on capital while competing in the marketplace to improve efficiency, and to bring capacity into line with its continuing share of the market. (*The Government's Expenditure Plans 1984/85 to 1986/87*, Cmnd, 9748, HMSO, London, 1983)

The NCB are continuing to pursue a policy of building a secure, high-volume, low-cost industry which will pay substantial wages to those who work in it. . . . the NCB plans to . . . achieve the required supply/demand balance and give the industry a stable base capacity of 100 million tonnes from which output could be expanded as market opportunities arise. (National Coal Board (1984) *Report and Accounts 1983/84, pp.1-2*)

The National Union of Mineworkers argues for production of 200 million tonnes a year. If opencast mining and private production were ended, that would mean additional NCB production of 95 million tonnes a year. At current productivity levels that would mean 188,700 additional jobs for miners. Such a level of employment in the industry would provide the basis for a rational long-term energy policy based on coal. . . Of course, a sustained recovery of employment in coal would require a different economic policy, one in which public sector spending led to a general economic expansion and jobs for all. Selective import controls would be required. . . (The National Union of Mineworkers (1984) *Campaign for Coal, Briefing Booklet I*)

The clash of perspectives over whether the size and structure of an industry should be determined by market forces or by government planning is starkly revealed in these quotations from the parties involved in the coalminers' strike of 1984/85. This chapter uses the coal dispute as a vehicle for exploring the nature of the *market mechanism* and *government planning* as methods of *allocating* and *distributing* resources. It introduces two important criteria for assessing the relative merits of markets and government as allocative mechanisms. These are *efficiency* and *distributional* considerations and they will be used throughout the book. The case of coal also illustrates how markets and government interact in practice to determine what is produced and how it is produced; who benefits and who pays the costs.

The Conservative government's policy towards the coal industry—and industry in general—was that there should be less support by government, both financial and regulatory, and a greater role for market forces. For an industry whose costs exceed its revenues, as was the case with the National Coal Board, a reduction of government support means that it has to cut costs, and this usually involves closing excess productive capacity. Even if the existing labour force is redeployed, as occurs when pits are closed, this policy still means a cut in the number of mining jobs. As many pits are concentrated in areas of high unemployment, the loss of mining jobs is likely to worsen local unemployment and lead to the dissolution of close-knit mining communities. The National Union of Mineworkers resisted this policy by striking against the pit closures planned by the NCB. As the NCB (which began trading as British Coal in 1986) can only maintain loss-making pits because it has access to government funds, its decisions regarding pit closures and the pay and conditions of its labour force are dependent on government policy. In turn, the finance the government gives the NCB is not fully in its control. If the NCB makes a loss the government has to fund the deficit since there are no provisions whereby a nationalised industry can go bankrupt, like a private sector firm, or even a public sector company such as BL, which is not nationalised but incorporated under the Companies Act.

Prior to nationalisation in 1946, the coal industry was in the hands of many individual owners. The Coal Industry Nationalisation Act 1946 gave the NCB a monopoly of coal production in the UK. Currently it produces 95 per cent of UK coal, the rest being produced by private operators under licence from the NCB. The Act specified that the NCB had the duty to make 'supplies of coal available, of such quantities and sizes, in such quantities and at such prices as may seem to them best calculated to further the public interest in all respects, including the avoidance of any undue or unreasonable preference or advantage'. Not surprisingly, the Act did not define that elusive concept 'the public interest'; a term which refers to some, usually unspecified, balancing of conflicting interests which is deemed to be in the interests of society as a whole. The miners' strike of 1984/85 was a violent clash of interests between miners and their communities, on the one hand, and coal consumers and taxpayers, as represented by the government, on the other. Nationalisation does not of itself solve the problem of what constitutes the public interest.

THE FORTUNES OF THE COAL INDUSTRY

Though the NCB has a monopoly of coal production, it still faces competition from other sources of energy. In 1950 90 per cent of the UK's energy was provided by coal compared to 35.6 per cent in 1983. The changing reliance on the different primary fuels is shown in Table 3.1. Technical change, combined with the increased availability of alternative fuels—in particular, oil and natural gas—caused a steep decline in the demand for coal during the 1950s and 1960s. As diesel engines replaced steam in ships and locomotives, and as households and industry turned to natural gas and oil, the main outlet for coal became domestic electricity generation, which now accounts for around 80 per cent of the NCB's market.

Table 3.1: Sources of energy in the UK 1950—83 (as percentages of total energy)

	1950	1960	1973	1983	1984
Coal	89.6	73.7	37.6	35.6	21.2
Oil	10.0	25.3	46.4	33.9	46.5
Natural gas	0.0	00.0	12.5	23.9	25.1
Nuclear	0.0	00.0	2.9	5.8	6.6
Hydro-electricity	0.4	0.6	0.6	0.8	0.6

Source: *Digest of UK Energy Statistics.*

The *demand* for a product—which is the quantity people are willing to buy—generally depends on its price relative to substitutes and on consumers' incomes and tastes. In the case of coal, the rapid decline in the demand for coal in the 1950s and 1960s was due to the advent of cheap oil and natural gas. The decline in coal's share of the energy market was arrested in 1973/74, when oil prices were quadrupled by the Organisation of Petroleum Exporting Countries (OPEC), which had formed a successful cartel to restrict output and so raise its price.

The demand for coal also depends on the general demand for energy and this will be higher the more output the economy is producing. The 1973/74 rise in oil prices made energy as a whole more expensive and the long-term response has been to find ways of conserving energy. As a result the amount of energy used per unit of national output has declined since the mid-1970s and continues to do so. Total UK energy demand in 1983 was no greater than in 1968. So even with a 30—40 per cent price advantage over oil, as in the early 1980s, and a modest rate of growth for national output, the number of tonnes of coal absorbed by the UK market has been declining, as shown in Table 3.2. By 1985 the NCB estimated the demand to be 100 million tonnes a year. Coal consumption in the UK has, in recent years, been less than the amount produced and this explains in part the losses incurred by the NCB since 1980.

Table 3.2: The demand and supply of coal in the UK 1959–83 (million tonnes)

	1950	1960	1970	1975	1979	1983	1985
Consumption (million tonnes)	206	200	157	122	129	112	101.2
Imports (million tonnes)	–	–	1.2	4.8	5.1	5.1	12.1
Exports (million tonnes)	17.2	5.6	3.0	1.4	2.5	6.8	3.3
Production (million tonnes)	220	197	145	126	123	105	104.5
Colliery manpower (000s)	691	602	287	247	233	192	154
No. of collieries	901	698	292	241	219	170	133

Source: *National Coal Board Report and Accounts*, 1984–85; 1985–86.

As the demand for coal has declined, so has the number of miners and pits. In 1947 the NCB employed 704,000 miners at 958 pits; by 1985 this had declined to 154,000 miners and 133 collieries. In addition to the decline in the demand for coal, international competition had intensified: US, Australian and South African coal can be shipped to Western Europe and still be cheaper than NCB coal. So even though an industry is a public sector monopoly it is not totally insulated from the operation of market forces: a decline in the market's demand for the product brings about some contraction in the industry. But an industry need not face the full rigours of the market if it is protected by government measures.

GOVERNMENT POLICY TOWARDS THE COAL INDUSTRY

Like all the nationalised industries, the NCB is set performance targets, or objectives, by the government. In contrast to this a private sector company would set its own objectives, like maximising profits or increasing its market share. The Nationalisation Acts of the 1940s required each of the nationalised industries to break even. In the case of the coal industry the Act stated that 'the revenues of the Board shall be not less than sufficient for meeting all their outgoings properly chargeable to revenue account. . .on an average of good and bad years'. However, the coal industry, in common with some others (steel, railways and shipbuilding), has been unable to cover all its costs. This means that it has been unable to finance investment out of its own resources. Since 1956 the nationalised industries have not been allowed to raise money on the Stock Exchange, but are lent money for investment by central government, which borrows on their behalf. As noted in Chapter 1, central government net lending to the nationalised industries is part of public expenditure which it is the Treasury's job to control. Thus a loss-making nationalised industry is much more dependent financially on central government than a profitable one, and is more likely to find itself constrained by the requirements of the government's macroeconomic policies.

Each nationalised industry is attached to a particular government department; in the case of coal, the Department of Energy. To obtain funds for investment and other purposes, the NCB has to persuade the Department of the strength of its case. The Department then negotiates with the Treasury in order to obtain the funding it thinks the NCB should have. In other words it acts as a go-between, presenting the NCB's case to the Treasury and implementing government policy with respect to the coal industry. Ultimately, government policy towards the coal industry is thrashed out at Cabinet level between the Prime Minister, the Chancellor of the Exchequer and the other spending ministers, though policy decisions are frequently taken at department level. What emerges from this decision-making process may not be entirely to the liking of the Department of Energy and it may be unpalatable to the NCB and even more so to its employees.

Planning Coal?

To what extent the policies thrashed out between the NCB and the central government may be described as *planning* is dubious, not least because of the uncertain meaning attached to the term. In a very broad sense planning is a process of setting objectives, gathering information as to how those objectives may be achieved and making decisions, in the light of this information, about the action to take in order to attain the objectives. Planning is therefore essentially *rational*, as it is purposive action designed to attain specific ends. In this sense planning is regularly undertaken by households and firms in the private sector and is not confined to government. Such planning uses the information provided by markets. For instance, a household, in planning which central heating system to install, would take account of the relative prices of coal, oil and gas. A private sector coal-mining company would plan its investment in improving existing mines or sinking new ones by estimating the future demand for coal, and this would require estimating the future prices of alternative fuels, the overall demand for energy, as well as the future costs of producing coal.

A more restricted definition of planning limits it to a government activity in which it decides on what to produce and in what quantities, using criteria other than the commercial profit and loss calculations of private sector firms. The government can plan to produce more coal than a private sector firm would because it has the means to finance the ensuing financial losses or to prevent them by keeping coal prices high enough by restricting the emergence of alternative suppliers. Advocates of government planning with respect to energy would have the government decide how much each fuel would contribute to the total supply of energy, direct each fuel industry to supply the planned amount and then fix prices and subsidies to cover production costs. The government might well use the relative production costs of the different fuels to decide how much of each should be produced, but other considerations would weigh heavily as well, such as relying extensively on a non-nuclear, indigenous fuel or preserving mining communities. This sort of planning would be comprehensive. The production targets for coal, gas, electricity and oil and the use of these fuels by other industries would be coordinated by a central planning authority and imposed by using statutory directives including the control of imports and exports.

Since the end of World War II there has been no such comprehensive planning of energy in the UK. But neither has the demand and supply of energy been left to market forces alone to determine. What we have had is a combination of market forces and government action. I prefer to use the term planning to mean the centralised coordination of the allocation and distribution of resources by a state organisation charged with this responsibility, and to call the type of piecemeal action we actually have, the rational basis for which is often unclear, *government allocation*.

Since its inception the NCB has, at regular intervals, produced documents called *Plans for Coal*. As it can take a decade to develop new capacity, planning investment in coal mines requires estimates of the future demand for UK coal. Thus the NCB's *Plans for Coal* have set out production targets based on the NCB's estimates of its future sales. It is on the basis of these plans that the NCB puts its case to central government in order to get its investment plans approved and secure the finance to carry them out. One notable feature of these plans is that the NCB has always overestimated future sales—by about 20 per cent on average over six *Plans*. This upward bias in its production targets is to be expected from a public sector enterprise which has to bid for resources from the government. The most famous of these *Plans*, the 1974 *Plan for Coal*, was drawn up in the aftermath of the oil crisis. With the quadrupling of oil prices, coal's future prospects took on a new lease of life as a much cheaper alternative fuel, particularly for generating electricity. The 1974 *Plan* projected coal sales of 134 million tonnes in 1985 and 135–200 million tonnes for the year 2000. To attain this target required considerable investment, not just to expand capacity but also to close old high-cost mines and replace them with new, low-cost mines such as Selby and the Vale of Belvoir. The 1974 *Plan* was agreed with the unions and endorsed by the government. The NCB was able to go ahead with its investment programme which, by 1984, had cost £7 billion (1984 prices).

In the event the sales targets proved too optimistic; from 1978 they were steadily revised downwards finally to 112 million tonnes for 1985—22 million less than envisaged in 1974. Apart from the natural desire of the NCB to overestimate future demand, other reasons were: assuming too high a growth rate for the economy as a whole, and not anticipating sufficiently the fall in the amount of energy required per unit of national output. The NCB also grossly overestimated the demand for coking coal by British Steel because it took on trust British Steel's own estimates for the future demand for its products, which proved to be far too optimistic. Consequently the NCB invested in unnecessary new coking coal capacity. This shows how attempts to coordinate planning within the public sector can compound the problems arising from ill-founded, often politically-motivated judgements. As a consequence of basing investment plans on overoptimistic forecasts and closing old capacity more slowly than originally envisaged, because of union resistance, the NCB found itself by 1980 producing more coal than it could sell. Coal stocks were growing and contributing to the NCB's deteriorating financial position. The Monopolies and Mergers Commission, who in 1982 were asked by the government to report on the NCB's efficiency, criticised the Board's planning and commented tartly that development plans had taken precedence over the requirement to break even.

As well as suffering from excess capacity the coal industry's costs had been rising relative to prices in general and relative to the price of coal on world markets. The Monopolies and Mergers Commission noted:

that in spite of increased operating deficits and mounting stockpiles of unsold coal, and against a background of reduced recruitment needs and a decline in natural manpower wastage, mineworkers' earnings have continued to increase relative to those of workers in most other industries. We have no doubt that this is a reflection of the collective bargaining pressures in the industry.

The cost of a tonne of coal in some collieries was considerably in excess of its domestic price. In 1981/82 the NCB reckoned that the worst 10 per cent of pits lost an average of £24 a tonne and 70 pits lost over £10 a tonne, compared to an average of £36.5 per tonne in revenue. As a consequence of these developments the continued implementation of the 1974 *Plan for Coal* would have required large and increasing sums of money from the government to finance the NCB's mounting losses.

The NCB was induced to change its plans when the incoming Conservative government in 1979 tightened the financial screws. Two aspects of the government's economic policy caused it to turn its attention to the NCB. First, there was its aim to reduce the total amount of public expenditure: reducing its net lending and payment of subsidies and grants to the nationalised industries was a major element in trying to achieve this aim. The second policy objective was to make British industry more efficient, and this aim has been especially targeted at the public corporations. If the cost of coal is reduced (or prevented from rising as much as it would have done) then electricity costs, of which almost half are attributable to coal, will be lower and industrial and domestic users will benefit.

The Conservative government sought to control the public corporations by limiting the amount of finance each can raise from external sources. These external sources are central government net lending, subsidies and grants, as well as borrowing from the private sector—either from banks or from abroad—as the public corporations are not allowed direct access to the British capital market. In August 1979 the NCB was set an *external financing limit* and the requirement to break even on its revenue account by 1983/84. The production targets of the *Plan for Coal* could not be met within the financial targets now set and so the NCB had to change course. It revised its estimates of sales down to 120 million tonnes, and early in 1981 announced a programme of pit closures.

There was an instant outcry from the NUM. Welsh coalminers went on strike and the other areas threatened to follow suit. The government backed down and increased its grants to the NCB so that the pit closure proposals could be withdrawn. It has been speculated that the then chairman of the NCB, Derek Ezra, and the NUM President, Joe Gormley, who worked quite closely together, connived at this outcome, enabling the Board to use the miners' industrial muscle to get more money from the government.

Stimulating Demand for Coal

Government involvement in the coal industry has gone further than agreeing with the NCB its investment and restructuring plans, setting financial targets and lending it money. The government has also over the years helped to maintain the NCB's market for coal. Although there have been no statutory restrictions on importing coal since the 1950s, this has been discouraged. Dock facilities for handling coal remain limited and the Central Electricity Generating Board has been pressured by central government to buy the vast proportion of its coal from the NCB. Given the absence of central planning, the government does not itself determine how much NCB coal the CEGB should buy: this is determined in bilateral negotiations between the two nationalised industries concerned. In the long-term contracts negotiated in recent years, the CEGB has stipulated that the price it pays for coal be related to changes in the retail price index, and to the prices of foreign coal and competing fuels. This ensures that the price the NCB can charge is constrained by market forces. After the increase in oil prices in 1973, the government implemented further measures to encourage the use of coal. These included grants to the CEGB for burning coal, subsidies for coke burning, and grants to private industry to convert from oil-and gas-fired boilers to coal. The Department of Energy also finances research into new processes for burning coal. The demand for coal is increased by the tax on heavy fuel oil, which raises the latter's price relative to coal. These measures are an indication of the many ways in which government can intervene by altering relative prices in order to encourage some activities and discourage others.

Subsidies to Coal

The government has also provided what are called social grants towards the cost of pit closures, which finance the NCB's expenses in relocating redundant miners to other pits. The government funds the Redundant Mineworkers' Payments Scheme, started in 1965. This enables the NCB to provide redundancy payments and early retirement pensions at terms more generous than those available under general legislation to workers in other industries. In addition the NCB has received operating grants for specific items such as the costs of selling surplus coal on foreign markets at a price below that it would get on the home market, or meeting subsidence claims. When the NCB's revenues have failed to cover its costs, after the social grant and the operating grant have been take account of, it has then been paid an additional deficit grant from the government. Table 3.3 gives some indication of the NCB's financial position and the money received from the government in recent years. Internally generated funds—the difference between what the NCB receives in revenues and its costs—have been negative so the NCB has had to meet the difference from outside sources—mainly from the government. Some has been met by the social, operating and deficit grants—grants because this is money that is not repaid. The rest is financed by borrowing—either from the private sector or from government. This is repayable—with interest—though in the past the government has written off NCB debts to it.

Table 3.3: The NCB's profits and grants and loans from government (£ millions)

	Operating profit	Internally generated funds	Redundant mineworkers' payments scheme	Other government grants[1]	Net borrowing from government
1981/2	−248	−292	49	575 '	974
1982/3	−275	−301	81	520	288
1983/4	−718	−769	192	1145	613
1984/5	−1455	−1610	199	2414	−300

Sources: *The Government's Expenditure Plans* Cmnd 9143; Cmnd 9428; *NCB Report and Accounts*; The Monopolies Commission (1983); the NCB.

Note: 1. these are for the social costs of closing mines plus a grant to cover the NCB's deficit.

The Conflict of 1984/85

As Table 3.3 shows, the various measures of government support for the coal industry gave rise to an increasing reliance by the NCB on government funding. In 1983 the government signalled the renewal of its policy to cut the coal industry's financial losses by appointing as NCB chairman, Ian MacGregor, a man openly committed to the government's view that the coal industry should be made to operate as a commercial undertaking. With a profit-oriented businessman as chairman, the consultative decision-making style of a management board dominated since nationalisation by consensus-seeking mining engineers, had come to an end. The recently elected President of the NUM, Arthur Scargill was committed to conflict politics. The NCB's announcement of the closure of Cortonwood colliery in March 1984 precipitated a strike which was to last for a year. While the strike failed to force the NCB and the government to withdraw the policy of closing loss-making pits, it resulted in a further weakening of the NCB's financial position in the short run for which the government had to pick up the bill. The Coal Industry Act 1985 provided the NCB with up to £2.65 billion in government grants over the next two years, whereas the government had intended in 1980 that the NCB should break even by 1986/87. In the year following the strike, the NCB reduced its pits by 33 and the number of miners by 21,000. Output per man increased by 30 per cent. Consequently it reduced its losses to only £50 million—the smallest since 1978. However the substantial fall in oil prices since 1985 has worsened the NCB's chances of becoming financially self-sufficient.

The interest of the coal dispute for the analysis of economic policy-making is as a case-study of two contrasting models of resource allocation. One is that market forces are the best determinants of the size and structure of an industry—I call this the *market efficiency* model. The other, which I term the *social efficiency* model, argues that an industry should be planned by government according to social criteria. The rest of this chapter examines these two policy models more closely, by considering the two key criteria, *efficiency* and *distribution*, against which the alternatives of market or government allocation are assessed. These criteria are not specific to the coal industry: they apply to any sector or to the economy as a whole and lie at the heart of the debate about how the boundary lines of the mixed economy should be drawn. They will be used subsequently at many points throughout the book.

THE MARKET EFFICIENCY MODEL

The central proposition of the *market efficiency* model is that *competitive markets* allocate resources more efficiently than either non-competitive markets or government. Economists define an *efficient allocation of resources* as a situation where it is impossible, given current technological knowledge, to alter the way resources are being used so as to produce more of one good without producing less of at least one other good. Given this definition, the coal industry is *inefficient* if it is possible to reallocate men and capital to different mines and produce more coal than with the existing allocation. An equivalent test of *efficiency* is that the coal industry is inefficient if it is possible to produce its current level of output using fewer miners or other inputs. If this can be done, then the average cost of a tonne of coal is higher that it could be if resources were used more efficiently.

In a *competitive market economy* the wages the NCB—or any other firm—pays to its employees and the interest it pays on the capital it invests would reflect the value that these resources have if put to *alternative uses*. The value the factors of production used to make a good would have, if put to an alternative use, is called the *opportunity cost* of the good. If resources are to be *allocated efficiently* then it must not be the case that the factors of production used to produce any good would be more highly valued if used to produce something else. So if the *opportunity cost* of producing a unit of output exceeds the *price* consumers are willing to pay for that unit of output, this indicates that resources are *inefficiently allocated*.

On this basis it was argued that the NCB was allocating resources inefficiently because the cost of producing a tonne of coal exceeded its price. This situation is shown in Figure 3.1. The curve CC indicates how the cost of producing a tonne of coal rises as output is expanded because of the impact of the contribution of the more costly pits. The *marginal cost of coal* is the increase in total cost when output is expanded by one unit (such as one tonne). For coal it rises as output is increased, using the current allocation of men and pits. At an output of 90 million tonnes a year the *marginal cost* of coal exceeds the price the NCB gets from selling a tonne of coal, the market signals that the coal is valued by consumers less highly than the alternative goods that could be produced with these resources.

A private sector firm would be unable to continue in business if it incurred losses and so would be forced in these circumstances either to cut output or improve its efficiency, or both. A privately-owned firm would have more incentive to maximise its profits, as this would directly benefit its owners. *Profit-maximisation* occurs when the difference between a firm's total revenues and its total costs is as large as possible. This occurs at the level of output for which *marginal cost equals marginal revenue*. *Marginal cost* is the addition to total costs of producing one more unit of output; while *marginal revenue* is the addition to total revenue from selling one more unit of output. To see that the equality of marginal revenue with marginal cost is the point of profit-maximisation, consider what would happen to the firm's profits if it moved away from this position. If marginal cost is rising and marginal revenue is falling or constant, then to increase output beyond the point where marginal cost and marginal revenue are equal means adding more to total cost than to total revenue, causing profits to fall. Starting from a position where marginal cost equals marginal revenue and then reducing output, means cutting total revenue by more than total cost. This move would also reduce profits. Hence the profit-maximising output occurs at the level of output for which marginal revenue equals marginal cost.

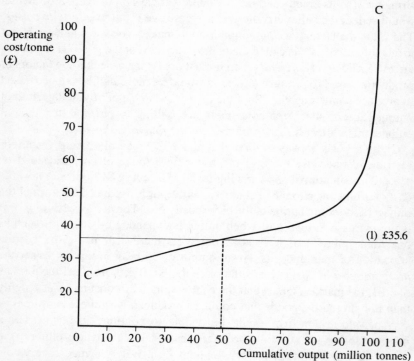

Source: MMC from NCB information.

(1)=Average net proceeds per tonne

Figure 3.1: Deep-mined coal production
Unit operating costs against cumulative output, 1981–82

The search for profit-maximising production levels by private enterprises is a crucial part of the mechanism by which an efficient allocation of resources is arrived at—so long as firms are operating in competitive markets. The *degree of competition* a firm faces depends on the extent to which it can raise its prices without losing its market share to rival suppliers. The greater the number of existing or potential suppliers the greater is likely to be the degree of competition. *Perfect competition* exists if each firm in the market cannot affect the price of the product by increasing or decreasing its own supply. Since the price of output is not affected by the amount the individual firm produces, then each additional unit it sells will increase the firm's total revenue by the amount of the price. In other words, a perfectly competitive firm's marginal revenue is constant as it expands or contracts output and is equal to the market price of the product. This means that a *profit-maximising, perfectly competitive firm would equate its marginal cost to the price of the product.*

In terms of Figure 3.1, let us assume that the CC curve represents the marginal cost curve and assume that the NCB operates in a highly competitive environment because consumers can easily obtain imported coal at world prices. Then, at the profit-maximising output where marginal cost equals price (at around 49 million tonnes in the figure) resources are *efficiently allocated* from the point of view of consumers. This is because the value of the resources used to produce the marginal tonne of coal—the marginal cost of coal—just equals the price of coal, which is the value consumers attach to the marginal tonne of coal. If less coal were produced then the price of coal would exceed the value of the resources used to produce the marginal unit of coal. Resources would then be inefficiently allocated because consumers valued extra resources devoted to coal production more than they valued their current use in alternative products. But if coal output exceeds the profit-maximising level, the marginal cost of coal is greater than the price of coal. In this case resources are also inefficiently allocated. This time because the value placed by consumers on the marginal unit of coal—as measured by its price—is less than the value of the resources if used to produce alternative products, which is measured by the marginal cost of coal.

Competition between firms is essential if markets are to allocate resources efficiently. The threat of competition from other firms prevents each firm from raising its price above its marginal costs. If price is above marginal cost, then consumers demand less of the good than if the price were equal to marginal cost and too little of the good is produced. Consumers value extra units of this product more than the alternative goods being produced with the resources as currently allocated. This situation could not persist for long in a competitive market because other suppliers would be attracted into the market by the prospect of earning a profit from selling the product at a price in excess of its cost. An increase in output would then cause the price to fall in order to induce consumers to buy more.

So, for consumers, lack of competition—*imperfect competition*—is undesirable, because it leads firms to charge prices in excess of the opportunity costs of their products and thus make *monopoly profits*. Such firms possess *market power*. But a firm may choose to enjoy its *market power* not as high profits, but in the form of higher costs. Lack of competition means that firms have less compulsion to keep costs as low as possible. As publicly-owned industries are less likely to be allowed to go bankrupt, the pressures to keep down costs are likely to be even less than in the private sector. The extent to which a firm's costs are greater than the minimum that could be achieved if the firm were efficiently run is termed *x-inefficiency*. Firms have *x-inefficiency* because this makes for an easier life. Getting costs down requires effort from both workers and managers. Higher costs can benefit workers as well as managers—if they get more pay and better working conditions, including a more leisurely work tempo. *Market power*, exercised either as high profits or as x-inefficient high costs, means higher prices for consumers. A conflict of interests between consumers and producers is inherent in any economic system. It is a complex web of conflicting interests since individuals are both consumers and producers. Economic policy in a mixed economy is frequently about how this conflict is resolved.

The view that resources should be allocated via competitive markets is biased towards the interests of consumers. Though if greater competition increases the efficiency with which a given quantity of resources is used it will increase the total amount of output available to be distributed to all members of society. Furthermore, if it encourages the searching out of new opportunities, new processes and products it will stimulate technical progress and so promote economic growth. However there will be groups within the economy who feel threatened by increased competition and are likely to become net losers, given the absence of a system which ensures complete compensation of those who are made worse off by policy changes.

So from the perspective of the *market efficiency model*, a state-owned monopoly is likely to be x-inefficient and to be run for the benefit of its workers and managers, rather than in the interests of consumers or taxpayers. Policy towards the coal industry informed from this perspective would be far more extreme than that adopted by the Conservative government. It sought only to put pressure on the NCB's costs by placing limits on its deficit financing, though it would be feasible to inject more competition by ceasing to discourage imports and giving the CEGB and British Steel a free hand in choosing whether to buy British or foreign coal. The industry could also be split up into much smaller units, as workers' cooperatives or privately-owned firms, so that collieries would have to compete with each other. Without state financing of surplus supplies of coal, the pits which could not bring their unit costs below the price of coal would have to go out of business.

SOCIAL EFFICIENCY

The *criterion for an efficient allocation of resources is that the market prices of goods should equal their marginal costs*. This criterion is the keystone of orthodox economic theory and provides the standard reference point for the economic analysis of policy measures. But it does not by itself imply that private sector firms operating in competitive markets will achieve an efficient allocation of resources. Nor does it always imply that a firm which is making a loss, as measured by accountants, is producing goods which are worth less to consumers than their opportunity cost. There are number of reasons why a competitive market solution may not result in an economically efficient use of resources. These were put forward by NUM to argue that, while there were loss-making pits, as reckoned by the NCB using standard accounting data, there were no uneconomic pits, i.e. no pits which were using resources which would be more highly valued elsewhere in the economy.

First, for it to be correct to count the total wage bill of a colliery as part of the opportunity cost of coal, it must be the case that no permanent increase in unemployment would result as the consequence of closing that colliery. To the extent that miners would remain permanently unemployed or take a job another unemployed person would have got, their alternative output is zero. So, assuming that leisure time when unemployed has no value to the individuals concerned, the opportunity cost to the economy of such miners is zero. The NUM, in arguing that there were no uneconomic pits, assumed that all mining redundancies would mean an equivalent permanent net loss of jobs in the economy, thus making the opportunity cost of employing miners zero.[1] They then valued the coal produced by every pit at the average price received for it by the NCB. This ignores any potential availability of cheaper imported coal and the existence of excess production which the NCB was having to stockpile, which would make the marginal value of NCB coal to the economy considerably less than its price. However, if one assumes miners have no opportunity cost and marginal coal has a positive value then, provided the non-labour costs of producing coal are less than its value to consumers, it is *socially efficient* to employ these miners to produce coal. The term *social efficiency* refers to the costs and benefits of an activity to society as a whole. In economic analysis an activity is said to be socially efficient if *it yields benefits to the economy as a whole which exceed its opportunity costs*. The money costs and money revenues of the firm undertaking this activity may be a

misleading guide to its social efficiency because they do not measure costs
and benefits to society as a whole.

Private and Social Costs

The costs that a firm or individual incurs in undertaking an activity are termed
private costs. Anything that a firm or individual pays for on a market is a
private cost. The wages paid to its employees and the money spent on raw
materials and capital goods are the NCB's private costs. Also, the use of factors
owned by the firm but not paid for in money, such as an owner-manager's
time, are private costs. So the private costs of any activity are those incurred
by the agent undertaking that activity and these may differ from the *total social
costs* of the activity to the economy as a whole. If it is true that miners' wages
are in excess of what they could earn in alternative occupations, then the private cost to the NCB of employing miners exceeds their opportunity cost to
the economy. The *opportunity cost* of miners to the economy—that is, what
they could produce in other industries—is their *social cost*. In general terms,
the social cost of an activity is the value of the resources it uses if they were
allocated to the next best alternative.

Private and Social Benefits

Similarly, *social benefits* are distinguished from *private benefits*. The
private benefits to a firm of its business activities are measured by the
money revenues obtained from selling its products. But the *social benefits*
of its products may be greater or less than its private benefits. The *social
benefits* of an activity are its *private benefits*, received by the individual or
firm undertaking the activity, plus any additional benefits to others. In the
case of coal, the NUM maintained that there are various considerations that
make the social benefits of coal greater than the revenues obtained by the
NCB. They argued that the social cost of nuclear power is much greater
than the CEGB or the government estimate, because of its radiation risks.
If this were the case, then the social costs of the nuclear power stations
planned for the future would exceed the costs of coal-fired power stations
and should not be built. Scrapping the nuclear power programme would
increase the future demand for coal. Another argument is that the current
generation should value the welfare of future generations more than
market-based calculations do. This value judgement justifies working
existing mines until they are exhausted, even if the current costs are high,
because of the benefits to future generations of delaying the exploitation of
the more cheaply worked deposits. A further social benefit, not measurable
by market prices, is the value of retaining closely-knit communities in their
existing locations. The social calculation of the NUM, not surprisingly,
yielded social benefits from retaining all collieries in excess of the social
costs of doing so.

Externalities

To decide whether the market or social efficiency approach is superior is easy if one comes to the question armed with personal prejudices. If not, it is necessary to weigh up the strengths and limitations of each. The weakness of the market efficiency approach is that it is narrow in the sense that it ignores costs and benefits that are not reflected in market prices. Mainstream economic theory—neoclassical microeconomics—teaches that even *perfectly competitive markets will not produce an efficient resource allocation if private costs differ from social costs and private benefits diverge from social benefits*. If this is the case, then there are said to be *externalities*. An activity undertaken by an economic agent which yields costs or benefits to other people that are not exchanged for money or for goods and services gives rise to an *externality*. An example of an *external cost* is pollution. For instance, the private cost of using coal does not at present include the cost of air pollution caused by the emission of sulphur dioxide from coal-burning. Such emissions exacerbate respiratory diseases and cause acid rain which is thought to damage vegetation. An example of an *external benefit* is the security of supply attached to using an indigenous fuel rather than relying on imports.

So, from the standpoint of the economist's standard definition of an *efficient allocation of resources*, the *social efficiency approach* is correct in principle. The problem is applying it in practice. The great stumbling-block is the quantification of external social costs and benefits. What value is to be given to decreasing the probability of nuclear contamination, to preserving mining communities, to saving cheap coal seams for future generations, or to the security of having indigenous fuels on tap? Economists have made valiant attempts to quantify these kinds of social costs and benefits, in a branch of applied economics called *cost-benefit analysis* (discussed in Chapter 10). But these attempts have not gone without criticism, especially by those adversely affected by the policies such calculations suggest. Because the quantification of social costs and benefits usually depends on making particular assumptions, which can be dubious, contentious and hidden, the social efficiency criterion is ripe for high-jacking by interest groups looking for statistical backing for their cause.

The *social efficiency criterion* is widely used by economists to justify government intervention in the workings of markets. The intervention justified comes in many forms; state-ownership, laws, subsidies and taxes, to name just a few we have come across in relation to the coal industry. Thus the social efficiency criterion is linked with *planning*, though it need not imply such a comprehensive and integrated form of government intervention. If resource allocation is to be determined by comparing social costs and benefits and trying to maximise the difference between them, then this calls for government intervention to replace or redirect market forces.

Economists working within the social efficiency perspective (an area of economics known as welfare economics) have, on the whole, paid little attention to the effect on resource allocation of the type of organisation undertaking the economic activity in question. Specifically, private production costs are assumed given at their achievable minimum, regardless of whether the firm is in a competitive or monopoly market, in the public or private sector. In other words, *inefficiency* is ignored in this approach. In contrast, the *market efficiency* approach strongly suggests that a competitive environment is essential if costs are to be kept low and innovation undertaken efficiently. This approach places greater emphasis on the dynamic response of firms to an ever-changing environment, whereas the *social efficiency* approach deals with resource allocation at one moment in time, or over a time-horizon for which future costs and benefits are known.[2]

DISTRIBUTION

The social efficiency criterion states that a *policy will increase economic efficiency if the social benefits it creates exceed the social costs it incurs*. The social benefits are calculated by summing up all benefits to all affected individuals. The sum of social costs is similarly arrived at. The difference between them measures the extent of the change in economic efficiency.

However, there are two important value judgements underlying this concept of social efficiency as commonly used in economics. The first is that a pound is valued equally by everyone. This assumption stems from requiring social costs and benefits to be quantified: money is the only common unit of measurement for all the goods and services that comprise social benefits and costs. A unit of money is made equivalent to a unit of welfare for want of any better measure of welfare. The second value judgement is that how the costs and benefits are distributed does not matter: all that matters is that the total of social benefits should exceed total social costs. But the people receiving the social benefits may be quite distinct from those bearing the social costs. In the coal industry example, the miners and other employees of the NCB stood to lose from pit closures, while coal consumers and tax payers would gain. The *distributional* implications of the government's policy towards the coal industry, in terms of both material well-being and political power, overshadowed the issue of efficiency.[3]

In principle, the *efficiency* aspect of a policy can be separated from its *distributional* implications. If the social benefits of a policy exceed its social costs, then it would be possible for those who benefit to spend some of their gains compensating the losers, so that the losers ended up no worse off than before. So long as the social costs are less than the social benefits, then there will still be positive net benefits left over for the gainers, even after they have fully compensated the losers. So in principle, a policy which is socially efficient, in that it produces an excess of social benefit over social cost, must also be capable of leaving nobody worse off because they can be fully compensated by the gainers; the gainers will still have sufficient left over to be better off than before. *A policy which increases the welfare of some people, while not making anybody worse off, is said to be Pareto-efficient.*[4]

Quite often economic policy measures are accompanied by some compensation for the losers, though frequently this is seen as inadequate by those who are adversely affected. Over the last twenty years governments have sought to compensate the coal-miners for the cost of redundancy through the social grant paid to the NCB and the Redundant Mineworkers' Payments Scheme. This has covered the redeployment of miners and financed voluntary redundancy and early retirement. How much the government pays miners to compensate for redundancy does not affect the extent to which closing mines results in a gain in social efficiency: the sum of social benefits and that of social costs (given that they could be estimated) and the difference between them is not affected by how these social benefits and costs are allocated between miners, coal consumers and taxpayers. But, of course, the *distributional* impact of a policy is still of prime importance to those affected by it and, in political terms, usually overshadows the criterion of *economic efficiency*.

CONCLUSION: EFFICIENCY AND DISTRIBUTION

This chapter has served two main functions. The first was to develop further the broad theme of this book, introduced in Chapter 1, of economic policy-making in the context of the *mixed economy*, where both *markets and government allocate and distribute resources*. The coal industry example shows how both market forces and government interact to determine the size and structure of the industry and the distribution of the costs and benefits associated with that industry.

The second purpose was to introduce the two basic criteria economists use in analysing economic policy. These are *economic* or *social efficiency* and *distribution*. The first criterion asks: 'What is the effect of a policy measure on social efficiency? Will it result in an overall increase in real output, interpreted in a wide sense to mean an excess of social benefits over social costs?' If it does, then this means that there is the potential for those who gain by the policy to compensate those who lose by it, so the losers are no worse off, while the gainers still experience an increase in their welfare. However this compensation need not occur for the policy measure to be deemed to improve economic efficiency. Quite often the efficiency criterion is not expressed so explicitly in terms of comparing changes in social costs and benefits. The effects of policy are posed in terms of its likely impact on output or employment, on the implicit presumption that any increase in these implies greater efficiency.

A narrower criterion of efficiency—that of *market efficiency*—was examined in the context of a policy aimed at making the coal industry more efficient by getting it to operate like a commercial enterprise, i.e. one which makes its decisions on the basis of profitability. The reasons for expecting greater competition in a market to promote the efficient allocation of resources were outlined. However, the existence of externalities which create discrepancies between private costs and benefits and social costs and benefits means that even perfect competition cannot guarantee a socially efficient allocation of resources. But, given the problems of identifying and measuring all social costs and benefits government intervention, in turn, offers no guarantee of achieving a socially efficient outcome. Furthermore, both the market efficiency criterion and the social efficiency criterion have implications for the distribution of income and other aspects of social welfare. Their use cannot be advocated without making a value judgement about distribution.

The *distribution* criterion asks how a policy measure affects individuals and groups. Who gains and who loses and by how much? To recommend a policy which benefits one section of the community at the expense of another, is to make an explicit value judgement. Quite often economists, in common with others, are concerned to promote *equity* or fairness. This objective often implies reducing differences in income, wealth and general welfare between individuals. A policy can be recommended because of its distributional effects, even if it is socially inefficient. Conversely, a socially efficient policy could make the wealthy better off without making the poor any worse off in terms of absolute income, but could be criticised for being inequitable.

The two broad concepts introduced so far—that of *markets and government as allocative mechanisms* and that of *social efficiency and distribution* as the analytical criteria for assessing economic policy—are closely interlinked. This is because the criteria of efficiency and distribution are used to assess whether, in particular instances, resources should be allocated and distributed by markets or by government. Different judgements of the relative merits of markets and government as allocative mechanisms underlie much of the disagreement over economic policy.

The next two chapters explore two key elements of the government's economic powers: the size and direction of its expenditure and the level and structure of taxation. Efficiency and distribution provide a way of assessing both the impact of government expenditure and taxation policies, and the nature of the policy-making processes by which expenditure and taxation decisions emerge.

NOTES

1. A. Glynn, *The Economic Case Against Pit Closures* (Sheffield, NUM, 1984).
2. What I have called the *market efficiency* approach thus incorporates *Austrian* arguments that the market performs well as an allocative mechanism because it is more efficient than government at gathering, disseminating and using information.
3. It is possible to combine a chosen judgement about distribution with a social cost/benefit calculation by weighting each individual's cost/benefit or each class of cost/benefit so as to reflect this particular value judgement. But this is not standard practice in cost-benefit analysis which attempts to replicate market evaluations.
4. The concept of *Pareto efficiency* is named after Vilfredo Pareto (1848–1923) who did pioneering work in welfare economics.

4 Government Expenditure

Within days of taking office, Labour will begin to implement an emergency programme of action. . . .We will:

- Provide a major increase in public investment, including transport, housing and energy conservation.
- Begin a huge programme of construction.
- Raise child benefits by £2 a week.
- Uprate the pension.
- Provide more resources for the health service with an increase of at least 3 per cent a year.
- Improve the personal social services.
- Spend more on education. Begin to develop comprehensive care for the under-fives.

The costs—an £11 billion expansion.

(Labour's Manifesto, 1983)

We shall maintain firm control of public spending and borrowing.

We have checked the relentless growth of local government spending. . .. We shall legislate to curb excessive and irresponsible rate increases by high spending councils.

We have more than matched our pledge to maintain spending on the National Health Service.

We shall continue to protect retirement pensions and other linked long-term benefits against rising prices.

We shall be ready to increase police establishments.

We have substantially increased our defence expenditure in real terms.

The national motorway and trunk network will continue to be developed and improved.

(The Conservative Party Manifesto, 1983)

Government expenditure is a major instrument of economic policy. It features strongly in election manifestos, as the political parties woo the diverse interests who benefit differently from the various public expenditure programmes. This chapter is about how government expenditure is determined. What are the main considerations brought to bear in determining its level and composition? How does government plan and control public expenditure? And what role is played by political interests both inside and outside government? These are the main questions examined.

THE COMPOSITION OF GOVERNMENT EXPENDITURE

The term *government expenditure* as used officially, is restricted to the expenditure of central and local government. It does not include the public corporations, except in so far as they receive money from central government as grants and loans. So, strictly speaking, the term should be general government expenditure.

There are various ways of classifying how government money is spent. One is the distinction between *goods and services*, on the one hand, and *transfer payments* to individuals and organisations, on the other. Government expenditure on goods and services is on items such as health, education, transport and defence. These goods may be produced in the public sector, in which case the expenditure includes the wages of government employees; or the government may purchase them from the private sector. The services provided include administering laws and regulations, which are another major instrument of economic policy. *Transfer payments* are payments the government makes to people for which it receives no goods or services in return. Pensions, unemployment benefit, student grants, subsidies to industry, the arts, or to agriculture, are all included under the heading of current grants and subsidies. Capital transfers consist of grants to the private sector to spend on fixed capital assets, and net government loans to the private sector and abroad. The third type of transfer payments is interest payments on government debt held by the private sector or by foreigners.

The proportion of government expenditure going to transfers has steadily increased over the years. In 1890 government expenditure on goods and services was three-quarters of the total: by 1938 it was two-thirds. Between 1955 and 1984 it declined from 64 per cent of the total to 52 per cent. Goods and services expenditure is subdivided between current expenditure—that is, expenditure on final consumption—and capital expenditure on investment goods. The proportion of expenditure going to public sector fixed investment has shown the most marked decline, from 12 to 11 per cent in the decade 1963–73 to around 4 per cent in the 1980s (or 5 per cent if council house sales are not subtracted from public investment).

As expenditure on goods and services has fallen over the years, so the proportion spent on transfers has risen. Current transfers on pensions, unemployment and supplementary benefits and the like had risen to 35 per cent of total government spending in 1984 and account for a good part of the rise in government expenditure as a share of GDP noted in Chapter 1. Another way of classifying government expenditure is according to the types of goods and services or transfer payments it provides. These are known as the public expenditure programmes—categories used by the government for planning public expenditure. As can be seen from Figure 4.1, over 60 per cent of public expenditure goes on four major programmes: social security, health and personal social services, defence, and education and science.

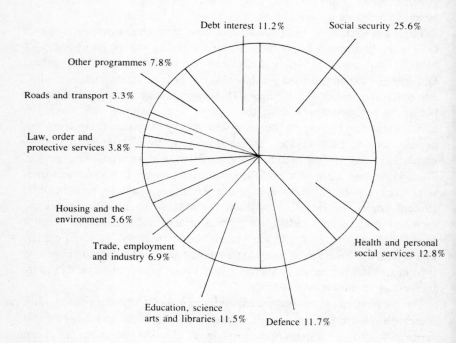

Source: *The Government's Expenditure Plans 1985/6 to 1987/8* Cmnd 9428: *Economic Trends*, August 1985.

Figure 4.1:   Government expenditure programmes as percentage of total spending, 1984—85

EFFICIENCY, DISTRIBUTION AND AGGREGATE DEMAND

The size of government expenditure since World War II (see Table 1.3) means that it has a decisive impact upon the allocation and distribution of resources and upon the functioning of the economy as a whole. The government, by undertaking capital investment and producing goods and services, which are then sold at prices above or below those a competitive market would charge, alters the allocation of resources. As we saw in the coal industry case, this may lead to a less efficient allocation of resources if state-owned businesses are x-inefficient. Or it could improve social efficiency if, for example, public enterprises succeed in removing discrepancies between private and social costs and benefits. Government expenditure is an important way of redistributing income, especially through transfer payments to people who cannot work and, less so, by providing free education, health and other social services. The redistributive impact of government is assessed more fully in Chapter 12. Government expenditure also has an overall effect on the functioning of the economy as a whole, since it is part of *aggregate demand*; that is, the total level of demand for goods and services produced in the domestic economy.

Keynesian Demand Management Policy

The central proposition of *Keynesian economics* is that the amount of aggregate demand is the major determinant of the quantity of national output produced with the nation's stock of capital and its labour force. The higher the level of aggregate demand the more output firms wish to produce and therefore the greater is the level of employment and the lower the level of unemployment. According to Keynesians, cyclical changes in the quantity of output and unemployment are due primarily to variations in the level of aggregate demand. In a depression, when unemployment is high and output low, an increase in aggregate demand is called for in order to raise output and employment. Once the economy is operating with a fully employed labour force then any further increase in aggregate demand cannot be met by raising output. Consequently prices rise and there is inflation; in at open economy imports will flow in to satisfy domestic demand and the balance of payments is likely to move into deficit. Under such inflationary conditions aggregate demand needs to be reduced.

In Keynesian thinking, the government should prevent depressions and avoid inflation by *managing aggregate demand*—raising it when unemployment is high and lowering it when excess demand threatens to cause inflation and a balance of payments problem. Thus the government manages the level of aggregate demand in order to *stabilise* the economy. One way it can do this is by altering its own spending in the required direction. Another way is by the government taking action to restrict spending by households and private sector firms. The major determinant of household consumption expenditure is the amount of income available for spending. The government can affect this by altering the amount taken in income tax or levied as taxes on goods. Interest rates also affect demand.

The higher they are the more costly it is to borrow to finance consumption and investment, which are thereby discouraged.

A government practising Keynesian economic policy responds to a downturn in economic activity by a combination of increasing its spending and reducing taxation and so enlarges the gap between the amount of government spending and tax revenues. This difference is called the *budget deficit*, and in the UK is officially termed the *public sector borrowing requirement* (PSBR). The PSBR can be financed either by the government borrowing from domestic residents or foreigners, or by an increase in the supply of money. Since the 1930s Keynesians have been highly critical of the view that the government should practise prudent housekeeping and always balance its budget. They argue that attempting to balance the budget in a recession is counterproductive as the consequent reduction in government spending or increase in tax just reduces aggregate demand further. Instead, the government should run budget deficits during depressions and a surplus only during boom periods.

Keynesian demand management policies were operated in the UK from the end of World War II until the mid-1970s. This was the period of *stop—go* policies. Although unemployment was low by today's standards—it averaged 1.7 per cent between 1948 and 1966—both Conservative and Labour governments would respond to a rise in unemployment by boosting aggregate demand. Unemployment would then fall, but inflation would accelerate and the balance of payments move into deficit. The government would then reduce aggregate demand and the whole cycle of events would be repeated. From the late 1960s, the trend of unemployment and inflation was upwards, undermining the Keynesian presumption that they were inversely related. With the quadrupling of oil prices in 1974 the world moved into its most serious recession since World War II and there was an upsurge of inflation. It was partly the inability of Keynesian policies to cope with these new problems that stimulated a revival of pre-Keynesian economics in the form of *monetarism* and *supply-side economics*.

Monetarism and Supply-Side Economics

Monetarists are particularly concerned with inflation and its relationship to high levels of government spending. *Supply-side* economists are critical of the Keynesian emphasis on aggregate demand and its neglect of those factors which determine the quantity and quality of the supply of output. Supply-siders stress the importance of the incentives for individuals to work and to save, maintaining that the expanded role of government has impaired incentives and so weakened the performance of the economy.

Both these critiques of Keynesianism focus on the problems of financing government spending. It has to be financed in one of three ways—taxation, borrowing or expanding the money supply. High taxation is said to reduce incentives—discouraging people from working or taking business risks or from saving out of taxed income when the returns are subject to further tax. They argue that government borrowing diverts resources from private sector investment by driving up interest rates. Finally, expanding the money supply to finance government budget deficits is inflationary.

Monetarism and supply-side economics are related but distinct approaches. *Monetarism* refers to the theories and empirical evidence associated with the idea that the quantity of money is the major determinant of the money value of aggregate demand and that inflation is ultimately caused by governments allowing the money supply to expand too quickly. A major reason for this, in the monetarist view, is government budget deficits. Hence monetarists tend to advocate balanced budgets or much reduced deficits. Furthermore, monetarists maintain that Keynesian policy is ineffective as well as inflationary: an increase in aggregate demand will, at best, lower unemployment only temporarily. Over the longer run workers raise money wages to compensate for the effects of price rises. Because there is therefore no permanent fall in real wages, firms will not increase the amount of labour they wish to employ and so there is no long-run fall in unemployment.

For the last decade there has been no consensus on the desirability of increased government spending as the cure for unemployment. The Thatcher government, under the influence of monetarist and supply-side arguments, came to power in 1979 with the intention of bringing down inflation by reducing the public sector borrowing requirement and controlling the growth of the money supply. This requires either raising taxation or reducing the amount of government spending. Supply-siders favour tax cuts on the grounds that these improve incentives and so increase national output. These policies are the converse of Keynesian ones. According to Keynesians the level of government spending and taxation should be determined by the amount of extra aggregate demand the government needs to create in order to achieve full employment. Under monetarist and supply-side policies the desired amount of government spending and taxation are subordinated to the task of reducing the PSBR and the growth of the money supply. The opposition parties in the UK advocate, to differing degrees, an increase in government expenditure in order to reduce unemployment by up to one million over three years or so.

CONTROLLING PUBLIC EXPENDITURE, 1976–86

The effective abandonment of Keynesian policies in the UK occurred in 1976 under a Labour government forced to cut back planned government spending in response to a severe balance of payments crisis. Between 1974 and 1975, in the wake of the first OPEC oil price rise and a rapid expansion in the UK money supply, inflation surged to 25 per cent. Government expenditures rose rapidly between 1974 and 1976, from a plateau of around 40–41 per cent of GDP in 1967 to almost 49 per cent in 1975. The Labour government, which had won power in 1974 in the course of the successful miners' strike of that year, continued the previous Conservative goverment's expansionary policies. These were reined back in 1976, amidst considerable acrimony within the Labour Party, as a condition of an IMF loan, negotiated to support the sterling exchange rate. Fears of the destabilising effects of ever-rising government expenditure triumphed over the Labour Party's traditional commitment to government spending on industry and the welfare state.

The Conservative government was elected in 1979 with the intention of reducing government expenditure in real terms. As stated in their policy document, *The Right Approach to the Economy* (1977): 'Our intention is to allow State spending and revenue a significantly smaller percentage share of the nation's annual output and income each year.' Its first full White Paper on the government's expenditure plans in March 1980 proclaimed:

The Government intend to reduce public expenditure progressively in volume terms over the next four years. This is a substantial change from the plans published by the previous Government in their White Paper of January 1979. The change of direction is essential to the achievement of the (government's) objectives. . . . These are: to bring down the rate of inflation and interest rates by curtailing the growth of the money supply and controlling Government borrowing; to restore incentives; and to plan for spending which is compatible both with the objectives for taxation and borrowing and with a realistic assessment of the prospects for economic growth. (Cmnd 7841, p.3)

The government set out targets for the years 1980/81 to 1983/84 with respect to total public expenditure, other than debt interest, in real terms and as a percentage of GDP, as well for the individual expenditure programmes. These expenditure plans, together with specific targets, for the public sector borrowing requirement and the growth of the money supply, were called the *medium term financial strategy*. The government has set great store by its adherence to the MTFS, in order to avoid the destabilising effects of continual and unpredictable changes in government policy. Although both the money supply and the PSBR targets announced in 1980 were not met and were subsequently revised, some reduction in money supply growth, the PSBR to GDP ratio and, in particular, inflation were achieved. And, as indicated in Tables 1.1 and 1.2, some contraction in the size of the public sector in terms of output and employment occurred by the mid-1980s. However, government spending in real terms—that is, taking account of inflation—actually rose rather than falling as intended.

The discrepancy between the plans and the actual out-turn for the public expenditure planning total (which excludes interest on the national debt) is shown in Table 4.1. The government's expenditure plans are published annually as a White Paper. These are listed in the left-hand column of Table 4.1. Each row records the planned total spending in that year's White Paper for the three future financial years. Going down a column shows how the expenditure plans for that year have been revised over time in subsequent White Papers. The final row shows the extent to which actual expenditure turned out higher than planned, especially in relation to the original intentions of 1980.

Table 4.1: Difference between expenditure plans and out-turn (£ billion in cash terms)

	1980−81	1981−82	1982−83	1983−84	1984−85
March 1980 White Paper, Cmnd 7841	91.2	101.0	106.4	112.4	
March 1981 White Paper, Cmnd 8175	−	104.4	109.9	113.6	
March 1982 White Paper, Cmnd 8494	−	−	114.7	120.7	127.6
Febry. 1983 White Paper, Cmnd 8789	−	−	−	119.6	126.4
Febry. 1984 White Paper, Cmnd 9143	−	−	−	−	126.4
Out-turn	93.0	104.7	113.4	120.3	128.1

Source: *The Government's Expenditure Plans 1985−86 to 1987−88*, Cmnd 9428.

The discrepancies between the plans for future spending on the major programmes set out in March 1980 and the outcome are indicated in Table 4.2. It can be seen from the last row that the government intended to cut the planning total—that is, public expenditure excluding debt interest—by an average of 1.2 per cent a year. The difference between the sum of the total programmes and the planning total is that the latter includes the contingency reserve—a sum set aside for meeting unexpected increases in individual programmes. But after four years, the planning total had risen by an average of 1.8 per cent a year, compared to the intended cut of 1.2 per cent a year.

From Table 4.2 it can be seen that the largest planned cuts were in the industry and trade, transport, housing, environmental services and education programmes and in the external financing of the nationalised industries. In the event, spending on industry and trade, transport and education actually rose, while other programmes, like law and protective services, increased more than planned. In the light of this experience the

Chancellor of the Exchequer's statement in his 1985 speech is hardly surprising: 'Controlling public expenditure is one of the most difficult tasks facing any democratic government in the modern world'. The process whereby public expenditure in the UK is determined, *planned* and *controlled* is now examined.

Table 4.2: Comparison of 1980 planned percentage changes in public expenditure with out-turn

Programme	Planned average annual change 1980–84	Average annual change out-turn 1980–84	% error between plans & out-turn 1980–84
Defence	3.1	3.6	1.9
Overseas aid and other services	5.3	0.0	−27.8
Agriculture, fisheries, food & forestry	−1.4	8.6	44.9
Industry, energy, trade & employment	−11.8	7.8	123.7
Nationalised industries external finance	−115.0	−12.7	401.1
Roads and transport	−3.3	2.3	25.0
Housing	−15.1	−14.6	−4.0
Other environmental services	−3.1	−0.5	11.0
Law, order and protective services	2.5	5.4	11.8
Education, sciences, arts & libraries	−2.7	0.8	15.1
Health and personal social services	1.1	3.3	8.8
Social security	0.9	5.7	20.1
Other public services	−1.9	−0.9	3.9
Common services	1.7	−8.2	−43.7
Northern Ireland	−1.5	0.9	10.1
Total programmes	−1.9	1.7	15.6
Planning total	−1.2	1.8	12.8

Source: *The Government's Expenditure Plans*, Cmnd 7841 and Cmnd 9428.
Note: the raw data from which the percentage figures are calculated have been expressed in comparable real terms by using the government's price deflator in Cmnd 9428.

THE FRAMEWORK FOR DETERMINING PUBLIC EXPENDITURE

From the point of view of the government and its officials, what counts as government expenditure is what has to be financed by taxation or by borrowing from the British public, foreigners and the banking system. It is this perspective that informs the gathering and presentation of statistics on public expenditure. Hence the expenditure that the public corporations finance out of their own revenues is not part of public expenditure. Since 1977 the capital expenditure of the public corporations has been excluded from statistics on public expenditure; what is included is the amount they finance by borrowing from the government or other sectors or receive in government grants. This total is known as the public corporations' *external financing limit*. This change in definition has reduced government expenditure by some 3 per cent.[1] Similarly, that part of the costs of goods and services produced by central and local government which is covered by user charges, does not count as public expenditure. So prescription charges, dental fees, council house rents and municipal bus fares are all subtracted to give the total that needs financing from taxation or borrowing. Thus *government expenditure* is the net expenditure of central and local government plus government lending and grants to the nationalised industries and so underestimates the amount which the public sector spends on goods and services, because it excludes spending financed by user charges.

The official definitions of government expenditure are determined by which items the government finances by taxing and borrowing. The official statistics also distinguish between *public expenditure* and *government expenditure*. The main difference is that the former does not include interest paid out on government debt. The reason for this is that all the items included in public expenditure are considered under the government's procedures for planning and controlling its spending. Debt interest, as it varies with the level of interest rates which the government cannot control, is therefore excluded. The public expenditure total is further reduced by the Conservative government's creative accounting practice of treating money received from the sale of public sector assets to the private sector as negative government expenditure. It would be more logical though, to present the sale of assets as a means of financing the PSBR and thus treat it as an alternative to borrowing.

The Private Government of Public Money is the telling title of a book by two American political scientists, Heclo and Wildavsky, who studied the British process of public expenditure planning.[2] It spotlights the highly centralised nature of this process within Whitehall. This is not to deny that public opinion and the sway of political interests is important in determining public expenditure, but to stress that the planning process itself is confined to a relatively small group of civil servants and ministers, in the Whitehall 'village'. Local authorities' powers to spend—and to raise revenue—are now even more circumscribed as a result of Conservative government legislation than they were previously. Not only does central government determine the amount of grant local authorities receive and earmark parts of it for specific purposes as before, but since 1985 it has resorted to rate-capping to restrict the amount individual local authorities can spend. Public corporations are also constrained in their spending by their individual external financing limits, which are set by central government and by the need to get government authorisation for their investment spending even if they have surplus profits.

As indicated in Chapter 2, Parliament plays only a minor role. Its authorisation of government spending is only required for money spent out of the Consolidated Fund, into which tax revenues are paid. EC contributions, judges' salaries and interest payments on the national debt do not require parliamentary approval, nor does expenditure financed by National Insurance contributions or borrowing. In the annual Appropriation Act, Parliament authorises about 60 per cent of government spending from the Consolidated Fund by voting money for specific purposes on the basis of 'supply' estimates, laid before it by the government and which it cannot increase on its own initiative. Parliament's approval of the government's expenditure estimates is usually a formality and ministers experience little difficulty in coming back for further votes of money should the estimates prove wrong. The Treasury and Civil Service Committee of the House of Commons does scrutinise the government's expenditure White Paper. This and parliamentary debates stimulate some public discussion, but the formulation of public expenditure plans is firmly in the hands of ministers and civil servants.

Implementation is, of course, another matter as we have just seen with the case of the Conservative government's failure to cut public spending. The actual spending of public money is much more diffused, through the provincial arteries of central government, the local authorities and public corporations and the private sector recipients of public funds. For central government the problem of control is seeing that the plans are adhered to and that spending does not rise more (or on occasions less) than intended. Some items of public expenditure are not planned by the Treasury and spending departments, in the sense that the amount spent depends on demand by recipients, as with social security payments. The government exercises some control, as it has some leeway in how much the benefit rises. As evident from Table 4.2, these kinds of programme do enter the planning total and their future amounts are estimated. Expenditure on some programmes, such as unemployment benefit, can change quite rapidly and unexpectedly, whereas the demand for old age pensions can be estimated with greater accuracy. Given time, the government can gain a greater degree of control over individual programmes by implementing policy changes, like dismantling regional investment grants.

THE PLANNING AND CONTROL OF PUBLIC EXPENDITURE

The framework for planning and controlling public expenditure and the way it is operated by civil servants and politicians has not changed in essence since the reforms of the 1960s which established the current system—the *Public Expenditure Survey Committee*—though certain aspects of it have evolved over time.

The Public Expenditure Survey Committee (PESC)

In the 1950s increasing dissatisfaction was expressed with the antediluvian nature of the public expenditure system. It had evolved without major reform since Victorian times when government expenditure accounted for only a small proportion of the nation's resources. It was described by Clarke, the Treasury official regarded as the chief architect of PESC, thus:

The main characteristic of the system was its diffuseness and decentralisation. The management and control of government expenditure was seen as the examination of a mass of spending proposals from departments, each to be considered on its merits.[3]

The system was designed to control public spending, in the accounting sense of ensuring that money is spent for the purposes intended, rather than to plan its level and allocation. Items of expenditure were considered in a piecemeal fashion, one year at a time. It was not a procedure for deciding on the overall allocation of government spending or projecting it several years ahead. There was no mechanism for applying the principle of allocative efficiency or of making a global assessment of the distribution of government spending. The Plowden Committee, set up to review the problem, recommended that

Public expenditure decisions should never be taken without consideration of (a) what the country can afford over a period of years having regard to prospective resources and (b) the relative importance of one kind of expenditure against another. This may appear to be self-evident, but in administrative (and, we would hazard the opinion, in political) terms it is not easy to carry out.[4]

In the wake of Plowden, the *Public Expenditure Survey Committee* (PESC) came into being. This term covers not just the interdepartmental committee of around 50 civil servants coordinating the planning of public expenditure, but also the whole annual cycle of producing figures for the next few years' public expenditure programmes. The basic principles are that a global total for public spending should be agreed for the coming financial year (April to March) and, less firmly, for the next five years (now reduced to three). Stabilisation considerations should determine the planned total. Is there sufficient slack in the economy for the government to be lax in allowing spending to rise, or do inflation or balance of payments and exchange rate conditions indicate the need for stringency? Having decided the ceiling under which spending should be constrained, expenditure has to be allocated to the individual programmes and this is the part of the decision process where *allocative efficiency* and *distributional* criteria play their key roles. There is an inevitable tension between the demands of the individual programmes for resources and the ceiling set for total expenditure. The demands of the programmes push up the ceiling, while the ceiling exerts downward pressure on the programmes.

The PESC cycle starts in November/December, when the Treasury informs the departments of what assumptions about overall economic policy they should use in formulating their expenditure projections. These economic policy assumptions depend on the objectives of the government and on the Treasury's assessment of future prospects for the economy. Each spending department then estimates the costs of its programmes for next year and, more hazily, for a further two years, on the basis of its current policies. Between March and May the Treasury scrutinises the departmental figures. The Treasury does not try to second-guess the departments by producing its own data: it relies on asking probing questions about the assumptions upon which the figures are calculated to ensure that departmental estimates are not inflated. The game whereby spenders try to increase their budgets and the Treasury to reduce them is played within a set of implicit rules and personal relationships between civil servants which relies on a degree of mutual trust. By bargaining with the departments, the Treasury attempts to get the individual programmes to come within the total ceiling. In May the Public Expenditure Survey Committee meets to draw up a report on the expenditure projections as they stand at this stage of the process. The discrepancy between the total projected sum for all the programmes and the Treasury's desired expenditure total and remaining disagreements between the Treasury and the departments are set out by the Committee.

The Role of Ministers
At this point the ball passes to the ministers, who thrash out the remaining disagreements in Cabinet and its committees and in bilateral negotiations between the Chief Treasury Secretary and the spending ministers. Again there are two distinct but related issues—agreeing the planning total and the size of the individual programmes within the total. Almost invariably the individual programmes sum to more than the ceiling the Treasury ministers want. Even if this ceiling is raised by the Cabinet, it is usually still less than sum of the individual programmes. Hence with seasonal regularity the Cabinet spends the summer months arguing about expenditure 'cuts'. Usually these are cuts in the departmental expenditure projections that have emerged from PESC, rather than a reduction of last year's spending on a programme in real terms. However these may still be fought over in Cabinet because spending departments want to expand their programmes.

Whatever party is in power, the ritual battlelines are drawn between spending ministers on the one hand and the Treasury ministers on the other. The Prime Minister holds the balance of power and without her support the Treasury will fail to hold the line. Thus Callaghan's support for his Chancellor in 1976 tipped the balance in favour of cuts to secure the IMF loan against left-wing spending ministers' opposition. The reasons for Cabinet disunity over spending decisions are first, that Cabinets are an often uneasy coalition of interests and viewpoints within the ruling party, some of whom are more in favour of public spending in general than others. And second, that the political career of a spending minister is judged, both within and outside government, in terms of his success at defending his department's interests. This can only be done by securing money for the department's programmes. Departmental civil servants judge their minister's performance in relation to his ability to defend their programmes in Cabinet. Each department acts as a channel for political interests which have a stake in its programmes. Thus in 1986 there is an alliance of construction companies, trade unions, NEDO and Keynesian economists lobbying for increased public spending on housing, roads, sewage and school and hospital buildings, which is gaining ground against the Chancellor's and Prime Minister's long-standing resolve to cut public spending to make room for tax cuts.

When it comes to deciding on priorities between expenditure programmes there is no rational formula to be applied, no weighing-up of social costs against social benefits from different allocations of resources to expenditure programmes. The final priorities that emerge will be influenced by the general preferences within the governing party for particular types of expenditure—be it law and order, defence, social services or subsidies to industry—and by the importance of particular political interests outside government to the party's ability to retain power. What does not occur is a clear articulation by government of detailed objectives prior to deciding how these objectives are best secured by dividing up the available resources amongst the different programmes. This *rational* approach to decision-making is virtually impossible within a political arena. Here the collective decision-makers have both complementary and conflicting interests. Decisions emerge as the result of a bargaining process between the decision-makers, conducted within a framework of procedural rules and accepted modes of behaviour. They are influenced by the dynamics of personal relationships and by the general political mood of the time as it responds to events and opinions conveyed in the media. As Joel Barnett, Chief Secretary to the Treasury in the 1974–79 Labour government recalls:

Expenditure priorities were generally decided on often outdated and ill-considered plans made in opposition, barely thought through as to their real value and never as to their relative priority in social, socialist, industrial or economic terms. More often they were decided on the strength of a particular spending minister and on the extent of the support he or she could get from the Prime Minister.[5]

The hard choices between competing uses for scarce public resources are made by sequential bargaining rather than by a collective determination of the government's priorities and a comprehensive consideration of all the spending programmes taken together. One aspect of the sequential consideration of programmes is that once the Cabinet has agreed a planning total, the Chief Secretary of the Treasury then attempts to get any outstanding disagreements between the spending departments and the Treasury settled by engaging in bilateral negotiations with various spending ministers. Programmes still in dispute return to Cabinet but they are again considered separately over a series of meetings. Decisions are made, reconsidered, made again, until exhaustion sets in. The spending objectives that emerge as the ones with highest priority are those for which people in particular ministers are prepared to fight. According to a Labour minister, Anthony Crosland, a minister wins resources 'by persuading, arguing, cajoling, exploiting his political position . . . above all by being persistent. . . whether you can exhaust your colleagues before they exhaust you'.[6] Another factor that militates against the Cabinet articulating a collective view on the overall priorities by comparing each expenditure proposal against all the others, is the reluctance of spending ministers to criticise each other's proposals so as to avoid receiving reciprocal treatment.

If exhaustion still has not produced decisions on all the outstanding areas of dispute, Prime Ministers have sought final agreement in a small Cabinet subcommittee of ministers. The problem here is finding suitable ministers with sufficient political weight. The Conservative's so-called 'Star Chamber', chaired by Viscount Whitelaw[7] and used since 1981, has been more successful than previous subcommittees of this kind. Labour governments have preferred to thrash things out in full Cabinet.

By autumn the Cabinet have ostensibly arrived at an agreed set of figures, which provide the basis for the Chancellor's *Autumn Statement* on economic policy. Some ministers and political interests will have done well, others fared badly. The Treasury will have been more or less successful in relation to their objectives, depending on the pressures exerted by the spending ministers in relation to external factors, such as sterling crises or by-election losses attributed to the unpopularity of Treasury stringency. Early in the New Year the PESC cycle is completed with the publication of the annual White Paper on the Government's expenditure plans, quoted from earlier in this chapter. It is at this point that Parliament, the rest of the public sector, and those of the electorate who choose to take an interest in such matters, are informed of the government's spending intentions for the next three financial years.

The political posturing, infighting and bargaining that form an integral part of the expenditure planning process are mostly about marginal changes to programmes, as in any one year about 98 per cent of expenditure is already determined by previous policies. The view that government activity is largely concerned with marginal adjustments to existing policies and that major rapid change is relatively rare is known as *incrementalism*. PESC itself has been described as a major exercise in *incrementalism*. Expenditures on programmes are estimated on the basis of what they will cost if current policies are continued. This makes it difficult for the Treasury to eliminate, or even cut, existing departmental programmes. So in order to contain total spending the Treasury is reluctant to permit new programmes to enter PESC. Thus radical reforms involving expenditure and revenue changes are held back.

Controlling and Monitoring Public Expenditure

Planning, controlling and monitoring public expenditure are distinct activities. Planning is the attempt to determine an appropriate level of public expenditure and to allocate it in relation to the government's priorities. Monitoring is concerned with seeing how public money is actually spent and comparing this out-turn with the plans. Control is making sure that the public expenditure programmes stay within their planned limits. Expenditure can be monitored without necessarily being controlled, since nothing may be done about observed discrepancies between intended and actual spending. As with the system operated prior to PESC it is possible to control public spending, in the sense of preventing it from rising rapidly, without planning it.

As noted in Chapter 2, formulating policy and implementing it are distinct aspects of policy-making. Governments can engage in planning exercises without controlling their expenditure, if the plans are not adhered to, as happened in the mid-1970s. Between 1971 and 1975 public expenditure was planned to rise in real terms by 15 per cent: it actually grew by 28.6 per cent.[8] Government expenditure as a percentage of GNP rose rapidly from 41.6 per cent in 1973 to 46.9 per cent in 1974 and peaked at 48.9 per cent in 1975. In December 1975 the House of Commons Expenditure Committee drew attention to evidence that in real terms public expenditure in 1974–75 had been £5 billion in excess of what the government had planned in 1971, and that the bulk of this excess could not be traced to announced policy changes. As Leo Pliatsky, Second Permanent Secretary at the Treasury in charge of public expenditure, pointed out, 'neither the previous Conservative government nor the present Labour government had paid any attention to their White Paper plans or allowed PESC to frustrate the will to spend'.[9]

Controlling expenditure involves monitoring it. The Treasury monitors the departments' spending by scrutinising weekly returns and can query particular items with a view to preventing an unauthorised expenditure. But the Treasury does not possess a detailed auditing capacity as in some countries, and relies on mutual trust in its relationships with the departments. Parliament monitors expenditure through its Public Accounts Committee, whose sole task this is, and also via its select committees, in particular the Treasury and Civil Service Committee. Auditing the public sector's accounts is the responsibility of the National Audit office, which reports to the Public Accounts Committee. However it has a relatively small staff (around 700 in 1980). Its main function traditionally has been to check that money is spent for the purposes intended by Parliament. Only more recently has it attempted value-for-money audits. It has been criticised by private sector accountants for lack of expertise in establishing management information systems which give early warning of financial mismanagement, instead of simply discovering it after it has occurred. By itself monitoring only draws attention to ways in which money has already been misspent. It is only effective in controlling expenditure to the extent that it inhibits fraud and incompetence and results in action being taken to prevent the recurrence of types of misspending discovered. Parliament can only bring pressure to bear on government, it cannot directly determine either the planning or control of public expenditure.

Central government has difficulty in ensuring that the public expenditure plans it announces are actually adhered to because, by and large, the people who do the planning are not those who do the spending. Even if in the course of the PESC cycle the Treasury has brought the spending departments to heel and the PESC figures have been collectively agreed in Cabinet, this is a political compromise and possibly a highly fudged one at that. The spending ministers may have acquiesced to a total ceiling for public spending and for their own programmes, but still intend to spend as much as they can get away with in the next financial year. As already noted, some items of public expenditure are determined by the demand for them. If, under existing regulations, people or organisations are entitled to benefits or grants, then the government has to pay up. If demand is wrongly estimated then actual expenditure will differ from the PESC projections. In addition, unplanned events occur, like the 1984–85 miners' strike, which increased government spending by about £2 billion.

A further problem, of greater political importance than demand determined expenditures, is the centralised nature of UK public expenditure planning. Included in public expenditure is local authorities' expenditure net of user charges and the expenditure of the public corporations which they cannot finance out of internal sources. Therefore a central government, which wants to control public spending, finds itself having to devise ways of restricting the spending of local authorities and public corporations. The mechanisms devised may not be effective, as with the NCB, which has on several occasions breached its external financing limit, or may pose other problems. For instance rate-capping has diminished the scope for local democracy and external financing limits restrict the ability of public corporations to operate as commercial enterprises—a problem taken up in Chapter 11.

'Funny Money' and Cash Limits

Another significant difficulty in making expenditure plans hold is inflation. The problem is what prices to use in measuring public expenditure when future years' prices are not known with any degree of certainty. If today's prices are used, then inflation will reduce the real value of expenditure in future years when this is not intended. Until 1981 the problem was tackled by measuring the expenditure in all the years in the annual survey in terms of the same set of prices called *survey prices*. The figures thus indicate the real value of projected future expenditure or, as it is alternatively called, the volume of expenditure. So for instance, if teachers' pay rose by 10 per cent but the number of teachers remained the same, the amount of expenditure on education in *survey prices* would be unchanged since the quantity of education being provided is unchanged.

However the problem with conducting PESC in survey prices was that it provided no indication of how much actual money the government would be spending in the next and subsequent years. This is why survey prices were called 'funny money', since they were not prices the government actually paid, but units of account. With government expenditure plans in survey prices, the monetary value of actual expenditure automatically rose with increases in the wages and prices paid by government. PESC set the real value of programmes but did not put any constraint on the ability of the spenders to pay more in money terms when public sector pay or purchasing prices rose: 'It was a system which placed emphasis on planning rather than control, on the medium-term future at the expense of the here-and-now, on so-called resources to the exclusion of money.'[10]

In order to secure greater control of public spending in inflationary times, the government introduced cash limits in 1976. After determining the real value of programme expenditures, the government then decides what rate of inflation it is prepared to finance and calculates what upper limit on cash expenditure this implies for the various programmes. Any expenditure over and above the limit due to higher costs is not automatically financed. It is intended that departments and their spending units should not breach the cash limits. About 40 per cent of public expenditure is covered by cash limits, as well as a further 20 per cent which is local authority spending.[11] Demand-determined programmes, like social security, are not cash-limited.

In a further bid to increase its control of cash spending, the government abandoned survey prices in 1981. The planning exercise was conducted in cash not volume terms: the government indicated how much it intended to spend in the next three years in cash terms in those years. There was an outcry, especially from the Treasury and Civil Service Select Committee, because it was now impossible to know what level of real expenditure the government intended to maintain. Subsequently the government has also provided projections of real expenditure, by deflating its cash planning figures by the rate at which it expects domestic output prices to rise.[12] This presentation has its problems too. Since the government aims to have a low rate of inflation it cannot reveal that it realistically expects a higher rate. On the other hand, pitching the allowed rate of inflation in the expenditure figures too low means a greater likelihood that actual expenditure will be higher than planned expenditure, since there is a limit to the extent to which real expenditure can be squeezed. But such discrepancies between plans and out-turn weaken the government's credibility. The year-by-year changes in survey prices, arrived at by different ways of adjusting the figures for inflation, make it extremely difficult to calculate how the real value of government spending on the various programmes has changed over time. The full mysteries of government accounting are difficult—if not impossible—to comprehend.

CONCLUSION

While the mechanism for determining government expenditure has, particularly since 1976, enabled much more systematic attention to be paid to 'what the country can afford over a period of years having regard to prospective resources', it has been much less successful as a rational procedure for deciding on the 'relative importance of one kind of expenditure against another'. This is not surprising, for there is no objective formula for determining what pattern of public expenditure is the most beneficial. As we have seen with the economist's criterion of social efficiency, that formula is based on an ethical judgement of how to measure social welfare. Even if that judgement were generally accepted, the problems of quantifying social costs and benefits leave plenty of scope for argument amongst the affected political interests. The dilemma between the desire to have a rational technique for social calculation and the desire to enable citizens to participate via their political representatives in the process of allocating and distributing resources is aptly summed up by Helco and Wildavsky:[12]

Avowed empiricists by profession, British political administrators are at times idealists. They lust after a philosopher's stone, the welfare function that would enable them to determine the relative worth of expenditures on one purpose versus others—highways versus hospitals versus schools versus houses. They love politics, but are secretly disappointed at their inability to substitute a rational formula for political conflict.

An examination of the process whereby government expenditure is determined reveals the triumph of the criterion of *distribution* over that of *allocative efficiency*. This is not to say that efficiency considerations are absent, nor that governments entirely neglect the problem of securing an effective use of resources. It is, however, the case that implantations of rational decision-making techniques, which emphasise efficiency and cost-effectiveness, do not flourish in a political environment. An inherent difficulty is the inability of political decision-makers to agree on definitions of efficiency, when these necessarily depend on assumptions about what is a desirable distribution of social welfare. To quote again from Clarke, who spent 22 years in the Treasury:

It must be accepted that there is no 'scientific' way to handle public sector expenditure and receipts. It is a mixture of politics (sometimes of the crudest kind and sometimes of the most far-sighted), economics and public administration . . . good administrative systems make it easier for good governments to make good decisions, and more difficult for bad governments to make bad decisions.[13]

NOTES

1. For definitions of government/public expenditure see P. Stibbard, 'Measuring public expenditure', *Economic Trends*, August (HMSO, London, 1985).
2. H. Heclo and A. Wildavsky, *The Private Government of Public Money* (Macmillan, London, 1981).
3. R. Clarke, *Public Expenditure, Management and Control* (Macmillan, London, 1978).
4. Plowden Report, *Controlling Public Expenditure*, Cmnd 1432 (HMSO, London, 1961).
5. J. Barnett, *Inside the Treasury* (André Deutsch, London,1982).
6. M.Kogan, *The Politics of Education* (Penguin, London, 1971).
7. Leader of the House of Lords and Deputy Prime Minister.
8. Heclo and Wildavsky, op. cit., p. xxi.
9. Leo Pliatsky, *Getting and Spending* (Basil Blackwell, Oxford, 1982).
10. Ibid., p. 137.
11. *The Government's Expenditure Plans 1984—85 to 1987—88*, Cmnd 9428 (HMSO, London, 1985).
12. Heclo and Wildavsky, op. cit., p. 360.
13. Clarke, op. cit., p. ix.

5 Taxation

We shall reform taxation so that the rich pay their full share and the tax burden on the lower paid is reduced. We intend also to bring down the starting point of the highest rates of tax, and to remove the present ceiling on earnings related National Insurance contributions. Capital taxes will be used to reduce the huge inequalities in inherited wealth. We shall reverse most of the Tories' concessions on capital transfer tax and introduce a new annual tax on personal net wealth. (Labour's Manifesto, 1983)

This Conservative Government has been both giving those incentives and clearing away the obstacles to expansion: the high rates of tax on individuals and businesses. . ... In the last four years we have made great strides in reducing and simplifying taxes. . ...This dramatic progress is all the more striking when compared to the vast increases in taxation which our opponents' policies would inevitably bring. (The Conservative Manifesto, 1983)

Taxation is the chief means by which governments finance their expenditure and so forms the major component of the revenue side of the government budget. Taxation differs from other sources of government revenue in that the power to tax is ultimately enforced by state coercion of its citizens. In a democracy it is presumed that this power is legitimated by general agreement that transfer payments and state-subsidised goods and services need to be collectively financed via taxation and that everyone has a duty to pay their share. But taxes have significant effects on the *distribution of income* and on the *allocation of resources*. These effects give rise to considerable disagreement on the appropriate level of taxation, on how the tax burden should be shared out, and on what is the best *tax structure*—that is, what kinds of taxes should be levied and what tax rates set. This chapter outlines the basic facts about the level and structure of UK taxes and assesses the UK tax system in relation to the general purposes which taxation serves and the standard criteria for judging the desirability of a particular tax. The considerable dissatisfaction felt about the complexity and incoherence of the British tax system is then related to the nature of the tax policy-making process in this country.

TYPES OF TAXES

As Table 5.1 shows, tax and national insurance contributions finance over 80 per cent of government expenditure. The next largest revenue source is government borrowing. This may take the form of borrowing from the domestic private sector, from abroad, or from the central bank. In the latter case this involves an increase in the money supply which, if carried on to any great extent, gives rise to inflation. Another source of government revenue is user charges, for such things as medical prescriptions, dental care and local authority recreational facilities. As user charges are excluded from the official measurement of government expenditure, only the gross profit, or trading surplus, from general government trading activities is included in Table 5.1.

Table 5.1: Sources of government funds 1985—86

	£ billion	% total funds
Taxes on income	35.6	22.5
Taxes on company income	17.8	11.3
Taxes on commodities	34.3	21.7
Taxes on capital	2.5	1.6
Local authority rates	13.7	8.7
National Insurance contributions	24.3	15.4
Other	8.6	5.4
Total taxes and NI contributions	137	86.6
North Sea oil royalties	2.1	1.3
Gross trading surplus and rent	2.9	1.8
Interest and dividends	6.4	4.1
Miscellaneous	2.9	1.8
Public sector borrowing requirement	6.8	4.3
Government receipts and borrowing	157.9	100.0

Source: Financial Statement and Budget Report 1986—87, HC273, p. 7.

The only tax not levied by central government in Britain is local authority rates, payable on the rateable value of domestic and commercial properties. The annual rate payable by the occupier of a property is its rateable value multiplied by the rate in the pound levied by the local authority. Local authority expenditure is considerably in excess of rate revenues. In 1984–85 local authorities spent around 23 per cent of total government expenditure whereas rates accounted for only 8.5 per cent of government revenues. Rates have proved an unpopular and inadequate form of local taxation. This has contributed to the increasing reliance of local authorities on central government grants which are around half their total revenues. Central government under the Conservatives has been replete with schemes to contain and reduce local government spending. It proposes to replace rates by a *community charge*—a fixed sum per adult. To describe in any greater detail the current system for determining local tax rates and government grants to local authorities is to incur a high risk of error, confusion and speedy obsolescence. This chapter concentrates on taxes levied by central government.

A common distinction is between *direct* and *indirect* tax. *Direct* taxes are those on income, profits, cash flows or wealth, including property. *Indirect taxes* are those levied on goods and services. An *ad valorem* tax, such as value added tax (VAT), is levied as a percentage of the value of the goods. Specific taxes, such as those on cigarettes, alcohol, petrol and oil, are levied as a specific sum on each unit of the good. National Insurance contributions are really a form of income tax, not a state insurance premium against sickness, unemployment and old ages, because the amount of NI benefit an individual expects to receive is not directly related to his contributions.

The amounts raised by different types of tax are shown in Table 5.2. In 1985–86 over half of tax revenues were obtained from taxes on income, including National Insurance contributions, and just over a third from taxes on commodities. Ten per cent came from taxes on company income, of which over 5 per cent was due to taxes on companies' North Sea oil revenues. Only 2 per cent of revenue was raised from taxing the transfer of capital. The major changes over the previous six years were the shift from taxes on income to taxes on commodities, as the deliberate consequence of the Conservative government raising VAT from 8 per cent to 15 per cent and cutting the standard rate of income tax to 30 per cent. The other major change was the advent of tax revenues from North Sea oil.

Britain is similar to most other developed countries in that the bulk of its tax revenues are derived from direct taxes on households, social security contributions and indirect tax. However, as Table 5.3 reveals, Britain raises proportionately more from indirect taxes than most other countries. When comparing changes in the tax structure over time, or in making international comparisons of taxes, one must be careful to allow for the effect of tax remissions. For example child allowances in Britain used to be received as a tax deduction—normally on the father's income—until replaced by child benefit, which is cash paid usually to the mother.

Table 5.2: Sources of central government tax revenue

	1979–80 £ billions	1979–80 per cent	1985–86 £ billions	1985–86 per cent
Taxes on personal income				
Income tax	18.8	36.8	35.1	29.4
NI contributions	12.0	23.6	24.3	20.4
Advance corporation tax (a)	1.4	2.8	5.0	4.2
	32.3	63.2	64.4	54.0
Taxes on company income				
Mainstream corporation tax	2.5	4.9	5.7	4.8
Petroleum revenue tax	0.2	0.4	6.4	5.4
Development land tax	0.01	0.03	0.1	0.1
	2.7	5.3	12.2	10.2
Taxes on transfer of capital				
Capital transfer tax	0.4	0.7	0.9	0.7
Capital gains tax	0.4	0.7	0.9	0.8
Stamp duties	0.4	0.9	1.2	1.0
	1.2	2.3	3.0	2.5
Taxes on commodities				
Value added tax	4.9	9.6	19.3	16.2
Oil and petrol	2.5	4.8	6.5	5.4
Tobacco	2.5	4.8	4.3	3.6
Alcohol	2.3	4.6	3.8	3.5
Betting and gaming	0.3	0.7	0.7	0.6
Car tax	0.4	0.7	0.9	0.7
Vehicle licences	1.1	2.2	2.4	2.0
EC own resources				
Customs duties	0.7	1.5	1.2	1.0
Agricultural levies	0.2	0.4	0.2	0.1
	15.0	29.3	39.3	33.3
Total	51.0 (b)	100	119.3 (b)	100

Sources: *Financial Statement and Budget Report 1979–80, 1986–87.*
Notes: (a) Tax on dividends; (b) due to rounding error subtotals do not add up precisely.

Conversely, investment grants, which were cash payments to qualifying companies, were replaced by investment allowances, which companies offset against corporation tax. Since governments can provide subsidies either by way of cash expenditure or by means of tax remissions, the latter are known as *tax expenditures*. The impact of the tax structure depends not only on what is taxed and at what rates, but also on what is not taxed. There are over 100 kinds of direct tax relief and exemption. The revenue lost is around half the government's tax revenues. There are further indirect tax remissions—VAT is levied only on about half of consumer expenditure.

Table 5.3: Sources of tax revenue as percentage of total tax: OECD countries 1982

	Direct paid by households	Taxes paid by companies	Social security	Indirect taxes	Capital taxes
Australia	45.6	10.0	—	44.3	0.1
Austria	27.8	3.6	29.6	38.9	0.2
Belgium	37.4	6.3	28.6	27.1	0.7
Canada	37.3	9.3	12.2	40.9	0.4
Finland	40.4	4.6	13.0	41.7	0.2
France	15.0	5.9	43.0	35.6	0.6
Germany	25.2	4.1	39.9	30.6	0.2
Italy	31.0	5.4	35.1	28.3	0.2
Japan	24.4	17.3	29.6	27.9	0.9
Netherlands	25.4	6.7	42.8	24.7	0.4
Sweden	40.8	2.7	27.4	28.9	0.2
Switzerland	41.6	4.6	29.7	22.1	1.9
United Kingdom	29.6	10.0	17.0	42.9	0.6
United States	40.6	5.9	23.4	29.0	1.2

Source: *Economic Trends*, February 1985.

THE FUNCTIONS OF THE TAX SYSTEM

The primary function of taxes is to raise revenue for the government to spend. Taxation directly transfers command over resources from the private sector to the government and so is not inflationary in the way expanding the money supply is. Until the rise of Keynesian economics and the welfare state, revenue-raising was regarded as the only function of taxation, which should be sufficient to cover government expenditure, so avoiding a budget deficit.

Short-Term Management of the Economy

Keynesian economics brought in an entirely different view of the functions of the government budget: that it provides the government with a vital leverage over the level of aggregate demand, as explained in Chapter 4. In theoretical models of the economy government spending and taxation are both equally effective as instruments for changing the level of aggregate demand. But in practice, as recounted in Chapter 4, government expenditure is difficult to adjust quickly: rapid cuts over the short term are particularly difficult to secure. Hence the main brunt of Keynesian short-term demand management was largely borne by taxation. In the years when Keynesianism dominated Treasury thinking (from about 1941 to 1976), tax revenue and tax rates were set in order to regulate aggregate demand at the level the Treasury considered appropriate for the current state of the economy.

The demise of Keynesian economic policy since the mid-1970s, and its replacement by avowedly *monetarist* policies, changed the role of taxation in the short-term management of the economy. The monetarist prescription of eliminating budget deficits in order to prevent inflation could involve either cutting government spending or increasing taxation. Because the Thatcher government has espoused the supply-side view that the relatively poor performance of the British economy is due to the excessively dominant role of the state in economic affairs, it has also sought to reduce taxation. This central aim was reiterated in the 1985 Budget:

Restraint in public spending is essential both to curb the encroachment of the state and to provide scope for reducing the burden of taxation. . . .. Lower taxation has an important part to play in improving motivation, efficiency and employment.[1]

The combined aims of reducing taxation and the budget deficit—the *public sector borrowing requirement*—can only be achieved by cutting government spending. But, as indicated in Chapter 4, government spending in real terms in fact increased between 1979 and 1986. Given their desire to reduce the PSBR, total taxation has risen since the Tories were returned to power, though the desire to reduce it became more pressing as election time approached. Under the Conservative government, the level of taxation has been determined by the amount of government expenditure, which has been higher than desired, and by the size of the PSBR considered appropriate in relation to the priority given to reducing inflation and the diagnosis that this can only be achieved by means of monetary control. Thus taxation itself has been regarded in a more negative light, as a necessary evil, whose harmful effects should be minimised, rather than viewed more positively as a tool for interventionist policies aimed at promoting redistribution or economic growth, as in the 1960s and 1970s.

Promoting Growth

In the 1960s attempts were made to design selective taxes which would stimulate economic growth. Selective employment tax was introduced by Labour in 1966 for this purpose, as well as to raise revenue. Firms were taxed on each employee, but firms in the manufacturing sector received a rebate for each worker. This tax was the brain-child of Nicholas Kaldor, an economist who gained considerable influence over Labour's economic policies in the 1960s. Kaldor's rationale for SET was that labour productivity in the service sector grows more slowly than in the manufacturing sector. Therefore a tax which favoured employment in manufacturing would increase the overall rate of growth of the economy. SET proved an unpopular tax and in the 1970 election the Conservatives pledged themselves to abolish it. On winning power they replaced SET and purchase tax in 1973 with value added tax.

Another tax which the 1964–70 Labour government introduced, hoping that it would promote growth, was corporation tax. The form of tax selected was that known as the classical corporation tax, under which all a firm's taxable profits, whether retained or paid out in dividends, were taxed at the same rate of corporation tax. As shareholders then paid income tax on their dividends, these were thus taxed twice. Thus the classical system of corporation tax was meant to encourage firms to retain profits and thereby stimulate investment. However the Conservatives took a different view: if firms pay out their profits as dividends, then financial investors will reinvest these in firms with the most profitable investment opportunities. Retention of profit encourages firms which are earning profits currently, but whose future profitable investment opportunities are limited, to invest in projects with a lower rate of return than those available to other firms which need to seek external finance to undertake such investment. If this is the case, then the classical system of corporation tax, by favouring less profitable investment projects, impedes economic growth. So in 1973 the Conservatives introduced the current imputation system of corporation tax. The firm pays corporation tax on all its taxable profits, but individual shareholders are deemed to have had the standard rate of income tax already paid by the firm on the dividends they actually receive.

In retrospect, it now seems that such elaborate tinkering with the tax structure in order to induce growth-promoting behaviour from economic agents, has little discernible effect on economic growth, while the upheaval of introducing new taxes causes considerable administrative costs. The more prevalent view now is that the disincentives to work, saving and risk-taking created by the tax system should be minimised and that this involves simplifying the tax structure, not complicating it by producing differential tax rates for different types of economic activity or different kinds of transaction.

Correcting for Externalities

Another possible function for the tax system is correcting the misallocation of resources due to *externalities* (see Chapter 3 pp. 55). In principle, activities with social costs in excess of private costs would be taxed, while those with social benefits in excess of private benefits would be subsidised. To ensure efficient resource allocation the rates of tax or subsidy on each good need to be set so as to equate the marginal social benefit of the good with its marginal social cost. This would require a complex system of differential tax rates. In practice the quantitative information needed to estimate the required rates of tax and subsidy is not available, so at best crude adjustments can be made via the tax system. Correcting for externalities is not an explicit official justification for particular taxes. However, using their conceptual apparatus economists can provide a rationale for certain taxes, like those on motor vehicles, petrol, alcohol and tobacco, being levied on goods which impose external costs. The practical and conceptual difficulties of estimating socially optimal tax rates open the way to special pleading by political interests who argue for favourable tax treatment, claiming that social benefits are at stake. Examples are the zero VAT rating for books and newspapers on the grounds that reading is good for people, and the favourable tax treatment of woodlands, in the name of national security. Whatever their justification, differential tax rates increase the complexity of the tax structure, give greater scope for special pleading, and create anomalies and loopholes in the tax system. Given that the available information permits only crude adjustments for externalities, this function for the tax system can only be a minor adjunct.

Redistribution

A much more important function of the tax system is that of *redistribution*. Together, government expenditure and taxation are the major instruments of redistribution and will be considered later in relation to the welfare state. Income disparities between households are reduced by making the better-off pay a higher proportion of their gross incomes in tax, by taxing the transfer of wealth (capital transfer tax) and the possession of wealth—though a wealth tax has never been introduced in Britain. Another, though less significant way in which the tax system has been used for redistribution is *regional policy*. In order to encourage investment in the less prosperous regions, the Industry Act 1972 enabled manufacturers to claim higher investment allowances against corporation tax for fixed capital expenditure in assisted areas. The scope and size of these allowances was reduced in the 1980s.

Not all the redistributive effects of the tax system promote equity, either because they were not intended to or because their effects on distribution are unintentional or unknown. One reason for the complexity of the British tax system is that it discriminates between different types of economic activity and different kinds of transactions. Until 1985, income from investment was taxed at a higher rate than earned income, while income from self-employment is taxed under a different schedule from income from employment, where tax is collected by the PAYE system. Because of the range of expenses that can be claimed against income from self-employment it is, in effect, taxed more favourably. As a consequence of these different tax schedules, people with the same income, but derived from different sources, are taxed at different rates. Businesses are also taxed differently, depending on the nature of their business activities. Farming receives particularly favourable treatment, having been exempt from local authority rates and from the standard rate of capital transfer tax. Manufacturing has been favoured over service industries, by means of special investment allowances.

The full redistributive impact of the tax system is not known because it is difficult to discover which people are worse off and by how much as the result of any given tax. How the ultimate cost of a tax is distributed is called the *effective incidence* of the tax. The agent who appears to pay the tax to the government, be it employers' National Insurance contributions, income tax or VAT, may well be able to pass on—or shift—the effects of the tax onto someone else. For example, the increased employers' National Insurance contributions for high-paid workers, introduced in 1985, will not be paid entirely by the employers if, as a result of their demanding less well-paid labour because of its higher cost, the salaries of such people fall relative to what they would otherwise have been. In this event part of the tax is shifted on to the employees in the form of lower salaries. Similarly, indirect taxes are shared between consumers and suppliers. Their *incidence* does not fall entirely on the consumer because as a result of lower demand due to the tax, suppliers find it worthwhile to boost sales by taking a cut in the price they receive for the good net of tax. Thus part of the tax is borne by suppliers.[2]

As can be seen from these examples, the reason why the *effective incidence* of a tax is different from the amount of tax formally paid by a firm, worker or consumer is that the imposition of the tax causes changes in the demand or supply of the taxed item which in turn, change its price. It is not possible accurately to estimate the full extent of all the price and quantity changes brought about by the imposition of taxes. Hence there is only incomplete knowledge of the *effective incidence* and *redistributive* impact of taxes. In fact most assessments of the burden of taxes, such as those reported later in the chapter, assume that the incidence of income tax falls on workers and that of indirect taxes on consumers.

ASSESSING THE BRITISH TAX SYSTEM

Is Britain Over-Taxed?

As government expenditure has risen as a proportion of GDP since the 1950s, so has taxation. As Figure 5.1 shows, over the decade 1954–64 tax receipts plus NI contributions hovered around 28–29 per cent of GNP (at market prices). Then the proportion of GDP taken in tax began to rise until it peaked at 37 per cent in 1970. In the 1970s it ranged between 33 and 36 per cent. Despite the Conservative government's desire to see taxation cut, the tax: GDP ratio rose from 34 per cent in 1978 to 38 per cent in the years 1982–84. The rise in the percentage of GDP taken in tax over the years has meant that more income-earners have been drawn into the tax net, which has gradually trawled further down the income scale. In 1985 a single person earning over £38.40 a week was liable for tax. In the 1980s the

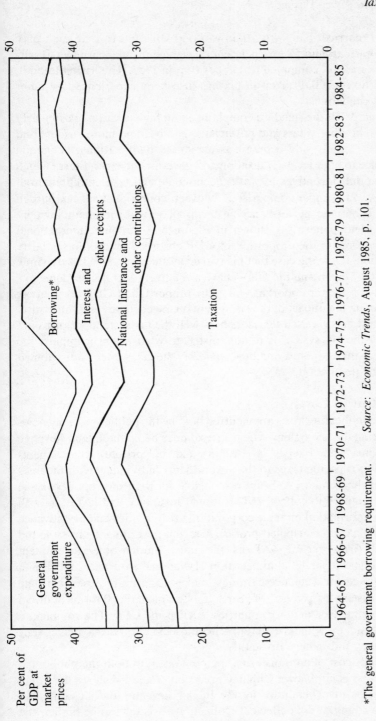

Source: Economic Trends, August 1985, p. 101.

Figure 5.1: Government expenditure and revenue sources as a percentage of GDP, 1964–84

archetypal married man with a non-working wife and two children only needed to earn around 58–59 per cent of average manual earnings to start paying income tax, compared to 133 per cent in 1953. This rising trend in the proportion of GDP taken in tax has also been experienced by other developed economies.

By the late 1970s the standard complaint about high taxation, particularly amongst right-wing voters and politicians, had become more strident and widespread. Supply-side economists attributed poor national economic performance to high levels of taxation and government expenditure, which are held to dull incentives to work, accumulate and take entrepreneurial risks. However, simple comparisons between countries' total tax burden and their economic performance in terms of growth or unemployment reveal no clear pattern, as shown in Figure 5.2. Britain's international ranking in terms of the proportion of GDP absorbed by taxation is fairly average, though it is the case that the two economies perceived as dynamic in the 1980s—Japan and the USA—have a relatively low tax burden.

Probably of greater importance than the proportion of GDP taken in tax in determining the impact of the tax system on the economy is its structure. The standard criteria used to assess how well the tax system performs are how costly the tax system is to administer, to what extent it impairs the efficiency of the economy, and how *equitably* the tax burden is distributed amongst the population.

Administrative Costs

The costs of collecting taxes are incurred both by the public sector agencies administering the tax system—the principal ones being the Inland Revenue and Customs and Excise in Britain—and by private sector agents responsible for paying taxes to the government. Individuals with incomes taxed other than under PAYE are responsible for their own tax payments. Firms are required to collect VAT, National Insurance and PAYE, as well as provide information on their corporation tax liabilities and pay advance corporation tax on distributed profits. A recent government survey found that small firms regard VAT as the most burdensome government regulation. The separate administration of National Insurance, PAYE and self-assessment for freelance earnings, makes for a more expensive state collection system than an end-of-year self-assessment on all forms of direct tax liability practised in other countries, such as the USA. The complexity of the tax structure with its different schedules and allowances, makes self-assessment by individuals difficult.

The overall cost of administering the tax system to both the public and private sectors is not known with any precision. Table 5.4 shows the direct costs in terms of expenditure by the Inland Revenue and Customs and Excise per pound of tax collected. Collection costs tend to be higher, the

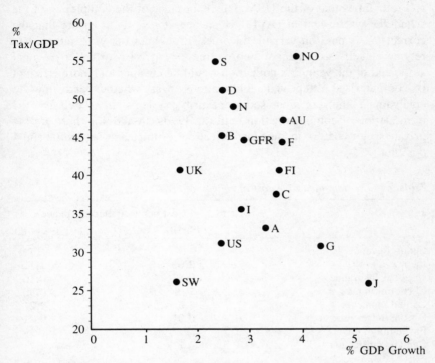

Notes: GDP growth is annual average percentage rate, 1970-82,
          Tax/GDP percentage is average for 1972, 1977 and 1982.
Source: OECD, *Economic Outlook; Economic Trends* February 1985.

Key

A = Australia	AU = Austria	B = Belguim
C = Canada	D = Denmark	F = France
FI = Finland	G = Greece	GFR = Germany
I = Italy	J = Japan	N = Netherlands
NO = Norway	S = Sweden	SW = Switzerland
UK = United Kingdom	US = United States	

*Figure 5.2: Comparison of tax as a percentage of GDP and average annual
rate of GDP growth 1970−82*

larger the number of collection points and the greater the enforcement problems. Thus customs duties are by far the most expensive to collect, followed by capital transfer tax and capital gains tax. Income tax costs over 2 per cent of revenue to collect. This is double that in Sweden and Canada, and four times that of the USA. This is because of the complexity of the schedular system and of PAYE, which operates so as to ensure that the correct tax is paid on variable incomes throughout the year, rather than relying on self-assessment and correcting for any over- or under-payment at the end of the year. Tax collection would be cheaper and more efficient if computerised. Repeated deliberations over whether and how to amalgamate the tax and social security systems have delayed the introduction of computerisation until the 1990s. In addition there are the private sector costs of income tax collection, estimated at between 2 and 4 per cent.[2]

Table 5.4: The administrative cost of collecting £1 in tax

Tax	Cost per £1 collected (pence)	
	1981–82	1984–85
Inland Revenue		
Income tax	2.06	2.13
National Insurance	0.17	0.16
Corporation tax	1.05	0.80
Capital gains tax	2.6	2.21
Petroleum revenue tax	0.01	0.01
Estate duty and		
Capital transfer tax	3.1	2.7
Customs and Excise		
VAT and car tax	1.25	1.04
Excise duties	0.41	0.32
Customs duties	11.03	10.62

Source: *The Government's Expenditure Plans 1985–86 to 1987–88*, Cmnd 9428.

The cost of administering a tax is an important consideration in determining whether it is worth levying. The problem with a wealth tax, usually desired on equity grounds, is that it is relatively expensive to administer, given that a self-assessment system of tax collection is not used. This had been one of the arguments against introducing a tax on the ownership of wealth. VAT is more expensive to collect both for the government and the private sector than the purchase tax it replaced, because it is collected at all stages of production, not just at the point of sale, as was purchase tax. A strong political argument used in favour of introducing it in 1973 was that it would harmonise the UK with the VAT systems used in the EC. Given that we now have the VAT administrative framework it would be more cost-effective to extend it to all goods and services.

An important element in the case for a simpler structure for income, wealth and corporation taxes, with far fewer special exemptions, is that it would be cheaper to administer, for both the public and private sectors. A significant element in the cost of operating the British tax system are the resources devoted to tax avoidance. (Avoidance is using legal loopholes to reduce tax liability, whereas tax evasion is illegal.) The complexity of tax legislation, with its many special exemptions, unintended loopholes and continual piecemeal amendments, means that both companies and individuals find it financially worthwhile to engage the services of tax lawyers and accountants to find legal ways of reducing their tax bills. The resources of skilled manpower absorbed by the tax avoidance industry are part of the cost of administering the tax system. The higher the rate of tax, the more incentive tax payers have for seeking out ways of avoiding tax. This is one reason why high rates of tax on unearned income and the transfer of wealth have not yielded much in the way of tax revenue. Thus a complex tax structure, combined with high rates of tax, make for an administratively inefficient tax system. A tax system composed of a few broadly-based, generally applicable taxes, levied at moderate rates, minimises the scope and incentive for tax avoidance and is therefore less costly to operate. However, the opportunity cost of tax avoidance activities is but one aspect of the impact of the tax system on the efficiency of the economy.

Efficiency
The strongest and most loudly-voiced charge against taxes is that they constitute a burden upon the community, distort market choices and, by discouraging work, saving and risk-taking, reduce national output. All these effects are aspects of the impact of taxes on efficiency. It is the standard practice of economists to analyse the effect of a tax by comparing a *perfectly competitive market*, which is allocating resources efficiently, before and after the imposition of a tax. Within this framework a tax produces a less efficient allocation of resources than its absence because it causes market participants to alter their choices and so 'distorts' the market. For instance, a tax on a commodity results in demand falling and so less being produced, making both consumers and producers worse off. There is one case in which the imposition of a tax does not distort market choices and thereby diminish social efficiency. This is when it is levied on a good in fixed supply, such as land. The quantity available of such a good is the same whatever its price, since once in existence it costs virtually nothing to produce and put on the market. The actual market price of such a good is determined solely by the demand for it. When a tax is imposed

there is no advantage to the owners in trying to raise its price by reducing the amount they put onto the market. So they cannot pass on to consumers even part of any tax by raising the price of the good. Taxes on land have long been advocated as *socially efficient* because their imposition will not diminish the amount of land put to use.[3]

There are, of course, not many goods in fixed supply. For most goods the effect of a tax is to change the quantity traded and thus to distort the market relative to its non-taxed state. Given the need to levy taxes and the absence of precise knowledge of the welfare effects of different taxes, the presumption is in favour of a common rate of tax on all goods and services so as to minimise market distortions. It would also reduce the scope for special pleading by consumers and producers of specific products. However, this principle is only partly adhered to: goods deemed socially harmful, such as alcohol and tobacco, are more heavily taxed; others, such as food, children's clothing, funerals, transport, fuel and power are not subject to VAT.

Much more concern is expressed about the inefficiencies brought about by direct taxes than by indirect taxation. There is considerable controversy over the extent to which income tax impairs the incentive to work and so reduces the supply of labour and national output. In so far as tax reduces people's disposable income, it is likely to increase the amount of work they do, as they work harder to recoup their living standards. A lump-sum poll tax on all persons of working age would have little effect on the supply of labour, as it would have to be paid regardless of whether an individual worked or of how much she/he earned. Such a tax would therefore be good from an efficiency point of view but would be inequitable.

High *marginal rates of income tax*—that is, the amount of each additional pound that is taken in tax—are most likely to deter work effort. If 80p of each additional pound earned goes in tax, then the financial rewards of working long hours or taking on additional responsibilities are relatively small. High marginal rates of income tax occur at both the bottom and top ends of the income scale. At low incomes this is known as the *poverty trap*. Because means-tested benefits, like family income supplement (FIS) and housing benefit, are lost as earnings rise, while taxation increases, there are low-income households who would have to double their earnings before being any better off. There are probably over half a million low-income households with *marginal income tax rates* of over 50 per cent. At the other end, the top marginal rate of income tax is now 60 per cent, having been reduced from 83 per cent in 1980. The standard marginal rate of tax, taking into account all taxes, including NI contributions, has been estimated at 62 per cent in 1985 compared to 55 per cent ten years earlier.[4] The cut in the standard rate of income tax from 33 per cent to 30 per cent and the raising of VAT from 8 per cent to 15 per cent in 1979 was aimed at lowering the overall marginal rate of taxation.

While academic opinion is divided on the disincentive effects of high marginal income tax rates on work effort, the way the tax system has distorted the allocation of savings is much more readily acknowledged, though stoutly defended by entrenched interests. The tax legislators have regarded certain forms of saving—owner-occupied houses, pensions and life assurance—as peculiarly worthy of tax exemptions. Interest payments on mortgages of £30,000 are offset against income tax, and this has encouraged personal investment in housing. To even things up council house tenants are also, to varying degrees, subsidised through lower rents, while they, and the few private sector tenants left, may receive housing benefit. Thus a complex system of housing subsidies, with its attendant administrative costs has arisen, with most households receiving some form of tax expenditure or subsidy.

Saving via life insurance was made attractive by the Inland Revenue contributing 15 per cent of the premiums, up to a specified limit, and by favourably taxing the income of life insurance companies. Pension fund contributions are exempt from tax, as is the investment income of pension funds. These tax concessions have encouraged individuals to save by means of long-term contracts with insurance companies at the expense of direct investment in businesses. Companies which do not issue shares have found it virtually impossible to obtain finance from the general public, and personal shareholding has also dwindled. Institutions have come to dominate the provision of finance to companies, while the proportion of household wealth held in housing and in life and pension funds rose over time, to stand at 86 per cent by 1978.[5] In 1984 the Chancellor took the first steps to remove the tax distortion of savings, by abolishing the investment income surcharge, removing the 15 per cent tax relief on new life assurance policies and reducing the exemptions available to friendly societies.

Corporation tax is riddled with special exemptions, for different classes of business or different types of expenditure. Since its inception in 1965, it has been continuously amended by governments in response to short-term problems and the appearance of loopholes exploited by tax advisers. It is replete with complex rules for determining what types of expenditure and what kinds of loss can be offset against profits in calculating taxable profits. In order to encourage investment, governments have granted tax allowances against certain types of capital expenditure, such as on plant and machinery. However, as 'plant' is not defined in the statutes, there have been numerous court cases concerned with ascertaining what is 'plant'. These have determined that items forming part of the setting in which a business is carried on are not plant and so do not attract relief, unless they do so as part of the building itself which, if of the right category, will attract relief. So lifts and central heating have been treated as plant while basic electric fittings and plumbing are not. Normal lighting in a shop has been held to be part of the building and so not allowable, whereas specific lighting to create an effect in an hotel has been deemed plant.[6] This example should make clear why tax legislation is grist to the tax specialist's mill; it pays firms to devote considerable effort to managing their finances in order to minimise their tax liabilities and to take investment decisions for tax rather than just commercial reasons. Some mergers, for example, have been undertaken to acquire losses that can be offset against the acquiring company's profits. In recognition that the tax structure had encouraged firms to invest in labour-saving methods which failed to stimulate employment, the Chancellor in 1984 announced the phasing-out of investment allowances, not, however, without loud complaints, particularly from cable TV businesses.

So even if one is not concerned that the level of taxation acts as a drag on economic activity, there is still a good case to be made that the structure of the British tax system, especially company taxation and the taxation of savings and investment, promotes inefficiency. Its continual interpretation and amendment absorbs skilled labour that could be used elsewhere. Its consequent impact on the allocation of resources is to a considerable extent both unintended and unknown, but in certain cases seems likely to encourage less efficient resource allocation. The eagerness of economists to recommend ingenious schemes of differential tax rates and tax exemptions, to encourage some activities and discourage others, has waned in favour of the less ambitious, but more realistic, task of devising a simpler tax structure, which aims at doing the least possible damage to efficiency.[7]

Equity

The last of the standard criteria for assessing a tax system to be considered is *equity* or *fairness*. *Horizontal equity* is the principle that people with the same taxable capacity should be taxed equally. The concept of taxable capacity is by no means clear-cut. For instance, are two people with the same potential earning ability to be judged as having the same taxable capacity if one of them chooses to work less hard? The possession of wealth indicates a capacity to pay on a par with that of having income, but what if it is wealth of an illiquid form such as one's dwelling or pension rights? This unresolved issue helped to prevent the 1974–79 Labour government proceeding with its wealth tax proposals.

Vertical equity is the principle that people of different taxable capacity should be taxed differently: specifically that the better-off should pay proportionately more tax. A tax which follows this principle is referred to as progressive, while a tax which takes a higher proportion of the incomes of poorer people is regressive. The progressivity of a tax is measured in two ways: by the extent to which the average amount of tax paid and the marginal tax rate rises with taxable capacity. Income tax and capital transfer tax are explicitly progressive in that both are not levied below a specific threshold and have graduated and rising rate bands. The income tax rates in 1986 have ranged from 29 per cent to 60 per cent in 5 per cent intervals. A tax is progressive even if it has a constant marginal rate, so long as it only becomes payable after a certain threshold is reached. This ensures that the average amount of tax paid rises with taxable capacity.

When in existence capital transfer tax ranged from 30 per cent to 50 per cent on life-time transfers, rising to 75 per cent on transfers of over £2.65 million at death. However, very high marginal tax rates on the rich are largely a charade, as ways of avoiding paying these rates are devised by setting up trusts, transferring wealth before death in suitable tranches, and converting income into capital gains, which are taxed at a lower rate. Hence, even from the point of view of those who wish to place a high priority on equity, high marginal tax rates are often counter-productive because they encourage avoidance and so reduce tax yields. As can be seen from Table 5.2, capital transfer tax contributes only 0.6 per cent of tax revenue. Over the years its provisions have been amended to make it easier to avoid paying very high rates at death, so that the tax came to resemble closely the estate duty it replaced in 1976. In 1986 the government announced its intention of abolishing capital transfer tax and returning to estate duty which only taxes transfers of wealth on death.

Table 5.5: The redistributive effects of taxes: percentage of gross income taken in tax (1983)

| | Quintile groups of households ranked by income | | | | | |
	Bottom fifth	Second fifth	Third fifth	Fourth fifth	Top fifth	Average
Income tax and employees' NIC	0.3	8.5	17.7	20.7	23.4	18.7
Indirect tax	26.8	26.2	23.2	20.2	17.6	20.6
Total tax	27.1	34.7	40.9	41.0	41.0	39.3

Source: *Economic Trends*, December 1985.

The largest redistributive contribution comes from income tax and National Insurance contributions. One indicator of this is given in Table 5.5, which shows the percentage of gross income (original income plus cash benefits) paid in *direct* and *indirect taxes* for households grouped in five bands, according to their incomes before tax. Direct tax, including NI contributions, is highly *progressive* up to the third quintile of households. Indirect tax is *regressive*, as it takes a steadily falling proportion of household income as income rises. Children's clothes and food are zero-

rated for VAT to make that tax less regressive, though the same argument
for exempting tobacco duties, which are regressive, finds much less favour.
The 1980 cut in the higher income tax rate bands reduced the average
income tax payments of households with over £30,000 (1982 prices).
However, for the middle 90 per cent of households, tax changes since 1980
have increased the progressivity of the tax system as a whole, compared to
the 1970s. This is shown in Figure 5.3. More tax was paid at all income
levels in 1985 than in 1974 but less than in 1970. The steeper slope of the
1985 line shows that the overall *marginal* tax rate was greater in 1985 than
in the other two years. This was due to raising income tax thresholds and
the greater progressivity and size of NI contributions.

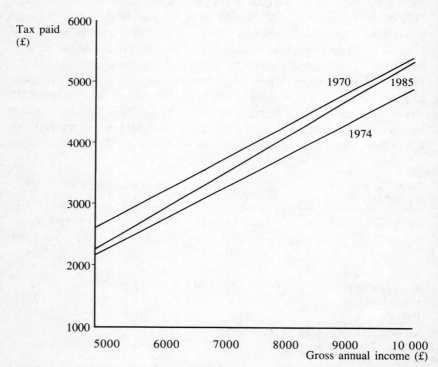

Source: J. Kay, *The Economy and the 1985 Budget*. (Basil Blackwell, Oxford,
1985), p. 66
Note: Excludes bottom and top 5 per cent of households.

Figure 5.3:   Total tax paid at different income levels (1985/6 prices)

In some measure, the desire to have a *progressive* tax system is incompatible with the objective of minimising its impact on *efficiency*. To the extent that high marginal rates are a disincentive to work, to accumulate, to make productive investments and to take entrepreneurial risks and, furthermore, nourish a lucrative tax avoidance industry, they will impair national economic performance. However a rationally designed tax system would endeavour to attain a given degree of progressivity at least cost to incentives. The problem with the British tax system is that much of its inefficiency is not attributable to the necessary costs of achieving greater equity. In the view of two leading academic commentators: 'if the present system did not exist it is inconceivable that anyone would propose that it should be introduced'.[8] Why has this state of affairs arisen; and why is reform of the tax system so that it achieves its 'basic functions of raising revenue and relieving inequalities in income and wealth without doing much damage in the process'[9] so difficult? Much of the answer to these questions lies in the nature of the tax policy-making process and, in particular, in the way it is conducted in Britain.

TAX POLICY-MAKING

The British tax system and the policy-making process that has produced it have for years been much criticised from the *rational* perspective. A *rational* tax-making process would involve the clear articulation of the functions, or objectives, required of the tax system and the adoption of taxes which best achieved those objectives. In a rational policy-making process much effort would be devoted to exploring the likely consequences of alternative tax structures for achieving the desired objectives and in ensuring that tax legislation was carefully drafted so that the intended effects of taxes were actually realised. In contrast to this, the actual tax system is not based on any unifying set of principles and so lacks coherence. It has been built up over the years by *ad hoc* measures, often hastily devised and then continually amended in the light of ensuing administrative problems or complaints from political interests, who have won the ear of the government of the day. The problem has not been just the inheritance of a tax system that has evolved over 140 years. New taxes, when devised, have shared the incoherence and complexity of earlier taxes, subject to frequent amendment and sometimes abolition and replacement. The economy has been unable to operate within a stable framework of taxation. In order to reach some understanding of why tax policy-making operates in this way we need to consider the institutional and political framework within which taxation is determined.

Finance Acts

The process whereby the rates of existing taxes are changed and new taxes created is circumscribed by the long-standing constitutional requirement that Parliament sanctions the power of the executive to collect taxes. Parliamentary approval for income and corporation taxes must be renewed annually, or the government would lose nearly half of its tax revenue. It is thus essential for the government to present a Budget and a Finance Bill annually at the beginning of the financial year. This is done on Budget Day (built up by the media as an important event) when the Chancellor unveils how much money he plans to take in taxes over the forthcoming year. The March Budget is normally the time chosen to alter the rates of the other 'permanent' taxes, amend the rules of existing taxes, repeal them or introduce new taxes.

The Treasury

Taxation is the undisputed domain of the Treasury. The two departments which administer taxes (the Inland Revenue and Customs and Excise) are attached to the Treasury; their views as to what is administratively feasible—or convenient—have an important influence on the structural features of tax changes. While the Treasury has to bargain hard to contain public spending, it has the whip hand in determining tax changes. The preparation of the annual Finance Bill is done by the Treasury, amidst great secrecy, justified by the argument that this prevents people securing financial gain by acting on prior knowledge of tax changes. The Chancellor is likely to consult closely with the Prime Minister, but may do little to consult or even inform other Cabinet ministers about the Budget. Thus the making of tax policy in Britain is even more centralised than the determination of government expenditure. Parliament cannot propose measures to raise a tax, though it can veto or amend new taxes or increases in existing taxes. The Chancellor's proposed changes to rates of existing tax are almost invariably ratified by Parliament, their rebellion over an extra 5p on derv in 1977 being a rare exception. Legislation for new taxes, which is usually included in the annual Finance Bill, may be amended in the course of its passage through Parliament, but it is unusual for the government to suffer a major policy reversal. The House of Lords cannot amend a Finance Bill—only throw it out entirely. Thus the Chancellor has a considerable degree of power in determining taxation, though as we shall see later, this is constrained by bureaucratic inertia and the desire to placate political interests.

Time-Scales for Tax Policy

Tax policy is oriented to the Treasury's annual budgetary cycle and is dominated by short-term considerations. The primary function of the

Budget is to ensure that the government raises the amount of tax revenue it considers necessary. In pre-inflationary, pre-Keynesian days, little year-by-year change would be necessary to ensure that the Budget balanced. But when there is inflation many tax rates require annual adjustment. Specific duties on alcohol, tobacco and cars require uprating or the real value of tax revenue will fall. Income tax and other kinds of allowances also need to be raised, otherwise the tax yield would swell automatically as inflation increases the nominal, but not the real, value of people's incomes, capital gains and wealth. The government could get by in terms of obtaining the amount of tax revenue it considers appropriate by altering the rates of existing taxes and these changes take up a considerable portion of the Budget. As far as short-term management of the economy is concerned, this is all that needs to be done.

The other objectives for the tax system, concerning its impact on the efficiency and dynamism of the economy and on the distribution of income and wealth, are long-term in nature and focus on the structure of the tax system. Furthering such objectives often requires the repeal or radical overhaul of existing taxes and their replacement by different forms of taxation. These are not year-by-year tinkerings with rates and exemptions, but structural changes intended to be long-lasting, like the introduction of corporation tax, capital transfer tax and VAT, or the Institute of Fiscal Studies' proposal for replacing income tax by an expenditure or realisations tax. [10]

During the era of *Keynesian demand management*, tax policy was even more subordinate to the requirements of short-term economic policy than in the 1980s. Taxation was seen primarily as an instrument for managing aggregate demand and there was an almost total divorce between the procedures that determined the expenditure side of the government's budget from those that set the level and structure of taxation. This was a constitutional inheritance from Victorian budgetary procedures, designed to ensure that Parliament legitimised the government's powers to tax, while quite separately it voted money for the government to spend. This separation of the tax and spending sides of the budget was not of much concern to Keynesian policy-makers, with their emphasis on taxation as the major instrument of demand management and their belief in unbalanced Budgets. In fact the annual Budget was seen as an impediment to *fine-tuning* the economy—that is, the continual raising and lowering of *aggregate demand* by government, which was then thought to stabilise the economy. A light foot on the accelerator or brake should be applied whenever necessary, not just in March. During this period, indirect tax rates were altered at other times of the year, using the powers the government still possesses, to lay such regulations before Parliament. Also mini-budgets were introduced part-way through the financial year, usually in response to a balance of payments crisis. Nevertheless, 1965–74 were years of considerable structural change with six major new taxes being enacted. The time, energy and manpower to enact and implement these taxes had to be squeezed into a timetable dominated by the imperatives of responding to repeated short-term crises of economic management.

Since 1979, the Treasury's emphasis on short-term tax changes for demand management purposes has been modified in several respects. In the Keynesian era government expenditure, together with the target level of real aggregate demand, determined the level of taxation. Under the medium term financial strategy, the government's desire to restrict the size of its budget deficit while, if possible, bringing down the level of taxation, has determined the Treasury's target for government spending. Although since 1975–76, much greater emphasis has been given to planning the level of government expenditure in relation to how it is to be financed, Britain still does not have a unified Budget, that is, one in which spending and revenues are considered side by side throughout the process of determining expenditure and setting taxes.

Another significant change in perceptions is the emphasis on improving the *supply-side* performance of the economy through direct measures, in contrast to the Keynesian assumption that supply would automatically respond to changes in demand. *Supply-side* policies include the long-term reform of the *tax structure* so that its harmful effects on efficiency and incentives are reduced. Nigel Lawson's Budgets in 1984 and 1985 contained a number of such measures, several of which have already been noted. They were intended to encourage investment in small businesses, stimulate wider share-ownership and increase the demand for labour. For instance, it was hoped that the discontinuation of investment allowances would bring about less labour displacement by subsidised capital and that the increased progressivity of employers' NI contributions would stimulate the demand for lower-paid labour.

The Treasury's Annual Cycle
Despite this shift towards a longer-term perspective for tax policy, it is all still conducted within the Treasury's annual cycle. Long-term structural changes are announced as part of the March Budget. As many tax adjustments are closely related to the current state of the economy, they are inevitably determined by short-run considerations which sometimes dominate the government's more strategic aims. Under the medium-term financial strategy, as under Keynesian demand management, the Treasury has to estimate what level of tax revenue it requires in the next financial year. To do this it needs to know what the level of government spending is likely to be and what size PSBR it wants to run. The PSBR is particularly difficult to forecast as it is the difference between two large cash flows—

government spending and tax receipts—neither of which is determined by government alone. While the government sets the tax rates, it cannot determine with any precision the tax revenues that will be yielded from a given set of tax rates. Revenues also depend on the size of the tax base—on incomes in the case of income tax and on consumer spending in the case of VAT. Petroleum revenue tax is particularly uncertain, as it varies with price and output of North Sea Oil. Government expenditure is not fully under government control: it varies with the take-up of entitlements, such as unemployment benefits, or with the size of public sector pay settlements. All these variables are in turn affected by government spending, taxation and borrowing, as well as by factors beyond the influence of government.

The Treasury uses an econometric model of the whole economy to provide forecasts and to stimulate the possible effects of setting taxes and government spending at different values. Even so, PSBR forecasts are notoriously error-prone; the Budget forecast for the PSBR in the coming year has ranged from £3.9 billion too high in 1977–78 to £4.7 billion too low in 1980–81. The average error between 1968 and 1983 was 1.4 per cent of GDP.[11] Thus the Treasury is certain neither of what level of tax revenues it wants for the coming year nor of what tax rates will achieve a given quantity of tax revenue.

The tax-setting cycle is coordinated with the expenditure planning cycle. Under the MTFS, the desire to reduce the level of taxation and the PSBR exert a downward pressure on the planned level of government spending. As the expenditure plans emerge in the autumn from bilateral bargaining between the Treasury and the spending departments, to be finally settled by Cabinet, the Treasury is then in a position to judge what the actual level of next year's spending is likely to be. They may well suppose that it will be higher than the published target and this will form part of their judgement regarding the appropriate level of taxes. The Treasury remains anxious to retain the secrecy of its deliberations, though over the years it has been forced to reveal more information. Under a backbench amendment to the Industry Act 1975, the Treasury is now required to publish both its model and its autumn and spring forecasts, and so has to reveal more of its background thinking with respect to the Budget than it used to. In response to the Treasury and Civil Service's Select Committee's agitation for greater participation and more open debate about budgetary policy, the Treasury began in 1982 to publish an Autumn Statement from the Chancellor to Parliament. This indicates the public expenditure targets, and the Chancellor's views on the current state of the economy and on the conduct of economic policy. The Treasury has steadfastly refused to reveal proposed tax changes prior to the Budget, arguing that these are always subject to last-minute changes in the light of current circumstances, such as exchange rate fluctuations or strikes.

From the autumn onwards, the Treasury begins to gear itself up for the spring Budget. Gradually, decisions are firmed up in the light of the relevant economic information gathered by the Treasury and the unfolding political scene. Decisions are made about changes in the rates of taxation which, it is forecast, will yield the revenue required. Obviously many different permutations would produce the revenue target, so how to distribute the tax increases or decreases—whom to harm and whom to benefit—is a vital issue. The pressure groups bombard the Chancellor both in public and private. The CBI and the TUC publish their Budget recommendations. Numerous other established pressure groups join the chorus. Whisky distillers, motoring organisations, the Child Poverty Action Group, trade unions, the Country Landowners Association, small business associations, financial institutions, accountancy bodies, academics. . . Some pressure groups are formed specifically to lobby on taxation, such as Heritage in Danger, which fought proposals to bring in a wealth tax in 1975, and the 1985 agitation by authors, journalists and broadcasters against the rumoured abolition of zero VAT rating for books and newspapers:

From the moment the Chancellor sits down after making his Budget Speech, he starts to receive suggestions about what he should have included in it and what should go into his next Budget. The volume of these representations begins to mount up from the late summer or early autumn. The letters and pages range from one side of manuscript to 40 pages of closely argued analysis. They come from individuals, from companies and from national organisations. Officials in the Treasury and the revenue departments gather and sort through all the suggestions, and comment on their implications, so that Ministers can evaluate them as possible candidates for the Budget.[12]

The Budget proposals are presented to Parliament in the Finance Bill. At the end of the Budget debate resolutions are passed to enable certain tax changes, like indirect taxes, to take effect immediately, even though the Finance Bill will take several months until it is ready for the Royal Assent. At the committee stage of passing a Bill through Parliament it is given detailed scrutiny by the House of Commons and each clause is debated and voted upon. It is at this stage that opposition and backbench MPs may be able to amend some of the government's proposals. Until 1967 the committee stage of Finance Bills was conducted on the floor of the House, but as the legislation become more extensive and complex, this procedure proved too cumbersome. Since then the more complex clauses are considered by a standing committee of the House. It is at this point that political interests who have failed to influence the Chancellor sufficiently prior to the Budget may have another go through the auspices of sympathetic MPs. Such representations usually succeed if the government modifies its proposed legislation, rather than because it is defeated on a vote over a clause. Quite often such amendments are not made immediately by the government, but are included by them in subsequent years' Finance Bills. It is by this process that some of the exemptions which complicate the tax structure come into being.

WHAT IS WRONG WITH TAX POLICY-MAKING?

There are various aspects of the process by which tax policy is made in the UK that are put forward to explain why it has not produced a more satisfactory tax structure. It is inevitably the nature of such explanations that judgements about their validity depend on detailed and, to some extent, subjective assessment of the evidence as to how policy is made and what effects this has.

The Dominance of the Short Term

The desirable characteristics of a tax system with respect to *administrative costs*, *efficiency* and *equity*, need to be embedded within the *tax structure* as permanent features. The adherence to *Keynesian demand management*, especially the *fine-tuning* variety, distracted attention from the longer-term effects on the economy of the tax system. However, even under the medium-term financial strategy, the Treasury still gears its entire tax policy-making efforts to the annual budgetary cycle. Inevitably the need to adjust taxes in response to short-term economic and political developments takes precedence over longer-term structural reforms. Even a Chancellor concerned with tax reform can only feed it bit by bit into the annual cycle of budget-making.

Bureaucratic Inertia

The predominance of short-term economic management in tax policy-making is only part of the explanation of why structural reforms are difficult to achieve. They require administrative changes, which are upsetting and inconvenient to those responsible for tax assessment and collection, both within the government machine and amongst the accountancy profession without. To what extent any proposed change in the tax system would impose an impossible administrative burden and to what extent this is just an excuse by administrators is difficult to judge. The reformer's perspective is put by Dick Taverne, ex-Labour Chief Secretary to the Treasury, arguing the case for a centre of fiscal expertise outside government:

Alternative proposals put up by Ministers against those favoured by the Inland Revenue had little chance because they were not backed by the practical expertise and knowledge of administrative problems which the Revenue could command. Indeed the Revenue proved itself expert at showing how all solutions other than their own were utterly unworkable and totally misconceived.[13]

Incrementalism (the slowness with which policy change is effected due to institutional and political factors) is by no means unique to tax policy. For many political scientists it is a description of the way policy is actually made, rather than a perjorative term. Indeed, incrementalism is no bad thing if it prevents badly conceived policies from being implemented, only to be reversed by the next government and replaced by yet more hastily devised measures.

Badly Conceived Taxes

Somewhat different is the criticism that new taxes have been badly thought out and hastily put together. The poor drafting of tax legislation, particularly when it is full of special exemptions, creates anomalies and loopholes which tax advisers exploit. Expensive litigation is utilised to interpret tax legislation and the government responds with further amendments to the law, either in an attempt to secure its original tax intentions or to appease complaints by taxpayers.

How this state of affairs comes about is traced first to the origins of proposals for new taxes.[14] Usually they emerge through the policy agenda-setting mechanisms of the main political parties. For party activists tax proposals serve political ends. Conservative supporters tend to dislike taxes, and have been particularly vocal in their condemnation of certain taxes—SET, double taxation of dividends and currently, rates. For egalitarian ends the Labour Party traditionally wants to tax capital and wealth. This is why they replaced estate duty with capital transfer tax and introduced the double taxation of dividends in 1965. In the mid-1970s as part of their 'social contract' with the TUC they were committed to the introduction of a wealth tax. However, these broad political aims have to be translated into effective legislation. Often the political commitment is made before the objectives of the tax or how they can be attained have been sufficiently analysed and debated. The Labour Party, not surprisingly, is particularly short of advice from supporters who are tax lawyers or accountants. Capital transfer tax, partly as the result of more recent Conservative amendments, failed to become the effective tax on inherited wealth it was intended to be. The state of corporation tax, with its complex exemptions and continual amendments, is partly attributed to its hasty creation by the Labour Government and repeal and replacement by the Conservatives. Mrs Thatcher committed herself to the abolition of rates, without any clear idea of what form of local tax should replace them.

How then do political commitments to alter the tax structure get translated into legislation? In some instances particular experts within a political party have devoted considerable effort to working out tax proposals. Usually, a government engages in some form of consultation before introducing a new tax. Often a Green Paper is issued, which sets out the current state of government thinking and invites comment from interested parties. The Inland Revenue or Customs and Excise are closely involved, and they in their turn consult with the accountancy bodies, in particular the Institute of Chartered Accountants with which there exist regular channels of communication.

Though the Treasury has opposed a standing House of Commons Select Committee on taxation, greater use was made in the 1970s of *ad hoc* select committees to investigate specific tax proposals—corporation tax, wealth tax and a tax credit scheme.[15] In the case of corporation tax, the committee did persuade the Chancellor to adopt the imputation method of taxing dividends instead of a two-tier rate. But the committees were sharply divided in their recommendations for the wealth tax and tax credit scheme, neither of which came to fruition. Usually the referral of such matters to a select committee indicates government indecision in the first place: the committee serves to highlight the difficulties of resolving the proposal's problems. This may well be useful if it prevents unsatisfactory legislation from being passed. Given that select committees are drawn from both government and opposition parties, they cannot serve as more than sounding-boards for proposed legislation. Thus the main responsibility for translating a political commitment with respect to taxation into legislation rests with ministers and officials. As already noted, MPs' ability and interest in scrutinising and improving the drafting of Finance Bills is limited.

Some believe that more informed public debate on tax policies, which is fed into the government's decision-making, would improve the outcome. The Treasury and Civil Service Select Committee, in a report on budgetary reform (May 1982) gave vent to a sentiment popular amongst those interested in policy making, but who are ouside the inner circle of government:

We believe that more open debate—'open' in the sense that more people and institutions are involved and in the sense that the discussion takes place before options are foreclosed—will, provided that such debate is properly informed, lead both to better decisions and to decisions which command wider respect and support.

However, believing in the principle of open government as an essential element of democracy, is not the same as believing that open government will itself lead to the adoption of policies more conducive to improving the overall performance of the economy. That this benefit will necessarily flow from more open government is doubtful because greater consultation by government, accompanied by public debate and controversy, increases the opportunities for diverse and conflicting political interests to influence the conduct of policy. The policies that thus emerge from bargaining amongst *political interests* are ineffective in attaining any specific objectives, because they are designed to appease incompatible demands from disparate interests.

Political Interests

Political interests impinge on all stages of tax policy-making; setting parties' election manifestos, lobbying the Chancellor about the contents of the Budget, influencing MPs with respect to amending the Finance Bill and contributing to the political environment to which ministers respond. Some interests maintain regular channels of communication with government departments, through which they influence tax policy. Often these interests are successful in gaining tax concessions: the Child Poverty Action Group campaigned for zero VAT rating for children's clothes, farmers for lower rates of capital transfer tax on agricultural land, industries and regions for more favourable investment allowances. Campaigns to retain existing tax concessions, such as those on books and pensions, are mounted on rumours that abolition is being considered.

As noted earlier in the chapter, a lot of the complexity of the tax structure, which makes it costly to administer and which promotes allocative inefficiency, is the outcome of tax concessions to particular activities and transactions. The problem is that once these concessions have been granted, even if they do not in the end result in much benefit to their recipients, their removal would make particular classes of taxpayer worse off. A prime example of this is mortgage interest relief. By subsidising house purchase, and so increasing the demand for houses, it has raised house prices and so home owners are in the end little better off. But having bought their houses at these higher prices, mortgagors, particularly those who have recently entered the market, would be badly hit by the abolition of mortgage relief. No political party dares risk so many floating votes by removing mortgage relief, even though it is a highly inefficient form of subsidy, which incurs the administrative costs of taking tax from people and returning it to them in mortgage interest relief.

Tax concessions, once granted, are politically difficult to remove. Some reformers have therefore recommended a gradualist approach, whereby the tax structure is altered slowly, but with a clear plan in mind.[16] Others have suggested a blitz on all fronts: concessions to all political interests are removed at the same time so that the net effect is beneficial to most interests.

CONCLUSION

This chapter has described the basic features of the UK tax structure in terms of the types of taxes levied. Tax policy falls into two distinct categories. Short-term tax policy is concerned with raising revenue to meet the government's ongoing expenditures and with the implications of the size of tax revenues for the short-term management of the economy. Even with the shift towards monetarist and supply-side policies, short-run considerations still take precedence over the long-term impact of the tax structure on economic performance.

The standard criteria for assessing how well a tax or the tax system as a whole performs its functions, namely its *administrative costs* to the public and private sectors, its impact on *efficiency* and the *equity* with which the tax burden is distributed, are all long-term considerations. They are *structural* characteristics of the tax system which form its basic framework. Given this framework, the actual rates of tax can be adjusted year by year with a view to obtaining the tax revenue the government considers appropriate. We have seen that assessed against these criteria, the British tax system is found wanting. Though there is bound to be disagreement about the tax structure, because people give different priorities to the objectives of efficiency and equity—which are to some extent in conflict—the tax system is criticised for failing to achieve a given degree of equity with less damage to efficiency.

Many of the reasons put forward to explain why the British tax system is unsatisfactory relate to the policy-making process by which taxation is determined. This process is highly centralised within the Treasury. This tendency has been accentuated under the Conservatives; with rate-capping, even local taxation is brought under central control. In conjunction with centralisation there is considerable scope for political interests, both within and outside the machinery of government, to influence tax policy, as is evident from the tax legislation that emerges. To what extent the weaknesses in the tax system are due to centralised tax-making power or government placation of diverse political interests is a matter of subjective judgement. Perhaps we have the worst of both worlds: governments with the power to make a continual succession of decisions, dictated by the pressures of short-term events and pluralist politics?

NOTES

1. *Financial Statement and Budget Report 1985—86*, p. 8.

2. The incidence of a tax would fall entirely on consumers if the demand for the good were perfectly inelastic (fixed whatever the price) or if the supply were perfectly elastic.
3. C.T. Standford, *Hidden Costs of Taxation* (Institute of Fiscal Studies, London, 1973).
4. J.Kay, *The Economy and the 1985 Budget* (Basil Blackwell, Oxford, 1985) p. 66.
5. J. A. Kay and M.A. King, *The British Tax System* (Oxford University Press, Oxford, 1983).
6. A. Homer and R. Burrows, *Tolley's Tax Guide* (Tolley Publishing Co., Croydon,1984).
7. Meade Committee, *The Structure and Reform of Direct Taxation* (Allen and Unwin, London, 1978).
8. Kay and King, op. cit., p. 35.
9. Kay and King, op. cit., p. 18.
10. Kay and King, and Meade Committee, op. cit.
11. Treasury, *Economic Progress Report*, No. 160, September (Treasury, London, 1983).
12. Treasury, 'Making a Budget', *Economic Progress Report*, No. 153, January (Treasury, London,1983) p. 2.
13. *Fiscal Studies*, November 1983, p. 5.
14. A. Robinson and C.T. Sandford, *Tax Policy-Making in the U.K.* (Heinemann, London, 1983).
15. The tax credit scheme was a Conservative proposal in 1972 partly to integrate the tax and benefit systems. It is described further in Chapter 13.
16. As suggested by the Meade Committee and Kay and King, op. cit.

6   Markets and Government: An Overview

Economic liberalism is opposed to competition being supplanted by inferior methods of coordinating individual efforts. And it regards competition as superior not only because it is in most circumstances the most efficient method known, but even more so because it is the only method by which our activities can be adjusted to each other without coercive or arbitrary intervention of authority. (F. A. von Hayek, *The Road to Serfdom*, p. 27)[1]

We reject the view that the operation of the free market—guided only by the operation of the forces of profit, self-interest and greed—can ensure that industry meets the needs of the community. (*Labour's Programme* (Labour Party, London, 1982), pp. 7-8)

Earlier chapters established the point that economic policy is about the use of markets and government as allocative mechanisms. The coal industry case-study showed how government and market as allocative mechanisms interact to determine the size and structure of that industry and the distribution of social welfare associated with it. The coal industry example also illustrates the sharp differences in value judgements over the relative merits of markets and governments. Different preferences between market and government allocation have for long been distinguishing characteristics of different political perspectives and political party programmes. A preference for government allocation implies higher levels of public spending, taxation and government borrowing, in contrast to market-oriented policies. Since the postwar consensus on the scope of the mixed economy evaporated, disagreement over the respective roles of market and government has intensified. In the 1980s, the Conservatives' *privatisation* policies have aimed at reversing the long-run trend for the public sector to encompass an ever-expanding share of economic activity.

This chapter is in the nature of a stocktaking. It serves to review and bring together the analysis on markets and government as *allocative mechanisms* already introduced, and to extend it further by explaining the major arguments for and against each of them, using the criteria of *efficiency* and *equity*. A third criterion, used much more in political than economic analysis, is the ethical appeal of the decision-making process itself. People may approve of the way allocative decisions are made, quite independently of the outcome. Market allocation is approved of by some because it enhances individual liberty, while being condemned by others for promoting the pursuit of self-interest at the expense of altruism and a collective concern for others' welfare. The efficiency and distributional criteria will be examined more fully in this chapter, while the third one is discussed more briefly. Distributional criteria and ethical evaluations will be re-examined in Chapter 12 in the context of the welfare state.

ASSESSING GOVERNMENT AND MARKET ALLOCATION

An allocative system is a decision-making mechanism for determining what goods and services are produced, what production methods are used to produce them, and how income, wealth and other factors that contribute to people's welfare are distributed. Any viable society must provide some means whereby individuals cooperate and coordinate their activities in order to increase their social welfare above that obtainable from self-sufficiency. This implies the division of labour, which in a free society can only occur if individuals exchange goods and services voluntarily. This requires the establishment of markets as well as a political system of *collective decision-making*—namely, government—in order, at a minimum, to enforce market contracts.

Markets and government provide different ways in which voluntary exchange takes place. In the market individuals exchange goods and services at a mutually agreed price, normally using the medium of money. The political basis of society is also held to rest on voluntary agreement, in the sense that citizens are conceived of entering into an implicit social contract whereby each surrenders the liberty to do whatever he wants and agrees to pay taxes and abide by laws in exchange for the advantages of living in a governed society, which provides him with law and order and, nowadays, a whole range of goods and services. In a liberal democracy government is held accountable to citizens by means of regular free elections, in which citizens choose between competing parties of politicians. As a government has to win majority support, the electorate have recurrent opportunities to change the nature of the contract between themselves and the state. Markets are the arena where the choices of individual economic agents determine allocation and distribution; government is the prime embodiment of *collective choice*.

How the Market Allocates

The market serves to bring together buyers and sellers to enable them to engage in mutually advantageous exchanges. Given that individuals undertake exchange voluntarily, it is presumed that they must thereby be no worse off and that at least one party to the exchange is better off as a result. This, of course, assumes that individuals have enough information to assess accurately the net advantages of the exchange, and this would include an assessment of the risks associated with the contract. It is also based on the value judgement that individuals are the best judge of their own welfare. The efficiency of market allocation is in question if either of these assumptions is judged not to hold.

In bringing together buyers and sellers and posting prices at which trade takes place, the market signals and transmits information to which buyers and sellers respond. The market enables individuals to signal their preferences, provided they possess something others want to exchange. Market exchange can therefore only occur when there are established *property rights* or ownership claims which can be exchanged. Except in the case of barter, a potential consumer requires money to register a preference on a market. With money obtained from owning real and financial assets and from working, households and individuals indicate their preferences for goods and services by the amounts they demand. *Demand* is the desire to acquire a good or service backed by the willingness and ability to pay for it.

Self-interest leads suppliers to respond to the demand signalled on the market by purchasers. Owners of labour and capital hire out their assets for a monetary reward or, in the case of labour, other attributes of the job may count as well. Firms are motivated by the profit incentive to produce those goods which command a value on the market in excess of the cost of the resources used to make them. It is the profit motive that drives firms to allocate resources to the production of goods and services consumers demand and thus respond to consumer preferences. The desire to earn profits also motivates firms to seek out low-cost production methods. This involves exploiting current knowledge about technology and methods of organising production, as well as seeking out and applying new knowledge.

The *competitive market* is advocated because it is held to promote efficiency in resource-allocation and the liberty of the individual citizen. Certain individuals also do well out of market distribution. Efficiency is a much used word in everyday speech, but for the purposes of policy analysis it requires careful definition.

EFFICIENCY CRITERIA

To start with it is important to distinguish between *productive efficiency* and *allocative efficiency*.

Productive Efficiency

Maximum *productive efficiency* is achieved if it is impossible to reallocate existing resources so that more of at least one good is produced, without producing less of any other good. This is illustrated in Figure 6.1 for the simple case of an economy producing two goods, X and Y. The quantities of X and Y are measured along the horizontal and vertical axes respectively. The curve PP' indicates the various combinations of X and Y that can be produced if all resources in the economy are fully utilised. Every point on curve PP' is *productively efficient*: it is only possible to produce more units of X if fewer units of Y are produced, or more units of Y if less X is made. The curve PP' is thus known as a *production possibility* curve or frontier. Now, any point inside the production possibility curve, like point A, is productively inefficient: X can be produced without giving up any units of Y. It is unambiguously the case that the value of output in the economy can be increased by reallocating productive resources or utilising them more fully. So a *productively efficient allocation of resources* is one where it is impossible to reallocate resources so as to produce more of one good without producing less of any other. When productive efficiency has been achieved, then every good has an *opportunity cost* which is the next best alternative use to which the resources used to make it could have been put. In a two-good world the opportunity cost of a unit of X is the amount of Y forgone in order to produce X.

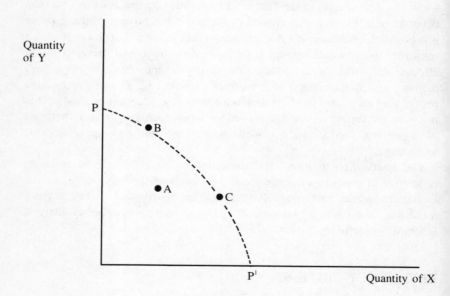

Figure 6.1: The production possibility curve

Given that the economy is *productively efficient*, the much more difficult question is which combination of X and Y along the *production possibility* curve should be produced, when all individuals are not unanimous as to which is the best combination for society as a whole. It is this question that economists have tried to answer by developing the concept of *allocative efficiency*. Their attempts to produce a solution to this perennial and knotty problem has also been constrained by the desire to avoid making judgements about whose welfare or values should be given greater priority.

Pareto Efficiency

The concept of *Pareto efficiency*, introduced in Chapter 3 (p. 57), underlies much of the economic analysis developed to make value judgements about policy measures. This is a branch of economics referred to as *welfare economics*. A *Pareto-efficient* resource allocation is one from which it is impossible to undertake any further adjustments that would make at least one person better off without making anybody else worse off. If it is possible to make at least one person better off without harming anyone else, then the existing allocation of resources cannot be *allocatively efficient* by the Pareto criterion. If resource allocation is not productively efficient, it cannot be *Pareto-efficient* either. Take point A in Figure 6.1. Any move upwards between lines AB and AC will yield more X or more Y or more of both X and Y, but there will be no reduction in X or Y. Thus such a move must make some people better off without harming others by depriving them of X or Y (assuming no envy!). But whether a move along the production possibility curve from B to C is *Pareto-efficient* depends on whether some people feel better off when the economy is at C, while nobody feels worse off. Without knowing everybody's preferences we cannot tell which of the points along the production possibility curve is *Pareto-efficient*. If a move from either point B or C makes somebody worse off then *both* B and C are *Pareto-efficient* allocations of resources to the production and distribution of goods X and Y. There are thus many *Pareto-efficient* allocations.

Because a policy measure is only judged worth undertaking on Pareto-efficiency grounds if it increases the welfare of at least one individual without making anybody else worse off, the Pareto criterion avoids making any value judgement about whose welfare should be preferred over that of others. But it avoids making interpersonal comparisons of welfare at some cost! It is a highly conservative criterion which weights the status quo very heavily and only allows a policy change to take place if all those affected by the policy are unanimously in favour, or indifferent. In other words each person has a veto. This means that as a practical criterion for judging policy measures it has little applicability. Most policies that are undertaken, and even more of those that are advocated, involve benefits for some and costs for others, as in the coal dispute. However the Pareto criterion does help to explain why some policy reforms are in practice so difficult to implement; certain interests will be harmed and their protests hinder any fundamental restructuring of policy in favour of inaction or ad hoc tinkering.

Maximising Net Social Benefits

This is why, in order to have a more widely applicable criterion for judging the efficiency of resource allocation, the definition in terms of a maximal value of output is favoured. According to this definition of *economic efficiency*, an allocation of resources is efficient if it is impossible to increase the value of final output by producing a different combination of goods and services. This, of course, presupposes that least-cost production methods are being used and so productive efficiency achieved. Thus a single policy measure is judged according to whether its *social benefits* exceed its *social costs*. If they do, then adopting the policy will increase the total value of economic activity. This is the criterion which I called *social efficiency* in Chapter 3, and on which the NUM based their economic case against pit closures. Sometimes this criterion is also referred to as *economic efficiency*.

There are two interrelated problems with the *social efficiency* criterion of maximum net social benefit. First is that it requires some valuation to be placed on the output of goods and services produced by each allocation of factors of production. If we rely totally on market valuation, then the value of total output will depend on the market prices for all goods and services produced and of the factors of production used in making them. In a market economy these prices will be determined by the interaction of demand and supply in all the interrelated markets that affect the economy. However these demands and supplies are themselves affected by the prior distribution of the ownership of the different types of capital and labour. Thus market prices depend on the prior distribution of resources, while at the same time they affect the distribution of income and wealth. An individual who owns few resources that are valued highly by the market will have little income or wealth. As the value placed on output by the market is not independent of distribution, the definition of what constitutes a socially efficient allocation of resources is not independent of distribution and so is not value-free. This is also the case with the *Pareto-efficiency* criterion, since what an individual in a given set of circumstances judges will improve or diminish his welfare depends on what he can sell his factor services for and what he has to pay for the goods and services he wishes to consume.

The second problem with the *social efficiency* criterion is that, unlike the Pareto criterion, it does rely on value judgements about whose welfare to satisfy. As pointed out in Chapter 3, a policy is judged *socially efficient* if the *social benefits* it yields exceed the *social costs*, even if those who bear the social costs do not get fully compensated and so are worse off as a result. All that matters is that the beneficiaries could, in principle, pay compensation to the losers so that the latter are no worse off, while they themselves are still better off than before the policy change. In other words, if social benefits exceed social costs there is a potential Pareto improvement. However the compensation required to secure an actual Pareto improvement need not occur for the policy, with its associated allocation of resources, to be deemed *socially efficient*, so long as the social benefits are valued more highly than the social costs. Thus the *social efficiency* criterion is based on a value judgement and its acceptability requires agreement on the ethical premise upon which it is based. This is that the losers should accept a measure which decreases their welfare, provided it increases the welfare of others by more than their own is diminished.

Is the Efficiency Criterion Useful?

If efficiency cannot be defined in a way that is independent of value judgements about income distribution, is it worth the effort of trying to treat *efficiency* and *distribution* as separate criteria? There are a number of reasons why it is. The first is that it gives a useful classification of the fundamental objectives underlying any policy change. It distinguishes between measures which are likely to increase the size of the kitty available for distribution and those which aim to divide up an existing kitty in a different way. Even if policy-makers' primary concern is to achieve a certain distribution of welfare, it is useful to know which measures will achieve this objective at least cost, i.e. which measures are efficient in attaining a given set of goals. In practice, as the coal case shows, efficiency and distributional criteria are thoroughly mixed up by the protagonists. Both sides in the coal dispute maintained that their policies would promote efficiency, using different definitions and measurements: these interpretations of efficiency had different distributional implications. For example, even if we accept the NUM's argument that the social benefits of keeping pits in operation exceeded the social costs of doing so, this still leaves the distribution of the social costs and benefits as a separate issue. The higher are miners' wages in relation to the opportunity cost of employing miners (which according to the NUM was zero), the more the costs of keeping old pits going are borne by coal consumers—in the form of higher coal prices—and taxpayers—in the form of subsidies to the NCB. The distinction between efficiency and distribution as criteria for judging allocative outcomes helps to clarify the issues.

Another reason for using efficiency as a criterion for assessing policies which is much favoured by conventional economists is in order to promote an analytic and objective approach to policy-making. The social efficiency criterion is put forward as a set of agreed rules for deciding between the rival claims of political interests. Its use is intended to promote a rational approach to policy-making; it turns the resolution of allocative and distributional problems by government into a technocratic exercise for disinterested experts and so removes it from the hurly-burly of political machinations in the corridors and committee rooms of power. Whether decision rules for allocating resources can actually be sanitised from politics is another matter, which is discussed further in Chapter 10 in the context of the Department of Transport's methods for deciding on road-building projects.

Efficiency thus provides one important criterion against which to assess how well markets or government perform their allocative function with respect to different types of goods and services. If the market does not achieve an efficient allocation of resources there is said to be *market failure*. Three main sources of *market failure* are generally distinguished. These are *externalities, imperfect competition* and *inadequate information*.

MARKET FAILURE DUE TO EXTERNALITIES

Examples of *externalities* as a source of *market failure* arose in the coal industry case-study. An *externality* occurs when the actions of one economic agent affect the welfare of others in a way that is not reflected in market prices. An *external cost* arises from coal burning because the emission of sulphur dioxide causes air pollution, for which the sufferers receive no compensation. Coal mining imposes costs on others because of subsidence, but this is not an external cost as the NCB is liable to pay compensation. The subsidence costs are incurred by the NCB and so are said to be internalised. Examples of *external benefits* attributed to keeping open existing pits are the preservation of mining communities and the benefits to future generations of having cheaply worked coal seams left to them. (The problem with the concept of external costs and benefits is that while they undoubtedly exist, almost anything can, with a bit of imagination, be classified as a cost or benefit.)

The *social costs* of an activity are its *private costs*—those costs incurred directly by the agent undertaking the activity—plus any *external costs* associated with it. Similarly the *social benefits* of an activity are the *private benefits* accruing to the agent engaged in the activity plus any *external benefits*. Private benefits and costs are reflected in market prices. For instance, the private costs of providing air travel are indicated by the price of air tickets. Consumers indicate the extent to which they value air travel by the price they are willing to pay. But the external costs of air traffic noise to those living and working around airports are not included in the price of air tickets. If social costs and benefits differ from private costs and benefits, then the market will fail to transmit the correct information about the costs and values attached to goods and services. The market will undervalue goods that yield social benefits in excess of private benefits and will consequently produce too few of these goods. Similarly the market overvalues goods which have social costs in excess of private costs. The price of such goods is less than it would be if producers had to take account of the external costs associated with the production of the good. Consequently, consumers demand more of the good than if its price reflected all social costs and so too much of the good is produced. Thus *discrepancies between social costs and benefits and private costs and benefits mean that market allocation is socially inefficient.*

The existence of externalities gives government a role in trying to correct for market failure. There are three main sets of instruments government can use: taxes and subsidies to private firms, regulation and public sector production. Goods with external costs, such as cigarettes, can be taxed in order to induce consumers to buy less. Additional output of goods which yield external benefits can be obtained by giving subsidies to private sector firms for producing them. Or those suffering external costs can be compensated: grants towards double glazing near airports is an example. Alternatively the government can try to produce the goods in the public sector in socially efficient quantities. This was the NUM's case for increasing government subventions to the NCB. Legal prohibition is an important way of either preventing individuals and firms from creating external costs, or forcing the perpetrators to internalise the costs and so reflect them in market prices. Planning regulations, pollution controls, speed and weight restrictions on roads, are all methods of reducing external costs. For example, the proposed EC limits on car exhaust emissions will require more expensive car engines or catalytic converters, so internalising the cost of air pollution by making motorists pay for preventive action.

But government intervention is not the only way to cope with the problem of socially inefficient resource allocation due to externalities. Private collective action is possible and does occur. For instance volunteer groups create external benefits by improving the appearance of the environment, through best-kept village competitions or reclaiming old canals. Local residents could band together and pay a local firm to reduce air or water pollution. The justification for government action on efficiency grounds is that the costs of organising private sector collective action are too great for this to occur in many cases.

Collective Goods
A further dimension to the externality problem concerns goods which yield external benefits from which people enjoying them cannot be excluded.

Common examples are national defence, and law and order. Everybody living in a country obtains the benefits (or disbenefits in the case of pacifists) of national defence and cannot be excluded from them. Street lighting and roads are another example, for although it is physically possible to exclude users unless they pay a charge, it is prohibitively expensive to do so, except for roads in great demand like motorways and major bridges. There are other goods which are held in common ownership, such as the air, the sea and common land, which it is difficult to prevent people from using because *property rights* in them are not assigned to individual owners. However the benefits of these goods held in common ownership are largely private, like using air to discharge smoke, taking fish from the sea, or grazing animals on common land. Goods that yield benefits, either external or private, from which it is difficult or costly to exclude consumers are termed *non-excludable*, in contrast to goods like food, clothing or housing from which people can be easily excluded unless they pay for them. So goods which yield either private or external benefits, or some combination of both, are further characterised by whether they are *excludable* or *non-excludable*.

Some goods with external benefits, from which it is difficult to exclude people, possess a further characteristic: the consumption of their benefits by one person does not reduce the amount available for others. This characteristic is known as non-rivalry in consumption. Defence again has this characteristic since the consumption of the benefits of a national deterrent by one individual does not in general reduce the amount available for others. The same is true of TV and radio channels. One person's reception of them does not reduce the ability of others to receive them. There are many goods which are partly *non-rivalrous* in consumption. Roads are one example. An additional vehicle on a quiet road does not reduce the amount of road space available for others. On a busy road, though, an extra car adds to congestion and so reduces the benefits other motorists are enjoying. Parks, golf courses, and concerts can all, up to a point, be consumed by additional users without detracting from the enjoyment of other users. In contrast, other goods, like food, electricity, the use of a personal computer, are *rivalrous* in consumption. Their consumption by one individual reduces the amount available for others. Goods which are completely *rivalrous*, by definition, cannot yield external benefits. Some goods can give private and external benefits. Education, for example, benefits those who receive it because it enhances their employment prospects or because they enjoy studying, but it is also held to yield external benefits in producing a socialised, literate and informed citizenry. These external benefits are enjoyed and so are non-rivalrous.

So there are two characteristics, *excludability* and *rivalry in consumption*, that we can use to classify goods. This gives the fourfold classification set out in Table 6.1. Goods which are *rivalrous* in consumption and *excludable*, are called *private goods*. Goods which are *non-excludable* and *rivalrous* in consumption are termed *common goods*. Those which are *non-rivalrous* in consumption—at least until congestion occurs—and *excludable*, such as road tunnels, motorways or parks, are called *toll goods* in Table 6.1, since it is feasible to charge for them. Finally, goods which are both *non-excludable* and *non-rivalrous* are known as *public goods*. It is important to appreciate that goods do not fall neatly into one of the four cells in Table 6.1. Rather, *excludability/non-excludability* and *rivalry/non-rivalry* in consumption vary along a spectrum.

Table 6.1: Private, common, public and toll goods

	Rivalry in consumption	Non-rivalry in consumption
Excludable	Private goods e.g. food, houses	Toll goods e.g. golf courses, motorways
Non-excludable	Common goods e.g. fisheries, wild animals	Public goods e.g. defence, public health

In fact there are very few goods that are *pure public goods*; that is, goods that yield benefits from which nobody can be excluded and for which the amount the individual can consume does not diminish as the number of consumers increases. Take defence, for example: the dispatch of the Task Force to the Falkland Islands in 1982 diminished the Navy's capacity to defend mainland Britain. Given the few nuclear shelters that exist in the UK, most people would be excluded from them. So this aspect of defence is quite close to being a private good as it is excludable and rivalrous, hence some households build their own shelters. While pure public goods are hard to find, there are many goods with a considerable *public goods element*: they yield external benefits from which it is costly to exclude people and are, to a degree, non-rivalrous in consumption.

The importance of this taxonomy of goods as *private*, or having a *collective* element (this embraces common, public and toll goods) is to determine whether markets will provide an *allocatively efficient* quantity of each type of good. In the case of private goods there are no significant external costs or benefits associated with their production and use and hence the market system can be efficient. In a *competitive market* the good's price will reflect both the cost of producing it, in terms of forgone alternatives, and its value to consumers. Hence a *competitive market* will produce a *socially efficient* quantity of *private goods*.

However the market will not provide a sufficient quantity of *public goods*. This is because people can obtain the non-excludable benefits of public goods without paying for them, as the history of Dungeness lighthouse bears out:

Dungeness was the obvious site for a lighthouse and Sir Edward Howard, Admiral of the High Seas, obtained a patent with permission to levy a toll of one penny a ton on all ships passing the light for a period of 50 years. James I gave the licence in 1615. The advantages to navigation were immediately obvious but the light dues were well nigh impossible to collect. Howard sold his lease to William Lamplaigh, who wisely enlisted the help of the customs to collect the dues. Trinity House tried to get the patent cancelled, they said it was a nuisance to navigation. The shipowners were in full support because they had no wish to pay dues. (Plaque at Dungeness)

Because its benefits are non-excludable, anybody providing a public good will find it difficult to get the other beneficiaries to pay for it. This is known as the *free-rider* problem. The social benefits of a public good are the sum total of the benfits enjoyed by all individuals, but because there are many beneficiaries, the benefit to each individual will be quite small. An individual cannot enlarge his benefit by producing the good and charging others for using it, because of the *free-rider* problem. So a private sector agent will only provide a public good if his private benefits exceed the costs of producing the good. Consequently too little of a public good will be produced by the market. Collective provision by government can solve the problem as the government has the power to tax everybody in order to finance the provision of public goods. The nature of public goods explains why defence and law and order were the first areas where government provision became dominant. It also explains why the bulk of basic research, which provides technical knowledge that is non-rivalrous in use and largely non-excludable, is funded by governments. However, because of the problems of discovering how much people value public goods, it is virtually impossible for government to determine the most socially efficient quantity of public goods.

Because *toll goods* can be made excludable, they may be provided by a variety of private sector organisations, such as profit-maximising firms or clubs and associations. Toll bridges, roads and canals were privately provided in the eighteenth century. Collective provision of services can be organised privately as in the case of golf clubs and motoring associations. However, collective provision is also provided by government which may charge a zero toll and finance the good out of tax revenues. This is how roads are funded and charged for in Britain, while in France and in parts of the USA tolls are charged for motorways. State provision of toll goods is justified on efficiency grounds if exclusion is relatively costly to enforce or too little of the good is consumed because people are excluded from using a good which is non-rivalrous in consumption.

The opposite problem arises with *common goods*: too much is consumed if there is no collective agreement to desist. Seas are overfished, pastures overgrazed, wild animals hunted to near extinction, or smoke released into the atmosphere, because it is not in the interests of one individual to reduce his consumption if others do not. The benefits of a single individual's restraint are experienced by all users and become negligible private benefits. The allocative outcome is inefficient because the social costs of depletion and usage exceed the social benefits from the extra consumption. One solution is to allocate *property rights* over the resources, so that the cost of the individual's use of them falls only on the individual. This is possible with land, but not feasible for seas and even less so for the atmosphere. Users can reach their own collective agreements on usage, but these may be costly to organise and enforce. Hence there is a role for government collective action to improve the efficiency of resource allocation by negotiating and enforcing regulations regarding the use of common goods. Examples are controls over the release of pollutants into rivers, seas and the atmosphere and international agreements between governments, as in the case of fishing limits and quotas or nuclear test ban treaties.

Providing Collective Goods

Government *allocation* with respect to public and toll goods need not involve public sector *production* of the goods in question. There is a considerable variety of ways in which such goods are financed and provided by a combination of private and public sector activity and different practices can be observed around the world. Government can perform any one of three functions with respect to public and toll goods: arranging for their provision, financing their provision, and undertaking the actual production.

Take broadcasting for example. Radio and TV waves are public goods in that the reception of signals is non-rivalrous and it is difficult to exclude consumers once they have reception equipment. However the use of radio and TV wave frequencies for transmitting programmes from the earth is rivalrous. So at a minimum government needs to arrange for broadcasting to be undertaken by allocating and enforcing private sector property rights in these frequencies. In Britain these are allocated administratively to the BBC, while independent broadcasters compete for franchises to operate programme channels and pay a levy for their use. The state also produces broadcasting services via the BBC but does not finance them. The private sector finances broadcasting either through the BBC TV licence or via advertising on independent TV and radio. The government tackles the free-rider problem with respect to the financing BBC services by legal means.

The alternative would be for the government to finance the state provision of broadcasting through general taxation. Another alternative would be for the state to pay private sector firms to produce TV and radio programmes.

The point is that various combinations of government and private sector organisation, finance and production are possible. From a social efficiency point of view, the methods chosen in any specific instance should be determined by efficiency considerations. This would mean a bias to methods which give consumers a way of registering their preferences and those which encourage competition amongst suppliers. Privatisation need not mean that the government no longer affects how a good is produced and distributed. Government can hand over the production of a good to the private sector while still financing it, as with refuse collection or cleaning and maintaining public sector buildings.

MARKET FAILURE DUE TO IMPERFECT COMPETITION

As has already been emphasised, markets need to be competitive if they are to allocate resources efficiently. The *degree of competition* in a market is an imprecise concept as it depends on those factors which force firms to take account of the possibility that their business will be lost to rivals if they do not satisfy their customers. The larger the number of firms already supplying a market and the more difficult it is for them to collude, the more competition there is likely to be. Competition is also related to the likelihood that new suppliers will enter the market if they perceive profit opportunities because the existing suppliers charge high prices or are *x-inefficient* and have high costs.

In order for markets to be *allocatively efficient*, prices must correctly reflect the *opportunity costs* of goods. This will not occur if lack of competition enables firms to keep their prices above the lowest attainable costs of production. Two ways in which this can occur were outlined in Chapter 3. One is that firms with *market power* will maximise their profits by charging prices in excess of *marginal costs*. As a consequence not enough of the good is produced. As price is in excess of marginal cost, consumers would value additional units of the product more highly than goods being currently produced with the resources that could be reallocated to the monopolised product. But rather than extract monopoly profits, firms can enjoy their market power by operating with higher costs so being *x-inefficient*. This also leads to higher prices for consumers.

Firms producing and selling output are not the only sources of market or monopoly power. It can be possessed by other types of seller, or by buyers if a few of them dominate the market. Trade unions exist in order to increase the market power of labour as otherwise most workers would face competition from other workers offering to work for lower wages or worse conditions. Many labour markets are now characterised by countervailing market power; there is bilateral bargaining between unions and large firms or employers' organisations.

Nationalisation and Regulation of Natural Monopolies

The kind of measures governments can adopt to combat the problem of allocative inefficiency due to imperfect competition, depend for their efficacy on the reasons for the lack of competition. Some markets are inherently monopolistic because of the nature of the production process. Industries like gas, electricity, telephone and water supplies are regarded as *natural monopolies* because duplicating their supply networks is extremely costly. One solution to the allocative efficiency problem posed by natural monopolies is public ownership, as in Britain in the postwar period. The main problem with this solution is that a public sector monopoly can be as x-inefficient as a private sector one, and may be more so, as the market sanction of bankruptcy has been removed.

An alternative solution, practised in the USA, is to keep the industries in the private sector but to *regulate* their performance in terms of such variables as profits, prices and quality of service, via special agencies. For instance, when the government sold British Telecom to private shareholders in 1984, it set up the Office of Telecommunications as the *regulatory agency* and limited the permitted rise in telephone charges to 3 per cent below the rate of inflation. There is another regulatory agency proposed for British Gas (sold to the private sector in December 1986). However the problem with regulation, as US experience testifies, is that the regulatory agency can become captured by the political interests of the industry it is regulating and fail to act as the guardian of consumers' interests. Furthermore, limits on profit rates dull the firm's incentive to reduce costs, as it gets no advantage in the form of higher profits, and so does little to combat x-inefficiency.

Competition Policy

If the industry is not a natural monopoly then in order to promote allocative efficiency the appropriate policy for government is to remove *barriers to competition* in the marketplace. Left to their own devices, sellers have an incentive to reduce competition in order to increase prices and profits and diminish uncertainty about the actions of rivals. Firms can collude to fix prices, to restrict sales outlets, to enforce tie-in sales or refrain from advertising, to mention just some of the *restrictive practices* by which firms and labour organisations reduce competition between existing sellers and erect *barriers to entry* from new competition. Buyers can also collude to strengthen their position *vis-à-vis* sellers. Under British and EC law various types of restrictive practices are illegal and firms are kept under surveillance by the Office of Fair Trading and the Competition Directorate of the European Commission. The Office of Fair Trading can investigate uncompetitive practices, both by individual firms and associations of firms, and put pressure on them to desist, or recommend government to outlaw specific practices. The recent abandonment of the opticians' monopoly of spectacles is one such instance. Another form of competition policy is to remove obstacles to competition from foreign firms, by reducing or eliminating import tariffs and quotas, or technical standards and government purchasing contracts which favour domestic firms.

Competition policy is generally restricted to measures applying to firms and the professions, such as solicitors, architects and doctors, and not to measures directed at trade unions. However legislation regarding the rights and duties of employers and the powers, responsibilities and liabilities of trade unions, greatly affects the degree of competition in labour markets. For instance Wage Councils, which set minimum wages in certain industries, prevent wages from falling due to competition from unemployed workers. The Thatcher government has reduced trade union power by limiting closed shop agreements and making unions liable to civil court actions in specified circumstances, such as secondary picketing. Widely interpreted, competition policy embraces a great variety of methods by which governments influence the operations of buyers and sellers on all forms of markets. Nor is government policy in general biased towards increasing competition: it often has the reverse effect because policies are brought in for other reasons than promoting allocative efficiency, as discussed later in the chapter.

MARKET FAILURE DUE TO INADEQUATE INFORMATION

The final type of *market failure* to be considered is that due to the market producing and transmitting insufficient *information*. The market participants are unable to undertake all the mutually advantageous exchanges that would be entered into if buyers and sellers possessed the requisite information. The market therefore does not produce a *socially efficient* allocation of resources. Many types of informational failure have been suggested, as this form of market failure has proved a fruitful source for critics of market allocation.

If market allocation is to be efficient, then the buyers and sellers must have enough information to be able to undertake voluntary exchanges that improve their welfare. Given that the outcome of market transactions is inevitably uncertain, though some transactions are more uncertain than others, the amount of information required for exchange to be efficient cannot be precisely established, leaving plenty of scope for argument. Consumer protection laws are justified on efficiency grounds, in order to prevent consumers making unwise decisions because of insufficient knowledge of firms' products. Products are obliged to meet specified safety standards and firms are required to inform consumers of the conditions attached to the sale of goods. Similarly, health and safety legislation can be designed to protect workers from agreeing to work in conditions which they do not realise are unsafe. Some of these regulations may not promote efficiency but be justified on paternalistic grounds: workers are held not to be the best judges of their own interests and so are prevented by law from taking risks they would voluntarily undertake for money.

Market failure due to informational inadequacies provides the underlying theoretical rationale for *Keynesian macroeconomic policy* as a cure for unemployment. In Keynesian analysis the labour market fails to clear: the supply of labour remains in excess of the demand for labour because market forces cannot bring about equilibrium. Because workers are unemployed, their incomes are low and so *aggregate demand* for goods is depressed. The market mechanism fails to provide a means whereby workers can signal to firms that they would demand more goods and services if only they could get jobs and so have more money to spend. Firms decline to take on more labour because the effective demand for their goods is deficient. So the government can correct for this type of market failure by increasing aggregate demand, either by spending more itself or by getting the private sector to increase its spending, through tax cuts or an expansion in the money supply and lower interest rates. However critics of Keynesian economics consider that labour markets would clear if government and institutional impediments to greater flexibility were removed.

Another source of informational inadequacy concerns uncertainty about the future. It is argued that private sector firms are too risk-averse and too concerned with short-term profits. Consequently they underinvest in long-term projects which take many years before they yield a positive return. It is further argued that financial markets fail to reflect the collective rate at which society wants to save and invest. Thus interest rates may be too high and so discourage investment, while what finance there is for investment is channelled into socially inefficient uses. According to these critics the government should put into effect society's desire to invest more so as to promote growth. Because of the scale of its command over resources, the government can spread its risks over many projects and so is justified in undertaking more investment in research and development than would occur if left to the private sector. These arguments have been used to buttress a wide range of government investments, such as Concorde, nuclear reactors, BL vehicles, microelectronics and computers. This rationalisation for state intervention on efficiency grounds presupposes that government can determine the socially desirable rate of investment and innovation, and that it can take a dispassionate, long-term view of these investment possibilities, rather than make short-run responses to the demands of political interests.

APPROACHES TO MARKET EFFICIENCY

Within economics there are two main approaches to assessing market efficiency—the *neoclassical* and the *Austrian*. The *neoclassical* approach is the one most favoured by mainstream economists and the one I have concentrated on so far.

The Neoclassical Approach

This is concerned with how markets transmit existing information about the preferences of buyers and sellers and the constraints under which they work, and reflect this information in prices. Markets are assumed to settle into an equilibrium in which demand and supply are equal. If there are externalities or imperfect competition or informational failures, then the actual equilibrium outcome in terms of prices and quantities is compared to the ideal or *optimum equilibrium*. This is the equilibrium which would prevail if the *marginal social benefit* of a good equalled its *marginal social cost*. The discrepancy between the two is the measure of *market failure*. The analysis of market failure, that typifies the neoclassical approach, is used to justify a wide range of government intervention in the working of markets. Indeed, it has been proved that, in theory at least, a centrally planned economy could be organised to achieve the same socially efficient allocation of resources that would be produced by a market economy in the absence of any market failures—provided the planners had enough information regarding the preferences of all individuals in the economy.[2] This, of course, is a tall order.

The Austrian Approach

The second approach to market efficiency is the *Austrian* one, associated particularly with von Hayek.[3] In this approach the market is inherently superior as an allocative mechanism to government because it is much better at seeking out and coordinating the information needed for making efficient allocative decisions. Austrian economists are highly critical of neoclassical economics for assuming that information is already known, and that all the market does is transmit given information. Thus market and government are assumed to have the same amount of information and their relative efficiency is judged by how well they succeed in equalising known marginal social benefits with known marginal social costs. For Austrian economists the neoclassical assumption of given and known information about social costs and benefits assumes away a vital function that any allocative mechanism has to perform. This is finding out information on individuals' preferences and on the opportunity costs of different economic activities. Thus an essential function of an allocative mechanism is seeking out and making effective use of the information needed to determine an efficient solution to the questions of what goods to produce, how to produce them and for whom. The neoclassical approach focuses on how an allocative mechanism calculates which allocation of resources is socially efficient, given that the required information is already known.

In the Austrian view the market is inherently more efficient at finding and making use of information. If a single central planning authority were to calculate the socially efficient allocation of resources, it would require a vast amount of knowledge, which in practice it could not obtain. The market is superior because it does not require any one decision-making body to have much knowledge. Each consumer, worker or firm possesses particular knowledge regarding their own tastes and specialist skills and how they can make best use of these in the marketplace. Self-interest leads individual economic agents to seek out and exploit opportunities for profitable trading. Since exchange is voluntary, every act of exchange must be to the advantage of the traders. So if a good is in short supply or over-priced by a monopolist, new suppliers will appear in response to profit signals, provided that government has not blunted, distorted or removed market incentives.

Austrians emphasise the dynamic nature of markets and the continual response they evoke to changing circumstances. This is in contrast to the neoclassical concern with the static equilibrium achieved when demand and supply are equal. Austrians focus on how markets both foster and respond to changes which give rise to differences between demand and supply. Market failure is very much a neoclassical and Keynesian concept. In Austrian eyes markets are superior to government in seeking out and using information, in contrast to the view that markets allocate inefficiently because of information failures. Imperfect competition would not be much of a problem if governments ensured that laws, regulations, taxes and subsidies did not impede the freedom of buyers and sellers to enter and exit from markets and conduct voluntary exchanges. The problem of externalities would be coped with by assigning property rights wherever possible so that market exchanges could take place.

DISTRIBUTION

Although economists stress the criterion of efficiency in assessing specific policy measures and judging whether market or government should be used as an allocative mechanism, much of government influence on economic activity is not related to this objective. While efficiency has been given greater prominence in economic policy in the 1980s, the impact of government on the *distribution of social welfare* is, I would judge, the major issue at stake. Even if policies are assessed in relation to their implications for economic efficiency, the primary concern within the political arena is their distributional impact on the various political interests.

Even if the market worked perfectly, in the sense that there were no *market failure*, the market mechanism would still be criticised for its inequitable *distribution* of income and wealth and other aspects of social welfare. In the marketplace an individual can only lay claim to goods if he can back his desire to consume goods with purchasing power. A want or need is not sufficient to register a demand on a market: it has to be accompanied by the ability and willingness to pay. In a pure market system an individual obtains the money needed to signal his demands for goods by possessing wealth, which is lent to others for a rate of return or sold outright, and also by selling his labour services, including those of entrepreneurship. In a market economy, the rate of return on capital, the wages of labour and the profits for entrepreneurship are determined by the forces of demand and supply. So if a person has no wealth and possesses labour services which command a low price, or cannot work or chooses not to, his purchasing power will be low relative to others. Hence there will be considerable inequality in individuals' purchasing power and those without access to income or wealth will be destitute. Apart from material wealth and income, people's well-being depends on intangible factors, such as the quality of the environment, the social relations they experience, the amount of influence and choice they can exercise. All these can be gathered together in the term *social welfare*.

The *distribution* of *social welfare* depends to some extent on chance; on the inheritance of wealth and personal ability, on the education and socialisation people receive, and on the opportunities available to them. Inequalities in the distribution of welfare due to such chance factors are regarded as inequitable. Some go further and regard disparities in income and wealth due to differences in ability and effort as also inequitable. Ideas about what constitutes an equitable or fair distribution of social welfare vary considerably, across individuals and according to time and place. Political credos differ in the extent to which they value equity, how they define it, and what means they are prepared to use to achieve it.

For ethical reasons people favour measures that reduce their own income and wealth in order to make the distribution of welfare more *equitable*. They are even more likely to favour measures that distribute welfare more evenly if the cost is borne by others—hopefully by the rich. Distributional issues are by no means concerned only with distributing social welfare more equitably. Quite often political interests are concerned to enlarge or preserve their own share of social welfare and this is probably the most powerful motivating force in political activity. In this book I am using the criterion of *distribution* to cover both *equity* and *self-interest*. The criterion of distribution is quite distinct from that of efficiency. A measure to *redistribute social welfare* necessarily takes from some and gives to others. A measure which improves *social efficiency*, in principle at least, is capable of increasing the social welfare of some without making anybody else worse off.

Criteria for Distribution

Equity, though a popular criterion of distribution, embued with considerable moral approval, is capable of several interpretations. In general it connotes fairness and often this is interpreted to mean *equality*: everybody should have the same amount of income and wealth or at least the degree of disparity between people should be reduced. However, for some there can be fair distribution without equality of outcome. *Equality* of opportunity is a widely accepted social goal, whereas the degree to which equality of outcome is desirable, given there is equality of opportunity, is more contentious. Another aspect of equity which embraces the notion of social justice is that each person should receive goods and services according to his or her *need* for them, as assessed through the political system, and not get only what they can afford with income from market transactions. This principle is enshrined in Marx's dictum: 'To each according to his need, from each according to his ability.'

Distributional goals can be targeted at goods rather than people. Goods that are deemed particularly worthy, independently of their market value, are called *merit goods*. On the basis of the value judgement that these goods have intrinsic merit, it can then be argued that the market does not produce enough of any particular *merit good* and that the government should ensure that more is provided. Examples of *merit goods* are education, cultural activities and the environment. Opera, drama, classical music and fine art receive government subsidies; the government helps with conservation, both by financial assistance and legislation restricting what can be done to the environment. State promotion of merit goods may work against a more equitable distribution of social welfare, as many of these merit goods are more extensively consumed by the middle and upper classes.

Distributional issues concern not only income and wealth in terms of money and publicly provided goods; they also involve a wider concept of *social justice* which embraces the distribution of economic power and how this is affected by the use of government or market allocation. Here sharp differences of opinion prevail. One strand of political thinkers, known as *libertarians*, who are closely associated with *Austrian* economics, idealise the competitive market system because is ensures the dispersion of economic decision-making power amongst myriads of market participants. The growth of centres of economic power, through the rise of large firms and trade unions and government bureaucracies, is inimical to individual liberty, which depends on the decentralisation of economic power.

Socialists see the libertarian ideal as both socially unjust and impracticable. They argue that market conditions necessitate the existence of large firms with excessive market power. The very nature of the market system is that some people do better out of it than others and have greater power, not only in terms of income and wealth, but in the ability to take decisions which affect the lives of others. One socialist solution to the concentration of economic power in private hands is the centralisation of such power in the hands of the state. The main motive for *nationalisation* orginally was to have public control over the 'commanding heights' of the economy—those industries deemed of greatest importance to the economy. As nationalisation has fallen out of favour, nowadays many socialists support decentralised forms of public control of firms, in which consumers and workers participate more actively in political decision-making. This could involve organising state-produced goods and services on a regional or community basis. These ideas will reappear in the later chapters on the public corporations.

ETHICAL JUDGEMENTS ABOUT A DECISION PROCESS

The implications of an allocative system for the distribution of economic power shade into ethical judgements about the nature of decision processes themselves, as distinct from judgements about their outcome in terms of efficiency and distribution. There are a number of moral considerations involved here. First, there is the question of whose preferences are taken into account. Mainstream economics accepts as axiomatic that it is the preferences of individuals that matter and presumes that the individual is the best judge of his own welfare unless strong counter-arguments prevail, e.g. as regards children, the mentally ill, criminals or, less clearly, the feckless. This contrasts with the notion that collective welfare or class interest exists quite separately from any aggregation of individuals' welfare.

Given the answer to the first ethical question posed above, there then follows the issue of how the decision process is to reflect individual or collective preferences. Is it to be through markets or the political system? If the political system is used, then how government institutions operate will influence the way the preferences of different individuals and collective interests in society are brought to bear on allocative decisions. In allocating resources in the NHS, for example, there is the question of how much influence politicians, administrators, medical staff, patients and the general public should have, and how institutional practices should be changed if patients, say, are to have greater decision-making power. These issues are examined at length in Part II.

A further ethical concern is with the nature of human relations embodied in or promoted by particular ways of allocating resources. Socialists dislike market relations on principle because they are based on, and hence promote, self-interest. Collective allocation by government is approved as an embodiment of social concern for others' welfare. So particular goods, like medical care or personal social services, are regarded as particularly unsuited to provision by markets. Private charity and even family provision is thought less preferable than state collective action. Market relations between individuals are particularly condemned in relation to the provision of basic needs, where one party is seen to be dominant. Thus the landlord–tenant relationship should be done away with as has largely occurred in Britain.

So those who subscribe to the notion of collective welfare and the promotion of altruism in human relations via state collective action, condemn market allocation as a means, independently of the ends it serves. Those biased towards individualism and the promotion of individual liberty, favour market allocation and dislike state collective action because of its coercive element and its insensitivity to individuals' preferences. If the decision process itself commands support, then people are prepared to accept particular outcomes that are not in their individual interests.

GOVERNMENT FAILURE

Although markets fail to achieve the most *socially efficient* allocation of resources or to distribute welfare according to subjective principles of *social justice*, there is no automatic guarantee that government action will improve matters, especially when the net effect of uncoordinated policies is taken into account. Much of this lack of coordination is inevitable, given the problems of acquiring information on the effects of policy measures and the impossibility, in a pluralist democracy, of taking highly centralised decisions over the whole range of state responsibilities. The concept of *government failure* mirrors that of *market failure* and encompasses a number of reasons why government is also unlikely to allocate resources with maximum social efficiency or sometimes to achieve the objective of equitable distribution sought from specific policies.

Information Problems
If markets fail to allocate resources efficiently because of the existence of *externalities*, then the first prerequisite for efficient government intervention is making good the market's informational failures. To apply the social efficiency criterion the government needs information on *social costs* and *benefits*. Given that the market has failed to produce the information, government decision-makers are faced with the problem of valuing social costs and benefits from evidence other than direct market prices. How this is attempted with respect to road schemes is discussed in Chapter 10. The social efficiency decision rule, that the optimal quantity of a good is produced when the amount it adds to social benefits (its marginal social benefit) equals the amount it adds to social costs (its marginal social cost) is difficult to apply. The best that can be hoped for is that government intervention improves the social efficiency of resource allocation, rather than achieving optimality.

Imperfect Competition
It is in the interests of particular groups of buyers and sellers to restrict *competition* between themselves. Their ability to do this is highly dependent on specific regulations affecting their markets and on the attitude of government to their uncompetitive practices. These interests try to persuade government and the general public that the restrictions on competition in their markets is in the public interest and is worthy of state support. Many professional associations, for example, ban advertising by their members and impose other restrictions on competition, arguing that this is in the interests of their customers. Some of these practices are protected by legal sanctions, as was, until recently, the reservation of house conveyancing for solicitors. Laws regarding shop and pub opening hours restrict competition. As part of their policy of increasing competition, the Conservative government removed some of these restrictions, but was defeated in its attempt to liberalise shopping hours.

There is no general consensus on the beneficial effects of competition on resource allocation in all circumstances. The legal limitations placed on trade unions and the extent to which particular markets should be protected from foreign competition are two particularly contentious areas. Public road transport is an example of a sector which has been highly regulated. Its defenders claim that this is necessary to protect the public from unsafe carriers and disorderly competition on popular routes, and to provide services on low density routes. However the present Conservative government has deregulated both long distance and local bus services in the belief that competition will make for greater efficiency. These are just a few examples: government-sanctioned restrictions on competition permeate the economy. The extent to which they actually promote social efficiency (because of externalities or informational failures of markets) or other social goals is hotly contested. Certainly for advocates of market allocation, government is a major source of imperfect competition which unjustifiably impedes voluntary exchanges between individuals and contributes to social inefficiency.

Bureaucratic Self-Interest

How well public sector employees perform in providing the goods and services their customers and clients want depends on the system of incentives and sanctions within which they operate. An important factor that affects this is the degree of *competition* from rival suppliers. As already noted, the absence of strong market pressures on public corporations with monopoly power weakens the incentives to keep costs at their feasible minimum. *X-inefficiency* can be even more of a problem in organisations producing *non-marketed goods*, like health and education, where it is extremely difficult to measure efficiency and where alternative sources of supply are not readily available, except to the affluent.

X-inefficiency can result if bureaucrats pursue their own self-interest, rather than the objectives of the electorate or the politicians, or of the clients being directly served by the organisation. In the absence of markets, the problem is to devise a means whereby state bureaucrats will respond to the preferences of those they are supposed to serve. A whole range of behaviour is subsumed under the umbrella of bureaucratic self-interest. Laziness, self-aggrandisement or status-seeking will all lead to the inefficient production of public sector output. Even more laudable behaviour, such as the pursuit of specific professional goals, can operate against the interests of the clients for whom the service is provided and the taxpayers who finance it. Doctors' desires to advance specialisms that they find intellectually exciting, university lecturers pursuing research at the expense of their teaching commitments, engineers wishing to develop technologically advanced products such as Concorde, are just a few examples of the kind of professional aspirations that lead to the misallocation of resources from the clients' or taxpayers' point of view. As public sector managers often benefit in terms of status, pay and conditions from the size of their bureaucracy, they will attempt to produce more of a non-marketed good that its customers would buy if they had to pay a price which reflected the cost of the good. The pursuit of self-interest by government employees results in allocative inefficiency and the subversion of the social goals that are sought via state collective action. These issues are discussed further in Chapter 8.

However human motivation is complex: people are not entirely driven by the desire for money or to do as little in the job as they can get away with. Many are attracted to public sector work by the desire to help others. The adherence to professional standards and the desire to do a job well are motives that induce workers to serve their employers and customers well. The problem of devising systems of incentives and sanctions that promote good performance from workers and managers is by no means unique to the public sector. Competitive markets provide one such system and their absence necessitates other institutional devices.

Political Interests

Yet another problem in securing efficient resource allocation by means of government, is the influence of political interests on allocative decisions. If such decisions were made by a benign dictator he or she would have a single set of objectives for society and, given sufficient information, could determine the allocation of resources which would maximise *social welfare*. In terms of Figure 6.1, the benevolent dictator would determine which point on the production possibility curve maximised social welfare. His decision-making procedures would be *rational*, since he would choose a set of policies aimed at maximising his definition of social welfare. Such policies would be efficient because they would ensure the best use of resources in terms of the dictator's objectives.

This is quite unlike political decision-making in a *pluralist* system in which a wide range of political interests influence decision-making. Political decisions emerge from the interaction of groups who have conflicting objectives as well as mutually advantageous bargains to make with each other. In contrast to the imaginary benign dictator, the decision-makers have no agreed set of objectives or common definition of social welfare. Pluralist political decision-making also contrasts with decisions taken by non-political units, such as households or firms, where the decision-makers are much more likely to have a common set of objectives and so are able to follow *rational* decision-making procedures. Because decision-makers in the political arena have conflicting objectives, policy measures are not chosen with a view to maximising some conception of social welfare, but emerge as the result of implicit and explicit *bargaining* between the political interests. The resulting allocative decisions depend on the relative strengths of the political interests involved, the tactics they employ and on the chance influence of time and place. So although the pluralist decision-making system is widely supported as a process in which diverse political interests can wield influence, the outcomes of the political bargaining process are frequently allocatively inefficient or fail to promote social justice. Again, these are issues examined further in Part II, in particular, Chapter 9.

CONCLUSIONS

Putting ethical judgements about the nature of an allocative system to one side, the issue of whether and how to use markets and government can be reduced to a functional problem of which measures will best achieve the desired policy objectives. If the aim is redistribution then the presumption is that government measures are required, given that private charity is inadequate. Government redistributive measures can vary from the very broad, e.g. cash transfer payments from tax revenues to those with low incomes, to highly selective, giving specific goods to particular categories of beneficiaries. When it comes to efficiency considerations, the presumption of mainstream economics is in favour of markets, provided any market failure problems can be overcome. Hence government will be more efficient at providing public goods than private ones.

Matters are further complicated by the frequent conflict between *distributional* objectives and *efficiency*. There is the perennial problem of the trade-off between *equity* and *efficiency*. One aspect of this trade-off is the extent to which taxing people's incomes from working and saving, in order to give other people benefits unrelated to their work efforts, inhibits the incentives to work and accumulate, and so adversely affects the level and rate of growth of output. It is also the case that measures to improve social efficiency frequently reduce the welfare of particular political interests, who are often by no means the less privileged groups. A notable example is farmers' resistance to proposals for reducing inefficient subsidies provided under the Common Agricultural Policy (see Chapter 14).

The analysis of efficiency and distributional criteria gives a rationalisation for the observation that pluralist, mixed economy democracies practise common forms of economic policy and have all experienced over time an increased economic role for government, which has only recently been widely questioned. The broad rationalisation offered is that economic policies are the means to achieving the aims of *social efficiency* in allocation and *social justice* in distribution. But this rational approach to explaining economic policy is not the whole story. To understand how economic policy is formulated and implemented also requires an appreciation of the political and institutional factors which influence decision-making in a pluralist mixed economy. The end-result is often policies which neither promote equitable distribution nor socially efficient resource allocation, though they usually benefit some sectional interest. The *Pareto criterion* is better at explaining why economic reforms are

difficult to institute—because some political interests will be harmed—than
it is in selecting policy measures on the grounds that they benefit some
while harming nobody.

The theoretical deductions and empirical evidence upon which these
observations are based are examined in greater detail in Part II on policy-
makers and policy-making. Government as an allocative mechanism is
investigated further by considering ideas and models concerned with the
roles of voters, politicians, bureaucrats and political interests in policy-
making. These provide the backcloth against which to assess the input of
the social efficiency approach to devising economic policies, as it is
practised by economists in their role as policy advisers.

NOTES

1. Among Hayek's best-known works are *The Road to Serfdom* (Routledge and
   Kegan Paul, London, 1944) and *Individualism and Economic Order*
   (Routledge and Kegan Paul, London, 1949).
2. Oskar Lange and F.M. Taylor, *On the Economic Theory of Socialism* in B.E.
   Lippincott (Minneapolis, 1938).
3. See note 1.

Part II:
Economic Policy-Making

Introduction

The chapters in Part II give a more reflective and theoretical consideration of the nature of economic policy-making. A basic premise is that policy-making is a process occurring over time into which are fed inputs in the form of decisions and actions by the individuals and groups with different preferences and interests. The end-result is a policy outcome, with effects which can be analysed in terms of *efficiency* and *distribution*. Part II is largely concerned with explanations of how economic policies are actually made, in contrast to the more traditional concerns of economists with prescriptive models of how policy ought to be made.

This concern with how policy is made means that the significance of the political institutions through which policy decisions are taken and implemented needs to be taken into account. The key political institution for a mixed liberal democracy is that of *representative democracy*. In this system citizens indicate their preferences for policies by voting for political representatives in regular, periodic elections. This is in contrast to direct democracy where citizens vote in referenda for or against specific policies. In a representative democracy citizens are given a choice of voting for a number of competing politicians who are free to advocate the particular policy bundles they favour. Most politicians belong to a political party and so support, to varying degrees, the set of policies advocated by their party. A politician's party affiliation and his/her own policy statements provide the basis for a voter's judgement as to how that politician would vote if elected to the legislative assembly. Elected representatives are not delegated by their constituents to vote in a predetermined way. In a parliamentary system the party (or coalition of parties) which wins a majority of seats in the legislative assembly forms the government. In a presidential system the successful candidate becomes the chief executive of government, but his/her ability to implement favoured policies depends on the political composition of the legislature.

The political constitution is important in determining how the policy preferences of citizens are translated into policy outcomes. As Britain is a representative democracy with almost no use of referenda, it is the implications of this system for policy-making that are investigated in Part II. This investigation starts by positing an ideal or perfect model of representative government, in which citizens' preferences are paramount, and then considers how actual representative democracy departs from this ideal. This comparison enables us to draw conclusions about the extent to which citizens' preferences ultimately determine economic policy relative to the preferences of politicians and the bureaucrats working in public sector organisations.

AN IDEAL REPRESENTATIVE DEMOCRACY

In the model of an *ideal representative democracy* the preferences of citizens alone determine policy. Citizens have a range of differing preferences for policy. Voting for political representatives, who in turn vote for specific policies, is the method by which the diverse preferences of individual citizens are aggregated into collective government action. As will be explained further in Chapter 7, the assumption that politicians and political parties seek to maximise votes leads them to tailor their policies to gain the support of a majority of voters. Vote maximising politicians are concerned with responding to citizens' preferences, rather than with winning power in order to further their own objectives for society or for a particular interest group. Thus an ideal representative democracy requires politicians whose sole motive is maximising their popularity at the polls. The role of public sector bureaucrats in an ideal representative democracy is to implement policy with complete detachment. The bureaucrats themselves have no preferences with respect to policy; with the neutral efficiency of a well-functioning machine they implement what the electors—via their representatives—have chosen. Thus the policy preferences of voters are translated via their elected representatives and appointed officials into policy outcomes without being distorted in the policy-making process by the actions of politicians or bureaucrats.

DEPARTURES FROM IDEAL REPRESENTATIVE DEMOCRACY

The ideal representative democracy, like the perfectly competitive firm, is a benchmark with which to compare reality. There are two crucial points in the policy-making process where the ideal form of representative democracy breaks down. One is the link between voters and politicians, examined in Chapter 7. If voters are ill-informed about policies and politicians and if, in addition, politicians seek power to implement their own favoured policies, then the preferences of politicians become important factors in policy-making. Chapter 7, on voters and politicians, takes as its key issue the extent to which the preferences of voters or those of politicians determine economic policy.

The second place at which the translation of citizens' preferences into policy outcomes breaks down is at the point of implementation by the public sector bureaucrats working with state organisations. Once the assumption that these are neutral cogs in the government machine is removed and replaced by the recognition that they have their own set of motivations and interests, their preferences too have an important influence on policy. The public choice approach to analysing political behaviour assumes that bureaucrats aim to maximise their *own welfare* which depends on different factors than those that determine the welfare of citizens, either as taxpayers or as clients of state-produced services. The extent to which bureaucrats subvert policy outcomes in this way depends upon the structure of the organisations in which they work, the sanctions and incentives provided and upon the professional, political and other attitudes with which bureaucrats are imbued. These issues are considered in Chapter 8 and the NHS used as an illustrative example of the impact of organisational structure upon policy-making.

In the model of ideal representative democracy voting is the only method of political representation. This ignores a vital feature of actual political systems—the activities of political interests and their organised form, the pressure groups. The importance of political interests has been emphasised in earlier chapters. Chapter 9 examines their role, both within government and outside, and presents contrasting views as to the value of their function in a liberal democracy.

The contribution of economics to the subject matter of Chapters 7–9 is in providing a methodology for studying policy-making; that is, making deductions about the nature of policy-making from a basic premise that the three classes of actors—citizens, politicians and bureaucrats—are made up of individuals who act to maximise their own welfare. Another term for welfare, especially when applied to an individual, is *utility*. The term refers to the satisfaction the individual gets from goods and services, broadly understood to include items such as the perquisites of a job or the furtherance of political principles, such as social justice. Utility is said to depend on, or be a function of, such factors. The assumption that voters, politicians and bureaucrats act as if they are in pursuit of personal utility-maximisation is a characteristic feature of the *public choice* approach to the analysis of policy-making.

RATIONAL POLICY-MAKING

But most of the work done by economists on economic policy has not been from the public choice perspective. Mainstream economics treats economic policy as if it were the outcome of *rational* decision-making procedures. In fact this is the distinctive approach of economics to policy, since no other discipline has nearly the same commitment to rationality. Economists therefore have their own idealised model of economic policy-making as a rational activity. This requires that policy-makers can articulate a clear set of objectives and determine priorities for those objectives. In order to do this the policy-makers must be able to agree on a set of preferences which the policy is to satisfy. Having agreed their objectives and the trade-offs between them, the next task for rational policy-makers is to seek the means that will best achieve the objectives and then implement them. The main role of economics, as an academic discipline, is providing the knowledge of what means are available to be exploited by policy-makers in order to attain their objectives to the maximum extent possible. As pointed out in Chapter 2, the role of the economist in this idealised view of rational policy-making is to offer advice on how to achieve the objectives; as an economist he has no special say in the choice of objectives. These are to be determined through the political process and taken as given by the economist acting in his capacity as technical adviser.

Thus the economists' ideal policy-making model can fit side by side with an ideal representative democracy, in that the economist provides knowledge about the attainment of policy objectives chosen by citizens. However he could equally well apply himself to attaining the objectives sought by politicians. However, economists as a profession are evidently not the detached technicians portrayed in this idealised view of their role. The uncertain character of economic knowledge and its close connection with value judgements about what constitute good social arrangements, mean that economists cannot separate their political views on the objectives of policy from their technical advice on the mechanics of manipulating policy instruments. The role of economists as rational optimisers is examined in Chapter 10, which assesses the limitations of rational optimising techniques for guiding policy choices in the political arena, where conflicts of interest have to be resolved.

The chapters in Part II are the core of this book. They develop the main argument—that economic policy-making is best understood as the outcome of political bargaining, with a subsidiary role for rational decision-making techniques. The ideas developed in Part II are then further illustrated in relation to specific policy areas in Part III.

7   Voters and Politicians

'It must be a conviction Government.'
(Margaret Thatcher, Interview in *Observer*, 25 February 1979)

What attracted me to work for [Mrs Thatcher] was her absolute commitment, a slightly reckless feeling that she had to achieve real change even though it meant, as a politician, living very dangerously. (Sir John Hoskins, BBC Interview, December 1982)

I am telling you, you cannot play politics with people's jobs and services. (Neil Kinnock, Labour Party Conference, 1 October 1985)

One of the principles underlying a liberal democracy is that what the government does should in some way reflect the wishes of the majority of individual citizens, while not unduly coercing those with minority opinions or interests. The central issue discussed in this chapter is how and to what extent citizens' preferences for policy are made effective by means of voting for representatives. In a representative democracy voting does not enable citizens directly to signal their preferences for specific policies. All that a vote enables a citizen to do is register a preference for one political party's bundle of policies over those of other parties. A person who favours the Conservative line on privatisation but Labour's policies on unemployment, has to weigh up these preferences together with those on other policy issues in order to decide which party's manifesto is the least objectionable.

In the Introduction to Part II an 'ideal' *representative democracy* was defined as one in which citizens' preferences alone determined policy choices. The chapter examines the role of the electoral system and the politicians in mediating between citizens' preferences for policies and the policies that are enacted. Citizens, of course, have widely divergent policy preferences. The political system is the means by which these differing individual preferences are aggregated and are thus reflected in policy-

145

making. A given pattern of citizens' preferences can be aggregated in many different ways. One factor that affects how these individual citizen preferences are aggregated and thereby reflected in policy, is the constitutional rules that govern voting, such as proportional representation. Another is the behaviour of the voters. Their motives for voting, how they perceive politicians, and the information they acquire about policies and politicians, are all facets of voter behaviour. The third factor, examined here, which determines the extent to which citizens' preferences influence policy is the behaviour of the politicians; in particular, whether they seek to maximise votes, or whether they aim for sufficient votes to secure power in order to implement their own preferred policies.

VOTING RULES

In Britain (as in other democracies), almost all political decisions are taken on the basis of majority voting—the election of constituency candidates and party leaders, the passing of legislation through Parliament and, in the case of the Labour Party, the adoption of party policy. Inevitably, majority voting leaves a dissatisfied minority whose preferences have been ignored and who will probably lose from the decisions taken. The only decision-making procedure that avoids this is unanimity, which is equivalent to the *Pareto* criterion for an improvement in social welfare. A policy measure that benefits some while harming nobody will command universal assent. However an extensive process of bargaining amongst all affected interests is required to negotiate compensating payments to those potentially worse off as a result of a policy measure in order to induce them not to vote against it. Negotiating unanimous agreement is costly and time-consuming, delaying decisions on issues which require attention. Hence in deciding on a voting rule a trade-off has to be made between the coercion of individuals who lose by a collective decision and the transaction costs of reaching agreement. Not surprisingly unanimity rules are relatively rare. The major constitutional ones affecting Britain are the Treaty of Rome, establishing the European Community, which cannot be amended without the agreement of all members and the Luxembourg Accord under which certain decisions can be vetoed by a member state on the grounds that its vital interests would be adversely affected.

When it comes to taking a course of action according to the preferences of the majority, there are a number of possible decision rules for determining what constitutes a majority. So far British elections have been contested on the basis of the *plurality* rule: the winning candidate is the one who is ranked first by the most voters: if there are more than two candidates a voter cannot indicate second or subsequently ranked choices. With uneven-sized constituencies and more that two contestants, a party can, in theory, secure office with less than one third of the votes cast.[1] Since 1922 only the 1931 election gave the winning party over half the votes cast. The 1966 election was the last one in which the victorious party had the support of over 48 per cent of the electorate. In 1979 the Conservatives obtained 43.9 per cent of the votes compared to 42.4 per cent in 1983 when, due to the opposition vote being split between the Labour and Alliance parties, they won the largest number of seats since the Labour landslide of 1945. The plurality voting rule leads to a disjuncture between a party's electoral support and its parliamentary representation. In 1983 Labour won 209 seats with 27.6 per cent of the votes, while the Alliance parties with 25.4 per cent of the votes took only 23 seats.[2] Hence a key aim of the Alliance is to change the electoral system to one of *proportional representation*, under which the proportion of votes cast for a party will be more closely matched to the number of parliamentary seats it obtains. Such a reform would obviously increase the probability of having a coalition government. Those in favour argue that this would increase stability and so improve the performance of the economy by preventing the oscillation between left- and right-wing policies. Those against fear that coalition governments are inherently weak because each minority interest can veto policies it dislikes and obtain pay-offs for supporting policies other groups want. This is one explanation for rising government expenditure and budget deficits: each group which benefits from an expenditure programme campaigns vigorously for it, but the general public, who ultimately finance it, have less incentive to agitate for lower state spending and taxation.

The electoral system, with its associated voting rules, influences how voters choose to translate their preferences into votes for specific candidates. In a contest between more than two parties voters may vote tactically and not for their first choice, in order to stop their least preferred candidate winning. The electoral rules also determine how a given pattern of votes is translated into parliamentary representation of the parties. Taking the electoral system as given, what then matters for the way electors' preferences influence economic policy is what determines how people vote—a matter that has proved fertile ground for academic speculation and which is of intense practical interest for politicians.

THE BEHAVIOUR OF VOTERS

A prerequisite of an ideal representative democracy in which citizens' preferences for policy are paramount is that citizens are clearly aware of what their policy preferences are and know how the political candidates would perform if elected. This supposes a rationality and purposiveness in voting behaviour that many political scientists and sociologists would deny.

The Sociological Theory of Voting

A long-standing theory of how people vote is the sociological theory. This holds that people loyally support the party which they perceive as representing the interests of their class. In this case electors would need to take little interest in economic policy issues as such: their party could be trusted to pursue policies in their supporters' interests. Consequently politicians' policy preferences, founded on their interpretation of their own class interests, would predominate. Which party formed the government and hence which policies were put into practice would depend on the class structure of society. If the Labour and Conservative Parties had roughly equal class support then the electoral outcome would hinge on the behaviour of the floating voters.

The sociological theory of voting behaviour has received only limited empirical support in survey studies of postwar electoral behaviour in Britain. While it is true that each party has a core of class support (in 1983 49 per cent of manual workers voted Labour, 71 per cent of managers and self-employed voted Conservative, and 35 per cent of semi-professionals voted for the Alliance) there is considerable cross-class voting and changing of party allegiance. In recent elections voters have perceived greater differences than in the past between the parties on key issues. The evidence suggests that voting is related to how closely voters can identify their own views with a particular party's stance. Thus policies are now thought to predominate over instinctive class allegiances in choosing how to vote.[3]

The Economic Theory of Voting

In the sociological approach voting is treated as instinctive group behaviour. In contrast, the economic theory of voting depicts the voter as a rational, calculating individual who votes for the party whose policies are preferred to those of other parties because of the satisfaction, or utility, the voter expects from these policies. Thus the voter is depicted as voting so as to maximise his/her *utility* or welfare. For an ideal representative democracy the voter needs access to complete and costless political information. S/he has to know the policy pledges in each party's election manifesto and be able to assess how likely these are to attain the policy objectives s/he considers both feasible and desirable. Then the voter needs to decide what credence to give to manifesto promises. Are they to be taken at face value as a reliable guide to what the party would do if it were in power? Or should the past performance of each party, in government and in opposition, be used to assess its likely future performance? In reality political information is not costless; it takes time and effort to acquire. In these circumstances the voter has to decide what costs it is worth incurring to be politically informed when the benefits of voting are low because one vote has a negligible impact on an election result. Hence in a world of costly information it is rational for the utility-maximising voter to be imperfectly informed.

It is fairly evident that voters possess extremely imperfect knowledge of the policy packages on offer, particularly in the field of economic policy where the experts themselves disagree on the technical analysis of how policy instruments should be used to achieve given objectives, like lower unemployment or reduced inflation. However, one cannot infer from this that voters instinctively support their class party rather than vote according to their necessarily imperfect perceptions of the policy issues and the alternative solutions offered by the competing parties. So both the sociological and economic theories of voting are somewhat extreme and the truth lies somewhere in the middle. Current research suggests that voters make their decision on the basis of vague impressions of how close each party's general stance is to their personal beliefs, and on the competence of the parties to carry out their policy promises and to practise good government.[4] This conclusion clearly implies a departure from ideal representative democracy. When voters are imperfectly informed about their own preferences and about what politicians are offering them, and vote on the basis of impressions, images and beliefs, the politicians are better able to impose their own preferences on policies and have less need to heed those of voters.

Voters' Preferences for Economic Policies
Because citizens in a representative democracy vote for a party and its associated policy package, voters' preferences can only have a significant impact on economic policies if these are regarded as important by voters relative to other issues, such as foreign policy (in particular defence and nuclear weapons), law and order, constitutional matters (regional devolution, local government organisation) or industrial relations (trade union legislation and industrial democracy). Though all of these have an economic policy dimension, they are not pre-eminently economic issues as are unemployment, inflation, government expenditure, taxation and privatisation/nationalisation.

However surveys of voters' attitudes do indicate that economic issues are regarded as important, especially in a postwar Britain increasingly preoccupied with its economic decline. In the 1983 election the most important issue to voters was the conflict between giving priority to reducing unemployment or keeping inflation down. The next most important issue was the choice between spending on the social services and reducing taxation. The third issue in order of importance was unilateral nuclear disarmament, followed by law and order and privatisation.[5] There is also empirical evidence that the popularity ratings of the governing party are positively related to the electorate's satisfaction with its economic performance. About one third to one half of a government's ratings in opinion polls can be explained by economic variables. Real income per head is the most significant economic variable over the postwar period, with unemployment and inflation only contributing to the government's unpopularity in certain periods.[6] The level of unemployment or inflation acceptable to the electorate has varied quite markedly over time, depending on what values were judged to be beyond the short-term control of the government. Even a year before the 1983 election, most political commentators did not expect voters to re-elect a government which had presided over a two-million rise in unemployment. So, while economic variables do appear at least partly to determine the popularity of the incumbent party, their explanatory power is somewhat erratic. Given that voters appraise the on-going economic performance of a government, they can use this information to decide how to vote—provided they do not suffer from complete amnesia. Voters' evaluation of past performance will help them to assess the ability of the incumbent party to honour its election promises in the future and to respond satisfactorily to as yet unknown future events.

Did the Voters Prefer Conservative Economic Policies?

In the light of the factors that may determine the way people vote, it is interesting to consider what evidence there is that in 1983 the electorate preferred Conservative economic policies to those of the opposition parties. The evidence summarised here is drawn from the 1983 survey of the British General Election, which assembled questionnaire and interview data from a representative sample of about 4000 electors in 250 constituencies.[7] It emerges from this survey that the Conservatives did not receive a clear lead in the proportion of voters preferring their policies over those of the major opposition parties. Table 7.1 shows the percentage of the voters placing each party as closest to their own position on the three issues which electors regarded as the most important. Labour clearly led on the issue of whether greater priority should be given to reducing unemployment or inflation. The Alliance were the most popular on the trade-off between spending on the social services or cutting taxes. The Conservatives had a slight lead on defence policy. Table 7.2 presents the answers to a slightly different question: 'Which party comes closest to your position on what you regard as the most important issue?' According to this information Conservative policy was most popular on defence, law and order and privatisation, though the latter two are ranked as the least important of the five issues. Labour did well on the unemployment—inflation and social services/tax cuts trade-offs, but was particularly unpopular on defence and nationalisation.

Table 7.1: Closest party on the three most important issues (%)

	Unemployment inflation	Taxes/social services	Defence
Conservative	28.45	31.27	37.30
Alliance	31.95	38.12	36.95
Labour	39.60	30.62	25.65

Source: Heath, Jowell and Curtis (1985).

Table 7.2: Closest party on the most important issue

	Conservative	Alliance	Labour
Unemployment/ inflation	490	602	887
Defence	373	226	91
Taxes/social services	102	164	204
Law & order	226	101	65
Nationalisation/ privatisation	71	21	8
Total sample	1262	1114	1255
% of total	35	31	35

Source: As Table 7.1

From information about the policy preferences of the electorate what inferences can be drawn about the way people would vote if these preferences were the only criterion used by voters in deciding which party to support? The great problem here is not knowing what weight the electors give to the different policy issues. This is a vital piece of information, given the clear evidence that many voters do not give their first preferences to one party on all policies, but favour one party on some issues and another on other issues. Making the very simple assumption that people vote for the party to which they are closest on their most important issue, produces the figures displayed in the last row of Table 7.2: Conservatives and Labour would have each got 35 per cent of the votes and the Alliance 31 per cent. The 1983 election survey researchers also estimated how the votes would have been distributed had people voted on the basis of their party preferences with respect to their two most important issues. This assumption gives the Conservatives 35 per cent, Labour 33 per cent and the Alliance 32 per cent.

The actual distribution of votes in the 1983 election was Conservatives 42.4 per cent, Labour 27.6 per cent and the Alliance 25.4 per cent. Given the evidence just presented on the policy preferences of the electorate, this suggests that other factors influence electors. However the hypothesis that electors decide how to vote only on the basis of policy preferences cannot be ruled out entirely because the survey did not have sufficient information on the weights given by voters to the various policy issues. It seems most unlikely that such information could be gathered anyway, as electors do not articulate such numerical weighting systems to themselves, even though this is what they must intuitively do if voting on the basis of policy issues when no one party ranks first on all issues. The authors of the 1983 election study conclude that voting is based on much more general and impressionistic perceptions of the parties than a careful appraisal of the relative merits of their policy packages: 'Factors such as policies, record in office, putative ability to implement a programme, leadership, unity of purpose may all come into it, but none is paramount' (p.99).[8]

THE BEHAVIOUR OF POLITICIANS

We have now looked at two sets of factors—the voting rules and the behaviour of voters—which make for an uncertain and attenuated link between citizens' preferences with respect to economic policy and what they get from government. The third consideration is the behaviour of politicians. To what extent do politicians respond to the preferences of voters in order to maximise votes? Or do they seek to put into practice their own preferred policies, constrained by voters' preferences only to the extent of seeking enough votes to gain office?

The Economic Theory of Democracy

One view of politicians' motivations is that they are primarily interested in securing power for its own sake. This implies the desire to maximise votes. Thus political parties compete for votes by trying to produce the most popular package of policies and by presenting themselves to the electorate as the most competent set of leaders. This approach models the political process on the lines of the market-place. Political parties are analogous to firms, except they aim to maximise votes rather than profits. The voters are consumers choosing between rival products on the basis of which is likely to give them the greatest utility. Because this approach, orginally developed by Anthony Downs,[9] applies the methodological assumptions of economics to politics, it is known as the *economic theory of democracy*. It predicts that the parties will be induced to present policies which appeal to the moderate centre and so will produce rather similar policy platforms. Consensual policies will therefore prevail.

These predictions are arrived at by assuming that the electorate are spread across an ideological spectrum that ranges from radical socialist intervention at one extreme to libertarian free marketeers at the other. If there are two parties competing for office then each can capture one or other of the extremes of the political spectrum by differentiating themselves as left-wing and right-wing parties. However the voters located in the middle of the ideological distribution—the *median voters*—are open to capture by either party. The party that is most successful at appealing to the *median voters* will win the election. Knowing this both parties will tailor their policy platforms to appeal to the median voter and so there will be little to distinguish the two parties in terms of their policies. The political competition then turns on which party can present itself as providing the most competent management team for the nation. This would explain why politics is so concerned with images, personalities, appearances and style.

Under certain conditions—in particular free and costless political information—Downs' theory of voting behaviour implies an ideal representative democracy. At first sight this may seem an odd deduction as vote maximising behaviour by politicians tends to be regarded with disapproval as self-seeking and cynical. But provided the voters are distributed evenly or normally along a left-wing/right-wing spectrum, vote maximising behaviour by two competing political parties enables the preferences of the median voters (the moderate majority) to be satisfied.

The Political Business-Cycle

When citizens are ill-informed about economic policy and unable to predict what politicians will do once in office, vote maximisation can produce far from ideal results. One possibility is the creation of a *political business-cycle*. In this scenario the governing party inflates the economy shortly before an election, taking advantage of the fact that unemployment tends to fall first and, only after a lag of a year or more, does the associated increase in the rate of inflation appear. This enables the government win the election before inflation rises, because the electorate are duped into thinking that boom times are here to stay. But once in power the government has to implement deflationary policies, because the boom cannot be sustained. Thus there is a cycle in economic activity caused not by random economic events but by the political process itself.

The existence of a political business-cycle is premised also on specific voter behaviour. It is assumed that voters judge the parties on their present performance rather than on the policy packages they present for the future. A boom in economic activity makes voters favourably disposed to the government: voting decisions are based much more on perceptions of politicians' competence to deliver good short-run economic performance than on any evaluation of the likely future outcome of policies. If the political cycle persists, this must mean that voters fail to learn from experience about politicians' deceptive ways. Various hypotheses about the generation of political business-cycles have been tested. The general conclusion is that though there have been specific instances of governments having a deliberately reflationary Budget prior to an election, there is little solid evidence in favour of a persistent political business-cycle.[10] This conclusion buttresses faith in the capacity of representative democracies to make sensible policy decisions.

The End of Consensus?

Downs' theory of democracy appeared in 1957 at a time when consensual politics was much more in evidence in the USA, the UK and other European countries that it is now. When the Conservatives returned to power in 1951 they had accepted the major delineations of the mixed economy drawn up by the 1945 Labour government. This consensus on economic policy was maintained by the 1964–70 Labour government under Harold Wilson: the only major extension of public ownership was the renationalisation of steel. The Conservative government of Edward Heath won power in 1970 with a manifesto commitment to free market policies— less state intervention in industry and the dismantling of prices and incomes policy. But after two years, panicked by rising inflation and the insolvency of Upper Clyde Shipbuilders and Rolls-Royce, the government did its famous U-turn, bringing back a prices and incomes policy and enacting the highly interventionist Industry Act of 1972.

It was not until the advent of the 1974 Labour government, committed to more nationalisation and to a 'social contract' with the trade unions in return for favourable union legislation, that the strong elements of consensus began to break down. Both the major parties began to desert the middle ground of politics. The left wing of the Labour Party became more influential in policy-making. They favoured unilateral nuclear disarmament, nationalisation, government control of investment, pro-union legislation, import controls and a substantial increase in state spending on welfare and industry. By 1981 the Labour Party had shifted sufficiently leftwards that some right-wing members broke away to form the Social Democratic Party. Over the same period the Conservatives were shifting rightwards. In 1975 Mrs Thatcher won the leadership of the Conservative Party in opposition to Edward Heath, who had pursued Keynesian and interventionist policies. In contrast, Mrs Thatcher favoured monetarism and free market policies. With like-minded colleagues, she gradually steered the party in these directions.

During the 1980s there has been a very evident lack of consensus between the parties on macroeconomic policy, on the appropriate levels of government spending and taxation, and on privatisation. The breakdown of consensus can be partly attributed to increased dissatisfaction with the results of consensus policies. The viability of Keynesian economic management was increasingly called into question as both unemployment and inflation rose in the 1970s. By 1976 the Labour Cabinet, faced with a sterling exchange crisis, adopted a monetarist approach. It announced monetary targets and cut planned public expenditure. Over this period the performance of the public sector was increasingly criticised, for poor labour relations, indifferent services and inefficiency.

Mounting scepticism grew at the ability of economics and other social sciences to provide policy makers with soundly based technical knowledge on how to employ policy instruments to achieve given objectives. In the face of the clamour from rival schools of thought, the scientific basis of such knowledge is increasingly placed in doubt, giving rise to greater perceived uncertainty about what specific policy measures will do. For instance, the widespread optimism that Keynesian economics could prevent mass unemployment has now largely evaporated. Disagreement is no longer concentrated solely on the objectives of economic policy. The means or techniques by which given policy objectives can be achieved are also in dispute. So it is not just a matter of disagreeing about whether lower inflation or lower unemployment should have greater priority: controversy rages over whether unemployment is best brought down by the Keynesian method of expanding aggregate demand, or by *supply-side* measures directed at reducing the cost of labour to firms and increasing its quality, in terms of skills and flexibility. With increased pessimism about the ability of the scientific method to produce an accumulated body of tried and accepted knowledge about economic and social behaviour, there has been a return to ideology (i.e. non-scientifically verifiable beliefs) as the basis for choosing between alternative policies. The lack of consensus in politics reflects that there is a lot more to disagree about and less recourse to genuine scientific knowledge as a non-political way of resolving such disagreements.

With the breakdown of the postwar consensus, the Downsian model looks less plausible than it did from the 1950s to the mid-1970s. However it still offers some insights. It explains the success of the Alliance in terms of capturing the middle ground of the median voters, deserted by the two major parties. Currently there are pressures within both the Labour and Conservative Parties to reoccupy the middle ground. At the same time the nature of the political debate has shifted. Both the Alliance and sections of the Labour Party are more favourably disposed to the concept of the 'social market economy'—one in which market forces are harnessed to promote efficiency while the government also intervenes actively to promote social harmony. Thus, after a period of realignment, a new political consensus may emerge out of the process whereby political parties strive to win votes.

Conviction Politicians

Provided that voters are able to make reasonably well-founded judgements about the parties' election pledges, then vote maximising politicians will be responsive to citizens' preferences, particularly those of voters able to influence the balance of power between the parties. The politicians will seek to satisfy the preferences of the moderate majority and the political system will be biased towards the ideal form of representative democracy.

But if politicians seek power for specific purposes rather than as an end in itself, then their sole objective is not vote maximisation. Securing votes is a means to the attainment of other objectives. These may be entirely self-seeking and concerned with enhancing the politician's personal life-style or with the pursuit of the sectional interests represented by the politician. The motivations may be more idealistic, embracing the politician's concept of how to promote some national purpose, be it the creation of a more just society, or one which harnesses individuals' talents to improve the country's economic performance. The three kinds of motive distinguished here merge into each other at the edges and are often difficult to separate when assessing any individual's motivations. Most politicians are probably imbued, to differing degrees, with all three types of motive. But whatever the combination, they are likely to conflict with the objective of maximising votes. This is because the more politicians pursue their own or sectional interests or their vision of the good society, the more voters they are likely to displease. Conviction politicians want power, not merely for its own sake, but to attain other ends. So they need to assess how far they can pursue their favoured political aims before failing to get enough votes to secure power. There is thus some trade-off for conviction politicians between the objective of getting votes and winning elections, and pursuing their favourite policies.

So in contrast to Downs' model, in which politicians are simply vote maximisers, they are more plausibly viewed as pursuing some combination of self-seeking, sectional and idealist objectives, constrained by the need to get votes in order to attain power. The more conviction politicians succeed in pursuing policies that voters dislike, while managing still to secure office, the greater the departure from the ideal form of representative democracy.

Politicians have only imperfect information about the nature of the trade-off between votes and political objectives. This trade-off lies at the heart of debates and divisions within political parties. As any major political party is a coalition of people with somewhat different interests and beliefs, there are bound to be internal conflicts between different views of the good society and between idealists and pragmatists. The different factions tend to argue that the policies informed by their own beliefs will prove more popular with the electorate. The leadership of the Labour Party, under

Neil Kinnock, moved the Party back towards the centre ground and disavowed left-wing extremists, in order to regain votes. The so-called 'wets' in the Conservative Party argue that Mrs Thatcher's policies are too extreme to be electorally popular.

Margaret Thatcher is a self-styled conviction politician: she is in politics to promote policies she considers necessary to revitalise Britain. She is described as an unusual Prime Minister: a powerful personality who leads from the front. She gradually acquired power to pursue her own convictions. Her methods contrasted with those of her predecessors, Callaghan, Wilson and Heath, who were consensual leaders, distilling the views of Party and Cabinet to arrive at decisions that would command consent and appear to be an appropriate pragmatic response to current problems.[11] A conviction politician will take greater risks with votes by pursuing objectives at the expense of consensual policies which are inconsistent with those objectives. Hence a conviction politician does not take the electorate's policy preferences as given but tries to change them by proselytising. If parties are led by conviction politicians, rather than Downsian vote maximisers, party competition will be openly about ideologies, not just about managerial competence. If the electorate's voting decisions are not entirely based on policy preferences, but on a more general evaluation of each party's performance, then the conviction politician's strategy may pay off. The pursuit of a coherent set of policies, in contrast to pragmatic U-turns, may present a sufficiently strong image of competent leadership to offset any failure to convert enough of the electorate to the politician's ideological position. The strategy of a conviction politician, whose policy preferences remain some distance from those of the median voters, is a high-risk one. It is vulnerable to erosion of the politician's power base or to cracks in the image of managerial competence. (Hence the significance of the Westland affair in 1985/86.)

Politician's Surplus
Citizens, even in an ideal representative democracy, will feel coerced by collective actions with which they disagree. The governing party, if it wishes to retain power, has to avoid coercing voters in such numbers and to such a degree that they lose the electoral support needed to remain in office. Given that a government accepts as binding the constraint of retaining sufficient votes to win the next election, it is still left with some scope for neglecting the preferences of voters in order to pursue its favoured interests and ideals. This gap between the maximum votes a party could attain, if that were its sole objective, and the minimum required to retain or acquire power, is a kind of *politicians' surplus*. It is analogous to the profits firms in imperfectly competitive markets can earn by keeping price above average cost. A firm can take these profits in the form of *x-inefficiency*. Similarly,

politicians can dispense with surplus votes by pursuing policies which benefit particular interests who support them or which promote their ideals, or do both simultaneously.

What factors determine the size of the *politicians' surplus*? The first set of factors are the rules that make up the electoral system. For instance, plurality voting, especially combined with a three-party race, enables a single party to form a government with only minority support. How small such a minority is depends on the pattern of voting in relation to the distribution of voters over different-sized constituencies. So, for example, rural and inner city constituencies are over-represented because they are smaller than average.

The second set of factors relate to the determinants of voter behaviour. If voters were a highly homogeneous group in terms of their preferences with respect to all policy issues, then the parties would be constrained to offer very similar policy packages. Only to the extent that a party could offer very clear superiority in management expertise, could it stray from the preferences of the median voters. However when voters are highly differentiated with respect to their policy preferences, they are forced to trade off policies they favour against those they do not, when deciding which party's policy bundle is the least objectionable. If, in addition, voters are poorly informed about what policies each party would implement if in power, and rely instead on vague perceptions of the competence of the parties to govern and further their class or sectional interests, then politicians' surplus is enlarged. So, for example, a government could pursue a relatively unpopular economic policy because its stance on defence and law and order is approved or because it is seen to provide competent leadership. The shorter are voters' memories, the longer a government can spend on less popular policies and hope to produce a winning set of new election promises.

The size of politicians' surplus depends on the motivations of the politicians. Those concerned with gaining and keeping power purely for its own sake, and hence whose sole objective is vote maximisation, will have no motive to seek a surplus. The vote maximising political party is thus equivalent to the efficient profit maximising firm. The equivalent of x-inefficiency occurs when politicians (like the workers and managers of firms in imperfectly competitive markets) seek further ends of their own, like satisfying the sectional interests and ideological predispositions of the party's activists. Many political commentators have noted that a party, on attaining office, tends to put into effect policies which are distinctly differentiated from those of their predecessors and which were campaigned for by their activists when in opposition. After a while these policies become muted or are abandoned, as the government seeks to reduce its degree of surplus in readiness for the next election. Thus the Wilson government of 1964–70 abandoned national planning after three years; the Heath government reneged on free market policies after two years; the Labour government of 1974–79 backpedalled on increased welfare expenditure from 1976 onwards; the Thatcher government failed to adhere to its initial announcement of strict monetary targets, and specific cuts in the PSBR, and real government spending. To carry on with the initial strategy in the face of mounting problems of implementation is judged to exact too much surplus to retain sufficiently the confidence of the electorate.

Increasing the Demand for Party Policies

So far I have implicitly assumed a given, though uncertain, relationship between a party's policies and the number of votes it can hope to secure. This is analogous to assuming a firm faces a given demand curve. However, political parties, like imperfectly competitive firms, can take action to increase the demand for their products, such as advertising and public relations. In the political market, parties attempt to change voters' preferences not only by overt advertising, but by many other activities— speeches, writing, constituency surgeries, supportive social research. The use politicians can make of the media is also of great importance, especially when voters are making judgements on the basis of impressions and images. To the extent that advertising and PR are successful, a political party can pursue its favoured policies without losing votes: it has altered in a favourable direction its trade-off between votes secured and policies pursued.

Another method firms use to expand sales is finding appropriate market niches to exploit. A political party can do the equivalent by searching for combinations of policies which will improve its trade-off between votes gained and the ability to pursue its favourite policies. Parties are presented with opportunities for such marketing tactics if some voters belong to minorities which feel strongly about a single issue, like rent control, animal rights or the environment. By putting such issues in its policy package a party can secure the support of this minority and so gain votes for its other policies. These tactics are known as *log-rolling*. A party of conviction politicians could secure their favoured policies by entering into a sufficient number of bargains with single-issue minorities. If no successful counter-coalition is mounted, then the majority against each of these issues taken singly will find itself coerced, while the governing party continues to enjoy its surplus.

THE ECONOMIC ANALYSIS OF POLITICS

The economic analysis of politics applies the analogy of the marketplace to the behaviour of voters and politicians. Voters are likened to customers and political parties to firms. Both are depicted as *utility* maximisers. Voters exchange their votes for a package of policy promises from a party. However this political transaction is crucially different from a market one. In a market it is presumed that no buyer or seller engages in a transaction if he is worse-off as a result. It is in this sense that a market participant is not coerced. In the political market, when collective decisions are made by majority rule, some individuals are going to feel worse-off as the result of specific decisions. It is in this sense that they are coerced. However they are prepared to accept this coercion, so long as they believe in the legitimacy of the system of representative government under which they live. In a similar way people accept the legitimacy of market allocation, even though they would be better-off under a different set of prices than those determined by the market. Living in ordered communities involves accepting rules which do not in all instances operate in one's favour.

In both the economic market and the political market the decision rules, the constraints and the behaviour of the participants determine the allocation and distribution of goods and services. Under market allocation the possession of goods or talents others value highly in monetary terms enhances the ability of an individual to satisfy his preferences. In the political market each citizen has a single vote, but those who happen to possess a casting vote have more influence. In both systems of allocation the extent to which the individual can get his preferences satisfied depends on the extent to which his preferences coincide with those of others. Consumers with minority tastes usually find them more difficult and expensive to satisfy. In politics those whose position coincides with the middle or median of the distribution of voters' preferences are likely to be the least coerced, especially if politicians are pure vote maximisers. In a Downsian two-party world the voters at the extreme ends of the political spectrum are more coerced as their vote is not competed for. Voters who perpetually support a minority party which never gains power are highly coerced and in some cases resort to non-legitimate means to secure their aims. Some minorities can succeed in getting their demands attended to if their support is required to form a winning coalition of interests. If parties are led by conviction politicians, the voters located towards the more extreme ends of the political spectrum will be intermittently satisfied when their favour party wins power and uses its political surplus to implement non-consensus policies.

METHODS OF AGGREGATING PREFERENCES

This chapter has concentrated on the implications of voting as the method by which citizens in a representative democracy influence collective decision-making. But there are other systems for aggregating preferences in society. Under direct democracy people vote in referenda for and against policy proposals. Both direct and representative democracy are concerned with distilling aggregate preferences from individual citizens' preferences. Other systems presume a collective preference which exists in its own right and is not an aggregation of individuals' preferences. *Corporatism* (see p.32) leans towards a conception of group preferences, based on functional representation by hierarchical labour and management organisations, who bargain directly with government. There is also the concept of a holistic will of the people, which is interpreted and attended to by its leaders. This underpins both fascist and communist conceptions of democracy.

Even in a representative democracy not all collective decisions are taken by politicians. Many collective decisions, particularly those concerned with the detailed implementation of policy, are to some extent removed from the political arena, and are taken by appointed officials or lay representatives. The value of doing this for decisions of a commercial nature has for long justified the setting up of public corporations and of government agencies which are not departments of state, like the Manpower Services Commission and the National Health Service. In the latter case an element of democratic accountability is sought by appointing local authority representatives to Community Health Councils. In many spheres the government shares collective decision-making with private sector agencies, professional organisations or trade unions, as in financial services, health, education, labour relations and wage determination, to name a few areas in which one or more of these groups shares responsibility with government.

Voting is not the only way of signalling preferences in the political marketplace and thus influencing government decision-making. Because of the transactions costs involved in constantly consulting large numbers of people and in changing leaders, voting occurs periodically. The most significant form of political participation, other than voting, is the activities of political interests, many of whom organise themselves as pressure groups. These activities occur continuously as the various political interests attempt to benefit or avoid losses from collective decisions. While the ability to command crucial votes is a strong asset for any political interest, its power to help or hinder the implementation of government policy is another important resource. Thus the activities of political interests are closely related to voting, as well as being a distinct and powerful influence on collective decision-making by governments. Political interests and pressure groups are discussed in Chapter 9.

CONCLUSION

The main focus of this chapter has been the question of how and to what extent voters' preferences in a represenative democracy influence economic policy. The main thrust of the analysis applies to any type of policy. However the economic performance of a government seems to be a major, if not the major determinant of its standing with the electorate: the electorate do regard economic issues as important in deciding how to vote.

The notion of an ideal representative democracy serves as a benchmark against which to locate key points at which the political system fails to translate the preferences of the majority of citizens into policy. One is the voting rules which determine how a given pattern of votes is transformed into the choice of elected representatives. Plurality voting in the UK has meant that no government since the 1930s has won power by obtaining over 50 per cent of the votes. The next stage at which citizens' policy preferences may fail to be translated into policy is in the act of voting. The evidence suggests that citizens are poorly informed about policies and politicians, and fail to articulate policy preferences in their own minds, voting instead instinctively or on the basis of vague impressions as to the competence of party leaders and the closeness of the party's policies to their own beliefs. About 20 per cent of voters do not bother to turn out at a general election, and the number of abstainers rises to around 60 per cent for local elections. Consequently citizens' policy preferences bear only a tenuous relationship to the policies chosen by their elected representatives. The third determinant of the extent to which citizens' preferences influence policy is the behaviour of politicians. Given a well-informed electorate, competing parties of vote maximising politicians will ensure that the policies offered to the electorate are those that command the support of the moderate majority of the electorate. However, conviction politicians will use their politicians' surplus to pursue their own preferred policies, constrained only by the need to secure the minimum number of votes necessary for power. This suggests that conviction politicians cause a greater departure from the ideal form of representative democracy than do vote maximising ones.

For clarity of exposition, voting rules, voter behaviour and politicians' behaviour have been discussed under separate headings, although they do interact. For instance, how people vote depends on the electoral rules and on the perceived behaviour of politicians. Whether politicians are simply vote maximisers, or seek power as an instrument to achieve ideological ends, determines how active they are in changing voters' policy preferences.

This chapter has concentrated on voting as the method of aggregating preferences for collective decision-making, and restricted this to voting in a representative democracy. Another important form of political participation, other than voting, is pressure group and political interest activity. These are taken up in Chapter 9. Meanwhile Chapter 8 examines another link in the chain between citizens' preferences and policy outcomes. This is the influence of public sector bureaucrats and bureaucracies in their function as instruments for implementing policy.

NOTES

1. A. Breton, *The Economic Theory of Representative Government* (Aldine, Chicago, 1974).
2. A.C. Heath, R. Jowell and J. Curtis, *How Britain Votes* (Pergamon Press, Oxford, 1985).
3. Ibid.
4. Ibid.
5. Ibid.
6. P. Mosley, *The Making of Economic Policy*, (Wheatsheaf Books, Brighton, 1984), Chapter 2.
7. Heath *et al.*, op. cit.
8. Ibid.
9. A. Downs, *An Economic Theory of Democracy* (Harper and Row, New York, 1957).
10. J.E. Alt and K.A. Chrystal, *Political Economics* (Wheatsheaf Books, Brighton, 1983).
11. A. King (ed.), *The British Prime Minister* (Macmillan, London, 1985).

8 Bureaucrats and Bureaucracies

In a constitutional sense the civil servant is there simply to manage, to implement and execute his or her Minister's policy . . ..The risk of a clash between the doctrine of ministerial responsibility and genuine managerial accountability and authority remains ever present. (Sir Frank Cooper, former Permanent Secretary to the Ministry of Defence, *Financial Times*, 10 May 1985)

Ministers should realise their ability to manage their departments is as important to the country as their performance on the floor of either House. . ... There is no clear orientation towards the achievement of effectiveness and efficiency at the higher levels of the Civil Service or in the government generally. (*Efficiency and Effectiveness in the Civil Service*, Third Report from the Treasury and Civil Service Committee (HMSO, London, 1982)

Public employees today are not only regarded as public servants working in the public interest; they are also seen as a class that benefits by working for government. (R. Rose, *Understanding Big Government* (Sage, London, 1984) p. 150)

According to bureaucrats, the only safeguard against political interference is a guarantee of structural autonomy. (D.M. Fox, *The Politics of Civil and State Bureaucracy* (Goodyear, Pacific Palisades, California, 1974; p. 13)

Democracy inevitably comes into conflict with bureaucratic tendencies which democracy has produced. (M. Weber, *The Theory of Social and Economic Organisations* (Free Press, New York, 1947) p. 226)

Economic policy is formulated and implemented by organisations and by people operating within organisations. This factor is not taken into account in either the ideal model of representative democracy or the rational model of economic policy-making, outlined in the introduction to Part II. These just take it for granted that the policies chosen by citizens and their elected representatives are implemented. In a similar vein, early writings on administration in the tradition of Weber, regarded state bureaucracies as structures designed for the efficient implementation of policy. If policies were formulated by politicians and impartially administered by officials, then the state bureaucrats would have, in effect, no preferences with respect to policy. But once it is recognised that bureaucrats do have policy preferences and that these affect policy outcomes, this highlights another point at which the link between citizens' preferences and policy outcomes is weakened.

This chapter investigates the impact of state bureaucrats and bureaucracies in the making of economic policy. Because bureaucrats implement policy, their cooperation and expertise is required by politicians in formulating policy. Policies affect bureaucrats' own interests, hence they seek to influence its formulation. Furthermore, as the extent of government intervention in the economy has grown, it has become increasingly difficult for the legislature to specify in advance rules which will govern all aspects of a policy when it is implemented. Much is left to the discretion of bureaucrats, who then formulate policy as they implement it. Thus there can be no rigid separation of policy formulation from policy implementation.

As in Chapter 2, the term bureaucrat is used here as a shorthand term to include all public sector workers. A crucial feature of a bureaucracy, in both the private and public sectors, is its hierarchical, pyramidical structure of authority, which relates superiors to subordinates. In order to process their work effectively bureaucracies are also organised according to specialist functions. Thus there are also horizontal relationships between different divisions within a bureaucracy.

Bureaucrats can be differentiated by their positions and functions in this hierarchy. More narrowly conceived definitions of bureaucrats restrict the term to administrators—civil servants, local government officers, health service administrators, and the like. Administrators are normally thought of as operating in non-market bureaucracies, in contradistinction to managers who occupy executive positions in firms, including public corporations. Here I treat administrators and managers as essentially the same kind of bureaucrat; they are in charge of running their bureaucracy and so are distinct from professional bureaucrats, such as teachers, doctors, engineers, soldiers, even economists, who are employed to exercise their professional expertise, acquired through specialist training. They possess technical knowledge of which most administrators, politicians and clients have little understanding. Although professionals, like doctors and teachers, are towards the bottom of the hierarchy that connects them to the government department responsible for their organisation, they exercise a large measure of discretion in their daily work, which is jealously guarded as clinical or academic freedom. State employees occupying relatively low hierarchical positions, doing manual, semi-skilled and clerical work, are also included as 'bureaucrats' here: their interests as workers are affected by government policy and their cooperation is required for the implementation of policy. Organised in trade unions, they can have a significant impact, particularly with respect to policies aimed at reducing the costs of running their organisations.

The chapter starts by considering the motivations of bureaucrats, using the economic analysis of bureaucracy which assumes that bureaucrats, like everyone else, are motivated by self-interest. From this assumption it is deduced that bureaucrats will allocate resources inefficiently and hence not produce policy outcomes which are entirely in accord with the preferences of citizens. If polticians are concerned to improve the performance of bureaucracies in satisfying the preferences of citizens then they need to attend to the organisational structure of government bureaucracies and the system of sanctions and incentives these give to bureaucrats. These problems are examined in relation to the National Health Service and, to a lesser extent, state education. This involves examining their organisational structure, as well as the problems of monitoring and making the executive arm of government accountable to the electorate.

THE IMPLICATIONS OF BUREAUCRATS' SELF-INTEREST

The distinctive approach of economics to the study of bureaucracy is the importance attached to the assumption that individual bureaucrats are motivated by self-interest. If individuals act to further their self-interest when they buy and sell in markets, there seems to be no plausible reason why they should suspend self-interested action in relation to their work in the state bureaucracies. This is not to claim that self-interest is the only motivating force for individuals, whether they are consumers or bureaucrats, but that it is an extremely important motive from which useful predictions and explanations can be derived. It is also difficult to conceive of an organisation having its own goals, unless the individuals within the organisation have agreed, even if implicitly, the objectives of the organisation.

As with theories about consumer behaviour and firms, economists represent self-interested behaviour in terms of *utility-maximisation*. The next step is to specify what gives bureaucrats utility. A considerable range of factors has been suggested—income, prestige, power, security, an easy life, perquisites like luxurious offices or trips abroad, interesting work, the promotion of personal values about professional conduct or the organisation of society, and so on. It is evident that some of these objectives are, or may be, mutually inconsistent. For instance, doing little work may well conflict with acquiring power, prestige or a high income. Individual bureaucrats pursue some of these objectives and not others, and do so to differing degrees.

A Model of Bureaucratic Utility-Maximisation

A well-publicised theory developed by Niskanen,[1] who was an economist in the US Defence Department, posits that many of these objectives are furthered by increasing the size of the organisation for which the bureaucrats work. This involves expanding the output of the bureau, which then requires a larger budget to finance its activities. A state bureau bids for its budget to politicians, who are depicted as the bureau's sponsors. They buy the collective good from the bureau on behalf of the citizens. The bureau's output and budget are higher than the politicians, as representatives of the citizens' interests, would choose if they were in full control of the policy programme.

The basis for this deduction is explained in Figure 8.1. It is assumed that, in principle it is possible to define a citizens' demand curve for the collective good in question, be it health services, education, policing or defence systems. The vertical distance between the demand curve and the horizontal axis indicates the maximum amount of money per unit of collective good, that citizens in total are prepared to pay for that particular quantity. This demand is really only a notional one, derived from a conceptual exercise. It is assumed that each citizen could specify the maximum he is prepared to pay for different quantities of the collective good and that these amounts are totalled to give the citizens' collective demand curve. Because the good is a collective one citizens do not pay a market price per unit for the quantity they consume; instead, they pay taxes which are transferred to the state bureau in the form of a budget. In this model it is assumed that the collective good is distributed to its clients at zero price. The quantity each client gets is determined by a combination of legislative rules, bureaucrats' discretion as well as customer demand.

The average and marginal costs of producing the collective good are, for simplicity, assumed to be constant as output changes, and are given by the horizontal line labelled MC = AC. Using the standard criterion of welfare economics, it is deduced that the 'socially optimal' quantity of the collective good is OQ^1. This is the quantity at which the *marginal social cost* of producing the good is equal to the *marginal social benefit*—the latter being the amount by which citizens as a whole value one additional unit of the good. At output Q^1 citizens value the marginal unit at AQ^1 ($AQ^1 = OP^1$). The 'socially optimal' budget allocation to the bureau is the rectangle OP^1AQ^1 which is the average cost per unit (OP^1) times the number of units produced (OQ^1).

But if bureaucrats obtain utility from enlarging the size of their bureau by producing more output than OQ^1, they will bid for a larger budget than the 'socially optimal' one. At the limit the bureaucrats will increase output to OQ^2 units and get a budget of OP^1BQ^2. If the bureau fails to produce the 'socially optimal' quantity of the good, then it is *allocatively inefficient*. In this particular example the citizen-customers are getting more of the good than they really want when they have to pay OP¹ per unit for it. If the bureau acted like a private sector monopoly firm and maximised profits then it would restrict output to below its 'socially optimal' level. This would also be allocatively inefficient.

But how does a state bureau manage to get away with producing a different quantity of output than the citizens want at the price they have to pay? What determines the extent of resource misallocation? The answers given to these questions by this analysis of bureaucracy rest on aspects of *market failure*, as outlined in Chapter 6, translated into the public sector. One important aspect of market failure is lack of competition. The analysis depicted in Figure 8.1 assumes that the state bureau in question is a monopoly supplier. Citizens have no other bureaux or private sector firms to turn to as alternative sources of supply. If there were such competition, then it is predicted that the state bureau would be constrained by loss of custom from supplying units of output at a price in excess of the citizens' marginal valuation of the good.

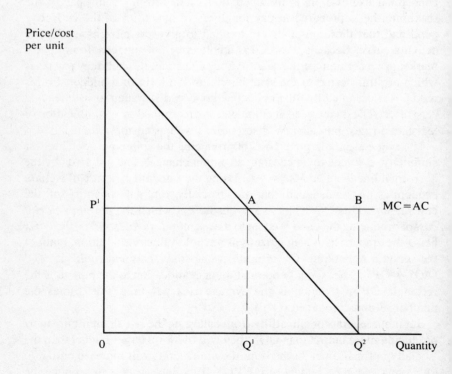

Figure 8.1: Allocative inefficiency in a bureaucracy

Imperfect Information

Another important aspect of market failure is imperfect information. In the sectors producing non-marketed goods, such as state education, health, defence, law and order, there is extremely limited information about both citizens' demand for the collective good and, on the supply side of the market, about costs. Satisfactory measures of output simply do not exist. Take education as an example. The grand goals of education—developing individuals to their full potential, providing equal educational opportunities, inculcating social values, improving the quality of the labour force—can at best be gauged approximately by measures such as tests of pupils' performance, examination results or the incomes earned by people of different educational attainments. Similarly with defence; there is no means by which an individual citizen or politician can assess, other than on intuitive or moral grounds, what quantity and quality of 'defence services' are being supplied or whether the price paid is reasonable or excessive.

Not only is the information required to evaluate the costs and benefits of collective goods inherently defective, what does exist is much more readily available to the bureaucrats producing the collective good than to politicians who in turn have better access to information about state bureaucracies than do individual citizens. Specialist bureaucracies exist because expertise can only be acquired and efficiently exploited by individuals and agencies concentrating on a relatively narrow area. Ministers and local councillors cannot have detailed knowledge of what goes on in the public sector bureaucracies for which they are politically responsible. Thus bureaucrats' possession and control of information is a potent source of their influence.

So when a bureaucracy applies to politicians for its budget to produce the quantity of services it considers desirable, using its preferred production methods, the politicians have limited information on what quantity and quality of services citizens want, what they are actually getting, and what the cost of producing such services really is. Thus it is possible for a bureaucracy to bid for a larger budget than politicians and citizens would choose if they possessed more of the relevant information. For these reasons it is deduced that a bureau will push its output beyond the 'socially optimal' quantity, OQ^1, as depicted in Figure 8.1.

Allocative and Productive Inefficiency in Bureaucracies

The model of bureaucracy depicted in Figure 8.1 deduces that a monopoly bureau will be inefficient because it produces more output than citizens would choose to pay for. This type of inefficiency is *allocative inefficiency*. The bureau depicted in Figure 8.1 is assumed to produce its output at minimum feasible cost, given by the cost function $MC = AC$, hence it is productively efficient. But many of the factors that give bureaucrats utility are not secured by enlarging the bureau, while producing at minimum unit cost. Goals like security, an easy life, perquisites, interest, professional prestige, are furthered by actions which result in output costs being higher than the minimum feasible level. The lack of market criteria makes it much easier for professionals to urge that the most technically advanced equipment must be used, in defence, in medicine, in scientific research, and so on. In the absence of any clear criteria of how much clients or citizens in general benefit from this equipment, these pressures are difficult to resist. Costs are also likely to be higher because a non-profit-making bureaucracy, which cannot go bankrupt, lacks the incentive to discover more cost-effective methods of production. The easy life for bureaucrats lies partly in not bothering to seek information on the opportunity costs of their various activities in order to find the most efficient production method. Supplying themselves with perquisites (e.g. generous travel and entertainment allowances, subsidised catering facilities, lucrative overtime rates, restrictive manning agreements) all raise production costs above the feasible minimum and so give rise to *x-inefficiency*.

Pressures exerted by politicians on a bureau's budget give it an incentive to improve efficiency. For example the BBC, when granted a £58 colour TV licence fee in 1985 instead of the £65 it had bid for and expected to get, set up a committee to investigate every aspect of its activities. It decided to save money by replacing in-house services and equipment by bought-in alternatives, thus eliminating up to 4000 jobs. Plans to build a £100 million new headquarters in central London were abandoned in favour of a cheaper alternative at White City.[2]

So there are many different ways in which a bureaucracy creates or fails to eliminate x-inefficiency. In terms of our model of bureaucracy, all the factors responsible for x-inefficiency are depicted as raising the cost function from its minimum feasible position of AC^1 to AC^2 in Figure 8.2. As a consequence, citizens pay a higher budget to the bureau for a given quantity of output than if x-inefficiency were less prevalent.

The distinction between *allocative* and *productive efficiency* is an important one. *Allocative inefficiency* is judged from the point of view of the citizen-customers of the bureaucracy. It exists if the customers of the service do not get the quantity, quality or mix of services which they would choose to have given the amount they pay to finance the bureau. Unless the collective good is a pure public good, which by definition benefits all citizens, it is necessary to distinguish between those citizens who are clients of state-provided private goods, like NHS patients or parents of state school pupils, and those who are taxpayers but do not use the service. Even if a taxpayer does not use a service he may still be concerned that its clients should get their preferred amount or quality of service, given its production costs.

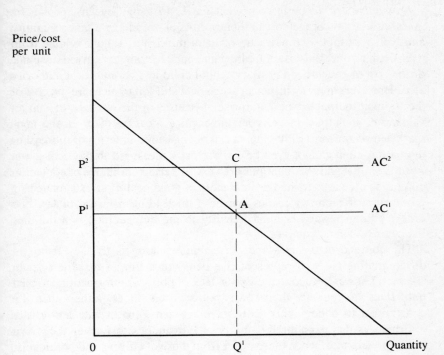

Figure 8.2: Productive inefficiency in a bureaucracy

The concept of allocative efficiency in relation to the mix of non-marketed goods produced by a bureau is impossible to quantify in any satisfactory way. It is not really possible to obtain a marginal valuation or demand curve for a collective good, as shown in figures 8.1 and 8.2. An individual citizen cannot meaningfully state how much he is prepared to pay for the bundle of medical services that make up the NHS; still less can politicians aggregate such valuations to produce a total demand function for expenditure on the NHS. Despite its quantitive imprecision, allocative efficiency is an important concept, if one makes the value judgement that consumers' preferences—in this case those of the clients-cum-taxpayers—are important. To some these preferences are paramount. From this perspective one can make a qualitative judgement about the allocative efficiency of a non-market bureaucracy by the degree to which customers can exert any influence or choice and the extent to which in the absence of any such choice, the customers express dissatisfaction. Thus the lack of influence of patients in the NHS, or of parents in the education system, is *prima facie* evidence of allocative inefficiency.

Productive efficiency is somewhat easier to gauge because it can be assessed in terms of the cost in money units of producing a given quantity and type of output. Estimates are made of the cost of a tonne of coal from a particular mine, the cost of treating an appendectomy in a given hospital, or the cost of educating a primary school child in a certain local authority area. However, in many instances, such data still fail to measure the cost of the ultimate output of the enterprises because, in the absence of market valuations of output, there is no satisfactory measure of it. In the non-marketed sector most of the inputs can be measured in terms of money but the output often cannot even be satisfactorily measured in physical units. Results of tests and examinations are very imperfect measures of education output; so are cases treated as indicators of good health; arrests made as a proportion of reported crimes can be a misleading measure of law and order; killing power (terminal lethality to the bureaucrats) is a dubious indicator of defence output.

The absence of costless and perfect information is the key factor in differentiating an ideal representative democracy from a real-life one. In Chapter 7, it was argued that citizens' lack of political information enabled politicians to pursue their own policy preferences rather than be constrained to adhere only to those of citizens. Inadequate and costly information also explains the ability of bureaucrats to further their own policy preferences, when these differ from those of citizens and politicians. In part these information difficulties are due to the problems of valuing the non-marketed output, and so are so especially acute with respect to the social services. However, they also exist in the market sector. The owners of private sector firms have information problems in monitoring managers and workers, and ensuring that they perform efficiently.

Two main, interconnected themes for this chapter have now emerged. The absence of good, costless information about the efficiency and distributional implications of policy measures, and the desire of bureaucrats to promote their own preferences in policy making. The power of bureaucrats to do this is based on their possession and control of information about policy, which generally exceeds that of the politicians and citizens. Politicians concerned to improve the delivery of policy by bureaucrats with respect to either their own or their constituents' preferences, need to pay attention to the organisational structures within which bureaucrats operate, and to the system of incentives, sanctions and professional values that motivate them. The rest of the chapter amplifies these points with respect to British government bureaucracy. The importance of hierarchical structure, with central government departments at the apex, and the significance of bargaining between the tiers that make up the hierarchy is discussed in the context of the NHS and education.

BUREAUCRACY AND BRITISH GOVERNMENT

The Civil Service

The *Yes Minister* series has done much to publicise the view that bureaucrats determine policy. It depicts the higher echelons of the civil service as manipulators of their ministers, trying to ensure that government is run according to civil servants' notions of what is in their department's interests. *Yes Minister* is an entertaining element in a wide literature which presents the culture, attitudes and ethos of the civil service community as important influences on policy-making.

A minister is in a department for a relatively short time compared with his officials. Although civil servants change departments, each department has over time developed its own philosophy, way of doing things and policy priorities. A minister is extremely busy with party political and constituency issues, as well as with running his department. He can only comprehend a small fraction of all the information appertaining to his department. Much of this is selectively filtered by officials as it percolates up the bureaucracy before finally reaching the minister's desk. As Lord Armstrong, former head of the civil service admitted:

The biggest and most pervasive influence is in setting the framework within which the questions of policy are raised. We, while I was at the Treasury, had a framework of the economy which was basically Keynesian. We set the questions which we asked ministers to decide arising out of that framework and it would have been enormously difficult for any minister to change that framework, so to that extent we had great power. I don't think it was used maliciously or malignly. I think we chose that framework because we thought it was the best one going. We were very ready to explain it to anybody who was interested, but most Ministers were not interested, they were just prepared to take the questions we offered them which came out of that framework without going back into the preconceptions of them.[3]

A number of former ministers, from Richard Crossman to Michael Heseltine, have remarked that civil servants aim to keep a minister from causing trouble by deluging him with paper-work. It takes a determined and well-organised minister to promote a policy which goes against the prevailing departmental line. It also helps if the policy was in the governing party's election manifesto and so is seen to have popular support. The Treasury's Keynesian framework which Lord Armstrong refers to above was jettisoned when the Conservatives returned to office in 1979, with a Prime Minister and Treasury team determined to foreswear Keynesianism and implement their medium-term financial strategy. Nigel Lawson, as Financial Secretary to the Treasury, rejected the Treasury's framework as useless for formulating the MTFS, and, under a new chief economic adviser, the Treasury model was revised along more monetarist lines.

Bureaucracy: Hierarchies and Networks

Apart from the problems a minister faces in managing and controlling his department and putting into practice his or her government's policies in the face of departmental foot-dragging, central government departments themselves have problems in seeing that the department's policies are in fact implemented by the agencies responsible for delivering them. Many forms of economic policy are not directly implemented by central government departments but involve a hierarchical network of organisations, some of which straddle the public-private sector divide, while others are outside it.

For example, monetary policy is operated by the Bank of England. Although nationalised since 1946, the Bank, like most other central banks, retains considerable freedom of action, based on its technical expertise in monetary matters and its close daily contact with the financial institutions and markets whose behaviour has to be influenced in order to implement monetary policy. Relations between the Bank and the government can at times be strained, as in 1980−81. The government had announced a target for the growth of the money supply of 7−11 per cent for 1980−81, and 6−10 per cent for 1981−82. The money supply actually grew by 19 per cent and 13 per cent in these two years, amid mutual recriminations. The Treasury felt the Bank was not trying hard enough, and some argued for a different technique of monetary control. The Bank maintained it was doing as well as it could under the circumstances and successfully resisted any significant changes in its mode of operation. Sections of the Labour Party and other radicals believe that the Bank of England asserts the interests of the City at the expense of the industrial sector in giving priority to defending the exchange rate and using exchange rate crises as a lever to secure more deflationary macroeconomic policies. This accusation was particularly pronounced during the Labour government's sterling crisis of 1976, which led to cuts in planned government expenditure.

Hierarchical relationships, in which the bureaucracies lower down the chain often possess a considerable degree of autonomy, characterise the nationalised industries, education and health services—to single out some main areas. In education the hierarchical line runs from the DES (or the Departments for Scotland and Northern Ireland) to local education authorities and then to schools and colleges, where headteachers and principals, as well as teachers, all influence delivery. Similarly for health, the DHSS allocates budgets to the fourteen Regional Health Authorities in England and indicates its policy priorities to them. The Regional Health Authorities, in turn, allocate budgets to their District Health Authorities, who have sole responsibility for hospital services. Community Health Councils, on which sit representatives of the DHA, local authorities and lay people, provide community health services, such as public health measures, clinics and health visitors. Family Practitioner Committees are independent employing authorities which contract for the services of doctors, dentists, pharmacists and opticians, and so have no management function. They are directly funded by the DHSS and are not cash-limited.

Implementation Problems in the NHS

The problems a central government department has in implementing its policies through the bureaucratic chain of communication are well illustrated by the case of the NHS. From the late 1950s, social reformers in academic circles and in the Labour Party complained that the allocation of health resources was socially unjust: some regions received more money on a per capita basis than others, while the quality of medical services for the mentally ill, the handicapped and geriatrics was poor. This pattern of resource allocation was largely dictated by history. Prior to the establishment of the NHS, London, in particular, had developed good medical facilites asociated with its many teaching hospitals. These attract ambitious and well-qualified medical staff who are adept at attracting resources and so reinforce the existing allocations. As the population of London declined, so the over-supply of acute hospital beds has itself become more acute. Other areas are also well-endowed with teaching hospital facilities or are attractive places for GPs to locate. The DHSS has no powers to direct GPs to practise in deprived areas and can only offer financial inducements for doctors to work there. The acute hospital specialities are more attractive to clinicians than are geriatrics or the mentally ill and handicapped. This is an example of how bureaucrats' preferences influence resource allocation.

After twenty years of operating the NHS, the DHSS began a concerted attempt to correct what it and many outside commentators perceived to be an imbalance in the allocation of resources between regions and between different types of health care. From the beginning of the 1970s the DHSS issued a series of White Papers and other documents on its priorities for the different types of health service. It set out a clear and quantified statement of its objectives in 1976 in *Priorities for Health and Personal Social Services*. The DHSS has sought to shift the balance of expenditure away from hospital services (which in 1983 absorbed 62 per cent of the NHS budget) to general medical and community health services. The aim is to treat people in the community rather than in hospital, and so was a reversal of the policies pursued since 1948, which benefited acute hospitals in particular. It implies raising the proportion of expenditure on mentally ill, handicapped and elderly patients relative to the acute hospital services, on which expenditure had increased rapidly in the 1960s with the hospital building programme.

One way in which the DHSS sought to implement this policy was through the NHS planning system, set up in 1976. The DHSS issued guidelines on its priorities, which initially were quite specific and quantified. The Health Authorities were expected to incorporate these priorities in their own plans for their services, drawn up in the light of their local circumstances. In the event the planning system did not operate as intended by the DHSS. Due to a lack of commitment and expertise, Health Authorities drew up inadequate plans or no plans at all. The attempt at operating a comprehensive and rational planning framework proved too complex to be put into practice except as a largely paper exercise.[4] As it became apparent that the DHSS's priorities were not being effected at local level, the department's priority statements became vaguer; quantification was dropped and the importance of local decision-making on priorities openly acknowledged. The DHSS's ambivalence was manifest in its 1981 handbook for DHAs on health service priorities and policies:

We want to give you as much freedom as possible to decide how to pursue these policies and priorities in your own localities. Local initiatives, local decisions, and local responsibility are what we want to encourage. . .
    but a national health service must have regard to national policies and priorities and I must ask you to take account of them, as set out in this handbook, in making your plans and decisions.

Another method by which the DHSS has tried to shift budget allocations from the regions with relatively high per capita expenditure to those with low expenditure is the Resource Allocation Working Party (RAWP), established under the Labour government and continued under the Conservatives. RAWP has aimed at 'equal opportunity for access to health care for people at equal risk'. Formulas are used to relate each region's budget to its 'need' for medical resources. Failing better statistics, each region's 'need' for medical resources is measured from its recorded mortality rates for various diseases. A 'fair' level of expenditure is estimated by relating the average amount spent in the UK as a whole on in-patient treatment for the disease to each region's measure of 'need'. Those with less than the 'fair' level of expenditure are allocated more money. The scheme has been applied to teaching hospitals and capital works; it enabled expenditure to the priority regions to grow at 3 per cent a year compared to half of one per cent for the least favoured regions. Only new resources were reallocated, and this not without protest and criticisms of the formulas.

After ten years of RAWP the disparities in per capita expenditure between regions have been reduced but not eliminated. As ever, incrementalism has prevailed in the face of the ubiquitous resistance of those who do worse out of budget reallocations. The crudity of the RAWP formula—yet another example of inadequate information—has been compounded by the further problems of allocating budgets within regions, which is in the hands of the RHAs. Thus some deprived areas, like inner London community health services, have suffered because they are within high-spending regions whose budgets are squeezed under RAWP. A further indication of the failure of the DHSS fully to implement its priorities is that the proportion of the NHS budget allocated to mental handicap and mental illness did not change between 1975–76 and 1981–82. The proportion spent on general hospital services declined slightly from 40.5 per cent to 38.1 per cent while that on primary care rose from 18.3 per cent to 19.7 per cent.[5]

It is therefore evident that the actions of state bureaucracies, such as the Health Authorities, are as important for resource allocation as the policy pronouncements of central government. Why this is so is due both to general characteristics of relationships within and between state bureaucracies, as well as to specific features of particular institutional arrangements.

Hierarchical bureaucracies, both in the public and private sectors, do not operate simply as a chain of command with orders coming from the top being fully obeyed as they are communicated downwards. The armed forces are the organisations which come closest to such a model, and even they, especially in peacetime, deviate from it. Instead bureaucracies are characterised by bargaining and negotiation between the various tiers in the hierarchy, and between bureaucrats who relate horizontally to each other at various points within the organisation. An example of a set of hierarchically-linked administrative tiers is the line from the DHSS to RHA, DHA, hospital and consultant. Different configurations of interests are brought to bear on decision-making at the different points in the hierarchy where bargaining between the tiers takes place. Most studies of NHS administration conclude that the power of the medical staff in decision-making is quite considerable and that of the lay representatives minimal. As one researcher concluded: 'Through a variety of channels, medical interests were able to influence what was decided, and overall the distribution of power was weighted heavily in favour of the professional monopolists.[6] Until 1984 the NHS side of a District Health Authority consisted of four appointed officials—an administrator, treasurer, medical officer and nursing officer—plus two elected medical representatives. These relationships were also characterised by negotiation and accommodation. Traditionally the NHS has practised consensual management. This was made explicit in the decision-making machinery established by the 1974 reorganisation; a DHA arrived at its policies by agreement amongst its members. This consensual style of management enabled medical interests to wield considerable influence.

The DHSS's main source of power is the allocation of budgets to the RHAs. The Health Authorities' trump card is their responsibility for the physical inputs used to provide health services. The DHSS has to bargain largely by exploiting its power to withhold or to grant money. The ultimate sanction of sacking or suspending Health Authority members is hardly ever used, because the costs in terms of non-cooperation of those supplying the human resources is far too great. For the reasons discussed in Chapter 7, a government department like the DHSS cannot have a clear mandate from UK citizens that its resource allocation plans are in any sense 'socially preferred' to alternative allocations. Thus, when in conflict, both the DHSS and the NHS bureaucrats can claim that they are futhering the interests of NHS clients. The dialogue between competing interests within and without the NHS is part of a pluralist decision-making process.

ACCOUNTABILITY AND MONITORING FOR EFFICIENCY PURPOSES

There is therefore a problem in ensuring that both politicians and bureaucrats deliver the policies that citizens have a right to expect; that is, making public servants accountable for their policies to the electorate. Democratic accountability is one of these vaunted, laudable principles. In the absence of any agreed criterion for aggregating citizens' preferences, it cannot be defined precisely nor made operational, except in rough-and-ready ways.

In a broad sense regular elections make politicians accountable to the voters. But there is no way in which all those responsible for the delivery of collective goods, such as health, education or defence, can be made directly accountable to the electorate. The transactions costs of such procedures would, in most people's judgement, exceed the benefits of individuals being able to signal clearly their preferences to the producers of collective goods. But there are various institutional devices for making some of these services to some degree accountable to elected representatives. Local councils provide education and personal social services, but local authority nominees and lay people form only part of the membership of Community Health Councils and DHAs. And, as has been noted, the NHS professionals exert the predominant influence.

In constitutional theory, a minister is accountable to Parliament for the conduct of his/her department. Thus the Secretary of State for Health and Social Services and the Minister for Health are responsible to Parliament for the NHS, though their actual authority with respect to the provision of its services is, as we have seen, somewhat attenuated. Parliament endeavours to obtain accountability by questioning ministers on the floor of the House and by taking evidence from ministers, officials and other informed sources in select committees. Ministers also try to ensure that the bureaucrats in the various administrative tiers for which they have direct responsibility are made accountable to them by means of rules, procedures, codes of conduct, guidelines, inquiries, provision of statistical, accounting and other information, and the like. All these combine to produce a set of explicit and implicit incentives and sanctions which form the material for exchanges between bureaucrats, and between them and their political sponsors. From the politicians' perspective all these are devices to make bureaucrats perform in ways that produce the policy outcomes sought by the politicians.

Monitoring of bureaucrats by politicians is an essential activity in securing accountability, and in inducing bureaucrats to be both allocatively and productively efficient. However, the traditional accountability and monitoring practised by Parliament is little concerned with efficiency. Its prime object is to ensure that public money has been spent in the past in ways authorised by Parliament. Nowadays, though, increasing attention is being paid to 'efficiency auditing' or 'value for money auditing'. Paliamentary select committees and the Comptroller and Auditor General have become increasingly critical of both policies and bureaucracies for not having explicit objectives against which performance can be assessed and for failing to establish management information systems that can generate the information needed for taking decisions which will improve efficiency. A bureaucracy cannot become more efficient if it lacks information on what are its actual and desired outputs, the opportunity costs of its activities and on the relationship between its resource inputs and what it produces. The hallmark of the Thatcher government has been its concern with improving efficiency throughout the public sector, in particular with reducing the unit costs to government of collective goods relative to what they would otherwise have been.

Promoting Efficiency in the NHS

In the context of government policy concerned with reducing the rate of growth of public expenditure, and even—in party rhetoric—with reducing it absolutely, the more efficient use of resources became a more pressing concern. Even with a government more convinced of the virtues of the welfare state, the rate of growth of welfare spending enjoyed in the 1960s and early 1970s could not be sustained without a substantial increase in the UK's rate of economic growth. Thus the greater attention given to efficient resource utilisation goes deeper than the party politics of the Thatcher government. The parliamentary monitors of the NHS have criticised its decision-making processes and its efficiency. The Select Committee for the Social Services has produced several critiques: in 1980 they recommended 'that the DHSS should give high priority to developing its capacity for devising coherent policy strategies for all the areas for which the Secretary of State is responsible.[7] The Comptroller and Auditor General has reported that millions of pounds could be saved by the more efficient deployment of nurses.

In recent years the DHSS has actively sought to increase the influence of its policies on NHS performance by means of institutional changes designed to improve monitoring, accountability and the efficiency of resource use, as conceived by the DHSS. In 1982 the NHS was once more reorganised to remove one layer of bureaucracy—the Area Health Authorities—which had mediated between the Regions and the Districts. This reduced the number of administrative jobs and simplified the communication chain between the DHSS and the final point of delivery of health services. A small team, led by Roy Griffiths, Managing Director of Sainsbury's, was appointed to advise on the effective use of manpower and management in the NHS. The *Griffiths Report*, published in 1983, commented that:

The NHS. . . still lacks any real continuous evaluation of its performance. . . .Rarely are precise management objectives set; there is little measurement of health output; clinical evaluation of particular practices is by no means common and economic evaluation of these practices is extremely rare. Nor can the NHS display a ready assessment of the effectiveness with which it is meeting the needs of the people it serves. (p. 10)

Griffiths, from the perspective of experience in running commercial organisations, diagnosed the root cause of these problems as the lack of a general management function at the DHSS and right through to regions, districts and hospitals.

Absence of this general management support means that there is no driving force seeking and accepting direct and personal responsibility for developing management plans, securing their implementation and monitoring actual achievement. (p. 12)

Griffiths concluded that the ability of the DHSS, at the pinnacle of the organisational hierarchy, to plan and implement an overall strategy for the NHS should be strengthened and that it should not dissipate its energies on supervising the details of implementation at the delivery end. This should be secured by creating an institutional framework, ethos and set of sanctions and incentives, such that individual bureaucrats, on their own initiative, take the appropriate decisions which contribute to the fulfilment of the DHSS's objective.

The Secretary of State, Norman Fowler, accepted Griffiths' recommendations that general managers be appointed at all levels of the NHS, with the responsibility for seeking to improve efficiency in the production and delivery of health services. The NHS is now run by the Health Services Supervisory Board, on which sit ministers, the Permanent Secretary at the DHSS, the Chief Medical and Nursing Officers and—for the present—Roy Griffiths. Its functions are to determine the purpose, objectives and direction of the NHS, make strategic decisions, appraise its budget and resource allocation, and receive reports on performance evaluations. Under them is an executive committee, the NHS Management Board, with a chairman who also sits on the Supervisory Board. The Management Board plans the implementation of policies determined by the Supervisory Board, gives leadership to the managers of the NHS lower down the hierarchy, and controls and monitors performance. Many of the initial board appointments were from the private sector, intended to bring into the NHS private sector management techniques, such as the appraisal of individual managers' effectiveness, in order to improve performance through the incentive of merit awards.[8] The tensions inherent in trying to run a politically accountable organisation as if it were a business were revealed by the resignation of the first board chairman, after only 18 months in the job, on the grounds of excessive political interference by ministers.

General managers have been appointed at regional and district level, from outside the NHS as well as largely from the existing personnel. Thus administrators, engineers, nursing officers, medical staff and other ex-specialists have become district general managers. Consensus management, whereby decisions were reached by agreement of all members of the team has been replaced by the general management function. The general manager is responsible for ensuring that his unit is run efficiently, and in accordance with the policy guidelines set by the DHSS and the Region. The DHSS hopes that this change will speed up decision-making and improve the efficiency and effectiveness of the delivery of health services. To do their job effectively general managers need the agreement or compliance of those supplying the various specialist services, from consultants to hospital porters. However, there will be occasions when this is not forthcoming and the general manager will judge that he has to use his authority to impose decisions. Conflict is thus more likely than in the days of consensual management, especially at first when all involved are unaccustomed to accepting the 'right of managers to manage'.

Griffiths also proposed the greater involvement of doctors in managerial decisions. Since it is their decisions 'that largely dictate the use of resources', cost reductions and improvements in patient services cannot be achieved without the active involvement of doctors. This requires that doctors have available the cost implications of their clinical decisions. To provide such information needs the development of a completely new financial information system. Work on such a management budgeting system, beginning with a few pilot projects and headed by financial managers recruited from the private sector, is underway. It seems to have got bogged down in the complexities of accurately relating inputs to ultimate health outputs, and in changing the practices of doctors, who regard themselves as an elite profession. They have traditionally looked to their professional peers as the sole source of appraisal, monitoring and information on how to conduct their work.

Apart from management budgeting, another monitoring device, aimed at providing more information to be used in improving efficiency, is the publication by the DHSS in 1983 of 'performance indicators'. These measures use readily available data, covering such areas as clinical services, finance, manpower and estate management, to produce statistics on costs per case treated, length of hospital stay, length of waiting lists, and the like. As the DHSS accepts, such measures do not necessarily indicate anything useful about the relationship between the input of real resources and the resulting output of health services to patients—hence the term 'indicators'. They are to be used as a starting point for a DHA's assessment of its performance in comparison with other authorities. Any wide deviation from average practice should trigger an investigation to see if performance can be improved.

Yet another institutional change was the introduction in 1982 of a simplified planning system to replace the failed attempt at comprehensive planning by means of a two-way flow of documents between the DHSS and the RHAs. The District not the Regional Health Authority is now the basic planning unit. The DHSS seeks compliance with its policies via a system of reviews of each DHA's strategy and performance, involving ministers, DHSS civil servants, and regional and district officers. Through a process of dialogue the DHSS seeks to discover the extent to which RHAs and DHAs are implementing government policy, whether there are good local reasons for any deviations, and to press for compliance where it thinks this justified.

The example of recent initiatives with respect to the way the NHS is organised and run are entirely explicable within the framework of the economic theory of bureaucracy. They represent attempts by the political sponsors of a state bureau to make it perform more in line with their notions of what constitutes allocative and productive efficiency. This is done by trying to devise a system of incentives and—to a lesser extent—sanctions, to which individual bureaucrats respond in ways which secure the sponsor's objectives for the provision of a collective good. The *sine qua non* of such a system of incentives and sanctions is adequate information. This is needed in order to define objectives in operational terms, for monitoring how well the objectives are being achieved and to provide the basis, at all levels of the hierarchy, for bureaucrats to take decisions which contribute to the achievement of the political sponsor's objectives.

Promoting Efficiency in Education

A similar pattern of initiatives has been taken by the Department of Education and Science, which set out its aims and proposals in *Better Schools*.[9] Here it stated two broad objectives: to raise standards at all levels of ability and to secure the best possible return from resources. However the DES has less influence over the English education system than the DHSS has over the NHS. Education is officially described as being the responsibility of a triumviral partnership between the DES, the local education authorities and voluntary bodies that run the schools, and the teachers' associations. Thus there is little that the DES can prescribe to local education authorities and teachers. Central government in Britain has never laid down a national syllabus, as in many other countries. The curriculum is the responsibility of the LEAs and governing bodies of schools. In practice it has been largely left to heads and teachers, constrained by the syllabuses of external examinations. Without an explicit curriculum and methods of assessing the extent to which pupils have been taught the curriculum, it is difficult put into effect the Secretary of State for Education's statutory accountability to Parliament:

to promote the education of the people of England and Wales and the progressive development of institutions devoted to that purpose, and to secure the effective execution by local authorities . . .of the national policy for providing a varied and comprehensive education service in every area. (Section I of Education Act 1944)

Since 1980 the DES has been actively engaged in getting its partners to agree a broad common curriculum. In 1981 the DES published a guidance paper, *The School Curriculum*, in which it advocated a set of commonly agreed principles for a 'broad, relevant, balanced and differentiated curriculum'. It recommended that LEAs should draw up policies for the curriculum in their areas, and that schools should set out their aims in writing and measure their achievement against them. After further discussions the Secretary of State announced in January 1984 further plans to define the main objectives of the curriculum in terms of measurable attainment levels at various ages and abilities; to introduce a new 16+ exam—the GCSE—which tests, not relative attainment as do GCE and CSE but absolute attainment levels against agreed national criteria; and to bring 80–90 per cent of all pupils at 16+ to the levels currently expected of average ability pupils.

There have been other strands to DES education policy. One is to increase the influence of parents over what goes on in schools by giving more explicit powers to school governing bodies and making greater parent representation mandatory. This is another instance of a measure aimed at increasing customer influence over the provision of a non-marketed good.

The proposal to introduce teacher assessment is another example of a monitoring device to make bureaucrats more accountable and to induce better performance by means of a stronger system of sanctions and rewards. The government has wanted a revamped salary structure for teachers, which would enable teachers in under-supplied subjects and with good teaching skills to be paid more; and which would embrace 'a new contractual definition of teachers' duties and responsibilities and the introduction of systematic performance appraisal, designed to bring about a better relationship between pay, responsibilities and performance'. [10]

However the DES has to negotiate this not only with the teachers' unions, but through the local education authorities who are the teachers' employers. So apart from exhortation, the main bargaining weapon the DES has used is its influence on the amount of money assessed for education in the rate support grant. It has used the sanction of refusing extra money to finance the teachers' pay claim unless teachers negotiate a new contract. The teachers' unions have resisted appraisal and payment by merit or skill. They have used industrial action to press their pay claim; and to resist the implementation of the government's proposals with respect to both teacher appraisal and implementation of the new GCSE, unless substantial additional finance is forthcoming. The current situation in education highlights the problems faced by politicians who try to implement policies which bureaucrats see as threatening their self-interest and accustomed professional discretion; especially when central government is not prepared to pay the price demanded by the bureaucrats for their cooperation.

DEVISING STRUCTURES FOR RESOURCE ALLOCATION

The 1985−86 teachers' dispute illustrates quite vividly that establishing and operating systems for accountability, control and monitoring incur costs. The costs in terms of money or real resources are tangible, if difficult to measure accurately. Others are intangible, such as the creation of resentment, low morale and uncooperative attitudes amongst the bureaucrats, which ill dispose them to be either allocatively or productively efficient. Bureaucrats are motivated by sentiments that are not always directly self-seeking, such as aspirations for professional good practice, for furthering their concepts of the public interest and for helping others. These motivations do promote allocative and productive efficiency, though not exclusively. However these aspirations, combined—sometimes unconsciously—with more self-seeking motives, inform working practices; they are built up collectively within professions and organisations, through the interaction of attitudes, expectations, custom, personal relations, reward systems and organisational structures. All these have to be taken account of in devising ways to promote efficiency in state bureaucracies. There are no precise formulas for working out the optimal structures and systems for ensuring allocative and productive efficiency in bureaucracies. It is largely a matter of informed judgement, not only about how people and institutions tick, but about the influence which different political interests do and should exert on policy-making.

The economic analysis of bureaucracy highlights the virtues of the market, as an efficient social organisation for producing and distributing goods, that are emphasised by the *Austrian school*: the market is efficient in its use of information. For a bureaucracy producing non-marketed goods to perform efficiently there have to be much larger two-way information flows, both vertically and horizontally, so that activities can be coordinated, so that officials higher up the organisation can devise appropriate policies for the lower levels to implement, and so that implementation can be monitored. Monitoring is an inherently costly activity; it involves duplication, as one group checks the activities of another—hence the efficiency arguments in favour of privatisation and competition for public sector organisations producing marketed goods. For the non-marketed sectors, privatisation has, so far, been largely limited to those services that can be bought in from the market more cheaply, like cleaning and catering.

If market provision is unsuitable for externality or distributional reasons, then increasing competition within the public sector is recommended by some. By having as large a number of agencies producing a given type of collective good as economies of scale permit, some element of competition can be created. At a minimum the performance of the different units can be compared, as is being attempted with performance indicators in the NHS. One academic proposal is the use of markets within the NHS whereby a health authority uses its government-funded budget to contract for specific health services for its clients from other authorities. Another is the creation of 'health maintenance organisations' which contract, either with the state or with state-insured patients, to provide clients with annual health care for a fixed fee. Doctors then have greater incentive to use less expensive methods of treatment, but patients have to take on more responsibility for judging the quality of care they receive and, if dissatisfied, complaining, suing or moving to alternative associations. Libertarians welcome such additional responsibility for the individual as an extension of his freedom. In opposition to such views, socialists reject market relations on ethical grounds for promoting selfish behaviour, which is to be especially condemned in the field of welfare services.

THE ORGANISATIONAL PROCESS

There are a number of different approaches to studying bureaucracy. Here I have concentrated on the economic approach to the analysis of bureaucracy, which is part of a branch of economics known as *public choice*. Its distinctive methodology is that it makes deductions on the basis of the assumption that bureaucrats, and other kinds of policy-maker, are self-seeking utility-maximisers.

An alternative perspective is to examine bureaucracies as institutional structures for processing policy. Rules and procedures determine what issues get considered, how they are dealt with, who influences decisions as they are processed through the organisation, and with what effect on policy outcomes. For example, the organisational process perspective focuses on the procedures of the Public Expenditure Survey Committee in relation to the annual cycle of expenditure and revenue decisions, as exerting an influence on economic policy, distinct from that of the various political actors or of the economic issues involved. The decision-makers, and those who influence them, are constrained by rules and procedures to act in certain ways, though they have some discretion in how well they deploy their skills in manipulating these to their advantage. The NHS and education examples both illustrate how bureaucratic structures, rules and procedures, influence the relative power of ministers and bureaucrats in determining the allocation and distribution of resources to state employees and to service clients.

IN DEFENCE OF BUREAUCRATS

This chapter has possibly overemphasised the malign influence of bureaucrats: they have been depicted as intervening between the policy preferences of citizens and the policy outcomes they get, with the politicians as representatives and champions of citizens' preferences. However, as discussed in Chapter 7, we cannot take for granted that politicians mirror the citizens' preferences without distortion or do so in ways which can be defined as 'socially optimal'.

There has always existed a strong argument that certain areas of policy should be taken out of the political arena and handed over to bureaucrats to administer in a depoliticised manner within a hierarchical bureaucracy, where rules, procedures, detachment and authority govern decision-making, rather than political bargaining. One manifestation of this view, examined in Chapter 11, is the Morrisonian model of the public corporation, which is run by a management board independent of central government. Another is the British practice that civil servants and local authority officers are not political appointments; senior civil servants do not engage in party politics.

What advantages does the depoliticisation of policy seem to hold? For one thing it speeds up decision-making especially in areas where quick decisions based on technical expertise are required. This explains why monetary policy is usually operated by central banks which enjoy a considerable measure of independence from central goverment. It is also notable that state organisations producing marketable goods and services, and which therefore have to respond to commercial pressures, are hived off into agencies which are, to some measure, independent of government departments. Depoliticisation also adds a measure of stability and continuity to policy-making. Departments are able to evolve policies which continue essentially unchanged, even though the party in power changes. Thus the DHSS's policy of redistributing NHS resources continued with a switch from Labour to Conservative government; the DES's concern with education standards surfaced under the previous Labour government. Of course, for those who want radical change, the continuity argument is not appealing; voices on both the radical right and left have called for politically appointed officials in central and local government, so that politicians can implement their policies more effectively.

Yet another reason—with powerful appeal to economists—is that decisions taken by bureaucrats will be more rational than those taken by politicians. A group of politicians, representing different views and interests, cannot establish an agreed preference ordering for their policy priorities. Given the impossibility of the task they do not even try, as we have seen with the PESC procedures for determining the level and allocation of government expenditure. Therefore the policy choices made are not the outcome of a rational decision-making process, whereby the means are selected that will best achieve the objectives. Instead policies emerge as the result of bargaining and negotiation amongst the politicians. A specialist bureaucracy, operating at arm's length from politicians, can more easily form a collective consensus on what are its objectives and its preference ordering over those objectives, since its bureaucrats are bound together by common attitudes and by the continuity of the organisation. They will more readily devise and operate rational decision-making procedures.

CONCLUSION

This rationalist view of policy-making, and the role of expert technicians in it, are examined further in Chapter 10. Two main critiques are offered of this depiction of policy. The first, examined in this chapter, is that bureaucrats are not philosopher-kings who pursue the public good in a disinterested manner. The second leads on from the first: it is the recognition that bureaucrats are also political interests. This breaks down the distinction between rational decision-making by bureaucrats and non-rational political bargaining by politicians. This theme is taken up in the next chapter which investigates the role of political interests and pressure groups in policy-making.

The main theme running through this chapter is that the influence of bureaucrats on policy is related to the absence of perfect, costless information about policy, which is particularly acute for citizens. In their role as policy implementers, bureaucrats have better access to information than the politicians who are electorally accountable for policy. The difficulties experienced by principals—politicians in this case—in ensuring that their wishes are carried out by their agents—the bureaucrats—is common to both the public and private sectors. Owners of firms have essentially similar problems in ensuring that managers and workers perform efficiently. However the agency problem is heightened in the non-market public sector by the absence of adequate measures of the effectiveness of economic policies in achieving the objectives set for them. It is rare to get clearly defined objectives and difficult in the absence of prices to measure the output of policy in relation to such objectives. Information on the resource costs of non-marketed output is the least difficult to obtain, but requires the establishment of good management information systems.

The paucity of information available to politicians and the costs of gathering it, give bureaucrats a certain leeway to pursue their own policy preferences and thus to further their personal and professional interests. This can be represented as utility-maximising behaviour on the part of bureaucrats, from which it is deduced that non-market bureaucracies will not be productively or allocatively efficient.

These somewhat abstract arguments were illustrated with examples from the state health and education services in Britain. While specialised and hierarchical bureaucracies are required in order to implement policies effectively, they also generate additional information flow problems. Implementation commands do not flow undistorted from the top of the hierarchy to the bottom. In fact, ministers and central government departments have only limited control of the bureaucracies for which they are responsible; the relationship between the bureaucratic tiers is more aptly described as a bargaining one. The structure of incentives and sanctions, the ethos and attitudes of professions and organisations are crucial in determining the kind of services the bureaucracies deliver to the citizen-customers.

An ideal representative democracy presumes the value judgement that the citizen-customers are sovereign in relation to their suppliers. Their preferences determine the allocation and distribution of resources. The necessary existence of government bureaucracies to formulate, process and deliver economic policies in a world of costly and imperfect information, results in an extremely attenuated connection between the preferences of citizens expressed through political participation and the policies delivered to them via politicians and bureaucrats. In the absence of markets, citizens have to rely for good service on the response of self-interested bureaucrats to the sanctions and incentives they face, on their professionalism and, ultimately, on their altruism.

NOTES

1. W. Niskanen, *Bureaucracy and Representation Government* (Aldine, Chicago, 1971).
2. 'The BBC adjusts its set', *Financial Times*, 22 March 1985.
3. P.M. Jackson, *The Political Economy of Bureaucracy* (Philip Allan, Deddington, Oxford, 1982), p. 9.
4. C. Ham, *Health Policy in Britain* (Macmillan, London, 1985), pp. 69–70.
5. Ibid., p. 131.
6. Ibid., p. 158.
7. Ibid., p. 132.
8. 'A private focus on staffing a public service', *Financial Times*, 4 November 1985.
9. *Better Schools*, Cmnd 9469 (HMSO, London, 1985), p. 55.
10. Ibid.

9 Political Interests and Pressure Groups

For good or ill the influence of interest groups is a characteristic feature of Britain today. The most important of them carry weight at the highest levels of decision-making and others, no less significant, thrust their way daily into the headlines to demand action from governments and politicians. Below these are many hundreds of less well-known organisations, persistently and discreetly lobbying, and steadfastly upholding minority and unpopular causes. (Directory of Pressure Groups)[1]

I attended the numerous—and often contentious—meetings of two high-level interdepartmental committees . . . . I now found myself in a different world both administratively and intellectually. For one thing, vested interests were involved in an obvious and indeed essential way. . . . Those sitting round the table were there as the representatives of the departments and agencies that were interested parties. Their role was to articulate and defend the interests of their own organisations, or those of the outside groups for which departments acted as sponsors or advocates within Whitehall. Officials appeared not as individuals, but as it were wearing masks, like actors in a Greek drama. (David Henderson, Head of Department of Economics and Statistics, OECD and BBC Reith Lecturer, 1985)[2]

The very word 'lobbying' still sticks in some people's throat. They seem to think there is something improper about it; that it is a sinister (perhaps even dishonest) practice, something that starts with an expensive lunch and ends with a lucrative slice of 'payola'. But lobbying, which is to say informing your elected representative of your real concerns is a perfectly proper part of the democratic process - so long as it is done honestly, openly, with integrity and professionalism. (Sir Terence Beckett, Director-General of the CBI)[3]

When Sir Edwin Nixon [Chairman of IBM] meets a minister or permanent secretary, it is like a meeting of heads of state. Both will have been briefed on the items the other wants to raise. . . . 'It's a professional meeting,' says IBM's government affairs specialist. 'We do not see it as a chummy relationship.' (Hazel Duffy, 'The art of lobbying is becoming a profession', *Financial Times*, 24 February 1986)

A directory of pressure groups for the UK lists some 600 such organisations which it defines as:

bodies concerned to promote a course of action or represent a defined group of people with the aim of bringing about changes favourable to that cause or group. Promotional and interest groups share in common the fact that they try to influence public opinion, directly through mass campaigns or indirectly through the media, and attempt to change the action of government. They compete against each other in the allocation of resources and the determination of priorities, and on occasions appear at odds with the rest of society.[4]

A great variety of organisations is included in the directory, from trade unions and trade associations to single-issue promotional groups such as Friends of the Earth, the Wider Share-Ownership Council, Campaign for Comprehensive Education, the Low Pay Unit and Shelter the National Campaign for the Homeless.

The interests of distinct groupings in society can be distinguished independently of the existence of organised pressure groups to promote them, and can be furthered by the political activities of those with a common interest without their using a pressure organisation set up for the purpose. There are a whole host of such interests—consumers, workers, businesses and taxpayers; and subsets of them—teachers, doctors, miners, rate-payers, patients, motorists, smokers, mortgagors. Such distinct interests are referred to as *political interests* when their furtherance involves some sort of political action, such as voting, expressing opinions in the media, or personal contacts with ministers and civil servants.[5] The term political interests includes pressure groups; their presence and some of their activities are a visible part of the political interaction between interests from which policy outcomes emerge.

There is no role for political interests and pressure groups in the ideal model of representative democracy sketched out in the introduction to Part II. In this voting is the only means by which citizens transmit their policy preferences to politicians. But the activities of political interests provide an additional means by which citizens' policy preferences are signalled and brought to bear on policy-making. Political interest activity enables citizens to signal their preferences in a much more discriminating way than does voting. They can indicate the intensity of their feelings on a selected issue and thus convey specific preferences in their roles as consumer, worker in a particular industry or public sector bureaucracy, client of a social service, or resident in a given locality. One significant consequence of political interest activity is that Parliament is no longer the sole channel of communication and influence between citizens and government. In many eyes Parliament is relatively insignificant in the policy-making process, because of the importance of the extra-parliamentary channels of influence between the executive branches of government and political interests outside Parliament.

An important link between Chapters 8 and 9 is that a group of bureaucrats, motivated by common conceptions of self-interest and shared professional goals, is a political interest. Many bureaucrats belong to pressure groups, in particular trade unions and professional associations. Civil servants establish links with pressure groups outside government to form a policy-making community. Thus a particular political interest, such as agriculture (examined in Chapter 14) is firmly meshed into both the public and private sectors, helping to blur the distinction between the two.

This chapter considers how the activities of political interests, as a different form of political participation from voting, affect policy-making. It starts by describing the main kinds of pressure group and their activities. A key question raised is whether the activities of political interests and pressure groups distort the transmission of citizens' preferences into policy outcomes. Do some interests thereby gain more influence than others? The economic analysis of pressure group participation, pioneered by Mancur Olson, suggests that this is indeed the case. Another key theme of the chapter—and of the book—is that the influence of political interests means that the process of economic policy-making is best understood as a political bargaining game, rather than as a rational decision-making procedure. Differing views as to whether interest group pressure and political bargaining are malign or benign are then outlined.

PRESSURE GROUPS WITH ECONOMIC INTERESTS

It is standard procedure to distinguish between sectional interests, that are primarily concerned with the material self-interest of their members, and promotional groups espousing some cause like nuclear disarmament, environmental protection, animal rights or the elimination of poverty. The former are patently concerned with their own economic interests and encompass major economic groupings, such as trade unions and trade and professional associations. But promotional groups also aim to affect economic policy, as their aspirations involve some redistribution of resources. For instance, animal rights and environmental protection legislation affect some interests adversely by raising their costs. Most social welfare campaigns, such as those of the Child Poverty Action Group, Shelter or the National Campaign for Childcare, call for more government spending. Many sectional interest groups also claim to promote causes that can benefit those outside the group, while promotional groups espouse causes that benefit at least some of their members. For instance, in 1985 more than forty trade unions, professional and voluntary bodies, mostly representing NHS workers and clients, formed Health Concern, an organisation to 'protect and promote the founding principles of the

National Health Service'.[6] Thus a great variety of sectional and promotional interest groups impinge on economic policy-making.

Peak Organisations

The major economic interest groups are often classified into those representing workers and those representing the managerial and capitalist classes. In Britain, as in many other liberal democracies, labour and management are each represented at national level by a 'peak organisation'—the Confederation of British Industry and the Trades Union Congress. The two have certain features in common. Each is made up of a federation of member organisations: some 11,000 companies belong to the CBI, while the TUC consists of over 100 affiliated unions. Each has only partial coverage of its potential membership. There are around ten million workers in the TUC affiliated unions—less than half the workforce. The CBI represents mainly large industrial companies: there are a number of separate small business organisations, as well as the Retail Consortium. The TUC and the CBI are both hierarchically organised, with central committees. TUC policy is established at its annual conference by the votes of union delegates. The CBI has a General Council of around 400 which meets about once a month, as well as an annual conference. Because both organisations contain a wide range of interests and views, their central officers have to work hard at securing a consensus for the organisation's policy objectives. Obtaining compliance from members is even harder. For instance, although TUC conference voted for industrial action to support the miners in the 1984 dispute, key member unions refused to comply.

Both organisations formulate economic policies they want the government to adopt and advise their members on current government measures affecting their interests. To this end they both have an economic research unit, fund additional research, gather information from members (for example the CBI *Industrial Trends Survey*), and publish regular economic bulletins and press releases. Though the CBI's outlook is more in tune with the Conservative Party than any other, it 'is not a party political organisation; it must deal with successive governments, whatever their colour'.[7] The TUC, though, has always had close links with the Labour Party; it sees Labour's election to office as its main hope for securing its desired economic policies. Via the Labour-TUC liaison committee and personal contacts between their respective leaders, joint policy proposals for Labour's election manifesto are put forward.

For the last twenty years the main bone of contention between Labour Party leaders and the trade union movement has been incomes policy. It is widely accepted that a government boost to aggregate demand, designed to secure a faster rate of growth and hence lower unemployment, is vitiated if money wages rise more rapidly so that the extra demand is converted into higher prices rather than into extra output and jobs. Labour governments in the 1960s and 1970s secured trade union agreement to wage restraint, but on each occasion this only lasted a couple of years. The TUC could not secure further compliance from member unions, nor could trade union leaders secure it from rank-and-file members. The *quid pro quo* for the TUC is favourable employment and social legislation. For the 1979 and 1983 elections the Labour Party failed to secure any tangible agreement on incomes policy, which had become an abhorrent term in the union movement. Attempts to paper over the cracks with vague promises of a 'national economic assessment' proved unconvincing. Hence the importance to Labour and TUC leaders of clinching a more convincing agreement on giving priority to expenditure on employment-creation and welfare, not to pay rises for those with jobs.

The CBI is not so closely involved with Conservative policy formulation, though its members and chief officers make good use of their personal contacts with Conservative politicians. Like the TUC, the CBI lobbies for economic policies which it considers will benefit its members. Hence in the 1980s it has called for cuts in interest rates, in the exchange rate, employers' National Insurance contributions and business rates. In the run up to the Budget both the CBI and the TUC make formal submissions to the Chancellor for policy changes and publicise these. In 1986 the CBI called for £1 billion more spending on job-creation—specifically on infrastructure projects which would benefit the construction industry. It favoured an increase in tax thresholds over a cut in the standard rate of tax. The TUC in its pre-Budget submission called for six billion pounds more expenditure on job-creation and the welfare state, financed by increased borrowing and taxation of the rich.

The *corporatist* elements in British policy-making were mentioned in Chapter 2. Their most institutionalised form is the National Economic Development Council where business representatives, trade unionists and government ministers and officials meet on a regular basis to discuss economic policy. On the NEDC itself the Chancellor meets industrialists and trade unionists to discuss aspects of government policy. Under the Thatcher government such corporatist approaches have been downgraded, in contrast to their encouragement by the previous Labour government, not only within NEDC but also through regular contacts between ministers and union leaders. The Thatcher government has severely limited the range of items on which it has sought union consultation, to the extent that the TUC withdrew from the NEDC for a while. The CBI also found itself ignored when it criticised macroeconomic policy. The NEDC has been used mainly as a talking-shop for airing industry complaints; on some of these the CBI and the TUC have seen eye to eye. The issues on which the government has sought genuine consultation have been limited to such items as the

Chancellor's 1986 budget proposal for tax relief on schemes linking part of employees' pay to their company's profits.

The activities of the CBI and the TUC in promoting their members' interests are mirrored, to varying degrees, by other pressure groups. The ways in which a pressure group seeks to affect government policy and its success in doing so are to some extent related, and depend on the aims and characteristics of the pressure group, and on the extent to which government is sympathetic to its aims or feels compelled to give in to its demands.

THE ROLE OF POLITICAL INTERESTS IN POLICY-MAKING

Consultation and Decision-Making

The extent to which a pressure group is influential in policy-making largely depends on the degree of legitimacy accorded to it by government. 'Since the 1940s it has been accepted that departments should consult with recognised pressure groups, most items of legislation being worked out in this way before they are placed before the legislature.'[8] Legitimate pressure groups enjoy a close relationship with government. Their officers are in regular contact with the politicians and bureaucrats involved in their policy area. The most favoured groups are not only consulted, their representatives partake in governmental decision-making. Many are themselves bureaucrats in the sense that they are employed in the public sector. Representatives of teachers' unions, medical associations, scientific bodies, and such like organisations, as well as representatives of purely private sector pressure groups, sit on Royal Commissions, Committees of Inquiry and Departmental Advisory Committees; there are some 500 of the latter.[9]

Thus resource allocation within any sphere such as agriculture, education, health or defence, is conducted by a specialist policy-making community consisting of ministers (or local councillors), civil servants (or local authority officers) and representatives of the legitimate pressure groups. Such a policy-making community shares some common objectives, such as expanding or protecting the budgets of their expenditure programme against the claims of other programmes for resources, as in the PESC budgeting procedures. In this way a policy community is a political interest. On other issues the policy-making community has divergent goals. In particular the minister and the departmental civil servants are often attempting to squeeze budgets to comply with central government constraints or to reallocate resources within a sector in ways which the bureaucrats delivering the service or the client pressure groups resist, as shown by the examples of health and education in Chapter 8.

The relationship betwen legitimate pressure groups and government is symbiotic: they need each other. It is difficult for those in government with political authority to implement policy without the cooperation of those who work in the public sector producing state goods and services. This source of bureaucratic power was pointed out in Chapter 8. But the same point applies to those in the private sector whose actions are affected by government policy, either as a by-product or as a deliberate aim of policy. For instance, governments are concerned to improve the performance of British industry, hence they need information on how to do this; on what are the effects of particular tax and subsidy systems; how to induce more rapid innovation; how to improve workforce skills, and so on. For example, the Financial Services Bill going through Parliament in 1986 in order to regulate the rapidly changing financial markets, has required extensive consultation to provide information on the likely effects of alternative measures; furthermore the market operators themselves will be required to implement the provisions of the Bill by means of self-regulatory bodies such as the Security and Investments Board. The affected interests have succeeded against the government's wishes in getting the Bill amended to grant SIB legal immunity from prosecution.

Political interests and pressure groups who are closely enmeshed into the internal process of government policy-making undertake discreet lobbying. The pressures they apply on government and the extent of their participation and influence are hidden from outside observers. Such groups are 'insiders' in the policy-making process, in contrast to groups who are not accorded the access to the corridors and committees of power that accompanies legitimacy. In return for a share in the power of policy-making, insider-group representatives are expected to be reticent and discreet, to the extent of withholding confidential information from their membership. The focus of this discreet lobbying is Whitehall; with respect to EC decision-making, it is Brussels. The European Commission, which is the executive institution of the EC, sought from the beginning to enhance its power by establishing a strong preference for consulting only European-based pressure groups. Hence many UK pressure groups are represented in Brussels and are members of an appropriate EC hierarchical organisation. Insider groups send representatives to the consultative and policy-making committees by which the European Commission arrives at the policy proposals it puts to the Council of Ministers, who take the final decisions. Thus the most effective activities of political interests take place not in a blaze of publicity, or through parliamentary channels, but within the internal workings of government bureaucracy.

Campaigning
Outsider pressure groups—those not accorded access to government

decision-making—are forced to adopt campaigning tactics to gain publicity and public support. Some go further and cause social disruption, including violence, to get government to yield to their demands. Insider groups also use selective campaigning tactics, as do the CBI and TUC. In any case, the insider and outsider distinction is not clear-cut; pressure groups are arrayed on a spectrum from those at one end who participate in policy-making to those at the other end, who are totally ignored by government. The pattern is more complex still, because a pressure group's status in policy-making varies according to the issue in hand and to the political complexion of the government. The Thatcher government has accorded the trade unions little influence on macroeconomic policy-making, in contrast to the previous Labour government, but their representations are heeded in other areas or their cooperation sought, as with the MSC's initiatives in youth training. But the more a political interest is denied access to the consultative and decision-making procedures of policy-making, the more it has to rely on campaigns. Many pressure groups start as campaigning outsiders and gradually gain access to the internal processes of policy-making. The National Farmers Union (NFU), for instance, obtained its influential position *vis-à-vis* the Ministry of Agriculture Fisheries and Food during World War II when the government needed a rapid increase in domestic agricultural production to replace imports. The insider status of the farming lobby is enshrined in the Agriculture Act 1947 which requires the government to consult farming interests in an annual review of the industry.

Parliament is an important focus of campaigning activity. At best a pressure group can persuade a Private Member to sponsor a Bill in their favour or induce Parliament to amend or reject government-sponsored legislation, which the group have failed to alter by lobbying ministers and civil servants. Similarly a pressure group can influence the way local councillors vote on an issue like school reorganisation, privatisation of services or planning permission. The most successful action of recent years was the Keep Sunday Special campaign which succeeded in getting enough Conservative MPs to vote against the government's Bill to liberalise shopping hours, that it failed its second reading. This campaign also illustrates another feature of pressure group activity—the formation of temporary coalitions of different political interests who share a common attitude to a particular issue. The Keep Sunday Special campaign was organised by church groups, trade unions (in particular the Union of Shop, Distributive and Allied Workers) and some retailers, using a public relations firm. The campaign mobilised congregations and clerics, arranged around 220 constituency meetings with Conservative MPs, and encouraged supporters to write letters—around 50,000 to the government against the Bill compared to 8000 in favour.[10] The rival campaign, Open

Shop, organised by retailers, failed to mobilise support amongst the many working families who would benefit from extended weekend shopping.

Alternatively, pressure groups use Parliament to gain media publicity, to build up an influential body of opinion in their favour, or to obtain information. This is done by asking MPs to put questions to ministers, to initiate debates, make supportive speeches, choose topics for select committee investigation and question witnesses at such investigations. Pressure groups also give evidence at select committee proceedings and employ experts to do this on their behalf. MPs themselves inevitably have their own political interests and many belong to pressure groups. In the 1983 Parliament there were 115 trade union-sponsored MPs, while over half the MPs, and the majority of Conservatives, had business interests, including farming.

Parliamentary lobbying has now become an industry with specialist government affairs and public relations companies. These firms, as well as pressure groups themselves, pay MPs retainers or commissions for specific services rendered. According to one political correspondent: 'Just before lunchtime each day, a number of limousines stop outside the Members' entrance at the Palace of Westminster—the lobbyists have arrived to whisk MPs away to meet their clients'.[11] MPs are required to register outside income sources. Around a hundred are listed as parliamentary consultants, and about twenty are directors of public affairs agencies.[12] A recent survey revealed that 41 per cent of firms use government affairs consultants.[13] Many large companies employ their own specialist staff, not only for lobbying politicians and civil servants, but also to keep them informed of what government is doing that might affect them.

Some campaigns are directed at local authorities. For instance the National Child Care Campaign (NCCC), which wants free state nurseries for all under fives, lobbies both the DES and local authorities. It is the latter that have the discretionary power to provide nurseries and some authorities are much more sympathetic to such provision than others. The NCCC's ultimate goal would be achieved if the government, via the DES, gave local authorities a statutory duty to provide free nurseries for all who want them. Many campaigns seek to influence the climate of opinion, both amongst those with a specific interest in policy-making, such as journalists, broadcasters and academics, as well as amongst the general public. One example of such a campaign is Charter for Jobs, set up in 1985 by a group of politicians, Keynesian economists and other academics, journalists, businessmen and one businesswoman. It aims 'to encourage decisive action to reduce unemployment' and, via its Employment Institute, to 'study and debate about the best methods of reducing unemployment without setting in motion an inflationary upsurge'. It has called for a substantial rise in public sector infrastructure investment, a cut in employers' National

Insurance contributions and a job guarantee on community projects for all long-term unemployed.[14]

Quite often a political interest within government welcomes, or even encourages, public campaigns by the pressure group element of its policy-making community. For instance, in bygone days, both a Conservative and a Labour Secretary of State for Education urged the National Union of Teachers to publicise the case for more spending on education in order to strengthen their hand with the Treasury.[15] Barbara Castle (Secretary of State at the DHSS, 1974–76) urged the newly-formed National Association of Health Authorities to 'become a pressure group for the NHS'.[16] A good number of pressure groups are funded by government. For instance, the NCCC in 1985 got £78,000 from the DES for running nurseries and £50,000 from the GLC. Only £2000 was from other sources, such as subscriptions.[17]

These are not isolated instances. They exemplify the point that a government is not a monolithic organisation with a single agreed objective function, but a constellation of competing political interests which, with a certain degree of distortion, mirror those in society at large. The political interests within government form shifting patterns of coalitions with each other and with those outside government in order to further their aims through their inputs into policy-making.

THE ECONOMIC ANALYSIS OF PRESSURE GROUPS

To further one's understanding of how political interests affect economic policy-making some key questions need to be considered. Whose interests are reflected in pressure group activity? Are some interests articulated more forcefully than others, so having a greater influence on policy-making? These fundamental issues are addressed by many different perspectives in the social sciences. Here I propose to examine them using the methods of economic analysis, pioneered in particular by Mancur Olson in *The Logic of Collective Action* (1965). From this perspective the key to answering the question of whose interests prevail in pressure group politics is to examine the choices made by rational individuals. What determines the extent to which rational, self-interested individuals can be mobilised to engage in pressure group activity?

Pressure Group Activity as a Collective Good

As explained in Chapter 6, individual action through markets will fail to provide a sufficient quantity of *collective goods* (classified as public, toll or common goods, according to whether they are *non-rivalrous* in consumption or *non-excludable*). Thus there is an incentive for individuals with a common interest in some collective good to come together to obtain its provision. Good examples of such collective action are trade unions, trade associations and business cartels. Workers form a trade union to improve their real wages and working conditions through collective bargaining with employers. Each member of a union incurs membership costs: dues have to be paid to employ trade union officials and finance strike pay; wages have to be sacrificed during strikes and time given up to attend union meetings. These costs are *private* ones. However the benefit of a higher real wage will be enjoyed by all eligible workers; the benefits are *external* to those workers who are not members of the union. There is little economic incentive for an individual to join a union, when he can enjoy the benefits without incurring the costs; and so the union has a *free-rider* problem. It cannot be effective in raising wages without getting a relatively high proportion of the workers to join the union. The same free-rider problem applies to firms setting up a cartel to raise output prices above their competitive level. (The Organisation of Oil Exporting Countries is a prime example.) Any individual firm in the industry will benefit if it cuts its price below the cartel price and gains a higher share of the market. If enough firms do this the cartel collapses.

To eliminate free-riders such organisations press for legislation which enables them to exclude non-members from collective benefits. Trade unions want to be able to enforce closed shop agreements. Professional associations practise similar tactics, though they are generally regarded as more respectable and designed to protect an ignorant public. Professions control entry; for instance the General Medical Council determines who is recognised as a qualified doctor and is highly critical of alternative medicine. The ability of firms to form cartels and engage in restrictive practices has been greatly circumscribed in the UK and the EC over the postwar period, but there still remain many areas where legislation permits or encourages restraints on competition.

The effects of an economic policy measure, such as a cut in a particular tax or an increase in a social benefit payment, or the levying of an import duty, are a public good to the political interest that benefits from it: its benefits are non-rivalrous and non-excludable. Examples of legislation benefiting particular interests are minimum wage laws, the internationally negotiated Multifibre Arrangement which protects the textile industries of developed countries by imposing quotas on cheap imports, and the import controls and government intervention which keep up the prices of agricultural produce.

To secure the introduction of beneficial policy measures the political interest usually has to organise itself as a pressure group to lobby government. This is often a costly activity which has to be paid for by the group's members. An individual or firm will subscribe to these collective costs only if the likely private benefits exceed the individual's share of the pressure group's costs. Ways of overcoming the free-rider problem and thereby increasing membership, are for a pressure group to provide additional private benefits from membership or to raise the costs of non-membership. Hence prior to the welfare state, trade unions provided private benefits such as unemployment insurance and medical care. Nowadays they provide a range of personal services—group discount schemes, financial advice, education and training, and legal aid and advice with employment matters. They raise the cost of non-membership or non-compliance by action against strike-breakers and by securing closed shop agreements.

Sectional pressure groups, more than promotional ones, need to provide their members with more than lobbying. Almost invariably they gather and circulate information useful to their members, as do the CBI and TUC. The Consumer Association's main offering is its magazine *Which?*. Often there is a social element to an organisation's activities, which members enjoy for its own sake. An organisation is less effective in promoting its group interests, the lower the private benefits it can offer its members and the less able it is to impose costs on free-riders. Thus some political interests fail to form pressure groups at all.

This analysis has some telling implications with respect to which political interests will be mobilised and hence influence policy-making. An effective pressure group is more likely to emerge the higher the individual member's benefit from collective action relative to his share of the costs, and the higher his private benefits from the organisation relative to the private costs of not being a member. Hence the smaller the natural constituency the more likely it is to be effectively mobilised because the individual's private benefits from lobbying are a relatively large fraction of the group's total benefits. Hence trade associations of a score or so firms proliferate widely. The more close-knit the interest the easier it is to reach a consensus, in contrast to umbrella organisations such as the CBI and TUC. To counter the weakness of disunity, the effectiveness of large organisations in lobbying government lies in their potential ability to command a lot of votes.

It is frequently noted that producer pressure groups are more numerous and more effective than consumer or general taxpayer groups. This can again be explained by the calculus of individual cost and benefit. The income from an individual's work or business is a very large determinant of his utility, whereas the utility from consuming a particular good or from a small percentage reduction in tax payments is relatively minor. Individuals in producer groups have cheaper access to the relevant information; much of it arises in the course of work and does not have to be especially sought as it does in the case of consumers. Representatives of producer interests are often in contact with politicians and officials as part of their daily work; and some are bureaucrats themselves. Hence trade associations, professional bodies and trade unions are more numerous and more firmly entrenched in the policy-making networks than consumer and taxpayer organisations with much larger constituencies; the latter are latent rather than active political interests. Similarly the recipients of social security payments have a greater incentive to press for higher benefits than have taxpayers to resist the resulting increase in their individual tax bills. The progressivity of income tax can be explained by the preferences of the majority who have modest means. Complex rules governing tax exemptions for specific circumstances abound for taxes paid by the well-off or by companies. For these political interests the individual benefits of lobbying for concessions are high relative to the costs; as is the benefit–cost ratio of acquiring the information needed to take advantage of complex tax rules.

An intriguing aspect of pressure groups is that 'pressure politics is essentially the politics of small groups'.[18] This can be explained, as above, by the calculus of individual costs and benefits. An additional factor is that even when pressure groups do represent a large number of individuals with a common interest, the active members—usually full-time paid officials— who do the lobbying are relatively few. Pressure groups with a large membership are hierarchically organised with local branches—as are trade unions and the CBI, for example. It is the small group of full-time executives who participate in consultation and decision-making. Promotional pressure groups, like the Child Poverty Action Group, Shelter or the National Council for One-Parent Families, are run by a small core of professionals with the backing of academic or political activists. The vast majority of those whose cause is being espoused do not even belong to these groups.

Political representation by voting is equally distributed: each citizen has a vote. Both the cost of using a vote to the individual and the personal benefit thereby attained are low. The extent of political representation by means of pressure group activity is unevenly distributed. The collective costs to an interest group of establishing a pressure group are relatively high, while the ratio of individual costs to benefits varies quite considerably across different political interests. Setting up an effective pressure group is a considerable investment in time and effort, in organising the membership and cultivating channels of influence. Most established sectional interest groups, especially the producer ones, have been around for a long time. Many promotional groups, such as those concerned with welfare services and the environment, are a relatively new phenomenon of the 1960s; but they are largely outsiders. Thus whether an individual finds his particular interests represented by an effective pressure group, depends not so much upon his own willingness and ability to pay the necessary membership costs, but upon the pressure group activities of others, both in the present and in the past. The contention that producer interests dominate consumer interests and that the interests of the specific beneficiaries of state expenditure predominate over those of the general run of taxpayers is supported by both deductive reasoning and observation. The view that some interests predominate over others in economic policy-making is widely held, though opinions as to which political interests wield a disproportionate amount of influence are much more divided. A long-standing view is that it is the interests of those with economic power, either in business or finance, or in trade unions which can impose effective sanctions on others, that have the predominant influence on economic policy.

POLITICAL BARGAINING

The importance of political interests in policy-making renders the rational model of policy-making non-operational. This is because the essential part of any rational decision-making procedure is the establishment by the policy-makers of a clearly agreed set of priorities with respect to the objectives their policy is intended to further. If a policy is being decided by a set of decision-makers, representing diverse and conflicting interests, who therefore have different preferences with respect to the policy objectives, then they cannot agree on their priorities as the first step of their decision-making procedure. This feature of decision-making is fundamental to the way in which the level and composition of government expenditure is decided, as discussed in the British case in Chapter 4. As Richard Crossman, a Labour minister in the 1960s, noted in his *Diaries* about this aspect of policy-making: 'We come briefed by our Departments to fight for our departmental budgets, not as Cabinet Ministers with a Cabinet view.'[19] Had Crossman been an economist he might have said instead that the Cabinet fails to establish a unique preference ordering over its objectives; instead each minister maintains his own preference ordering.

At the end of the day, of course, decisions about expenditure are made by the Cabinet. They are published in the annual public expenditure White Paper and indicate the priorities the Cabinet has agreed. But the major difference between this decision-making process and the rational one, is that the priorities are not clearly agreed and articulated as the first step in deciding on the level and allocation of government spending. They emerge as the outcome of a process of bargaining between ministers, each of whom represents a different set of political interests, which largely reflect those of his particular department. Each minister, to a greater or lesser extent, presses for more spending on his department's programmes in competition with other departments and against the Treasury's own departmental remit to control spending. Ministers who fail to do this, because they attempt to take a less partisan stance and support the general government line on public expenditure, as did Sir Keith Joseph (Secretary of State for Education, 1981–86), are condemned by their policy community for failing to defend their interests.

Decisions about public expenditure emerge from a complex set of interactions between different political interests, within central government and the rest of the public sector, as well as in the private sector. Government departments themselves arbitrate between the competing claims of the political interests in their sphere of influence. Sometimes they act for these interests as their ambassadors with the rest of government and, on other occasions, ignore their demands. Departments use the campaigns of outside pressure groups or indicators of public opinion to support their case. In 1986 the spending departments used the unpopularity of the government in the polls taken early in the year to argue for increased expenditure on the welfare state which was subsequently announced in the Autumn Statement of that year. Priorities are in a constant state of flux, as government reacts to the pressures exerted by many diverse political interests, as they form new coalitions and seek to take advantage of the unfolding sequence of political events. Aspiring rational planners have a hard time making much headway against the swirl of political interests.

Political Bargaining as a Game

The importance of conceptualising a social process is that it enables one to see a common pattern that applies to many instances of the process. With such a framework one is better able to understand and explain how and why outcomes are arrived at. This can be done with *political bargaining* as a policy-making process by conceptualising it as a game played between the relevant political interests. Seeing policy as an outcome of a political bargaining game helps in explaining why a particular policy outcome occurs. This applies both to a single instance of a past policy issue as well as to continuous or repeated policy-making. The model of policy-making as a game, played by political interests, suggests a number of key questions: the answers to these help in explaining how and why policy outcomes occur.

The first question determines what the game is about. This involves establishing who the players are, which political interests are involved and what their objectives are. In some issues, say, the determination of public spending, it would be impossible to catalogue all the political interests involved, but one can specify the major ones—the Treasury, the government departments, local authorities, public corporations and their respective clients, and the members of the governing party. The task is somewhat simpler if a more limited policy issue is examined, say, the liberalisation of shopping hours; making the coal industry more efficient; or restructuring the social security system (examined in Chapter 13).

Another feature of the game is the relative strengths of the players, and what resources can they use in order to further their objectives. As policy decisions are the result of some form of agreement between the political interests, concluded after a process of bargaining, what each interest has to exchange with the others in return for what it wants is important in determining the outcome. The economic analysis of pressure groups indicates the conditions under which a political interest can be effectively mobilised. A legitimate political interest is accorded this status because it has something useful to offer government in exchange for its access to policy-making. The more firmly entrenched is a political interest in the internal governmental processes of policy-making, the greater is its influence on policy outcomes. Political bargaining, even with legitimate pressure groups, can be conducted with considerable animosity, as in the miners' strike or even the teachers' disputes. The bargains involve the exchange of threats; hence, how much damage one side can inflict on the other is a bargaining resource. A government's chief weapons are money and laws; their protagonists' is their refusal to work. Both vie for general public support as the ultimate source of the votes which grant legislative and public spending powers.

Another factor which determines the outcome of the game are the rules which govern the procedures by which decisions are made. For example, the rules of the game which govern the PESC system of government budgeting are very different from those which exist in the USA. In Britain central government decides overall budget allocations and the Chancellor of the Exchequer is the major decision-maker with regard to tax changes. This means that the political interests have no direct access to budgetary decisions. They have to lobby government departments or create a climate of opinion in their favour through Parliament and the media. In the USA, Congress make the budget decisions. The President puts his proposals to them and has to lobby congressmen as do all the political interests outside government. In the coal dispute the rules of the game included the NUM rules regarding the power to call miners out on strike. Because a national ballot was not held to obtain the required majority for a strike the Nottingham area weakened the strike by continuing to work. The government's new employment legislation limited secondary picketing and enabled the courts to sequestrate NUM funds.

The rules of the game are an important factor in determining how the game is played. Part of the skill of the players is using the rules to their own advantage. The teachers, for instance, found that withdrawing from non-contractual duties was a form of industrial action which lost them no pay and gave them more free time. The established partnership of teachers, local authorities and central government in managing education, determining its funding and establishing teachers' pay has so far severely constrained the DES in its attempts to implement its policies. Another aspect of playing the game skilfully is forming coalitions with other political interests on a particular issue, as in the Shops Bill case. Coalitions between political interests are sometimes permanent, though quite often they are temporary alliances with respect to a specific issue. A very common coalition is that between unions and companies in an industry pressing the government for import protection or subsidies.

Typical examples of such coalitions occur on the industry sector working parties of the National Economic Development Office. The management representatives on the Consumer Electronics Sector Working Party come from the firms who belong to the industry's trade association—the British Radio and Electronic Equipment Manufacturers Association. In 1977 BREEMA and the industry's unions jointly agitated against the plans of the Japanese firm, Hitachi, to enter the industry by building a TV assembly plant on a greenfield site in a development area in Durham. The local politicians and local trade unions welcomed the plans, as did the Department of Industry which wished to encourage foreign direct investment. As there was some 40 per cent excess capacity in the industry, the established manufacturers in BREEMA and their unions campaigned against the Hitachi plan on the grounds that existing jobs in their TV assembly and components factories would be lost. Consequently, Hitachi withdrew its plans and eventually took over GCE's loss-making TV assembly plant in Wales. BREEMA and the associated unions also used their channels of influence via NEDO and the Department(s) of Trade and Industry[20] to secure import protection. In 1977 they succeeded in getting a three-year import quota placed on monochrome TVs from Taiwan and South Korea, although such discriminatory measures are a violation of the GATT rules. Since the import quotas lapsed BREEMA has reached an annual agreement with these countries to limit their exports 'voluntarily'. Exporters comply with these restraints because the alternative may be UK government- or EC-sanctioned import restrictions.

A significant feature of the political bargaining game is how often the game is played. Some policy issues are discrete events; say, the conditions attached to the privatisation of a particular public corporation. Others occur at regular intervals, as does the PESC budgeting round or the annual setting of agricultural prices by the EC. Some games are replayed at irregular intervals or in slightly different contexts—the miners' dispute, for example. In highly regular, frequently repeated games the rules are usually clearly laid down. The players are familiar with the rules and with each other's strengths and weaknesses. The number of times a game is to be played affects the players' tactics. Moves which invite an unacceptable retaliation are not attractive tactics in repeated games. So spending ministers are reluctant to attack other spending ministers' bids for money. In repeated games players have a greater need to develop a degree of trust in the other players so that they have better information on what can be exchanged. Government departments do not bid for budgets to the Treasury greatly in excess of what they realistically hope to secure since such discrepancies are detected after several replays and would adversely affect the budgets in subsequent rounds.

The extent to which policy decisions are formed by political bargaining is itself one important rule, which differs over policy areas or between countries. For instance the US system of federal government budgeting allows greater scope for political interests to wield their influence than does the British system. The large US budget deficit that emerged in the early 1980s, and is set to continue into the 1990s, resulted from President Reagan's desire to reduce taxes combined with the reluctance of Congress to cut expenditure.[21]

The larger the policy-making community, the more political interests it contains and the more divergent those interests, the less likely it is that rational decision-making procedures can prevail or agreement be reached quickly. So, for instance, decisions about monetary policy are taken by a relatively small set of policy-makers. Only its broader context, which determines the general stance of government macroeconomic policy, is subject to a wide set of political influences. It is notable that reform of the Common Agricultural Policy (discussed in Chapter 14), which requires the consensus of twelve states, is very slow to appear, despite the mounting budgetary crisis that it is causing.

Some aspects of policy-making are much more insulated from the interaction of political interests than others. This can be a deliberate policy choice or be result of historical accident. For example, as Chapter 11 discusses, the extent to which the activities of commercial enterprises should be governed by political bargaining has been debated for decades. The establishment of public corporations, supposedly independent of government departments, was intended to limit their exposure to political bargaining. Taking decisions out of the political arena and giving them to specialist bureaucracies is an attempt to increase the degree of rationality in their decision-making. Another way to reduce the exposure of allocative decisions to political bargaining is to place them in the market. For some this is a justification of privatising public corporations.

IS POLITICAL BARGAINING A GOOD POLICY-MAKING MECHANISM?

Calls for more democratic decision-making, for more people to participate in policy-making and for more open public debate prior to policy decisions, are frequent and appealing rhetoric. But is extending the role of political interests in policy-making necessarily beneficial? Two distinct strands of thinking have developed. One, associated with *pluralism*, is favourably disposed to pressure groups; the other, partly though not exclusively related to *libertarian* thinking, regards them with a more jaundiced eye.

Pluralism

Pluralist thought developed in the nineteenth century, attained ascendency in the USA in the 1950s, since when it has retreated. It developed as a reaction against the idea of a sovereign monolithic state whose task is to promote a common conception of the national interest. Pluralists fear that such a state, even if the powers of government rest on winning a majority in free elections, will disregard the legitimate interests of the many diverse groups in society. Pluralists believe that citizens' liberty can only be protected against state tyranny by the existence of a multitude of interest groups which mediate between their individual members and the state. The role of the government is to hold the ring, to legitimate and operate the rules of the political bargaining game. It is not the government's task to impose a single view of what is the public interest; its role is to arbitrate between the diverse interests and to help in resolving conflicts.

As with all schools of thought, the pluralists' normative ideas of how society *should* be organised are closely linked with their positive views of how it actually *does* operate. Pluralists conceive of society as an organism made up of interacting groups—as 'a society of societies'. As stated by a leading pluralist, 'Pressure is always a group phenomenon. It indicates the push and resistance between groups. The balance of group pressures *is* the existing state of society'.[22] Thus pluralists see policy as the outcome of the interaction of many political interests. The more sanguine of them also believe that in liberal democracies all legitimate interests can have an impact on policy-making. If an issue is sufficiently important to the interests of a particular group, it is able to organise itself and thereby pressure government. All interests have some resources to mobilise—if not money then numbers—and so can influence policy-making.

In their normative prescriptions for how policy-making should be conducted, pluralists stress the desirable characteristics of the policy-making process itself, and not its outcomes. What is important is how policy is made rather than what actual policy is adopted. For the political system to deliver acceptable policies it is crucial that the vast majority of political interests accept the procedures whereby policy is made, and thereby acquiesce to policy outcomes they dislike. They are prepared to do this if they can participate in the policy-making process. In terms of the game analogy, it is important that all the players agree with the rules of the game and hence accept losing a game with good grace. Provided a political interest wins some games or scores some points in losing games, it is prepared to carry on playing under the rules. In this way all interests accept the legitimacy of government. Good policies are those that command agreement rather than those that achieve a given set of objectives efficiently.

Corporatism

Related to pluralism, but distinct from it, is *corporatism*, discussed in Chapter 2. Corporatism stresses the importance of economic interests. Those who control production on both sides of industry wield the greatest power. The prescriptive conclusions from this are that economic policy cannot be successfully implemented unless it is accepted by the major economic interests. For government to secure this consensus, the economic interests need to be organised by means of a well-defined hierarchical network so that government can bargain with a few representatives of the peak labour and management organisations. A corporatist system of policy-making cannot operate successfully unless the peak interest representatives can deliver the policies negotiated with government by securing the compliance of their members. For this to occur the representatives must be able to reflect effectively the interests of their constituent members, so that their bargains are accepted and implemented by their membership. These aspects are mutually reinforcing, since the more important is the corporatist element in policy-making, the greater the incentive for individual members to belong to their interest organisation and to comply with its requirements.

Incomes Policy

Corporatism has featured most strongly in the UK with respect to incomes policy. This is a prime example of an area where there are external and hence collective benefits from individual action but no discernible private benefits. Each individual trade union member benefits by obtaining an increase in his money wages. However, when all unions are doing this and prices rise as a consequence, the increases in real wages are nullified. But if any single union desists from pressing for the maximum wage increase it can secure, when others do not, its members' incomes would fall relative to those of others. If all practised wage restraint there would be general benefits in terms of lower inflation or unemployment.

A general agreement to desist from raising wages and prices is one way of resolving the problem. Between 1961 and 1978 Conservative and Labour governments tried various kinds of prices and incomes policy, both statutory and voluntary. Some statutory policies were successfully resisted by trade unions, while voluntary policies needed union–government accords, with unions naturally requiring something in return. For example, under the so-called 'social contract' of 1974–78, the unions promised wage restraint in return for favourable labour legislation and increased expenditures on the welfare state. By 1978 the unions could no longer assure wage constraint. In the view of the then Labour Chief Secretary to the Treasury, Joel Barnett, 'the only give and take in the contract was the government gave and the unions took'.[23] The CBI also tried to deliver a prices policy to the Heath government in 1971 by committing its members to limit price increases to no more than 5 per cent, but inflation rose to 10 per cent.

In the 1980s leaders of the Labour Party have been trying to secure some form of TUC agreement on incomes policy. The term itself is anathema to many trade unionists, and so has gone under vague pseudonyms, like a national economic assessment, to indicate that unions would get a say in macroeconomic policy making as a *quid pro quo*. It is notable that the Alliance, which has no corporatist links with the unions, recommends using taxation of excessive wage increases as the best incomes policy instrument. Their general policy stance, however, with its emphasis on consensus and working together, is distinctly pluralist with strong corporatist undertones. Corporatists thus seek to make a virtue of the existence of political interests, enhancing and harnessing their power by incorporating them more fully and directly into economic policy-making.

A Critique of Pressure Groups

The economic analysis of pressure groups casts them in a much more malign light than do pluralists and corporatists. Olson deduces that pressure groups are primarily concerned with redistributing national income in their favour rather than with increasing it. If a pressure group is relatively small then it would only get a very small share of any increase in overall national income that it achieved by its actions. However it will appropriate most, if not all, of any redistribution of national income in its favour. Given the earlier deduction that numerically small interests have a greater economic incentive to get mobilised, it follows that pressure groups are largely concerned with distribution and not with efficiency. In fact producer pressure groups are likely to obstruct efficiency improvements because of the welfare losses they bring to producers using old technologies and producing old-fashioned goods. If this kind of assessment is correct then political bargaining is a zero or negative sum game: all the winner's gains are taken from the losers and the total gains may even be less than the sum of the losses. In contrast, in a positive sum game, the net result of play is that the winners' gains exceed the losers' losses. Thus 'on balance, special interest organisations and collusions reduce efficiency and aggregate income in the societies in which they operate and make political life more divisive'.[24]

Other condemnations of deleterious effects of pressure group politics have relied on political or sociological analysis, such as Samuel Beer's *Britain Against Itself.* He diagnoses the problem as 'pluralist stagnation' which manifests itself in various ways. Attempts at reform are blocked by too many interests defending the status quo; because there are so many fragmented interests there is no incentive for any one group to incur costs in order to bring collective benefits or to refrain from immediate short-run benefits which will give rise to collective costs in the future. Hence the scramble for higher money wages, and for grants and subsidies from the state, which in totality are self-defeating and turn politics into a zero or negative sum game.

CONCLUSION

Chapters 7 and 8 considered how the transmission of voters' preferences can be distorted at two points in the transmission chain—between voters and politicians, and between politicians and bureaucrats—and thus permits politicians' and bureaucrats' preferences to influence policy. This chapter has added another factor—political interest activity—which operates alongside the voting system as an additional means for bringing the preferences of different interests to bear on policy-making. The nature of pressure groups and their activities were described to show how they impinge on policy-making. Of particular importance is the observation that government is itself a conglomeration of interests, some competing and some in coalition with each other. A particular political interest is often represented both inside government and without, thus forming a policy-making community for a specific area of policy, like farming, banking or education. Bargaining occurs both within a policy-making community and between them.

There are considerable differences of opinion as to whether political interest activity enhances or detracts from the functioning of representative democracy. On the positive side pressure groups enable citizens to express their policy preferences with greater selectivity than voting for politicians does. In addition it permits the signalling of intensity of preference, since the greater the desire for some policy the more this will be reflected in pressure group agitation. Pressure groups mediate between the individual and the state, and so prevent the majority from denying liberties and resources to minority interests. Pressure groups are also useful to government; they provide information which helps government to formulate and implement viable policies, which have the support of those who operate them and those who are affected by them.

On the negative side, political interest activity is seen as distorting the pattern of citizen preferences that would be revealed by voting. In contrast to votes which are equally distributed, the power of interest groups to influence policy is unequally distributed. This point is argued from a variety of perspectives. Here I have selected the economic analysis of politics (or public choice theory) to deduce that producers—including bureaucrats—are better represented than consumers; as are the beneficiaries of specific public sector programmes or tax expenditures relative to tax payers in general. Pressure groups are held to be primarily concerned with redistributing social welfare in their favour and so are engaged in a zero or negative sum game, which is mutually self-defeating. They are accused of inhibiting efficiency gains and clogging up the political mechanism, thereby preventing the enactment of policies which could improve economic performance.

The significance of political interests indicates that economic policy-making is conducted as a political bargaining game, rather than being a rational decision-making procedure. This is because government is itself a collection of diverse interests, competing for limited financial and legislative resources. Consequently the policy-makers cannot agree a consistent set of priorities for their objectives and so cannot undertake the first essential step for a rational decision-making process. Instead policy instruments are selected and implemented while the debate over priorities continues.

However, the primary role of economics and economists in policy-making is in providing the knowledge and techniques required to conduct rational decision making. The role of economists as technocrats, employed to exercise their professional expertise acquired from the study and practice of economics as a specialist discipline, is examined in the following chapter.

NOTES

1. P. Shipley, *Directory of Pressure Groups* (Bowker, Essex, 1979).
2. D. Henderson, *Innocence and Design* (Basil Blackwell, Oxford, 1986), pp. 8–9.
3. CBI, *Working With Politicians* (CBI, London, 1985), p.3.
4. Shipley, op. cit.
5. A much quoted and excellent definition of politics is 'those interactions by which values are authoritatively allocated for a society'; D. Easton, *A Systems Analysis of Political Life* (London, 1965), p. 21.
6. *Financial Times*, 11 December 1985.
7. CBI, op. cit., p. 41.
8. J.P. Mackintosh, *The Government and Politics of Britain* (Hutchinson, London, 1982), p. 29.
9. G. Wootton, *Pressure Politics in Contemporary Britain* (D.C. Heath, Lexington, Mass., 1978).
10. *Financial Times*, 29 March 1986.

11. *Financial Times*, 17 December 1985.
12. *Financial Times*, 24 February 1986.
13. *Financial Times*, 23 December 1985.
14. Charter For Jobs, *We Can Cure Unemployment* (London, 1985).
15. R.D. Coates, *Teachers Unions and Interest Group Politics* (Cambridge University Press, Cambridge, 1972).
16. B. Castle, *The Castle Diaries 1974−76* (Weidenfeld and Nicolson, London, 1980), p. 459.
17. National Childcare Campaign, *Annual Report*, 1985.
18. Mancur Olson, *The Logic of Collective Action* (Harvard University Press, Cambridge, Mass., 1965), p. 145.
19. R. Crossman, *The Diaries of a Cabinet Minister* (Hamish Hamilton, London, 1975), vol. 1, p. 275.
20. They were then separate departments.
21. For a racy account of US political bargaining games over the federal budget, see D.A. Stockman, *The Triumph of Politics* (The Bodley Head, London, 1986).
22. A.J. Bentley, *The Process of Government* (Principia Press, Evanston Ill., 1949), pp. 258−9.
23. Joel Barnett, *Inside the Treasury* (André Deutsch, London, 1982), p. 49.
24. M. Olson, *The Rise and Decline of Nations* (Yale University Press, New Haven, Conn., 1982), p. 74.

10 Economists: the Rational Optimisers

The crucial issue of principle is whether there can be, and whether there ought to be, economic criteria that are entirely independent of political decisions. If it can be cogently argued that there can, and ought to be such criteria then there is nothing absurd or perverse in the economist's declaring a policy to be economically inefficient even though it is approved of by the electorate. (E. Mishan, *Introduction to Political Economy* (Hutchinson, London, 1982), p. 26)

Once the economist knows the aggregation rule and once he knows what function is to be maximised, then he can apply his standard tools for the optimisation of social choice. (C.V. Brown and P.M. Jackson, *Public Sector Economics* (Martin Robertson, Oxford, 1982), p. 67)

Saying that a policy is optimal implies that it is the policy which is preferred to all other possible policies. Since individuals have different preferences, one person's optimal policy may be a long way from best as far as another individual is concerned. Optimal economic policy therefore implies agreement as to the preferences that are to govern policy choices. Such agreement should involve compromise among the different preferences held by different individuals. (Committee on Policy Optimisation)[1]

The aim of any evaluation process is to identify objectives and to assess the extent to which these objectives are attained. In an economic evaluation the most satisfactory way of assessing the preferences of individuals is, where possible, by direct observation of their behaviour. This provides a guide to how people evaluate one thing against another. . . .Where it is impractical to obtain values in this way, we believe that it is nonetheless good discipline to quantify the effects in whatever units are appropriate, and thus reduce the number of arbitrary value judgements which would otherwise need to be imported into the assessment. (Sir G. Leitch, *Report of the Advisory Committee on Trunk Road Assessment* (HMSO, London, 1978))

These quotations are all about economic policy as an exercise in rational decision-making aimed at devising socially optimal government interventions. This view of what economic policy is about typifies the approach of economics to policy problems. This chapter outlines the

214

economist's theory of economic policy as a rational exercise by which policy-makers aim at maximising social welfare. To do this they search for and then employ those policy instruments which best achieve the policy-makers' objectives. A fundamental problem is discovering which objectives policy ought to be directed at, because this inevitably means deciding whose preferences should be satisfied. The problem of deriving policy objectives from the preferences of citizens has for long preoccupied welfare economists. Some of the major approaches to this problem are outlined at the start of this chapter. This treatment builds upon and extends the economic analysis presented in Chapters 3 and 6 on the concept of *social efficiency*.

The technique of *cost-benefit analysis*, touched upon in Chapter 3, is an attempt to make the concept of *social efficiency* applicable to practical policy problems of resource allocation. How well it has fared when exposed to bureaucratic and political realities is examined, using the Department of Transport's trunk road appraisal procedures and the 1970 Roskill Inquiry into the third London airport as case-studies. These cases reveal quite clearly that a rational optimising technique does not win general acceptability as a depoliticised decision-making tool which can insulate an area of public sector resource allocation from political bargaining. Similar tensions between the demands of rational policy-making and the invasiveness of political bargaining, are discussed in relation to *economic planning*.

The desire to improve the efficiency with which economic policies are delivered to citizens is an ever-present element of policy-making. The rise of quantitative economics in the 1950s and 1960s held the promise that its techniques would be a significant advance to this end. This optimism was misplaced due to the problems of quantifying social efficiency and the lack of a consensus in favour of the value judgements upon which the concept is based. In the 1980s the techniques of the accountant and the management consultant are to the fore in government attempts to secure 'economy, efficiency and effectiveness'. These attempts are assessed towards the end of the chapter in order to contrast them with the rational techniques emanating from the concept of *social efficiency*.

THE THEORY OF ECONOMIC POLICY

What economists call *the theory of economic policy* conceives of policy-making as a rational procedure by which policy-makers aim for their most preferred outcome given the constraints imposed on them by factors beyond their control. This optimising model of economic policy consists of two distinct elements, one subjective and the other objective in nature. The subjective part of the model is the preferences of the policy makers—the objectives they have in mind and the priorities they attach to different objectives which have to be traded off against one another. Inevitably, this involves making value judgements about whose preferences and interests economic policy should serve. The branch of economics concerned with what policy choices ought to be made is known as *normative economics*: it forms the purely subjective part of the theory of economic policy. In technical language its focus of concern is devising an expression for *social welfare* for the policy-makers to maximise. As explained in Chapter 6, *social welfare* relates to the *utility* members of society receive from the consumption of goods and services, broadly interpreted to include intangible items like the environment and the well-being of others. This relationship between social welfare and its determinants is called a *social welfare function*.

But knowing how to benefit the chosen sections of society requires objective knowledge of the relevant economic relationships. Faith and ideology are insufficient for effective action. If a government wants to reduce inflation or make income distribution more equal it needs to know the most effective means of pursuing its objectives. This kind of knowledge is provided by the study of *positive economics* which is concerned with explaining and predicting the behaviour of economic agents and hence, that of whole economies or sectors. Positive economics provides policy-makers with information about which economic variables can be manipulated as policy instruments to achieve given objectives, and attempts to quantify the changes required. Economists' models of how the economy and its constituent sectors function also provide information on the constraints which limit what policy-makers can do. However, positive economics is not value-free; an economist's ethical judgements of what constitute good social arrangements influence how he interprets the evidence available from theoretical and empirical work in economics and other disciplines. This is especially so when, due to the absence of laboratory testing, the empirical validity of economic propositions is difficult to establish with great confidence.

In order to apply the theory of economic policy-making two sets of information are required. The first set concerns the *social welfare function*, the derivation of which is the province of normative economics, as it necessarily involves making value judgements about preferences. The second set of information is on the constraints that existing economic relationships, or the way the economy works, place on the policy-makers' ability to maximise *social welfare*. The economic relationships which policy-makers have to accept as unalterable determine the set of feasible policy alternatives from which they choose the one which maximises (or optimises) social welfare. As this book concentrates on economic policy-making it is not particularly concerned with the information provided by positive economics (much of it controversial) on the way economies function. This is the subject matter of most economics textbooks and can be readily found there. Suffice it to say here that the absence of an agreed body of knowledge about how the economy actually works, together with different conceptions of the good society, gives rise to fundamental disagreements about the conduct of economic policy. So dissension between *Keynesians* and *monetarists* on how the economy should be managed are related to different perceptions of how government expenditure, taxation and the money supply affect economic activity. These do not necessarily have any direct connection with value judgements about the importance of personal liberty relative to securing equality through government intervention, though there is a distinct tendency for monetarists to favour *libertarian* ideals.

THE PROBLEM OF DEFINING A SOCIAL WELFARE FUNCTION

A central and continuing problem in normative economics is deriving an acceptable *social welfare function* for the policy-makers to maximise. Should such a welfare function reflect the preferences of individual citizens and, if so, how are their preferences to be aggregated? Or should the policy-makers themselves define a social welfare function on behalf of society? The presumption of most economists, who belong to the mainstream of the discipline, is that the social welfare function (i.e. the preferences of society with respect to the objectives of economic policy) should reflect the preferences of individual citizens, rather than be determined by a holistic concept of the national interest or the will of the people. The political system, as well as the market, are devices for transmitting individuals' preferences into allocative outcomes. Hence economists' predisposition to individualism is not necessarily associated with a prior preference for the market. Most economists, other than adherents of the *Austrian school*, consider that there are widespread *market failures* which justify government intervention, but that such intervention should be designed to reflect the preferences of individual citizens.

An Individual's Utility Function
Individuals have different preferences and this gives rise to the fundamental problem underlying collective decision-making of deriving a social welfare function which reflects the preferences of the individuals who make up society. An individual's welfare function, or *utility function*, is relatively easy to define. Preferences for different combinations of goods and their

distribution amongst the various members of society can be readily represented by a *utility function*: the individual's *utility* or satisfaction depends on the quantities of the various goods consumed and may include the utility or disutility derived from other people's consumption. For choices involving two goods the utility function can be depicted diagrammatically, as in Figure 10.1, by means of *indifference curves*.

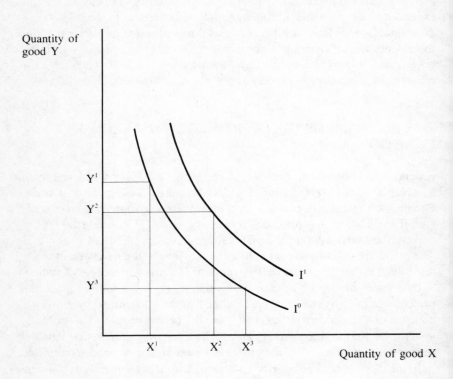

Figure 10.1: Indifference curves for an individual

Each *indifference curve* shows all the combinations of two goods, X and Y, which give the individual the same level of utility because they are equally preferred. Thus combination X^1,Y^1 is equally preferred to combination X^3,Y^3; the individual is indifferent between the two bundles. However combination X^2,Y^2 is preferred to either bundle X^1,Y^1 or bundle X^3,Y^3: indifference curve I^1 indicates combinations of X and Y which give a higher level of utility than the combinations along I^0.

We can combine information about an individual's preferences for policies which deliver different quantities of goods, with objective information about the constraints on the choice of goods bundles given by the productive capacity of the economy. The production constraint is represented in Figure 10.2 by a *production possibility curve*, P^1P^2, identical to the one in Figure 6.1 (see page 114). Now, given information about the individual's preferences, and assuming a one-person economy, it is possible to define an *optimal allocation* of goods. It is the quantities of X and Y that the individual prefers above all the other combinations that are available given the production constraints. The *optimal allocation* in Figure 10.2 occurs where the production possibility curve, P^1, P^2, just touches or is tangential to the indifference curve. Thus the *optimal allocation* is combination X^2, Y^2 on indifference curve I^1. This is the highest indifference curve that can be reached, given the production constraint. The individual's utility is maximised with X^2 units of good X and Y^2 units of good Y.

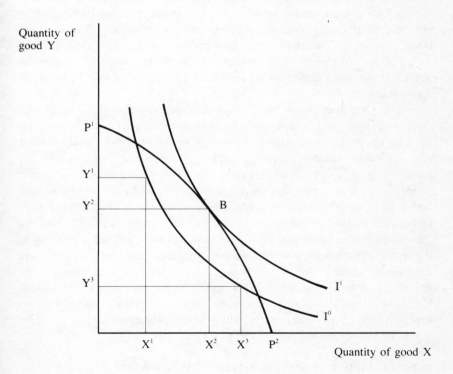

Figure 10.2: The optimum allocation of goods for an individual

Deriving a Social Welfare Function From Individuals' Preferences

Reaching an *optimal allocation* of goods for an economy composed of two or more people is more problematic. As a first step we need to derive a *utility function*, or *social welfare function*, for society as a whole. This social welfare function could be represented in the two-goods case by a set of indifference curves. But this cannot be done without making some value judgements about how one is to reconcile the different preferences of the individual members of society. This requires agreement on the basic principles that should govern the rule whereby the preferences of the individual members of society are aggregated into a social welfare function that represents collective preferences. One such principle is the democratic one that each citizen's preferences should have equal weight, as ensured by giving everyone the same number of votes to register their preferences for the different bundles of goods and services. To ensure equality of influence no one individual should be able to determine policy choices by having his/her preferences dominate over others. In other words, there should be no dictatorship. Another common desideratum is that the social welfare function should be a *consistent* ordering or ranking of preferences. If society prefers policy outcome A to outcome B and prefers B to C, then to be *consistent* it must then prefer A to C and not rank C above A. Yet another principle, which welfare economists have favoured, is avoiding making judgements about which individuals' preferences should be favoured above those of others.

In 1951, Kenneth Arrow[2] showed mathematically that it is not always possible to aggregate individuals' preferences by means of majority voting in order to obtain a social welfare function which does not violate at least one desirable ethical property, such as consistency or absence of dictatorship. Majority voting, as an aggregation rule, has undesirable properties; it is often possible for one individual to dictate to others because he has the casting vote and so can bargain with each side to secure the most favourable outcome for himself. Majority voting can also lead to inconsistent preference rankings or to rankings which differ according to the order in which the alternatives are compared and voted on. (This is known as cycling.) The implications of Arrow's work is that even if we know the detailed preferences of individuals, we cannot in general aggregate them by majority voting in order to obtain a social welfare function, unless we make some value judgements about which ethically desirable properties we are willing to forgo.

A Social Welfare Function Based on Policy-Makers' Preferences

There have been two broad responses to the problem of deriving an ethically acceptable social welfare function by aggregating individuals' preferences through voting. One is to abandon the attempt to relate the social welfare function to individual citizens' preferences and, instead, to base it on the preferences of the policy-making elite, who are presumed to act as philosopher-kings in judging what is best for society. For some, the philosopher-kings are not politicians but planners—bureaucrats who are specialised technicians in planning the economy and designing optimal forms of state intervention. Other scenarios presume that policy should be based on the preferences of politicians who have been elected to office.

The Committee on Policy Optimisation,[3] reporting in 1978, grappled somewhat inconclusively with the problem of establishing a social welfare function, or criterion function as they called it. Here is a sample of their deliberations:

How is acceptable compromise among the many conflicting preferences of the people in the United Kingdom to be achieved? Discussion of optimal economic policy often assumes that it is the task of the Chancellor of the Exchequer to form reasoned preferences. These preferences should obviously not reflect simply his personal tastes, or his individual economic interests, but would embody his considered opinion about the best interests of the nation, . . .different ways of determining his criterion function have been proposed. One method is to put him on a couch and ask him a series of hypothetical questions. For instance he might be asked whether, at a stated level of unemployment and rate of inflation, he would prefer a 1 per cent decrease in the rate of inflation to a 1 per cent decrease in the level of unemployment. Armed with his replies the technicians in the Treasury should be able to construct the Chancellor's criterion function. This scheme has been seriously proposed to us in evidence, but the Committee were not convinced that it would be feasible for reasons we explain below. . .

As we have been told in evidence by politicians, and civil servants, who have worked closely with ministers, Chancellors would not commit themselves on hypothetical questions. It is easy to see why. If the Chancellor's criterion function became known, as it easily might, his actions could be anticipated, and argument about the appropriateness of the criterion, in the Cabinet, in Parliament, and in the country at large, could inhibit its use without replacing it by anything equally decisive.

Whatever the difficulties of constructing a criterion function on the basis of the Chancellor's preferences, there remains the more fundamental problem that the criterion function should represent the national interest . . ..The goals of national economic policy vary from one interest group to another. . .. There are those who see the essential role of the democratic process as the resolution of these competing goals. . .. But complete agreement on a single national criterion function is not to be expected. Debate about the ends of national policy should never end. But our system of government makes it possible for us in effect to agree to adopt national goals, which may be changed from time to time as the balance of opinion changes, or as knowledge and understanding increases. A national criterion function would be no more, and no less, than such an expression of goals. If formulated its use should be the outcome of parliamentary democracy. . .

Most of the evidence took it as axiomatic that a satisfactory representation of the national welfare could not be arrived at. Other evidence was, however, not quite as pessimistic. The optimists argued that, under the present system, the Chancellor announces planning strategies and budgetary measures which, he claims, are in the best interests of the nation. Although these policies are not derived by using any explicit criterion function, there must nevertheless implicitly be some underlying criterion function. The Chancellor does and says things which must have a rational basis; if we could uncover this basis we would then have a criterion function. (pp. 60–3)

The Policy Optimisation Committee's discussion of deriving a social welfare function ranges from using the preferences of a single minister to those conveyed through the institutions of representative democracy which, as we saw in Chapter 7, imperfectly reflect individual citizens' preferences for different policies. Between these two poles, the social welfare function could be derived from the preferences of Cabinet ministers acting jointly as a single decision-maker, or from those of civil servants or professional bureaucrats who, it may be argued, are able to take a long-term and non-partisan view of social welfare.

The Pareto Criterion for Maximum Social Welfare
The alternative to deriving the social welfare function on the basis of the preferences of politicians and bureaucrats, is to maintain that the preferences of individual citizens are paramount. But as these preferences cannot be reliably aggregated into a consistent and non-dictatorial social welfare function, economists have fallen back on the *Pareto criterion*, introduced in Chapters 3 and 6. According to the Pareto criterion, an allocation of resources is socially optimal if any movement away from it would make at least one individual worse off. If it is possible to make one or more people better off without harming anybody else, then the current allocation of resources is not Pareto optimal as it is possible to improve social welfare. The Pareto criterion has considerable appeal to economists because it avoids making value judgements about whether some people should be made worse off in order to make others better off. A policy which makes some individuals better off and others worse off is not an improvement in social welfare according to the Pareto criterion. To say that such a redistributive policy is socially optimal would require one to compare different individuals' utility and decide on whom one wished to favour. The Pareto criterion is designed specifically to avoid making such interpersonal comparisons of utility.

However the Pareto criterion has several drawbacks. One is that a Pareto-optimal resource allocation may well be judged as distributionally inequitable by those not averse to making interpersonal comparisons of utility. The alternative is to derive a social welfare function on the basis of explicit value judgements about the desirability of different income distributions. These judgements may be personal ones or they may reflect the preferences of economic planners or elected representatives for the welfare of society. A further drawback to the Pareto criterion is that it requires unanimity before a policy can be undertaken. So long as even one individual is worse off as the result of a policy proposal, he can veto it. Obtaining unanimity lengthens the time-scale and increases the transactions costs of collective decision-making The bias is towards inaction.

The Net Social Benefit Criterion of a Potential Pareto Improvement

In order to make the Pareto criterion operational for policy purposes, economists have adopted the *social efficiency criterion*, already discussed in Chapters 3 and 6. A *socially efficient* policy choice is one which yields a sum of social benefits to individuals in excess of the social costs it imposes on the same or on other individuals. If the total social benefits exceed the sum of social costs, then it is in principle possible for the beneficiaries to compensate the losers fully and still be better off. However, this compensation need not occur for the policy to be deemed socially efficient: all that is required is a *potential Pareto improvement*, not an actual one. Thus interpersonal comparisons *are* made under the social efficiency criterion. It is judged that £1 is valued equally regardless of who receives it or who pays it. As utility is measured in money terms, it can be summed up or *aggregated* over different individuals.

Thus the ethical premises of this type of social cost-benefit analysis are that individuals' preferences count, individuals are the best judges of their own welfare, and individual utility can be measured in terms of money and thus aggregated. Individuals' utility from consuming a good or service is measured either by the amount of money they are prepared to pay for it, or by the amount of money compensation they need in order to be deprived of the good but feel as well-off as before. These valuations of individual and social welfare are not independent of income distribution, since what a person is prepared to pay for something, or be compensated for doing without it, depends on her existing income.

Social cost-benefit analysis is a technique developed by economists to enable policy-makers to reach socially efficient allocations of resources when market failure in any of its forms makes market prices an inappropriate signal for such decisions. The technique has been developed and applied over a number of years by the Department of Transport in deciding where and how to build or improve trunk roads. This serves as a useful case-study for examining the strengths and limitations of a technique for rational economic policy-making.

COST-BENEFIT ANALYSIS AND TRUNK ROAD APPRAISAL

Roads are a *public good*, as defined in Chapter 6, in that their benefits are *non-rivalrous* until congestion occurs, while the expense of excluding users by charging tolls is too great to be worthwhile except on certain popular or long-distance routes. In Britain, there are no direct charges for using public roads (apart from some bridges and tunnels), so there is no direct market indicator, in the form of prices, to measure how much users value an existing or proposed road. Furthermore the costs and benefits of a road scheme are unevenly distributed. A new motorway confers a number of benefits such as speedier journeys for road users, lowering transport costs for manufactured goods and improved conditions on roads from which traffic is diverted. The costs, in the form of noise, disruption, destruction of housing or farmland, and landscape despoliation are borne mainly by local people or by environmentalists concerned at the loss of attractive views and natural habitats. Some of these costs—noise, disruption or landscape despoliation—are *externalities* and cannot be directly costed by the market-setting prices for them.

Thus, a decision to invest in a new motorway involves balancing the conflicting interests of those who lose against those who benefit. Furthermore, if the allocation of resources to road building is to be socially efficient then the government must avoid incurring social costs arising from road building and maintenance which exceed the total amount road users would be willing to pay for the resulting benefits they enjoy. It must also provide or maintain all roads which the beneficiaries value in excess of the roads' social costs. As part of a rational decision-making procedure for taking road investment decisions, the Department of Transport has, since 1967, developed a computerised system of cost-benefit analysis, called COBA. By applying COBA the Department quantifies those social benefits and costs of a proposed road scheme which it considers amenable to measurement in terms of money.

The ethical premise underlying COBA is the standard individualistic one of most cost-benefit analysis. This is that social costs and benefits are the sum of individuals' costs and benefits as measured by the affected individuals' willingness to pay. Some of the costs are private and can be measured in market prices. This applies to the costs of acquiring the land for a new road, and of constructing and maintaining it by employing private sector contractors. However, the benefits are not valued by market prices because no charges are made for using a road. In principle, as a road is a public good, the total social benefit from a proposed motorway is the sum of the maximum amount each potential user would be willing to pay for using the road over its lifespan. Similarly, the external costs of a new road would be the sum of money all adversely affected individuals would be prepared to receive in compensation to be at the same level of welfare as if the road had not been built. Thus this type of cost-benefit analysis tries to replicate a market valuation system for goods and services for which a direct market does not exist. This is a demand-based valuation system because it values goods and services according to individuals' willingness and ability to pay for them. Consequently, the social valuation arrived at reflects the existing distribution of income and wealth, and this is one objection to it.

The Department of Transport's COBA

It is, of course, generally impracticable to obtain a direct valuation of social costs and benefits as indicated by the affected individuals' willingness to pay or receive compensation. COBA has therefore to provide a system for indirectly assessing how much road users would be willing to pay for using a proposed road. Hence estimates of the value of time saved by travelling on the new road are used as proxies of the beneficiaries' willingness to pay for it. The idea is that if by travelling on the new road a car user saves, say, half an hour a day which he could have spent earning £6, then he would be willing to pay up to £6 for using the road for that journey. Thus the benefits of shorter travelling time are estimated by making assumptions about the opportunity cost of travellers' time. For example, it is assumed that working time is valued more highly than leisure time and that the working time of different kinds of road user is not equally valuable. For instance car passengers' time is assumed to be worth twice that of bus passengers. These variations are derived from differences in the hourly average wage rate of the different types of road user. The value of time savings, which account for about 80 per cent of the benefits of a typical trunk road, also depend on how many hours in total are likely to be saved by faster travel. To estimate this requires a forecast of the number of vehicles and travellers which will use the road over the next thirty years—the estimated lifespan of a new road. Another benefit to road users, which is given a monetary value, is lower vehicle operating costs due to shorter and less congested journeys. A further benefit is fewer accidents, valued by an estimate of the consequent reduction in lost earnings and medical expenditure. The estimated number of lives saved is also given a notional value. Given the long time-span over which the social benefits are expected to accrue and the uncertainty attached to their likely size, a wide range of error is attached to their estimated annual values.

The main categories of the cost of a road scheme, which are readily assessable in money terms, are the initial capital costs of buying the land, for which compulsory purchase orders can be issued, and of constructing the road, including noise baffles, access bridges or other expenditures on reducing the adverse environmental impact of the road. COBA does not include any monetary evaluation of the social costs of extra noise or landscape despoliation, though economists have attempted such evaluations in other applications of cost-benefit analysis.

After all the social costs and benefits that can be readily quantified in monetary terms have been estimated, the net social benefit (i.e. benefit minus cost) for each of the thirty years of the road's estimated future lifespan is calculated. In the early years the net social benefits will be negative as the construction costs will not be matched by any benefits. In the early years of the road's use benefits will outweigh maintenance costs, though later on there may be years in which heavy renewal costs reduce net benefits significantly. At this stage of the analysis COBA has produced a thirty-year stream of estimated annual net social benefits, which are negative in the early years and positive in the most of the later years. But it is still not evident whether the road investment would be socially efficient.

The problem for any economic evaluation of an investment which brings in different annual streams of net returns over a number of years is how to value net returns in the immediate future relative to those obtained in the second, third and more distant years. It is generally accepted that people prefer jam today rather than jam tomorrow. The preference for having a given quantity of goods now rather than in the future is called *time preference*. Because of the existence of interest rates £100 today is preferred to the same sum in a year's time. If received today, the £100 can be invested at the current rate of interest and be worth more next year. If the rate of interest is 10 per cent then a person will be indifferent between having £100 now or £110 in a year's time. This is because an individual who is certain of getting £110 in a year's time could borrow £100 and repay it with interest in a year's time. The sum due for repayment in a year's time would be £100 + (£100 × 0.1) = £110. Thus £110 received in one year's time, when the current rate of interest is 10 per cent, is worth £100 today. The value today of a sum of money to be received at some future date is known as its *present value*. To work out the present value of £110 received in a year's time we need to discount by the rate of interest. Thus £110 divided (or discounted) by (1 + 0.10) is £100. The rate of interest in this context is known as the *discount rate*. If the rate of interest or discount rate in this example rose to 12 per cent then the present value of £110 received in a year's time would be £110/(1 + 0.12), which is £98.2. In this case, it would not be worth buying an asset costing £100 which would yield £110 next year, when the alternative of investing £98.2 at the market rate of 12 per cent would give one £110 next year. Only if the present value of an investment is greater than its cost is it worthwhile going ahead with it.[4]

Under COBA the present value of the estimated future stream of annual net social benefits from a road is calculated by discounting them by an appropriate discount rate. A positive net present value indicates that the resources are valued more highly when invested in the road scheme than in their next best alternative use. It would therefore be socially efficient to undertake the investment. The value of the discount rate is therefore important because it affects which road schemes are deemed to have positive net present values. In general one would expect that the higher the discount rate the fewer road schemes will pass the social efficiency test: a high discount rate reduces the value of the more distant future benefits relative to the costs which are mainly incurred at the start of the scheme.

Hence the choice of discount rate is a significant matter. In the private sector the appropriate discount rate to use for evaluating an investment project is the opportunity cost to the firm of raising finance on the capital market. The choice of an appropriate discount rate for public sector investment appraisal is more problematic. Some argue that the rate of interest which the government has to pay in order to borrow money on the capital market is the appropriate one to use, since it reflects the opportunity cost of alternative investment in the private sector. Others, less enamoured of market signals, argue that the public sector discount rate should reflect society's preference for having goods today rather in the future. Advocates of government intervention often argue that society has a greater preference for goods tomorrow than that revealed on financial markets, which determine the rate of interest and yields on financial assets according to the demand for and supply of them. Hence it is argued that the social rate of discount must be chosen by the government via some political process. Thus the choice of a discount rate reflects value judgements; there is no indisputable formula for deriving it.

Fortunately for the cost-benefit analysts at the Department of Transport, they have not needed to ponder over the philosophical problems of choosing an appropriate rate of discount to reflect the correct opportunity cost of public investment. The Treasury did it for them, as part of their attempt in the late 1960s to institute a greater degree of control, consistency and rationality in the appraisal of public sector investment projects. To this end, the Treasury introduced a common *test rate of discount* to be applied in appraising all public sector investment projects using the discounted cash flow technique of investment appraisal. The test discount rate was chosen to reflect the government's cost of borrowing; it was initially set at 8 per cent and then raised to 10 per cent. But uniformity in using discounted cash flow investment appraisal did not fully prevail across the public sector and this goal has now been abandoned by the Treasury. Some organisations, such as the Department of Transport, have continued to use the test discount rate as part of their appraisal procedures.

Assessing the Environmental Impact of a New Road

COBA is only the economic appraisal part of the Department's formalised procedure for deciding which road schemes to build. It deals only with those costs and benefits that can be quantified in money terms. Other methods are used to assess the social costs which the Department considers cannot be valued in money terms. Following an internal review in 1976, the Department adopted a standard format for the presentation of environmental factors—noise, air pollution and visual amenity. Noise is the most easily measurable environmental variable. In evaluating a scheme the numbers of each type of property that will experience a perceptible change in noise levels, measured in decibels, are recorded. The Department has to provide double-glazing or equivalent compensation for a given increase in traffic noise caused by a new road scheme. In addition it estimates the number of properties affected by atmospheric lead pollution.

The Department has not found an acceptable way of quantifying the visual effects of a road and so relies entirely on subjective judgement, using its own landscape architects and consulting with local interests and professional expertise, such as those of the Landscape Advisory Committee. The intrusion of a proposed road on nearby properties is measured by the amount of the onlooker's view taken up by the road. The severance of farm land or local urban communities by a proposed road is noted but not measured in any way. Not all road schemes harm the environment: by-passes around old towns and villages are designed to improve the environment by diverting heavy traffic. Here reduced noise and air pollution are again quantified, but the overall visual impact is subjectively judged.

Even though the environmental effects have been quantified or subjectively assessed, there is no obvious formula for comparing them against the estimated monetary net social benefits of a new road. In some cases different sets of environmental costs have to be weighed against each other as in the case of the controversial Okehampton by-pass which, to relieve the town, will cut across part of Dartmoor. Quantification is in the end only an aid to exercising subjective judgement and balancing conflicting interests: it does not provide an automatic formula for resolving these issues.

The Role of Political Interests
An additional input into the trunk appraisal procedure is consultation of affected interests. Some will make representations to the Department in favour of a road scheme, in order to get it into the first stage of the evaluation procedure. This is the preparation pool from which schemes are selected for COBA and environmental analysis. The usual lobbyists in favour of road schemes are towns wanting by-passes, peripheral regions seeking a spur to their economic development and the road users' organisations, such as the British Road Federation and the Automobile

Association, urging shorter journey times on congested routes. Once the Department has selected a few alternative routes for a given scheme it undertakes public consultation of local interests. Information leaflets are distributed and an exhibition held. The objective is to gain information on local reactions to the costs and benefits of alternative routes. On the basis of these consultations, the COBA evaluation and environmental assessment, the Department selects a preferred route for the road. At this stage the minister is required to hold a public inquiry into the proposed route at which interested parties can submit evidence before an Inspector. On the basis of the evidence submitted by the Department and by supporting and opposing outside interests, the Inspector makes his recommendations concerning whether the proposed route should be adopted and with what modifications. The report is not binding on the minister, who is empowered to make the final decision, for which he or she is formally accountable to Parliament.

During the 1970s considerable opposition built up to the Department of Transport's road building activities, orchestrated by environmentalist groups, such as the Conservation Society and Transport 2000. They see the Department as a particularly biased in favour of road transport. To them it is significant that the Department of Transport not only finances roads but is the trunk road building agency. In contrast, rail and water transport are run by separate nationalised industries. Though the Department provides part of their funding, the professionals in charge of rail and waterways are not part of the internal departmental interest group structure and so are held to be in a weaker position than the road builders. The road interests are seen as a legitimate interest group, in contrast to the environmental activists, who have to campaign loudly outside the magic circle of inner influence that includes road engineers within the Department and organisations such as the British Road Federation.

A prominent aspect of the anti-road lobby's campaign during the 1970s was the disruption of public inquiries. They were highly dissatisfied with the limited remit of the public inquiry, which could not investigate the primary question of whether the road was justified in the first place. The inquiry accepted that the road was needed, and merely heard evidence for and against the Department's preferred route. The environmentalists therefore could not put their case to a public inquiry that a trunk road through a beauty spot, such as the Aire Valley, was not justified whatever route it took.

They argued that the Department's entire formalised procedure for appraising roads was biased in favour of justifying road schemes and attacked cost-benefit analysis. A typical critique was offered by the Oxford University Transport Studies Unit:

Cost-benefit analysis in the way it is embodied in COBA does not seem applicable to the average road scheme. It simply clothes it in an aura of scientific precision which looks logical and seems to be more rational than any other method of evaluation. The apparent sophistication nevertheless may be a myth which not only obscures the basic assumptions but also hides the implicit judgements being made by the evaluator himself.[5]

Environmentalists dislike cost-benefit analysis because the environmental factors they consider so important are not amenable to monetary valuation. Either a cost-benefit study attempts such a monetary evaluation and has to make many heroic assumpions that can be shown to be unsatisfactory, or, as in the case of COBA, it does not include them. Environmentalists maintain that the costs and benefits which are evaluated in money terms under COBA are given undue importance by the Department compared to the environmental costs which are quantified in their own physical units or not at all.

At a fundamental level, the criticisms of cost-benefit analysis of the type practised by the Department of Transport are objections to the ethical presumptions underlying it. The premise that environmental factors can be valued according to individuals' willingness to pay for them is rejected in favour of the prior assumption that these are *merit* goods which cannot be valued in money terms and which should receive higher priority than that given to them by the Department of Transport. For instance, the Town and Country Planning Association have argued that the effects of a road scheme on a wider range of environmental factors—traffic congestion, speed, cyclists, pedestrians, safety, noise, quality of the environment, public transport, regional development, and so on, should be routinely assessed in non-monetary terms. In effect, this is an argument for downgrading the economist's approach of monetary quantification, which conceals conflicts of interest by aggregating money valuations of costs and benefits into one grand total—net social welfare. In the environmentalist approach the inherent conflicts of interest would be more fully exposed and different value judgements regarding their respective merits asserted. This approach dethrones the attempts of cost-benefit analysts to obtain objective valuations in favour of a more explicit exercise of subjective judgement by bureaucrats acting in the interests of society as they perceive them.

In response to the environmentalist agitation the Department of Transport set up the Advisory Committee on Trunk Road Assessment—the Leitch Committee—to hear evidence from the pro- and anti-road lobbies, the Department of Transport and other, less partisan, experts, and to make recommendations. As with most official reports, a good dose of *incrementalism* was advocated, couched in language designed to appeal to as many interests as possible. Leitch upheld the Department's use of economic appraisal. As the quotation at the beginning of the chapter shows, Leitch approved of it as a rational decision-making procedure for road assessment. They also liked it because it made for consistency in decision-making by bureaucrats in a hierarchical and geographically dispersed organisation. However, Leitch also concluded that the Department had not taken into proper consideration all the affected interests and that its assessment of those factors not readily quantifiable in money terms should be improved. The Department took up this recommendation and now, as discussed above, includes a wider assessment of the environmental impact of a road. The Department also modified the public inquiry procedures. The inspector is now appointed by the Lord Chancellor and not by the Minister of Transport, and the scope of the public inquiry has been widened to encompass the local need for a road. However, certain significant features remain. A public inquiry does not have decision-making powers: it advises the Minister. National transport policy and the methods of appraisal, including COBA, are not considered by a public inquiry. Instead, the government introduced a regular White Paper on Roads, in order to stimulate public debate in Parliament and elsewhere on road policy.

While these concessions have to a limited extent appeased the anti-road lobby, a more significant factor accounting for the diminution of protest in the 1980s has been the cuts in road expenditure and hence in road building. Schemes such as the M23 through rural Oxfordshire and the Okehampton by-pass across the Dartmoor National Park have angered environmentalists. On the other side, road users' organisations complain of the time taken for a road proposal to pass from the preparation pool to completion—now an average of thirteen years.

THE ROLE OF COST-BENEFIT ANALYSIS IN POLICY DECISIONS

From the perspective of economics, social cost-benefit anaysis is an important decision-making technique. Much effort has been expended by economists in refining its theoretical foundations and developing appropriate methods for measuring social costs and benefits in money terms. In the 1960s economists were particularly enthusiastic in selling the newly burgeoning technique to practising policy-makers. Academic proponents, such as Mishan, quoted at the start of this chapter, offered it as a depoliticised decision-making technique which allows socially efficient policy outcomes by circumventing interest group pressures. Cost-benefit analysis based on replicating competitive market valuations for items subject to market failure provides a set of rules which are independent of political interests' evaluations. Provided the rules are generally agreed, they can then be applied to produce an acceptable outcome in which some interests lose in order to benefit others to a greater extent. However, as the trunk road case-study reveals, the ethical basis of the Department of Transport's cost-benefit analysis is not accepted by the anti-road lobby, many of whom are not fully conversant with the theoretical foundations of the technique to which they object.

The Siting of Airports

Cost-benefit analysis reached its apotheosis in the 1968–70 Roskill Commission into the third London airport. It was set the task of inquiring into 'the timing of the need for a four-runway airport to cater for the growth of traffic at existing airports serving the London area, to consider the various alternative sites and to recommend which site should be selected'.[6] The government appointed the Roskill Commission in order to demonstrate that a thorough and rational investigation had taken place into determining the best airport site. This followed an earlier public outcry at the government's selection of Stanstead which it consequently withdrew in 1968. A research team was attached to Roskill which examined about forty sites before selecting four—three inland sites and one coastal site at Foulness—for a detailed cost-benefit analysis. The research team's evidence, together with that of other interested parties, was presented in public hearings before Mr Justice Roskill.

The research team concluded that Cublington, in Buckinghamshire, was the site which yielded the highest net present value of social benefits minus social costs. The worst site, Foulness, on a remote stretch of Essex coast, had lower environmental costs than Cublington, but the latter's accessibility to potential air travellers gave it higher social benefits in terms of total travelling time gained relative to more distant Foulness. The net gain from Cublington was estimated to be £100 million (around £600 million in 1986 prices). The Commission came out in favour of Cublington, with vociferous minority dissent on the part of one member, a professor of planning, backed by others from his academic community.[7] A vigorous local campaign by opponents to Cublington reached a crescendo of protest and the government selected Foulness instead. The whole project was later abandoned in a round of government spending cuts, when the economic case for the imminent need of a third major airport was rejected. In the 1980s the government renewed its search for additional airport capacity and conducted an inquiry into Stanstead. This came out in favour of a new runway there despite much local opposition.

The airport saga shows that cost-benefit analysis failed in this instance to provide a workable depoliticised rational decision-making technique. In general the impact of cost-benefit analysis in actual policy-making situations has been somewhat limited. It is used to assess the returns to investment in education and to different forms of health care, but has not become in general an accepted part of a routine procedure for allocating resources, as it is in trunk road appraisal. Even here it is used in conjunction with other assessment methods, which also take account of the views of the different interests. The limited use of cost-benefit analysis stems ultimately from the absence of a general acceptance of its ethical presumptions. As, Mishan,[8] one of its foremost proponents admits: 'under conditions of consensual collapse . . . the task of the normative economist is practically impossible to discharge conscientiously. His criterion for determining the economic efficiency of alternative policies or projects has all but evaporated.'

However other economist practitioners[9] see the proper role for cost-benefit analysis as simply an input into essentially political decisions. It serves to identify and measure the costs and benefits of a policy to the affected individuals, and to alert them and others to their likely magnitude and distribution. The responsibility for deciding who will benefit and who will lose, and by how much, is for political-cum-administrative decision processes. An alternative to valuing items in a cost-benefit calculation according to individual citizens' preferences, is for politicians or bureaucrats to put their own weightings on the various costs and benefits. Though the use of individuals' valuations, replicating those of a perfect market, is the most popular valuation system amongst UK practitioners, alternative weightings, which reflect the preferences of planners or politicians on behalf of society, are used, especially in project appraisal for developing countries.[10]

NATIONAL ECONOMIC PLANNING

Another area in which there is a tension between a technique of rational economic policy and the pressures exerted by political interests are schemes to plan the national economy. The essential features of national economic planning are that the government, in conjunction with a state planning agency, establish economic goals for the next five years or so, such as a certain overall rate of economic growth and consistent growth rates for the various sectors of the economy. Measures to achieve the plan's targets, such as specific rates of investment in various sectors, changes in the labour force and expenditure on public sector programmes, are then worked out and implemented.

Planning is a quite different method of public sector resource allocation from that of political bargaining. Planning is undertaken by a policy-making elite, with a clear and agreed set of priorities, who can therefore establish some form of social welfare function which they attempt to maximise. Highly centralised planning does not occur in mixed liberal democracies, since these do not accord their political and administrative elites the necessary degree of power. The two countries most cited as examples of planning in a mixed economy—France and Japan—have a cohesive policy-making elite well integrated with their equivalents in the private sector. Even in these countries, postwar planning has decreased in importance, as their economies became more developed and increasingly open and, in the case of France, integrated into the European Community. The increased complexity of their economies and the uncontrollable and often unpredictable impact of changes emanating from abroad have diminished the scope of planning.

Planning has never taken root in Britain. Apart from the highly controlled World War II economy, the only attempt at comprehensive planning was the ill-fated National Plan of 1965–67 of the Wilson Labour government. This was a hastily devised and poorly thought-out concoction of the newly created and short-lived Department of Economic Affairs. An ambitious 4 per cent growth target for real national output was set, when the average rate of growth achieved in the past was 2.5 per cent. The implications for the various sections of the private and public sectors of the 4 per cent target growth rate were then projected. Hence government expenditure was planned to rise by at least 4 per cent a year, in line with the intended growth in national income. However there were no reliable policy measures which could ensure 4 per cent real growth in private sector output. The hope was that a firm statement of intent by the government to expand at 4 per cent per annum would stimulate a corresponding increase in private sector investment and output. This type of planning, which relies on emulation by non-governmental agencies, who are not directly controlled by the planners, is known as *indicative planning*. In Britain the planners also had limited control of the public sector. When the economy ran into yet another balance of payments crisis in 1967, the government was forced to devalue sterling and reduce aggregate demand. Thus the government itself failed to adhere to the policies implied by the National Plan, which was subsequently abandoned.

The next Labour government (1974–79) was reluctant to launch another full-scale attempt at economic planning and instead pursued a low-key approach to industrial planning, whereby the government tried to influence directly the behaviour of firms. Two aspects of this policy were planning agreements and the National Enterprise Board. The intention of planning agreements was that private sector firms would enter into binding agreements with the government over their investment, output and employment policies in return for government favours in the form of finance or the absence of unpleasant constraints on their actions. Only one agreement was signed—with the Chrysler motor company, which was in desperate need of state finance. The National Enterprise Board was intended to revitalise British industry by taking up equity and loans in companies which might be fully or partially state-owned as a result. However the bulk of the NEB's portfolio consisted of holdings in state-owned Rolls-Royce and BL, and it never had enough finance to make much of an impact on British industry. The subsequent success of its investments was somewhat mixed. Some companies, like Ferranti, returned profitably to the private sector, while others, like Nexos, created to develop advanced technology office equipment, failed. The NEB was gradually wound down when the Conservatives won office in 1979. Currently the Labour Party plans yet another exercise in state investment via a public sector investment bank and restrictions on investment abroad.

EFFICIENCY INITIATIVES

The enthusiasm of the 1960s and early 1970s for policy optimisation techniques has waned. In fashion in the 1980s for promoting rational and effective public sector decision-making are auditing and managerial efficiency studies. These are the methods of accountants and management consultants rather than economists, though the latter are encompassing them within their field of interest.[11] The general concern is with economy, efficiency and effectiveness—concepts all somewhat narrower than the economist's notion of social efficiency. Economy here refers to keeping down expenditure; and efficiency to reducing the cost in money or input terms of producing a given unit of service. Effectiveness is the most difficult to gauge as it is the efficiency with which the objectives of a particular public service are attained. So, for instance, hospital economy and efficiency would be improved by reducing the number of days a patient occupies a bed, but effectiveness would be diminished if earlier discharge meant prolonged convalescence or readmission. In contrast to cost-benefit analysis, which is usually applied to assessing the return on a future commitment of resources, efficiency auditing is concerned with investigating current practice with a view to suggesting improvements.

This concern with public sector efficiency in a managerial sense, applying the methods of the private sector, has been a hallmark of the Thatcher regime. On becoming Prime Minister in 1979, with a commitment to reduce waste in the public sector as one element in containing its size, she appointed Derek Rayner, from Marks and Spencer, as her Advisor on Efficiency, with a small efficiency unit to assist him. A wide range of 'Rayner efficiency scrutinies' were carried out and continue under his successor. A number of specific organisational reforms have also been undertaken, in particular the Financial Management Initiative launched in 1982. This aims to create an organisational system and culture where public sector managers at all levels have clear objectives, information about the costs and consequences of their actions and a clear personal responsibility for ensuring value for money. A visible manifestion of the policy is that the annual Government Expenditure White Paper now proclaims official departmental objectives. In many areas the problem of translating broad goals, like raising educational standards, into measurable and hence assessable objectives, remain. Merely articulating objectives at the apex of a hierarchical bureaucracy does nothing to promote their achievement unless they can be translated into assessable objectives for those in the lower echelons.

There have also been other developments. In 1983 the Exchequer and Audit Department, which had been a government department, was replaced by the independent National Audit Office under the Comptroller and Auditor General. This is solely accountable to Parliament and reports to the Public Accounts Committee. It conducts value-for-money studies in central government departments and is beginning to consider wider issues of efficiency and policy effectiveness. Since the Local Government Finance Act 1982, local authority activities are scrutinised by the Audit Commission for England and Wales. It has investigated specific services like refuse collection and education. It is able to ascertain existing best practice and so inform less efficient authorities on how to improve their performance. Under the Competition Act 1980, nationalised industries first became subject to efficiency studies by the Monopolies and Mergers Commission. Efficiency studies have been done on individual sectors, like the universities and the NHS. The government's attempts to improve the latter's efficiency and accountability have already been discussed in Chapter 8.

There has thus been a plethora of activity in promoting efficiency in the public sector. A good deal of it has been in the form of different kinds of investigations into current practices, leading to suggestions for securing improved efficiency. This activity is in itself costly, both in the time of the outside investigators and of the organisation being scrutinised. Only about 40 per cent of the identified savings have so far been realised,[12] and the returns from the costs of changing organisational procedures and structures are by no means easy to assess. An efficiency study of the effectiveness of efficiency initiatives seems in order!

WHAT HOPE FOR POLICY OPTIMISATION?

There is an ever-present tension in collective decision-making between the desire for rational policies and the need to appease conflicting interests so that they all continue to participate in or acquiesce in the decision procedures and their outcomes. Rational policy decisions require some form of collective agreement on the priorities to be accorded to the various objectives the policy is intended to promote, as some of the objectives are usually mutually inconsistent and have to be traded off against one another. In other words, the policy-makers have to articulate an operational *social welfare function* and then assess the various policy alternatives with a view to selecting the one that attains the highest level of social welfare.

To What Extent Can Economic Policy Be Rational?

In the course of Part II I have discussed a number of ways such a social welfare function might be articulated. Policy alternatives can be put to the electorate by their politician advocates. Those policies gaining the majority of votes are then automatically implemented by the politicians and bureaucrats. Alternatively the elected politicians can select them on the basis of majority voting amongst themselves. However, as the work of Arrow[13] and other theorists has shown, there is no guarantee that such majority voting will conform to certain desirable characteristics for a social welfare function, like consistency or absence of dictatorship. Another alternative is that a small policy-making elite can act as a single decision-maker because they have essentially the same preferences, due to similar political outlook in the case of a Cabinet, or due to a shared professional ethos in the case of a group of specialist bureaucrats, like doctors, economic planners or teachers. Because of their professionalism or dedication, they can be trusted to pursue the welfare of society as a whole. Social cost-benefit analysis tries to have the best of both worlds—a policy selection technique operated by professional bureaucrats, following pre-set rules that enable them to elicit the preferences of individual citizens.

The previous chapters in Part II, as well as this one, indicate why the main strength of the rational policy-making model is its prescription for how good policy *ought to be made*, whereas it is of limited validity as an explanation of how economic policy *is actually made*. Its chief weakness as an explanatory approach is that it relies on the objectives or ends of policy being agreed upon by those with decision-making power. But when the decision-makers have different policy preferences and fail to reach an explicit and binding agreement on the objectives policy is designed to serve, then ends and means get confused. Decisions about what to do are taken before any explicit agreement on ends is reached. The decisions themselves are the outcome of a political bargaining game played out between decision-makers representing different interests. The chief players in the game are politicians, bureaucrats and lay members of political interest affiliations. One feature of the resulting policy outcomes are that objectives are attended to sequentially as the fortunes of the various interests fluctuate. For example, full employment is pursued for a time and low inflation neglected as an objective, only for the priorities to be reversed later. This contrasts with the rational approach, described by the policy optimisation committee, in which an explicit trade-off between inflation and unemployment would be declared by the government. Government expenditure is not allocated on the basis of an explicit agreement on priorities by the government but by a continual process of bargaining between ministers and in response to the pressures to spend emanating from public sector budget holders. The debate over priorities is never-ending, but the function of the political system is to reach decisions which are translated into some form of action while the debate continues.

There are considerable differences of opinion regarding the extent to which economic policy-making can be seen as the outcome of rational decision-making processes or as essentially non-rational because it results from political bargaining. It is a question of emphasis as to which explanation is dominant, rather than a stark choice between mutually exclusive explanations. There are certainly features of rationality in the organisational structures and procedures of the institutions through which economic policies are formulated and implemented, and which thereby impose some pattern and consistency on economic policy. Examples are the hierarchical structure of government departments, such as the DHSS, and their links with other public sector agencies, such as the NHS. Their procedures for policy-making do attempt to articulate priorities for objectives and to allocate resources according to such priorities, as with the NHS RAWP formula. In this context cost-benefit analysis is but one of a number of techniques to be used in this way.

Are Policy Optimisation Techniques Desirable?

There are also considerable differences with respect to value judgements concerning the desirability of determining public policy issues through the rational decision-making procedures required for the application of policy optimisation techniques. One influential brand of criticism of rationality has come from *pluralists*, who deny the existence of such a concept as overall social welfare and recognise only the diverse interests of different groups within society. In the pluralist view, public policy-making procedures should be designed to enable those interests, who feel strongly, to participate in the decision so that they agree to or acquiesce in the final outcome because they feel the decision process has itself been reasonably fair. From this perspective the efficiency of a policy outcome in terms of achieving a set of stated objectives is of secondary importance. From the rationalist perspective of economics it is the outcome of policy in relation to criteria of efficiency and, more vaguely and controversially, of social justice that is of primary significance, and forms the characteristic contribution of economics to the analysis of policy.

Are Planning and Democracy Compatible?

A related and long-debated issue is whether democracy is compatible with planning as a method of achieving efficient and equitable economic policies. For pluralists the answer is relatively clear: liberal democracy is paramount because its pluralist decision-making processes justify the resulting outcomes. Socialists, on the other hand, have largely favoured state economic planning as the only rational way of organising economic activity to ensure both the growth of material output and a just distribution of economic rewards. However, planning presupposes that economic objectives can be clearly defined and adhered to over a relatively long time-scale, otherwise there is no rationale on which to base planned actions. Democratic voting procedures, with their inherent problems of inconsistency, cycling of vote-winning alternatives, short-term political horizons, and accompanied by political bargaining amongst influential political interests, offer little hope of producing a consistent and stable set of revealed citizen preferences which the planners can then satisfy to their best ability.

Recognising that democracy is inconsistent with rational planning, especially that which aims at a fundamental change in the distribution of economic and political power, one strand of socialist thinking favours decision-making by a political and bureaucratic elite on behalf of the interests of the working class. This view is much less popular in socialist circles than thirty or more years ago. Experience with centralised economies and with running enlarged public sectors in the mixed economies, has led to a distrust of public sector bureaucrats' ability or willingness to take decisions which are in citizens' interests. Among socialists there is a widespread expectation that extra-parliamentary systems of democratic control and accountability can be devised, and that these can reconcile the demands of economic and social planning with those of democracy. One suspects that many such believers have not fully thought through how an increased degree of political bargaining, which further democratic decision-making implies, can be consonant with planning, which requires a clear and consistent articulation of priorities, and the search for and implementation of the most effective means of attaining the stated objectives.

Particularly to a sceptic, the potential for planning in a liberal democratic mixed economy to achieve what its advocates hope for seems minimal. The prerequisites for planning cannot take root in a system dominated by political bargaining as the primary method of decision-making, and where there is no consensus in favour of planning. To those who see the rationalist ideals of planning as unattainable in a liberal democracy, the absence of such consensus is hardly surprising.

The Contribution of Economics to Policy-Making

Compared to other participants in policy-making, the economics' perspective on its rational pedestal is somewhat detached from the political and administrative aspects of policy-making, in which the human element features much more strongly. This position gives the economics' perspective its characteristic merits, in that it clarifies policy issues by determining the nature and size of the likely costs and benefits as well as their distribution. In doing this, it can correct misleading arguments promoted by political interests to serve their own ends. However economics has a somewhat tarnished image amongst non-economists for dissension and wrong advice. The economic mode of argument is, with the help of partisan economists, exploited by political interests for their own ends. For example, social cost-benefit analysis can be used to justify various positions, from working loss-making coal mines to building motorways through beauty spots. As economists have not been able to build up a scientifically sound, and hence generally accepted, body of knowledge about how the economy works, economists of different schools advocate different policies, as do monetarists and Keynesians with respect to the problems of unemployment and inflation.

Economists are prone to offer naive and potentially disastrous policy advice when they neglect the importance of political and administrative factors in the selection and implementation of policy. For instance, cost-benefit analysis, or discounted cash flow investment appraisal techniques for nationalised industries may give efficient resource allocation in theory, but will fail to do so in practice if the bureaucrats or politicians manipulate the figures to suit their own ends. On the credit side, a measure of rationality in policy-making, a concern with clarifying the objectives sought by policy-makers, and trying to attain them efficiently, are valuable inputs into policy-making, provided political and administrative factors are taken into account. Economists are now more conscious of these than twenty years ago, when confidence in the new applications of quantifiable economics to designing optimal public policies was at its peak.

NOTES

1. R.J. Ball, *Report of Committee on Policy Optimisation* (HMSO, London, 1978).
2. K.J. Arrow, *Social Choice and Individual Values* (Wiley, New York, 1951).
3. Ball, op. cit.
4. The formula for the present value of £X received in N years' time, when the discount rate is R over the period, is $£X/(1+R)^N$.
5. Sir G. Leitch, *Report of the Advisory Committee on Trunk Road Assessment* (HMSO, London, 1978), p. 54.

6. *House of Commons Official Report*, 20 May 1968, cols. 32—9.
7. For example. P. Self, *Econocrats and the Policy Process*, (Macmillan, London, 1975).
8. E. Mishan, *Introduction to Political Economy* (Hutchinson, London, 1982), p. 232.
9. M.E. Beesley and P. Kettle, 'The Leitch Committee's recommendations and the management of the road programme', *Regional Studies*, vol. 13, pp. 513—29.
10. S. Marglin, *Public Investment Criteria* (George Allen and Unwin, London, 1967).
11. D. Mayston and F. Terry, *Public Domain, A yearbook for the public sector* (Public Finance Foundation, London, 1986).
12. National Audit Office, *The Rayner Scrutiny Programmes, 1979 to 1983* (HMSO, London, 1986).
13. Arrow, op. cit. (see note 2 above).

Conclusion to Part II: Rationality and Politics

The last chapter in Part II concentrated on the rational model of economic policy that typifies the economists' approach to policy-making. When economists are employed as policy advisors they rely extensively on rational decision-making tools such as cost-benefit analysis and the computerised models of the economy used for economic forecasting. Orthodox treatments by economists of economic policy concentrate on this rational approach to the exclusion of the impact of the political and institutional contexts within which economic policy is made. Here these political and institutional factors have been emphasised by analysing in some detail the roles of voters, politicians, bureaucrats and political interests in the process of policy making.

This analysis has used two 'ideal' models as benchmarks with which to compare the realities of policy-making—the ideal representative democracy and the rational model of policy-making. The Introduction to Part II and the following chapters indicated the crucial ways in which an actual representative democracy departs from its ideal form and the implications of this with regard to whose preferences get reflected in policy outcomes. This concluding piece considers how the actual policy-making process differs from the economist's rational ideal and what the role of rational decision-making techniques may be.

A rational, optimising policy-making procedure requires as a first step the establishment of clear priorities with respect to the policy-makers' objectives. In the economists' jargon this is termed defining a *social welfare function*. The declared stance of the economics profession is that the economist, in his professional capacity as a technician, has no special say in determining the social welfare function. His job is to seek out ways to maximise the social welfare function which is determined in some sense by society as a whole. Economists adopt one of two approaches to the problem of seeking out the social welfare function. One is to look to the political process to determine it. The objectives are decided by the elected

242

representatives, who are accountable to the electorate for their actions. The alternative way of obtaining a social welfare function is to bypass the political machinery altogether and to elicit citizens' preferences directly by determining their willingness to pay for goods and services. This is the method of cost-benefit analysis. It aims to replicate market valuations of resources in those areas where market failure makes market prices misleading indicators of socially efficient resource allocation.

The major weakness of the rational approach is that the political process is usually unable to define a social welfare function with sufficient clarity. The root cause of the problem is the difficulty of deriving a consistent set of collective preferences for society when the policy-makers have different interests and hence divergent preferences. Broadly interpreted, policy-makers embrace citizens-as-voters, politicians-as-legislators and bureaucrats-as-implementors. One way of understanding policy-making is as a linear process whereby the preferences of each class of policy-maker are fed into specific stages of decision-making. Thus there is no grand agglomeration of preferences to establish a social welfare function at the beginning of the policy-making process, as in the rational approach. Instead the different political interests are continuously engaged in asserting their preferences in competition with other interests, as decisions on the use of policy instruments are being made. What emerges from policy-making as a *political bargaining game* is a series of resource allocation decisions that reflect the on-going accommodations made between the various political interests. Thus there is no clear and direct link between the policy instruments that are actually employed and a single, well-specified social welfare function.

By-passing politics to quantify social efficiency by eliciting citizens' preferences from their revealed willingness to pay, can at best only be applied to a relatively narrow area of choice. Because of the problems of quantifying social costs and benefits, cost-benefit analysis can only be applied to comparing, say, different trunk road schemes, but not to making the more fundamental choices between schools, health centres, submarines, private consumption, and so on. Even with restricted choice, as with trunk roads, cost-benefit analysis is only part of a decision process that tries to accommodate a variety of political interests: it is rejected by some because they are unwilling to accept its ethical presumptions. Similarly, the large-scale computer model used by Treasury economists for forecasting is only a small part of the whole process of determining economic management policies. The major policy variables, the level and structure of government expenditure and taxation, are not unilaterally determined by ministers, aided by economists. These variables, too, emerge from bargaining between political interests who operate within a framework of rules and procedures, such as the annual budgetary cycle, and who are constrained by economic relationships beyond their control.

The main conclusions regarding the nature of economic policy-making have been established in Part II of the book. Part III amplifies these conclusions by presenting further examples of specific areas of economic policy, which illustrate the applicability of the ideas developed in Part II. Their common thread is that they all involve government intervention to produce or redistribute goods and services within the economy. The areas chosen are public corporations, by which government produces marketed goods on its own account; welfare policies, whereby the government provides non-marketed goods and redistributes income; and agriculture, as this exemplifies extensive government intervention in the private sector. Efficiency and distribution are again used as criteria against which to assess the impact of policy, and the role of political interests in the formulation and implementation of economic policy is brought out.

Part III

11 The Public Corporations

To secure for the workers by hand or by brain the full fruits of their industry and the most equitable distribution thereof that may be possible, upon the basis of the common ownership of the means of production, distribution, and exchange, and the best obtainable system of popular administration and control of each industry or service. (*Constitution of the Labour Party*, 1918, clause IV, section 4)

The Conservative Party has never believed that the business of Government is the government of business. (Nigel Lawson (1981) *Hansard*, vol. 1 (8th series) col. 440)

The consumer is sovereign in the private sector. In the public sector he is dethroned by subsidy or monopoly. (Sir Geoffrey Howe, Speech to Selsdon Group, July 1981, Conservative Office Press Release 533/81)

One major form of government intervention is the public ownership of business enterprises which produce *marketed goods*. As we saw in Chapter 3, a public corporation is subject to both market and government allocative mechanisms and thus to a complex mixture of commercial and political considerations.

This chapter examines the objectives sought from nationalised industries and from their privatised form, and compares these to the realities of policy-making. Policies towards the nationalised industries illustrate many of the themes of Part II, in particular the role of bureaucracies and political interests, as well as the attempts by economists to devise socially efficient criteria for guiding decision-making with respect to nationalised industries.

THE SCOPE AND SIZE OF THE PUBLIC CORPORATIONS

Public corporations in the UK produce a wide range of marketed goods and services. They include public utilities: electricity, water and sewage, broadcasting, postal services, telecommunications (until 1984), gas (until 1986), as well as public transport, aero engines, motor cars, military equipment and ships. In the 1970s the variety of goods and services produced in the state sector was even greater, ranging from hotel accommodation, pubs and travel agents to machine tools and electronics. Non-marketed goods and services, like defence, health and education, are produced directly by central and local government, not by separate organisations classified as public corporations. In 1984 there were over 50 public corporations.[1] Their relative importance in the economy has declined in the last few years, especially in terms of employment, as can be verified from Tables 11.1 and 11.2.

In terms of size, the major type of public corporation are the nationalised industries. These have been established by statute and so the nature of their activities, including their existence within the public sector, can only be changed by Act of Parliament. This is an important characteristic since it means that a nationalised industry cannot be declared insolvent or be sold to the private sector without specific legislation. No nationalised industry has ever been allowed to go bankrupt. Other public corporations, such as BL or Rolls-Royce, which are constituted under the Companies Act in the same way as private sector companies, can go bankrupt and some have, for example, the machine toolmakers, Alfred Herbert. The nationalised industries' statutes also protect them from competition by giving them legal monopolies or restricting the entry of other firms.

The second characteristic of a nationalised industry is that it is managed by an independent board, appointed by the sponsoring minister. This is also true of Companies Act public corporations but not of the third category of public corporation, which are enterprises run directly by a government department, called trading funds, such as the Royal Mint or, until recently, the Royal Ordnance factories. Similarly Passenger Transport Executives, run by local authorities, are not nationalised industries, whereas the National Bus Company is because it has an independent board. Particular undertakings have moved from one category of public corporation to another. For example the Post Office was from its inception a government department until 1961, when it became a nationalised industry. In 1981 it was split in two, with the creation of British Telecom, which was sold to the private sector in 1984/85. The current situation is extremely fluid as the Conservative government prepares certain public corporations for transfer to the private sector, while the Labour Party promises to renationalise them.

A third characteristic of all public corporations is that they are wholly or almost completely owned by the state. Firms in which the government has only a partial ownership stake, even if it exceeds 50 per cent, are officially classified as part of the private sector. There are few partly state-owned

Table 11.1: the Nationalised industries; size and finances

	Turnover £m	Capital employed (CCA basis) £m	Workforce 000s	Fixed investment £m	Government grants £m	Government net lending £m	Internally generated funds £m	Total external finance £m
	1981–82	1981–82	1981–82	1983–84	1983–84	1983–84	1983–84	1983–84
Electricity[a]	9043	32605	164	1867	11	−778	2110	−758
British Telecom	5708	16099	246	1572	0	−154	1919	−225
British Gas	5235	10955	105	1138	0	0	1147	−45
National Coal Board	4727	5891	279	720	731	613	−795	1183
British Steel	3443	2502	104	193	0	396	−146	318
British Rail	2899	2746	227	270	952	−22	−663	811
Post Office	2636	1347	183	123	0	−30	171	−62
British Airways	2241	1338	43	250	0	−42	339	−174
British Shipbuilders	1026	655	67	48	33	281	−243	306
National Bus Company	618	508	53	63	66	−8	−8	65
British Airports Authority	277	852	7	132	0	−5	112	18
Civil Aviation Authority	206	162	7	20	3	−5	16	−8
Scottish Transport Group	152	157	11	17	11	−9	4	15
British Waterways Board	16	50	3	4	40	1	−37	41
Water Authorities	na	na	na	823	49	279	460	350
Total	42,792	83,178	1627	7309	1896	516	4564	2285

Source: *The Government's Expenditure Plans 1985–86 to 1987–88*, Cmnd 9428; M. Beesley and S. Littlechild (1983) 'Privatisation: Principles, Problems and Priorities', *Lloyds Bank Review*, no. 149, July.

Note: a. Includes CEGB, Council and Area Boards, North of Scotland Hydro-Electric Board and South of Scotland Electricity Board.

companies left: they were the easiest ones for the Conservative government to sell to the private sector, as no specific legislation was required. In the 1960s and 1970s, government part-ownership of private sector companies was an important instrument of industrial policy and is still so regarded by the Labour Party.

The nationalised industries, as of 1984, are listed in Table 11.1. The data on turnover, capital employed and workforce, indicate their relative size. The next column shows their fixed investment, with electricity, telecommunications, gas, coal and water having the largest investment programmes. Government grants are paid mainly to cover losses. Here coal and railways stand out as significant recipients. The industries finance their investment out of government lending and internally generated funds. The last column, total *external finance*, shows the amount of its expenditure each industry does not finance internally from its revenues but has to raise by borrowing on its own account, or from government lending and outright grants. As explained in Chapter 4, the total *external finance* of the public corporations forms part of public expenditure and, as such, is under Treasury surveillance. Positive external finance means that the industry is a net recipient of government funds. Coal, steel, railways, shipbuilding and water are in this category: the first four have been chronic loss-makers for years; coal and railways since the 1950s. On the other hand, the net contributers to the Exchequer are electricity, telecommunications and gas with, in recent years, postal services and airways. Overall in 1984, government net spending on the nationalised industries was over £2 billion. The nationalised industries have remained a charge on the Exchequer for years, despite the Conservative government's intentions to change this.

REASONS FOR PUBLIC OWNERSHIP

The public ownership of productive assets has always been a vital element of socialist aspirations, as indicated in clause IV of the *Labour Party Constitution*, quoted above. The primary motive has been to secure economic power for the representatives of the workers, both in order to redistribute social welfare in their favour and to promote a more efficient allocation of resources. The pre-war advocates of nationalisation, without the benefits of hindsight, were particularly critical of competition as a means of securing efficient resource allocation. Sidney Webb, whose work greatly influenced early Labour Party thinking, inveighed against 'the waste and inefficiency' of a 'jostling crowd of separate employers'. Similarly, Herbert Morrison, the Labour politician regarded as the father of the nationalised industries, who successfully campaigned for the creation of the London Passenger Transport Board in 1933, condemned the disorderly services provided by private carriers, competing for passengers on busy routes and neglecting less popular ones. Not only would public ownership improve the customers' lot; even more importantly, it would benefit the workers in the enterprise who would no longer be exploited by capitalists. Public ownership would eradicate worker alienation and so improve industrial relations. Coal and docks, which had a long history of poor labour relations, were early candidates for nationalisation. A further reason is to enable the economy to be *planned*. In 1960 the Labour Party clarified the famous Clause IV by stating that it aimed for 'an expansion of common ownership substantial enough to give the community power over the commanding heights of the economy.' Hence, it has in the past aimed at complete public ownership of the energy and transport sectors and has more recently set its sights on the financial sector, in order to direct investment.

Less politicised reasons for public ownership are provided by the economic analysis of *market failure*, discussed in Chapter 6. In particular public ownership is an appropriate instrument for correcting market failure due to *natural monopoly*. Hence nationalisation is suitable for electricity, telecommunications, gas, water, canals and railways. A more contentious reason is to correct for allocative inefficiency due to *external costs* and *benefits*. For example it is argued that subsidised rail and bus travel is justified in order to reduce road congestion and the other environmental costs of private road transport. Nuclear power is too risky to be left in private hands: national prestige requires a state airline; airways and airports need to be regulated by a state agency. All these are examples where the existence of *externalities* is said to justify public ownership.

As pointed out in Chapter 6, the arguments in favour of state intervention that invoke the concept of *social efficiency*, and the claimed discrepancies between social and private costs and benefits, merge into *distributional* arguments. It is often held that a particular good yields positive net social benefits but because its private costs exceed its private benefits it is not produced in sufficient quantitites, if at all, by private firms. The market therefore fails to produce enough of such goods. Public corporations need not follow the private profit-maximising criteria and so can be used to produce goods that the market would neglect, such as telephones, mail and public transport in areas of sparse demand. It can be argued that providing communications and transport to all parts of the country promotes national cohesion and so yields external benefits to all citizens. The policy therefore is justified on social efficiency grounds. Alternatively, it can be argued that such policies further social justice by reducing the cost of living for poorer people in rural areas and so is supported by the population as a whole. Such policies will also be campaigned for by the political interests who benefit and will be favoured by politicians seeking to retain or gain power by securing the support of these interests.

However public corporations are often expected to finance loss-making goods from profits earned on their other lines. For example the price of sending a letter a few miles in an urban area or several hundreds of miles to a remote part of the country is the same. The Post Office uses the surplus of revenue over cost on urban mail to cover its losses on delivering rural mail. Public transport undertakings practise similar forms of *cross-subsidisation*. Private sector firms do produce loss-making goods when paid an explicit subsidy by the government, as do bus companies for instance, but are unlikely to be willing to do so by cross-subsidisation, unless this is the condition of the monopoly they are permitted to have. Cross-subsidisation as a means of redistributing social welfare is popular with politicians because it is concealed in prices. It is not so transparent, and hence not so potentially unpopular, as the alternative way of financing subsidies—taxation. However *cross-subsidisation* is *allocatively inefficient* as it means charging prices for goods that are out of line with the marginal costs of producing them.

Another aspect of the distributive aims served by public ownership is the preservation of jobs in particular industries or regions by the state taking over loss-making private sector firms that are threatened with bankruptcy or by continuing to maintain excess capacity in public enterprises. This became a more prominent feature of state enterprises in the 1970s under both Conservative and Labour governments, with the state takeover of BL and Rolls Royce and the nationalisation of shipbuilding. In this decade shipbuilding and steel joined the railways and coal as the public sector's chronic loss-makers. Employment objectives have always featured prominently in the coal, shipbuilding and steel industries, with their strong regional location in areas of high unemployment. Invariably arguments in favour of job preservation are buttressed by claims that national prestige or security requires the maintenance of a particular industry. As Joel Barnett noted with respect to Rolls-Royce: 'when national prestige and jobs combine, logic and common sense are not allowed to stand in the way.'[2]

THE OBJECTIVES OF NATIONALISED INDUSTRIES

When one looks at particular industries and firms that are in the public sector and at the goods and services they produce, there is often no clear economic reason why these enterprises are located there. One has to turn to political and historical explanations. However, from the amalgam of reasons that have promoted the public ownership of business enterprises, three basic objectives can be distilled that have underlain policies towards the nationalised industries. These are *efficiency*, *social objectives* and the overall *management of the economy*. The history of government policies towards the public corporations has been bedevilled by the frequent inconsistencies between these objectives, the difficulty governments experience in determining priorities for these objectives and in establishing an institutional framework for achieving them.

Efficiency

The concept of efficiency in relation to a nationalised industry was examined in Chapter 3. The first requirement for *economic efficiency* is that the industry should achieve the minimum attainable production costs for a given level of output: in other words there is no *x-inefficiency*. Without the elimination of x-inefficiency there cannot be full allocative efficiency. But allocative efficiency also requires that output prices be related to *marginal costs*. This means that public sector monopolies must not abuse their market power by charging prices in excess of minimum attainable costs. This criterion for allocative efficiency should also determine public corporations' investment programmes, so that fixed capital is committed to producing goods for which consumers are willing to pay prices that cover all production costs, including capital charges. There should be neither excess capacity nor unsatisfied demand.

Social Objectives

The efficiency conditions outlined above are those that a competitive profit-maximising private sector firm would satisfy, constrained by competition from existing and potential suppliers in its markets. Such a firm would not take account of *external costs* and *benefits*, unless induced to do so by government regulations or by taxes and subsidies. But a government could expect a public corporation to promote *social efficiency* by its own internal administrative means, that is, a public corporation could be expected to relate social costs and benefits in a way a private sector firm would not.

However, as has been stressed in several places in this book, the enormous problems attached to quantifying social costs and benefits make it extremely difficult to separate measures taken on *social efficiency* grounds from those adopted for *distributional* motives. Therefore I think that it makes for greater expositional clarity to include under the heading of *social objectives*, measures for correcting market failure due to externalities, together with those aimed more explicitly at securing a non-market distribution of social welfare. Hence protecting the environment, providing employment, producing loss-making goods for particular categories of customer, enhancing national prestige and security, are all included here in the term *social objectives*. The term efficiency, in relation to nationalised industries, is here restricted to the notion of *market efficiency*; that is, selling goods at prices which reflect the minimum attainable costs of production. So this reference-point for public corporations' efficiency is the level of costs and prices which could be expected from a competitive private sector firm and not the wider concept of social efficiency.

Overall Management of the Economy

Governments have sought to use the nationalised industries as instruments of more general economic policies. The current government has tried to increase the overall market efficiency of the economy by putting pressure on the public corporations to cut their loss-making activities and by loosening the regulations limiting competition in some nationalised sectors, like long-distance buses, express letters and telephones. As noted in Chapter 4, the public corporations have been expected to reduce their claims on public expenditure. Loss-makers have been set lower *external financing limits* while the profitable concerns have been expected to pay more to the Exchequer in terms of larger negative EFLs, even if, as in the case of water and gas, this has meant charging higher prices than justified by their costs.

Nationalised industries are also subject to formal and informal prices and incomes policies. The Heath government of 1970–74 required them to hold down their prices in an attempt to reduce the general rate of inflation and paid subsidies to finance the ensuing losses. As with the more recent example, the efficiency criterion for pricing in relation to costs was sacrificed in the interests of the government's macroeconomic policies. Nationalised industries have also been the battleground for wage claims, which the government has tried to resist in order to prevent emulation elsewhere, as well as to restrain public expenditure.

The public corporations' investment programmes have been affected by the government's macroeconomic policies. Since controlling the level of public expenditure became of overriding concern, the industries have complained of their inability to plan their investment programmes, because of the short time-horizon within which the government determines public expenditure, or to finance commercially desirable investment projects on their own account. Even industries earning a surplus are required to pay predetermined sums (their negative EFL) to the Exchequer, and have to get their large investment projects approved by the government. So far the Treasury has successfully resisted all pleas by the nationalised industries that they should be able to raise long-term investment finance on their own account on the open capital market. In a different age—the mid-1960s— nationalised industries were required to bring forward their investment projects as part of the Labour government's attempt to stimulate economic growth. When this failed to materialise, industries, such as electricity generation, were left with excess capacity on their hands and cut back on ordering new plant, so disrupting the production plans of their private sector suppliers.

The expectation that public corporations should pursue social objectives and act as instruments for general economic management injects an inescapable political dimension into what are also regarded as business enterprises, which should be run efficiently. The conundrum posed by this mixture was once aptly expressed by Sir James Bowman, former Chairman of the National Coal Board: 'What are we? We are not flesh, fish nor good red herring. We are not a commercial undertaking; we are not a public service; we are a bit of each.'[3] Thirty years on, the problems of combining the market mechanism with the process of political decision-making are still being addressed.

THE RELATIONSHIP BETWEEN GOVERNMENT AND NATIONALISED INDUSTRIES

The institutional framework within which public sector enterprises operate can take many forms. At one extreme a public enterprise can be run directly by a government department or local authority. At the other end of the spectrum it could be completely independent of government and operate just like a private sector company, except that its shareholders are the government. As we have seen, public enterprises in the UK are strung out along this range from public limited liability companies in which the government has a minority shareholding to those it wholly owns, through to nationalised industries, trading funds, government departments and local authorities at the other end.

This chapter concentrates on the nationalised industries because they are the most important type of public corporation. Also the problems associated with the formulation and implementation of policy towards nationalised industries have much in common with those related to the other forms of public corporation. From a rational perspective, the political and organisational framework within which the nationalised industries operate needs to provide a way of determining what objectives they are to pursue, and to ensure that the enterprises carry out the objectives desired by the political decision-makers.

The Morrison Model
When the 1945–50 Labour government embarked on its ambitious nationalisation programme it had, not surprisingly, no thoroughly worked-out blueprint for these new organisations. The most influential ideas were those of Herbert Morrison who, as Leader of the House of Commons, steered through the nationalisation legislation. For Morrison, nationalisation involved eliminating competition by combining all private undertakings in the industry into a publicly-owned monopoly and handing

it over to a management board of able men with proven business ability to run as a commercial enterprise. As the private profit motive had been eliminated, the board would run the business efficiently but in the public interest. Workers' and consumers' interests and that of the nation as a whole would be encompassed within that vague concept, the public interest. So the objectives for Morrison were business efficiency combined with the public interest—objectives that command a wide measure of support when expressed in such vague terms. The problem then was to devise institutional arrangements for securing these laudable aims.

Morrison was concerned that the nationalised industries should be removed from the political arena, which is why he placed so much reliance on an independent board of able businessmen. He held that the public corporation

must feel that it is responsible to the nation accordingly and that it cannot be the instrument of this or that private or sectional interest. . . .. The management must. . . be able to stand its ground in the interests of the undertaking which is committed to its charge.

He was concerned that if sectional political interests, particularly those representing the workers and customers of the enterprise, were allowed to participate in decision-making, then it would not be possible to run the business efficiently or in the general public interest. Hence there was to be no worker participation in running the industries nor direct parliamentary accountability.

However, as the industries were nationalised precisely in order for them to be run in the public interest there had to be political control and accountability. In the Morrison model this was vested in the minister of the department sponsoring the industry. The Morrison nationalised industry was modelled on the private sector public limited-liability company translated to the public sector. The private shareholders were replaced by the general taxpaying public with the minister as their representative. The minister was empowered to give general directives to the board regarding what the government considered to be in the public interest. But to protect the industry from the demands of sectional political interests, ministers should not intervene in day-to-day management.

With the exception of the limited duties legally imposed upon him the minister will have no right to interfere with the work of the board. It would be quite unwise to concede him the right to send for the board or its chairman and say, 'Here is something you are doing wrong; you must mend your ways and pursue the following policy'. . .. A mischievous and not too competent minister could easily ruin any business undertaking if that were permitted, whilst a weak and inefficient management would protect itself against public criticism by spreading the story that 'there is too much minister in the running of this show'.[4]

Morrison's views were strongly reflected in the statutes that set up the various nationalised industries and which continued to govern them more or less unchanged until the 1980s. The general powers and obligations laid down for each industry in the Nationalisation Acts are as follows.

1. The industry was required to produce certain goods and services, taking account of customers' and workers' interests and often granted a monopoly.
2. The industry's revenues should on average cover its costs, including depreciation and interest and repayment of debt.
3. The minister was to appoint the chairman and members of the management board and was empowered to issue directives to the board.
4. The industry had to publish its accounts and an annual report.
5. A consumer council was set up for each industry, to provide a channel for consumer interests, but they are consultative bodies with no powers.

The Morrison Model in Practice

While Morrison was very perceptive about the problems and tensions inherent in running nationalised industries, the organisational framework he devised did not prove an adequate solution. Despite various tinkerings with that framework over the last thirty years, the general view persists that the problem of devising a satisfactory relationship between government and nationalised industries remains unresolved. Customers complain of poor service, governments of inefficiency, trade unions of inadequate resources to pay higher wages, managements of too much political interference, Parliament of insufficient accountability. . .

Morrison's framework was based on the premise that, free of the capitalist profit motive, a public-spirited board of professional managers would run their nationalised industry as an efficient business, while acting jointly with the minister as guardians of the public interest. Three interrelated problems emerged: how to set efficiency criteria and get the industries to conform to them; how to determine what is in the 'public interest' as distinct from purely sectional interests; and how to reconcile the requirement of efficiency with political and social objectives.

The pre-war advocates of nationalisation had largely presumed that the industries would earn sufficient revenues to cover their costs, including new investment. Morrison thought that this responsibility could be safely left to the management boards and so no financial targets or efficiency criteria were specified in the Nationalisation Acts, apart from the very general stipulation to break even. As the 1950s progressed it became evident that this was insufficient guidance. Some industries, like coal and

258 Economic Policy-Making

railways, operating in declining markets, made losses and the industries as a whole were able to finance only a third of their investment from internally-generated funds. The government did little in the way of scrutinising nationalised industries' investment to ensure it would earn an adequate rate of return. The increasing reluctance of financial investors to take up nationalised industries' loan stock prompted the Treasury, in the Finance Act 1956, to undertake all Stock Exchange borrowing on the industries' behalf. The House of Commons became increasingly exercised about the industries' lack of parliamentary accountability. The Select Committee on Nationalised Industries was set up in 1956 to investigate the industries. It called for the establishment of more precise financial and economic criteria for guiding the industries' pricing and investment decisions.

In response the government, in 1961, issued a White Paper, *The Financial and Economic Obligations of the Nationalised Industries* (Cmnd. 1337), in which it stated the general principle that

although the industries have obligations of a national and non-commercial kind, they are not. . . to be regarded as social services absolved from economic and commercial justifications. (para. 2)

In an attempt to set clearer objectives and ensure less financial profligacy, the nationalised industries were set *financial targets*, in terms of rates of return on their capital assets and the explicit requirement to break even over an average of five years.

The problem with financial rate of return targets is that they do not by themselves ensure allocative efficiency even on the limited definition of market efficiency. A monopoly can attain such a financial target by charging high prices rather than by cost efficiency. A further problem, which much exercises economists, is that allocative efficiency requires prices to be set in relation to marginal costs and not average costs, as was the practice of the nationalised industries. Furthermore, even if a nationalised monopoly achieved the same price and output levels as would an equivalent perfectly competitive firm, social inefficiency would persist if private costs and benefits in the industry diverged from social costs and benefits.[5] Hence setting financial targets ignores the so-called *social obligations* expected of nationalised industries. If an industry undertakes commercially loss-making activities in order to fulfil social efficiency criteria, then it will be less able to earn a commercial rate of return on its assets. On the other hand, an industry can use its social obligations as an excuse for making losses that are due to commercial inefficiency—not keeping down costs, failing to innovate or neglecting market opportunities for satisfying consumer wants.

Thus the financial targets were criticised for failing to promote either market efficiency or the wider concept of social efficiency. Under the influence of academic economists the civil service prepared a further White Paper in 1967, *Nationalised Industries: A Review of Economic and Social Obligations* (Cmnd 3437). Financial targets and covering accounting costs were retained, but supplemented by pricing and investment rules, derived from the theory of *optimal resource allocation*. Prices were to be based on *long-run marginal costs*. These are the additional costs, including the capital costs, of producing an extra unit of output. Because *cross-subsidisation* violates the principle of *marginal cost pricing*, the White Paper was critical of its use to finance activities which were not commercially viable but desired for social and political reasons—activities euphemistically called the nationalised industries' social obligations. To make it clear that nationalised industries are primarily commercial undertakings and not social services, each industry should be paid earmarked government grants for fulfilling specific social obligations. The White Paper also required nationalised industries to use the *discounted cash flow* technique of investment appraisal (see Chapter 10, p.226). Investment proposals should be adopted only if they were estimated to bring in a rate of return at least equal to a specified *test discount rate*. This was initially set at 8 per cent (later raised to 10 per cent), and was supposed to reflect the opportunity cost of capital by reference to what it could earn in the private sector.

In retrospect the attempt to apply the principles of optimal social resource allocation was a dismal failure. There is little point basing prices on long-run marginal costs, if the industries' actual costs are well above the minimum attainable because of x-inefficiency. In addition the industries had problems in measuring long-run marginal costs. Using a test rate of discount does little to weed out low-return investment projects when the industry does its own investment appraisal on the basis of over-optimistic assumptions. An industry desiring to secure investment finance from the government has every incentive to overestimate future demand and underestimate future costs. Neither the sponsoring ministry nor the Treasury has the capacity to do its own independent investment appraisals. And if they had, they would be duplicating the work of the industries and undermining the purpose of having them run by independent management boards. Central government's scrutiny of the industries' investment appraisals relies mainly on asking probing questions about the assumptions upon which the figures are derived. In the event the rates of return actually achieved on investment fell well below the test discount rate. British Steel is a notorious case of an industry overinvesting on the basis of excessively optimistic assumptions about its future sales. As we saw in Chapter 3, the NCB invested in new capacity without solving the problem of its existing high-cost pits. In 1985 the Comptroller and Auditor General reported critically on the quality of investment appraisal. He pointed out weaknesses in the sponsoring ministries' scrutiny of the industries' assumptions and lack of checks to see whether the estimated rate of return on an investment project was actually achieved.[6]

The 1967 White Paper's proposal that nationalised industries should be paid an explicit grant for undertaking loss-making activities to satisfy social and political objectives, rather than practise cross-subsidisation or record poor financial results, was implemented, though both cross-subsidisation and missed financial targets persist. As noted in Chapter 3, the NCB has received a social grant for the Redundant Mineworkers Payments Scheme since the late 1960s. The Transport Act 1968 enabled British Rail and bus companies to receive government grants for running unremunerative services. These have become much more extensive than originally envisaged. By the early 1980s the social railway, as these subsidised services are called, was receiving almost £1 billion in government grants. The electricity boards have received grants for burning more NCB coal than they otherwise wanted to, and British Airways for buying British-made aircraft instead of their preferred US models.

The nationalised industries present these grant-aided activities as social obligations they are required to perform by the government for social reasons. As the social grants count as revenue they enable the industries to undertake these activities without recording them as loss-making. Nationalised industry boards have frequently complained that they are leant on by ministers to do things the government wants for political reasons but which harm the efficiency of the enterprise. However, it is also in the interests of an industry to acquire social obligations. These enable the business to be larger than it would be without them and to employ more people at higher wages. Thus social obligations are demanded by unions as well as by the customers of loss-making services. A nationalised industry can therefore form a powerful coalition of management, unions and consumers, exerting political pressure on government to use public money to further their interests.

One example of this is provided by Sir Richard Marsh, former Labour minister and one time chairman of British Rail. As part of his efforts to secure more money for the social railway, he showed the Conservative Minister of Transport

a complete map of the existing British Rail network. We then removed that and put up a much smaller British Rail network on which we superimposed the political map. He suddenly realised that all the closed lines were in rural areas and, by sheer coincidence, happened to be Conservative seats.[7]

A large chunk of the social railway consists of the commuter lines into London, which run through Conservative and marginal constituencies. It has been shown that rail subsidies discriminate in favour of the better-off, who travel by train much more than do the poor, particularly on commuter lines.[8] So although nationalised industries are officially deemed to have social obligations, it is by no means self-evident that these are in the national interest nor that they promote social justice. As has already been noted, the economists' concept of social efficiency has come to be readily used by political interests for their own ends, a development that was encouraged by the creation of grant-aided *social obligations* for the nationalised industries.

The attempted reforms of 1967 had some limited success. In some areas the principle of marginal cost pricing has been adopted, as with two-part electricity tariffs; the standing charge covers fixed costs, while the different day and night tariffs per unit of electricity consumed reflect the higher marginal cost of generating electricity at times of peak demand. Using the recommended discounted cash flow investment appraisal method has enabled industries to compare alternative production methods with greater rationality: it has, for example, tipped the balance in favour of electric rather than diesel trains on certain routes.

The failure of optimal resource allocation rules to provide a satisfactory set of depoliticised criteria for the pricing, output and investment decisions of the nationalised industries was partly due to the political naivety of the rationally-minded technocrats who developed them. The rules assume that objective data on the industries' minimum attainable costs for various output levels, both current and projected, and their likely future revenues are readily obtainable, rather than being malleable figures, produced under the influence of sectional interests. A further related reason is the lack of political will behind the adoption and application of these decision rules. According to Richard Crossman,[9] a member of the Labour Cabinet in 1967, the Cabinet took only twenty minutes over the White Paper. In reply to Crossman's opinion that it was a poor Paper, the Chancellor, James Callaghan, replied: 'It's only read by a few dons and experts. I take no responsibility and took no part in composing it.' Having been greeted with apathy by one government, the rules were then completely undermined by the next, which instructed the industries to keep down their prices as part of the government's counter-inflation policy.

By the mid-1970s, both the optimal resource allocation rules and the financial targets had been ignored, largely due to government attitudes and policies. In 1974–75, the industries were paid £1725 million in government grants to subsidise their losses, of which over £1 billion went on subsidised gas, electricity and postal prices. As a result of the public expenditure crisis of 1975–76, the government put some pressure on the industries to stem their losses. But with rising unemployment and the Labour government's reluctance to breach the implicit terms of its 'social contract' with the unions, this pressure was distinctly muted.

During the 1970s both Labour and Conservative administrations undermined the attempts of the 1960s to clarify and strengthen the framework inherited from Morrison. The principle that nationalised industries should be politically sanitised and operate at arm's length from government, within a framework of clearly established objectives which reflected both their commercial and social responsibilities, had failed to find an operational form. Under pressure from the industries' consumer and employee interests, and buffeted by the recurrent crises of general economic management, the clear message emanating from government was that nationalised industries are instruments of short-term economic policy and firmly within the political arena.

The State of Play in the 1980s

A third attempt at setting objectives for the nationalised industries was made in a further White Paper, *The Nationalised Industries* (Cmnd 7131), issued in 1978. In recognition of the failure of the 1967 rules, long-run marginal cost pricing was downgraded and the test rate of discount supplemented by the overriding requirement to earn a 5 per cent real rate of return on the investment programme as a whole. Much more importance has been given to *financial targets* based on standard accounting information rather than on economists' allocative efficiency criteria. Each industry is now set its own financial targets. For profitable concerns these take the form of specified rates of return on existing assets. Loss-makers are required to break even by specified dates. While these financial targets served to exert pressure on the industries to become more efficient in the commercial sense, they do not of themselves provide the government with sanctions against public corporations which fail to meet their targets.

As discussed in Chapter 4, the concern of governments since 1975 to control public spending led to the adoption of *cash limits*, which for a public corporation is its *external financing limit*. Under the Thatcher government, with its much publicised intentions to reduce public spending, the *external financing limits* became the main instrument of government control of the nationalised industries. They have served the dual function of limiting public expenditure as an objective in its own right, to which the public corporations were expected to contribute, and as a means of exerting pressure on the industries to improve their commercial efficiency. The impact of this policy on the NCB was examined in Chapter 3. Overall, by 1984–85, the Conservatives had cut the total external finance of the nationalised industries by 35 per cent in real terms compared to 1979–80, though this was much less than originally intended. If a nationalised industry breaches its EFL, as did the NCB, British Rail, the CEGB and British Steel, as a result of the miners' strike, there is little the government can do but pay up and not reappoint the chairman once his contract comes to an end.

There is no doubt that the EFL is a blunt instrument of control, and that it flies in the face of the criteria for efficient resource allocation, even of the limited kind which ignore externalities. It is, however, better suited to forcing industries to reduce their costs and so curb x-inefficiency. EFLs have also been used as a source of government revenue. By setting stringent EFLs—in some cases negative ones—the Treasury has put pressure on secure monopolies, such as water, gas and electricity, to charge prices in excess of marginal costs, in order to milk them for the Exchequer through a concealed form of taxation. To some extent this pressure has been resisted in the PESC bargaining sessions by the industries and their sponsoring ministers.

Despite the Conservatives' promise, when in opposition, that 'we aim to protect the management of nationalised industries from constant Whitehall interference',[10] relationships between government—particularly the Treasury and the Prime Minister—and the chairmen of the nationalised industries have been strained. Not only have the chairmen chafed at the constrictions and short-term planning horizons of the EFLs, they have resented the further attempts to extend central government scrutiny and monitoring of their activities. In coalition with their sponsoring ministries, they have successfully resisted Treasury attempts to introduce surveillance by a specially recruited group of businessmen. The Treasury wished to introduce new umbrella legislation to replace the nationalisation statutes by comprehensive and stronger statutory powers, including the setting of financial targets and the dismissal of chairmen. In the face of hostility from the chairmen and a distinct lack of enthusiasm from the sponsoring ministries, the government went no further with the proposals, which one industry had described as horrendous and turning them into a department of state.[11] Both parties have now turned to *privatisation*, where feasible, as a solution to the impasse.

Basic Issues in the Control of Public Enterprises

Over the last thirty years, dissatisfaction, both with the performance of the public corporations and with successive governments' policies towards them, has rumbled on. There are inevitable tensions in the relationship between government and state industries. It is generally accepted that if the state produces goods and services of a commercial nature, then a separate business organisation, rather than a government department, is more likely to undertake this activity efficiently. There is also a limit to the number of activities central departments of state can cope with. Having delegated production to a separate organisation, central government is then faced with the problem of getting these organisations to perform well. Firms which no longer face the sanction of bankruptcy and which are often monopolies to boot, have less incentive to keep down costs than private firms in competitive markets. However central government cannot double-check the activities of nationalised industries, as this would be wasteful duplication of effort. Monitoring and control must be kept to manageable proportions. Hence the need to devise an efficient and effective system of rules, sanctions and incentives to induce desirable standards of performance in state firms.

But matters are further complicated when public corporations are expected to do other things than perform with the efficiency of a competitive firm. Though not all would agree with this, public corporations are used as instruments of social and general economic policy. Those who favour state planning and intervention to improve the performance of the economy, see nothing incompatible in principle between this and the commercial efficiency of state enterprises. But the way nationalised industries have been used in the UK, as instruments of general economic policy, has impaired their performance as businesses. The provision of social services by public corporations is inconsistent with their commercial objectives, though in principle this can be overcome by the payment of explicit government subsidies.

In a democracy, it is difficult to use public corporations as instruments of social and general economic policy without placing them in the political arena. The alternative of having them run by professional public servants, who are trusted to determine the public interest, abjures any form of democratic control, even if such model persons exist. When the political element enters into the running of state industries they become subject to the pressure of political interests. Morrison saw this danger quite clearly, but the relationship he advocated between minister and management board failed to insulate the industries from political interests, both inside and outside the industry. Using the industries as instruments of social and economic policy serves to enlarge the opportunities for political interests to exert their influence. Measures that favour a sectional interest are presented as being in the national interest or being socially efficient or socially just. Both minister and management board act as channels for transmitting the influence of political interests. The management boards form coalitions with their employees, who want higher wages and more jobs, as in the coal industry in 1982, and with customers, who like subsidised services, in order to put more effective pressure on government for the necessary finance. In 1979 the industries coordinated their efforts by forming their own pressure group, the Nationalised Industries Chairmen's Group. On the other side, ministers seek to win political support from sectional interests by requiring nationalised industries to adopt policies that favour these interests. The industries complain that politicians want them to do things that are against their commercial interests, while government, especially the Treasury, complain of the industries' inefficiency due to their capture by sectional interests.

Central government itself is no monolith with a single point of view with respect to the nationalised industries. The sponsoring ministries tend to pursue different ends and represent different political interests than does the Treasury, whose overriding concern is controlling public expenditure and so reducing the demands of the nationalised industries on the Exchequer. The Treasury is therefore particularly keen to improve the commercial efficiency of the industries, cut their losses and, where possible, raise their profits in order to contribute to government revenue. However the Treasury has no direct contact with the nationalised industries. The sponsoring ministries mediate between it and the industries: they represent the Treasury to the sponsored industry and the industry to the Treasury. Thus the sponsoring ministries act as channels of representation for the industries' political interests within government and so are frequently in conflict with the Treasury. Examples already mentioned are the size of EFLs, nationalised industries' prices and legislation to alter the framework of control.

Dissatisfaction with the performance of the nationalised industries and with the difficulty of controlling them, coupled with the desire to extend the influence of market forces, led the Conservative government to turn to *privatisation*.

PRIVATISATION

Privatisation is a term of relatively recent origin which refers to a wide range of measures designed to extend the influence of market forces *vis-à-vis* the public sector. *Privatisation* with respect to the public corporations involves both selling public sector businesses to private owners and *liberalisation*—removing regulations which restrict competition in areas served by public sector enterprises. These two aspects of privatisation need to be carefully distinguished, since changing to private ownership in the case of monopolies does not by itself increase the degree of competition. Conversely, competition can be increased by *liberalisation* without transferring productive assets to private ownership.

As with public ownership, there are several diverse reasons for advocating privatisation. For *libertarians* it is an end in itself, since a large public sector is seen as a threat to individuals' liberty because it subjects individuals to a wide measure of collective choice and diminishes their own freedom to choose. Another primarily political reason for privatisation, emphasised by the Thatcher government, is to extend private ownership, particularly of houses and shares. Hence small private investors have been encouraged to acquire shares in privatised firms, either by giving preference to small subscriptions or by selling the enterprise to its employees, as in the case of the National Freight Corporation.

The other reasons for privatisation relate to its use as an instrument rather than an end in itself. The primary reason is to improve efficiency. Here the usual arguments as to why competitive market forces make firms perform more efficiently, covered in Chapters 3 and 6, apply. X-inefficiency is thought to be particularly rife in the public sector because the sanction of bankruptcy is weakened or removed, as in the case of nationalised industries and trading funds. The fear of a Stock Exchange takeover if the firm's profit performance is poor relative to its potential, which is held to constrain managers to make profits, is also absent. However if the firm is a monopoly, then the fear of bankruptcy is much diminished. The x-inefficiency arguments in favour of privatisation are therefore much stronger if the privatised firm is to operate in a competitive market. Hence private ownership needs to be accompanied by liberalisation if the efficiency gains are to be fully realised.

From the point of view of government, privatisation solves the problem of having to monitor and control public sector firms in order to limit their x-inefficiency. The job can be left to competitive markets and private sector agents who operate in them. Provided the market can be made competitive, privatisation is also a solution to the problem of securing allocative efficiency, since competition will keep prices in line with costs. Market failure due to externalities can also be corrected without resorting to public ownership, by means of taxes, subsidies or regulations. Taxes and subsidies can also be employed if the government wishes to use private sector firms as redistributive agents. However, privatised natural monopolies are liable to exploit consumers and misallocate resources by charging prices in excess of opportunity costs. As already noted, the alternative to public monopolies is *regulation* of private sector monopolies.

All these arguments are grist to the economist's mill. But to the politicians in power a second set of arguments has proved equally appealing: selling public sector assets has been a way of achieving the Thatcher government's goal of cutting public spending and reducing the size of the public sector borrowing requirement. If loss-making public enterprises can be turned round sufficiently to persuade the private sector to take them over, a drain on public funds has been stemmed. This, though, has been a minor element, since most enterprises that the private sector is willing to acquire are already profitable. The major source of public revenue from privatisation has been from the sale of assets. The government has treated the money received from such asset sales as negative public expenditure and deducted it from the PSBR, thus making it appear that both the objectives of reducing government spending and that of cutting the PSBR have been more closely achieved than if asset sales were treated as revenue.

The aim of selling public enterprises to raise revenue and that of privatising them in order to maximise efficiency, by placing the firms in a competitive environment, are in conflict. The greater the market power of a newly privatised firm, the higher are likely to be its profits and so the greater its stock market valuation. If a public enterprise has its market power reduced by being broken up into several parts and has its protective regulations dismantled, it will be unable to earn monopoly profits. As its share value on the Stock Exchange will be lower it will fetch less for the state coffers.

Another factor that has pushed the government in the direction of privatising public corporations in their current monopoly form has been the attitudes of the industries themselves. It is difficult for the government to implement privatisation without the cooperation of the organisations concerned. Nationalised industries, notably British Gas, resist privatisation, if this involves breaking up their business or stripping it of its protective regulations. However, after decades of political interference and several years of particularly sharp conflict over government expenditure restrictions and Treasury surveillance, the nationalised industry chairmen have warmed to privatisation, provided that their industries remain intact. The British Airports Authority is to be sold as one concern rather than as separate airports. British Gas is being sold as a single business. Alternative proposals involve breaking its monopoly of gas showrooms or separating the gas pipelines, which are a natural monopoly, from gas production and wholesaling, which are not. A public corporation could continue to own the distribution network, while private gas producers, and wholesalers paid for using the network.

Thus the privatisation programme has evolved as a blend of aspirations for improved social arrangements, the pragmatism of daily politics and bargaining between interconnected coalitions of political interests, both within and outside the machinery of government.

The Privatisation Programme

The Conservative government's privatisation programme has been more extensive than any previous administration's and is now extending beyond British Telecom to other industries with a strong element of natural monopoly, like gas and, possibly, water and electricity. The government started with *liberalisation* measures, and began selling major public corporations only in its second term. The Transport Act 1980 deregulated long-distance coach travel. Licence restrictions on operators entering the market were removed and limited to safety standards. In response to the threat of entry from private sector companies, the National Bus Company, which dominates the market, lowered fares and introduced new services. The Telecommunications Act 1981 permitted certain types of private equipment to be connected to the British Telecom network and allowed a newly-formed private consortium, *Mercury*, to compete in inter-city telecommunications. As a result, BT cut its charges on inter-city routes. The Post Office's monopoly of express mail has been removed. Among professional services, opticians' legal monopoly over dispensing spectacles has been removed as has solicitors' monopoly of house conveyancing.

The government's programme of asset sales started with the disposal of land, property, oil licences and shares in partly-owned companies and then moved on to the disposal of larger public corporations, the major ones being sold in stages. The assets sold and the sums obtained to the year 1984/85 are shown in Table 11.2. Further major sales are intended: e.g. British Airways and the British Airports Authority. Plans to privatise water, BL and the Royal Ordnance factories have been withdrawn for the time being. If all the most likely candidates went (excluding electicity), there would still be left some 60 per cent of the assets vested in the nationalised industries (listed in Table 11.1).

WHAT FUTURE FOR PUBLIC ENTERPRISE?

If the privatisation programme goes through as indicated, then the most radical changes since 1945−50 will have occurred in the contribution of public corporations to economic activity in Britain. In the thirty years after the major nationalised industries were created, the main political parties maintained a rough-and-ready compromise regarding the extent of public enterprise. The Conservatives accepted that it had a major role, while the Labour Party, despite the rhetoric of the Left, did not extend its boundaries beyond a few additional industries.

The Labour Party has strongly opposed the sale of public assets. The extent to which it would renationalise the privatised concerns is difficult to gauge. There is quite a widespread recognition of public disenchantment with centralised, state-run monopolies: customers complain of poor service, taxpayers of financing losses, while labour relations have been no better, or even worse, than in the private sector. This recognition has led those who are critical of private enterprise to seek alternative forms of collective enterprise, which would be more responsive to consumer demands and motivate their workers better. The 1985 TUC Conference adopted a resolution which recognised the 'limitations of post-war approaches to nationalisation', and called for 'a new definition in order to regain its acceptance both by workers and the electorate'. This revised approach should encompass decentralised forms of public enterprise, such as cooperatives and municipal undertakings, which would be democratically accountable both to their workers and to the community. How the conflict between consumers' and workers' interests would be resolved in the absence of competition is not clear. What is clear, though,

Table 11.2: Sale of public corporation assets

£ million

	1979–80	1980–81	1981–82	1982–83	1983–84	1984–85
British Petroleum	276		8		543	
British Aerospace		43				
British Sugar Corporation			44			
Cable and Wireless			182		263	
Amersham International			64			
National Freight Company			5			
Britoil				334	293	
Associated British Ports				46		51
National Enterprise Board	37	83	2			
British Telecom						1352
British Rail Hotels				30	15	82
British Gas (oil interests)						380
Enterprise Oil						40
Sealink						297
Jaguar					43	168
British Technology	1					
Drake and Scull Holdings	22					
Suez Finance Company		195				
North Sea Oil Licence Premia				33	11	
Sale of oil stockpiles			63	33	4	
Sale of commodity stocks			19	7		
Sale of land and property	34	84	107	35	28	
Total	307	405	494	488	1142	2370

Source: The Government's Expenditure Plans 1985–86 to 1987–88, Cmnd 9428; Financial Times, 7 November 1985.

is that with a change in government, policies with respect to public enterprise will be in for another upheaval. Despite this, the essential features of the relationship between government and the remaining nationalised industries are likely to persist under a different administration, as they have done in the past.

CONCLUSION

Economic policy with respect to the public corporations is distinct from that towards the social services, because the former organisations produce marketed goods. Thus the objective that public corporations should operate according to commercial criteria has loomed large, though tempered by the requirement of allocative efficiency that their monopoly power should not be exploited against the consumer. The public corporations have been looked to as a means for securing social and political objectives, while they are also subject to the vagaries of macroeconomic policy.

The tensions between the objectives of commercial efficiency, allocative efficiency, social goals and political accountability have remained at the heart of the relationship between government and public corporations. Public corporations provide another example of the relationship between sponsoring politicians and the bureaucrats employed in a state agency. Changes in organisational structure, in decision rules, and in the degree and form of monitoring, are all aspects of the politicians' attempts to make the bureaucrats perform more to their liking. The rational decision rules for social efficiency devised by economists have had limited value as a solution to these problems.

More recently, the libertarian principles of promoting competition have failed to be properly implemented in the privatisation programme, largely for political reasons. The politicians have used privatisation as a quick solution to their pressing problems, while the bureaucrats in charge of the nationalised industries have sought to turn privatisation to their advantage. Nor does privatisation of itself necessarily remove the political element in the relations between government and the enterprise. When a public monopoly is replaced by a private one, the government has to devise and implement some form of regulation to prevent the abuse of monopoly power. It is also open to pressures to adopt policies towards the firm which favour British industry, such as persuading it to buy from British suppliers.

The alternative scenario to privatisation is the creation of different forms of political accountability for public enterprises, by decentralising them and somehow making them more accountable to both workers and the community. These ideas are still at the stage of vague outlines and small-scale local experiments. How they would reconcile the conflicting interests of consumers and workers is far from clear. No solution has clearly resolved the inherent tensions of operating policies towards business enterprises which are exposed, because of natural monopoly or by political history, to political bargaining as the primary mode of policy-making.

NOTES

1. See Chapter 1 and *Economic Trends*.
2. J. Barnett, op. cit., p. 3 (Chief Secretary to the Treasury in 1974 – 79 Labour government).
3. In evidence to the Select Committee on Nationalised Industries, 1958.
4. H. Morrison, *Socialization and Transport* (Constable, London, 1933).
5. The welfare arguments for setting price equal to marginal cost were outlined in Chapter 3, pp. 49-51. The theoretical proof of this proposition requires that all markets set price equal to, or proportional to, marginal cost. One cannot state with certainty whether getting one industry to adopt marginal cost pricing, when there are others that do not, would improve social welfare. This is known as the problem of the second best.
6. *Financial Times*, 29 March 1985.
7. R. Marsh, *Off the Rails* (Weidenfeld and Nicolson, London, 1978), p. 167.
8. J. LeGrand, *The Strategy of Equality* (George Allen and Unwin, London, 1982).
9. Richard Crossman, *The Diaries of a Cabinet Minister* (Hamish Hamilton and Jonathan Cape, London, 1975), p. 524.
10. A. Maude *et al.*, *The Right Approach to the Economy* (Conservative Central Office, London, 1977).
11. 'A closer control proposed for state industry', *Financial Times*, 18 September 1984.

12 Welfare Policies and the Welfare State

The achievement of social equality depends upon the development of a more generous and universal system of social security and social services, and upon strengthening the powers of the local community within that system. . . .Means tests for public benefits and services within the welfare state; private and occupational benefits and services, distributed by the market according to people's ability to pay; and powerful bureaucratic and professional structures, both public and private, all have to be disentangled from British life.

A transformation of the welfare state to meet our universal ideals would necessarily involve the reduction and eventual abolition of private and occupational welfare. . . .We . . .hope that a Labour government would take into accountable common ownership the semi-socialized wealth of the pension funds and insurance companies. . .. This would allow the government to create a truly universal social security scheme. . .. It could provide protection for every crisis in life from the cradle to the grave: maternity, disability, sickness, unemployment, dependency, single parenthood, widowhood, old age and death. . .. An increase in child benefit is the most immediate and effective way of reducing family poverty among those in work. (F. Cripps *et al. Manifesto: a radical strategy for Britain's future* (London, Pan Books, 1981), pp. 198–201)

There is inefficiency and waste in state production, mainly because monopoly inflates costs.

There is inefficiency and waste in state consumption because there is over-provision or underprovision of goods and services, except in 'public goods'.

The cure in principle for waste in state production is ultimately complete privatisation. The cure in principle for waste in state consumption is to transfer consumption to the citizen, except for public goods.

To help the poor a Negative Income Tax for those in work should replace the current Family Income Supplement, etc.; for those out of work there should be a limit on unemployment benefits relative to income in work.

Taxation can be brought down by savings to the Exchequer from these reforms. Tax thresholds can be more than doubled, child benefits more than trebled, National Insurance Contributions abolished and VAT cut by 4 per cent.

The NHS, except for its element of public goods, should be replaced by competitive health insurance. State education should be replaced by competitive private education. Other central and local government services should be privatised.

These reforms should benefit rich, poor and middling because of the massive reduction in economic waste. Only pressure groups will lose. They are essential if the British economy is to regain its dynamism. (Patrick Minford 'State expenditure: a study in waste', *Economic Affairs*, April/June 1984, p.xix)

Welfare policies are concerned with the role of government in the allocation and distribution of welfare services, the production of which absorb a considerable proportion of the nation's resources. Thus welfare policies are an important category of economic policy, as well as having significant implications for the economy and for the conduct of macroeconomic policy. This chapter considers what constitutes the welfare state, what objectives have been sought from it and the role of different allocative mechanisms, including the welfare state, in furthering those objectives. While the welfare state serves as the main instrument of redistribution, the objectives that welfare policies should serve and the means used to secure such objectives arouse passionate disagreement. As the two extracts reveal, there is a vast gulf between radical socialist and libertarian welfare policies. Differing views on the relationships between the economy, the welfare state and economic policy are outlined in the course of this chapter. A further issue considered is resource allocation decisions in the non-marketed part of the public sector, where the price mechanism has been replaced by administrative (government) allocation.

WHAT IS THE WELFARE STATE?

The welfare state we actually have is somewhere between the two polar models extolled in the opening extracts. It is an essential ingredient of the mixed economies of western liberal democracies. While it takes different structural forms and varies in its size, the welfare state in these countries possesses strong common features. One is the social security system which consists of a set of cash payments and tax expenditures made by the government to individuals and households who are deemed to have insufficient income, because of old age, sickness, disability, unemployment or childcare responsibilities, or who are categorised as having special expenditure needs, because they are bringing up children, have high housing costs relative to their current incomes, or due to old age or disability.

The second element of the welfare state is the state provision of what are termed social services. These are services which are regarded as so important to the quality of life that no one should be debarred from them due to insufficient income, or to personal or parental fecklessness. The usual services included under this heading are state-provided education, health, housing and personal social services, such as residential and daycare for children, the elderly or handicapped, meals-on-wheels and home helps. Employment services, such as state-run employment exchanges and job-creation programmes, are usually also included. There is no agreed and watertight definition of what is classified as a social service: the definitions depend both on the social context and on subjective judgements. The definition of what constitute 'needs', which the state should provide free or at subsidised prices, has tended to widen over time. Public transport and domestic heating are nowadays widely regarded as having a social service element.

The third aspect of the welfare state consists of laws and regulations designed to protect people from ill-treatment or exploitation by others. Health and safety regulations, legislation to protect tenants from eviction and to control rents, laws to protect children from neglect and ill-treatment and to regulate their working hours, are all examples. However, such legislation can have undesirable side-effects because it limits competition and so impedes the provision of alternative or less costly services.

A BRIEF HISTORY OF THE WELFARE STATE

The fully-fledged welfare state, consisting of a reasonably comprehensive social security system and state provision of education, health, housing and personal social services, dates from the end of World War II. Prior to that it had gradually evolved from the nineteenth century as a succession of piecemeal social reforms. In Britain, the 1834 Poor Law reform provided state subsistence to the destitute in the workhouse, in return for hard labour, plus outdoor relief for the deserving poor—the old, sick and disabled. In the course of the nineteenth century, Factory Acts were passed to limit the use of female and child labour and to restrict working hours. The Education Act 1870 made primary schooling compulsory, set up local board schools, and provided state finance for voluntary schools. In 1910 a means-tested old age pension was introduced, followed in 1911 and 1920 by compulsory national insurance against sickness and unemployment. However when unemployment rose, this scheme proved inadequate and a means-tested supplement was added, financed out of taxation. In the 1920s local authorities began building houses for rent.

During World War II the coalition government began to plan the social reforms that would be required once peace returned. The postwar social security system, enacted in 1948, was based on the famous 1942 Beveridge Report on Social Insurance and Allied Services. The two major social services, the state education system, enacted in 1944, and the National Health Service, created in 1948, plus an ambitious postwar programme of local authority house building, completed the major structural features of the British welfare state. Some of the state's welfare services are consumed by the majority of the population: the NHS provides 91 per cent of hospital beds; state schools educate 94 per cent of pupils; all the workforce receive state pensions and for 40 per cent of them this is their only pension. Others are consumed by a minority, like means-tested benefits and council housing, which now accounts for less than 30 per cent of the housing stock.[1]

Postwar Developments in Welfare Spending

Although the main constituents of today's welfare state were in place by the end of the 1940s, the size of the welfare state has continued to grow in real terms and as a proportion of GDP, in Britain as well as in other developed economies. The annual average rate of growth in real terms of the major welfare programmes in Britain is shown in Table 12.1. Welfare expenditure as a whole has grown more rapidly than total government expenditure and considerably in excess of the rate of growth of real GDP. As economic growth faltered in the mid-1970s, welfare spending came under increasing pressure, as did all the public sector programmes. Under the Conservatives, welfare spending, while still rising in real terms, has slowed down relative to overall government expenditure.

Table 12.1: Average annual percentage rate of growth of real welfare expenditure[a]

	1951−63	1963−68	1968−73	1973−78	1978−85
Social Security	6.3	8.1	3.1	6.9	4.9
National Health Service	2.1	7.3	4.4	4.7	2.8
Personal social services[b]	—	7.5	11.7	5.9	NA[c]
Education	6.0	8.5	5.5	0.4	0.0
Employment services	0.4	36.6	5.6	30.5	9.2
Housing	4.1	11.9	8.6	1.3	−5.8
Total welfare spending	4.5	8.7	5.0	4.3	2.0
Government expenditure	3.0	7.4	3.3	2.2	2.1
GDP at market prices	3.2	3.4	3.5	1.2	1.5

Sources: *UK National Accounts; Economic Trends.*
Notes: a. Estimated using implied GDP deflator; b. Included with NHS 1951−62; c. 1.4% 1978−83.

Since welfare spending has grown at a faster rate than GDP it has risen as a proportion of GDP. As Table 12.2 shows, welfare spending has grown continuously over the postwar period, from 14.8 per cent of GDP in 1951 to around 26 per cent in the years 1983−5. The proportion of government expenditure on the welfare state has stabilised at around 56 per cent since the late 1970s. In 1951 it took only 40 per cent of total government spending;

by 1963 this had risen to 46.6 per cent; it then climbed to 51.5 per cent by 1973. The largest programme in terms of expenditure is social security, which by 1985 accounted for about half of the total welfare budget. The next largest programmes are the NHS and education with around 19 per cent each. The changing allocation of the welfare budget over the postwar period is shown in Table 12.3.

Table 12.2: Welfare spending as percentage of GDP (at market prices)

	1951	1963	1968	1973	1978	1985
Social Security	5.0	6.5	7.6	7.5	9.5	13.0
National Health Service	3.7	3.4	3.9	4.0	4.7	5.0
Personal social services[a]	—	0.6	0.7	1.0	1.2	NA[b]
Education	3.3	4.2	5.0	5.4	5.2	5.0
Employment services	0.1	0.1	0.3	0.3	0.7	0.9
Housing	2.6	1.9	2.6	3.2	3.2	1.9
Total welfare spending	14.8	16.7	20.0	21.4	24.4	25.8

Sources: As Table 12.1.
Notes: a. Included in NHS 1951–62; b. 1.2% in 1983.

Table 12.3: The share of welfare programmes in the welfare budget

	1951	1963	1968	1973	1978	1985
Social Security	34.0	38.9	38.1	35.2	39.0	50.2
National Health Service	24.8	20.2	19.3	18.8	19.1	19.5
Personal social services[a]	—	3.6	3.6	4.5	4.8	NA[b]
Education	22.5	25.1	24.9	25.4	21.4	19.2
Employment services	1.0	0.7	1.3	1.3	2.8	3.5
Housing and community services	17.8	11.6	12.9	14.8	13.0	7.4

Sources: *UK National Accounts.*
Note: a. Included with NHS 1951–62; b. 4.6 in 1983.

The 'Crisis' in the Welfare State

Since the mid-1970s the rate of growth of the welfare state in developed economies decelerated, with the general slowdown in world economic growth. Britain's experience, relative to that of other major mixed economies, is shown in Table 12.4. Even without such a faltering in the momentum of economic growth, welfare expenditure could not have continued indefinitely to grow at a faster rate than the economy as a whole. Deceleration and retrenchment, after years of expanding budgets, have brought acute adjustment problems to the welfare state and particularly to the bureaucracies that run it. In addition to slower-growing budgets, demands on the social security system have increased, with rising numbers of unemployed and old people.

Table 12.4: Welfare expenditure in mixed economies, 1960−81

	Welfare expenditure as percentage of GDP		Annual growth rate of real welfare expenditure %		Annual growth rate of real GDP %	
	1960	1981	1960−75	1975−81	1960−75	1975−81
Canada	12.1	21.5	9.3	3.1	5.1	3.3
France	13.4	29.5	7.3	6.2	5.0	2.8
Italy	16.8	29.1	7.7	5.1	4.6	3.2
Japan	8.0	17.5	12.8	8.4	8.6	4.7
UK	13.9	23.7	5.9	1.8	2.6	1.0
USA	10.9	20.8	8.0	2.9	3.4	3.2
West Germany	20.5	31.5	7.0	2.4	3.8	3.0

Source: OECD (1985) *Social Expenditure* 1960−1990.
Notes: Welfare expenditure excludes housing and, for France (1960), education.

Since the late 1970s there has been much talk of a 'crisis' in the welfare state of the mixed economies. It has become a source of intense dissatisfaction to both socialists and libertarians, whilst its popularity with the unpoliticised masses can no longer go unquestioned. For socialists it has failed to live up to hopes that it would eliminate poverty and promote social equality. Furthermore, they feel that the welfare state has alienated the underprivileged, because the services delivered to them are controlled by professionalised bureaucracies. The kinds of policy advocated by socialists are illustrated at the beginning of this chapter. They go hand-in-hand with a full range of economic policies designed to diminish the role of private sector institutions, particularly firms and financial institutions. The libertarian diagnosis of what is wrong with the welfare state is not so dissimilar. To them it is hardly surprising that state welfare has not produced social equality of the kind desired by socialists, since state bureaucracies are bound to be captured by the political interests that work in them and by those clientele groups that are politically powerful. The libertarian solution is to strengthen the role of private sector institutions, especially markets, so that consumers of welfare services can have much more influence over the kinds of service provided and the quantities in which they are produced. This policy, of reducing the role of the state and returning economic activities to the private sector, has become known as *privatisation*.

To appreciate why current policies with respect to the welfare state are conducted in the crossfire of ideological weaponry, we need to disentangle differences over policy objectives from differences over the means used to attain given objectives. The welfare state attempts to serve a variety of overlapping and partly inconsistent objectives. This is not necessarily a criticism: it could be construed as an inevitability. From the *pluralist* perspective on policy-making, this is the expected outcome as institutions and policy programmes evolve incrementally over time in response to the give-and-take of political bargaining. To substantiate this view I shall now consider in greater detail the main objectives which people think welfare policies should serve. I then outline arguments for and against state intervention as the best means of attaining these objectives, drawing on the analysis developed in Chapter 6.

THE OBJECTIVES OF WELFARE POLICY

Eliminating Poverty

Probably the primary objective underlying the creation of the welfare state was the elimination of destitution and poverty. There is no agreed and satisfactory definition of poverty. One common definition is a standard of living below subsistence level; that is, an income less than that required to obtain the quantity of food, clothing, shelter and other items judged necessary for living. However even the subsistence definition of poverty is a relative, and not an absolute, standard. The income judged necessary for subsistence in developed economies is far more than the income of most people in the world's poorest nations. Many of those concerned about poverty in their own society argue that it has to be defined in relation to the normal lifestyle of the mass of the population. People are poor if their income is too low to enable them to participate in normal social activities. This definition obviously produces a higher poverty income level than the subsistence definition.

Reducing Income Inequality

A closely related objective for the welfare state is reducing income inequality. Bringing everyone up to a minimum poverty level does decrease income inequality, but it still leaves a considerable gulf between low and high incomes, the size of which depends on the guaranteed minimum income. Making incomes more equal requires more than setting a minimum poverty level. The objective of ensuring that the welfare state provides a safety net, through which people cannot fall due to lack of income, is almost universally subscribed to. But the extent to which the state should do more than this and intervene to reduce income inequality is much more controversial. One form of such intervention is using taxes and state benefits to compress income differentials. Another is to limit what people can buy with their income, by banning the private sector production and allocation of goods and services deemed important for living standards, like health care and education. Many have looked to a free state education system to reduce income disparities by giving all children the opportunity to acquire skills which will earn them reasonable incomes. The failure of this objective after 40 years of state education is, for egalitarians, one of the disillusioning aspects of the welfare state.

Promoting Social Equality and Social Justice

The concept of social *equality* extends far beyond incomes to the distribution of resources, power and status. All these are imprecise concepts, not amenable to quantification. Any assessment of the evidence about their distribution is highly dependent on personal judgement. The extent to which people perceive that these attributes are unequally distributed and that this matters, or much can be done about it without excessive costs, vary greatly with political attitudes. Socialists stress the goal of social equality; that is, the equal distribution of income, wealth, status and power, often referring to it as *social equity* or *justice*. But social justice is not necessarily the same ideal as equality, since it concerns feelings about the fairness with which people are treated. Fairness does not necessarily imply equality; it may well involve treating people with different circumstances differently. For some, social justice is ensured if everyone has equal opportunities for social advancement, though differences in ability and in the personal exercise of choice will result in different levels of income and status. Providing minimum standards of housing, health care and education are guaranteed by the state, it is not socially unjust for those who choose to spend extra on these items to do so. For others, these differential outcomes are manifestations of social injustice.

Social Integration

Related to the objectives of social justice and equality is the use of the welfare state to promote social integration and cohesion. Some see increasing the degree of social equality as an essential aspect of making people feel part of the same society and hence accepting the legitimacy of its decision-making process. For others, the two objectives are much more distinct. The state can promote social cohesion through a common state school system, as in the USA, or through special measures to integrate ethnic minorities, without espousing the socialist vision of social equity.

Providing for People's Needs

Much of the activity of the welfare state is concerned with providing for people's needs. As stated in the White Paper setting up the NHS

The Government . . .want to ensure that in the future every man, woman and child can rely on getting all the advice and treatment and care which they may need in matters of personal health; that what they get shall be the best medical and other facilities available; that their getting these shall not depend on whether they can pay for them, or any other factor irrelevant to the real need. (Cmnd. 6502)

'Need' is a morally-loaded word. It conveys the notion that individuals have a much stronger claim to whatever they 'need' than to things they might 'want'. Hence it is frequently argued that the state should provide for needs. The consensus that the state should ensure at least subsistence needs has already been considered under the objective of eliminating poverty. The concept of social justice usually embraces the principle that nobody should be deprived of basic needs, though what precisely these consist of is much more contentious: food, housing, health care and education are normally placed in this category. This still leaves plenty of scope for disagreement as to whether the state should cater for minimum needs and what this minimum is, or whether, in the pursuit of social equality, it should allow only a common standard available for all. There is also disagreement as to what goods and services should be placed in the special category of needs and this has tended to widen over time with social change. For instance mobility and access to services, such as shops, are now often regarded as 'needs'.

Providing for people's needs, independently of their ability to pay, is part of furthering the other objectives, but it is not always consistent with all of them. The welfare state often provides for people's needs because they belong to particular categories, quite independently of their income. The well-off and articulate get free state education, including university tuition, free medical treatment and child benefit. These universal benefits, particularly those whose receipt depends on individual consumer demand, like health and especially education, do little to redistribute real income to the poor. Thus a significant feature of the welfare state is that it serves the needs of the vast majority. This may well promote social cohesion and the general popularity of the welfare state, but it reduces the proportion of welfare expenditure that directly benefits the most needy.

Income Maintenance

Yet another objective for welfare policy is to maintain people's incomes when they experience events, like sickness, unemployment and old age, which prevent them from earning their usual income. While this objective goes in tandem with those of eliminating poverty, reducing income inequality and promoting social justice, it is a distinct objective in its own right and is not always consistent with these other objectives. This is because of people's desire to maintain their income relative to the income they earned when working. This avoids the very sharp reduction in living standards that the better-off would have to experience if everybody received the same flat-rate benefits. Statutory sick pay is income-related, and occupational sick pay is even more generous; the state earnings-related pension scheme, originally introduced in 1978, aims to give additional pension rights related to earned income. However a positive relation between the state benefit an individual receives and his past income is inegalitarian. The political pressure to introduce such benefits has come from middle-income earners who want the advantages that high-income earners get from their private or occupational insurance schemes.

Promoting Ethical and Political Values

The objectives for welfare policy considered so far concentrate on the outcome of allocative processes as they affect distribution. If the argument were only about the achievement of specific outcomes in terms of distribution, then a relatively objective analysis of policy instruments would be possible in order to find out which were more likely to achieve given objectives. Arguments about the nature and extent of the welfare state would revolve around whether state or private sector agencies are more effective at achieving specific outcomes. To some extent this is one aspect of the debate about welfare policies. But the controversy over the use of policy instruments cannot be separated from often strongly held views about the ethical basis for human relationships and behaviour, that are reflected in economic and political institutions, such as the market and the state. Because of its ethical connotations, the welfare state, more than most aspects of economic policy, arouses political passions.

A common basis for *socialist* views on distribution is that since no individual is self-sufficient, because each person's standard of living is dependent on the actions of others, both now and in the past, the market's distribution of income has no ethical justification. All, whatever their role, have a right to an equitable share in national income. The welfare state is the institution above all others that distributes according to non-market criteria, according to people's needs and to the principles of social equality and justice. Furthermore, the collective provision of welfare through political participation is the embodiment of cooperative methods of organising economic activity, which are held in high ethical esteem. Because the market harnesses individuals' self-interest in competition against others, it is especially unethical to use it for providing human needs. Private charity is disliked because it accentuates the dependence of some individuals on others, who are only in a position to give charity because of the capitalist social and economic structure. Some also dislike dependency relationships within families. It is preferable for people to feel that they get their income from the state as a citizenship right. For some the welfare state embodies desirable social values because it represents the collective expression of altruism.

Quite the opposite view is taken by *libertarians*. To them collective state action is coercive: the sanction of elected governments, embodying in some way the will of the majority, cannot justify state action which limits the freedom of the individual to do as he/she thinks best, provided it does not detract from the liberty of others. To a libertarian, competitive markets are the guarantors of individual liberty; they offer consumers choice and respond to their preferences. The bureaucracies of the welfare state are entrenched monopoly suppliers, run in the interests of those who work in them. These bureaucrats have bolstered their power through professional associations and trade unions which, by appealing to spurious arguments about the public interest, have secured legislation to strengthen their monopoly power, and state finance to promote their own ends. The use of markets and voluntary action to provide welfare services not only produces better services for consumers, but for a libertarian is good in itself because it increases individual freedom and responsibility. Libertarians condemn paternalism, either of the socialist or patrician variety, because it denies individuals the right to exercise their own choice. Thus libertarian values place a high premium on liberty. Human dignity is impossible unless individuals are free to exercise choice and be responsible for themselves and their families.

The contrasts between socialist and libertarian welfare policies are not entirely due to different objectives; they both wish to use state intervention to redistribute income to those who do badly out of the market system or out of contemporary social institutions; both wish to enhance the power of the consumer of welfare services against that of the supplying bureaucracies. However, they are sharply divided on the methods of achieving these ends. In addition there are distinct differences in objectives—in the extent to which redistribution should occur and in the desirability of an egalitarian society or one which values the individualistic concept of liberty. Libertarian ideas gained ground during the 1970s and influenced the dominant group in the 1979 Conservative government. Socialists perceive Conservative policy as highly threatening to the welfare state. From a less committed perspective, the libertarian strand in Conservative thinking is just one element in the *mélange* of competing ideals, confused objectives and sectional self-interest that mould welfare policies.

THE MIXED ECONOMY OF WELFARE

The analytical core of this book—that economic policy is about which allocative mechanism to use for particular purposes—is just as relevant to social policies as to those policies more conventionally thought of as 'economic'. The production of welfare services, like education, health, personal care or insurance, is just as much economic activity as the production of steel and motor cars. All are, at least partly, *marketed goods*. However if produced by the state and provided free or if produced within the family, they are then *non-marketed* goods. Furthermore, if produced within the family, as is most domestic work and personal care, they are not even recorded as part of the national product, because of the absence of any monetary measure of their value.

Welfare services can be provided by either the public or the private sector; and within the private sector they may be produced by the market or by non-market means. The latter take a variety of forms. Within the family, which I define to include friends and neighbours, personal services are exchanged between people; since money is not used the market does not feature as an allocative mechanism. Marriage is an unwritten contract in which the partners share out tasks, usually practising a sexual division of labour. All the services normally undertaken within the household, such as cleaning, childrearing, home maintenance, can be bought on a market and are also now provided by the state in the form of home-helps, health visitors, day and residential care for children, the handicapped and the elderly, or maintenance of local authority housing. (I can only think of one personal service not yet available from the welfare state.)

Apart from the family, there are other non-market private sector institutions providing welfare services. Mutual aid organisations are collective arrangements whereby people pool funds or personal effort in return for a share of the resulting benefits. Trade unions, credit unions, play groups, and self-help groups for people sharing common problems, are all examples. Prior to state intervention in health and unemployment insurance, working-class people organised these for themselves through trade unions and mutual aid associations. Trade unions still provide a range of welfare services for their members, such as holiday and convalescent homes, and education. Charities operate on a different principle: people give others money or personal time without receiving anything tangible in exchange. Charitable services are provided mainly out of altruism, in contradistinction to the exchange of personal services that takes place within families and mutual aid associations.

Within the private sector the market also supplies welfare services. Education, medical care, over-the-counter medicines, housework and child-care can all be bought on the market by individuals. Occupational welfare provided by employers has become increasingly important. Some occupational welfare services are made mandatory by the state, like the payment by firms of statutory sick pay and maternity pay to their employees, which firms can recoup from their NI payments. Others, like occupational pensions, are encouraged by tax concessions. Many are provided by firms as payments in kind to their employees or as part of their conditions of service. Of particular importance are company and public sector sickness benefit schemes for employees, which are more generous than the minimum stipulated by law.

The welfare state is not just an alternative to the market: it is an alternative to all non-market forms of private sector welfare provision. It has taken over or supplemented many of the services previously undertaken within families or by mutual aid associations. Thus welfare policies are not just about which welfare services should be provided and for whom, but also about which allocative mechanism should be used. Not only is the welfare state part of the mixed economy but we have a mixed economy of welfare. The role of the state in this mixed economy of welfare is highly varied. Government organisations can produce welfare services and distribute them at zero price (NHS and schools) or it can charge (swimming pools and dentists). It can finance, entirely or partly, the provision of services but leave them to be produced by the private sector, either by firms (ethical drugs, residential care for the elderly) or by families (child benefit to help with child-care, invalidity allowance for looking after the disabled) or by charities (grants to the NSPCC for day-care nurseries). The government uses firms to administer the tax and social security system. Firms collect PAYE taxes and NI contributions and, since 1982, are required to administer statutory sick pay. Some of the state finance for private sector provision is via *tax expenditures*, such as tax-free occupational pension contributions and tax concessions for registered charities, which include private schools and hospitals.

Since the coming of the postwar welfare state, we have had a complex and overlapping mixed economy of welfare. If we look at any single objective for welfare policies we find that it is served by a variety of allocative mechanisms. For example, income maintenance is done by social security, by the market via pension funds and sickness and life insurance, by help from families and charities. Similarly 'needs'—health care, education, personal care—are provided by the state and by market and non-market private sector institutions. *Privatisation* policies with respect to the welfare state are a concerted drive to alter the balance of the mixed economy of welfare in favour of the private sector.

THE ECONOMIC RATIONALE FOR THE WELFARE STATE

I have already outlined some of the ideologically-based arguments for using or not using the government allocative mechanism for providing welfare services. Mainstream economists, working within the neoclassical tradition, have endeavoured to develop more instrumental criteria for assessing which mechanism is the more suitable in given instances. These have already been reviewed in Chapter 6, which examined the general arguments for using market or government as an allocative mechanism. The instrumental criterion is which allocative mechanism is likely to be *socially efficient*. It is firmly rooted in the concept of the mixed economy: in some instances markets are socially efficient; in other cases government. This perspective adds another objective for the state production of welfare services—to improve allocative efficiency.

As discussed in Chapter 6, where are three main sources of *market failure*: externalities, imperfect competition and informational inadequacies, which justify government provision of social services in order to improve social efficiency. The *externality* argument is probably the least convincing. Health services and education are largely private goods: they are both *excludable* and *rivalrous* in consumption. Health services have a public good element with respect to the prevention of contagious diseases, which account for only about 5 per cent of NHS spending, and medical research. However inoculation programmes could be financed by the state but provided by a private sector medical industry. Economists who wish to justify state production of social services on efficiency grounds stretch the externality argument much further. Education yields external benefits because it produces a more productive workforce and more civilised citizenry. Even redistribution is rationalised on externality grounds: people get external benefits from the satisfaction of knowing that others' needs are provided for, but are not willing to pay for this unless others are forced to do so through taxation.

Imperfect competition, due largely to informational inadequacies, provides a more convincing rationale for a state medical service than do externalities. It is feared that doctors have a monopoly of medical knowledge: patients have insufficient knowledge to make correct decisions regarding the services they would buy from doctors. If a market relationship operates then the doctor can exploit the ignorance of the patient to his own advantage. This evidently is not thought to be a disadvantage to the more affluent who choose private medical treatment because they consider it to be of higher quality. So there is a hint of paternalism in this argument: the mass of the population do not have the personal resources to find out which doctors and which treatment suit them best. This is disputed by libertarians, citing pre-NHS arrangements as showing how mutual aid associations, by employing their own doctors and charging their members set fees, provided consumers with greater choice than the NHS and kept doctors' fees competitive.[2] Informational failures provide a widely-held justification for state education, in opposition to libertarian arguments that all the state should do is make education compulsory for children and ensure through cash transfers, or education vouchers, that all parents have sufficient income to pay for their children's schooling. The paternalist view is that many parents are unable or unwilling to make informed choices about their children's schooling: such children are better off in a state system, run by teachers and administrators, in which consumer demand has little part to play.

The most compelling reasons for the existence of the welfare state are the various distributional objectives it serves. The economic efficiency arguments for the state production of welfare services have to be seen in the context of a climate of opinion in favour of the welfare state. Similarly, the rebuttal of these arguments and the emphasis on the failure of government as an allocative mechanism, as discussed in Chapters 6–9, are associated with a much more critical attitude to the welfare state. *Government failure*, due to inadequate information about consumer preferences, state monopoly power and sectional self-interest amongst the welfare state's bureaucrats and clients, is also analysed as a cause of allocative inefficiency.

Thus the economic analysis of markets and government as allocative mechanisms does not provide any clear set of guidelines as to which mechanism is best suited to producing particular types of goods and services. All one can discern is a general pattern in mixed economies; non-market mechanisms, including government, are relatively more important in producing welfare services than other types of goods; and this can be related to the political importance attached to distributional objectives in the allocation of welfare services. Though alternative market methods of allocation can be devised, they still require some combination of state finance, cash transfers and regulations to achieve the mixed bag of distributional objectives that command widespread political support.

THE WELFARE STATE AND ECONOMIC POLICY

The distributional and efficiency objectives sought from welfare policies cannot be considered in isolation from the rest of economic policy-making. As noted in Chapters 4 and 5, there is a two-way relationship between welfare policies and the level of taxation and government spending.

The Pressures on Welfare State Expenditure

The existing structure of state welfare provision, and the demands from its clients for their entitlements within that structure, commit the government to a large amount of spending which they can neither estimate precisely nor control in the short run. To the extent that expenditure is demand-led, it is not subject to *cash limits*. Over the longer run there is continual upward pressure on welfare expenditure. Client groups, like the elderly, the unemployed, potential entrants to further and higher education, or one-parent families, grow and seek higher benefits. Pensioners in particular, of whom there are now over nine million, are an influential interest group: state pensions have risen relative to other benefits. The professional groups employed in the welfare state, often in conjunction with their clients, demand higher standards of service, involving more expensive capital equipment as in the health service and scientific research, or more labour-intensive methods, as in education. There is pressure for expanded provision, taking in a wider clientele, as with the campaign for more state nursery schools. As state welfare services are *non-marketed* goods, the demand for them is not limited by their customers' willingness to pay a price which covers the cost of their provision, as with marketed goods. The amount supplied is usually less than the quantity demanded at zero price and so has to be rationed by various administrative and political means. The limit to the quantity of state welfare services produced is set not by equilibrating demand and supply via price, but by the amount of welfare spending sanctioned by the political process. The pressures which constrain the upward march of welfare expenditure are the unpopularity of rising taxation or inflation, if the expenditure is financed by an excessive expansion of government debt and the money supply. The more rapid the rise in real national output, the easier it is for governments to finance an expanding welfare state, since social expenditure can be increased without needing to reduce the amount of resources allocated to other sectors.

The Supply-Side Attack on the Welfare State
Set against the demands for greatly increased welfare expenditure, is the opposing *supply-side* diagnosis that the poor economic performance of the developed economies since the 1960s is due, at least in part, to the enlarged welfare state. There are several strands to this contentious argument, which can only be touched on briefly. One is that the *non-marketed* sector is larger than its consumers really want, because they have no market in which to express how much they value the resources used to produce welfare services compared to their opportunity cost—that is, the alternative marketed goods that could have been produced instead. The expansion of the state sector, at the expense of the marketed private goods people would like to consume, sets up pressures for increased money wages. These pressures make it impossible to use Keynesian methods for increasing output and employment without causing inflation and a subsequent reactive policy of demand contraction.

Another supply-side argument is that the provision of state welfare benefits, together with the high level of taxation required to finance them, destroys people's incentives to work and to save. Consequently fewer people take employment, they work fewer hours or they take less risky and less demanding jobs. State benefits, for sickness, unemployment and old age, paid out of taxation, reduce the need for individuals to save; this lowers the rate of accumulation for the whole economy, resulting in slower economic growth.

This analysis of the deleterious effects of the welfare state is rejected by most of its defenders as invalid. They also emphasis the dependence of the sectors producing marketed goods on the welfare services, in particular the health and education of the workforce. The policy conclusion of the supply-side critique of the welfare state is that governments should encourage the private sector to secure the objectives of welfare policies; the provision of welfare services should be privatised as far as possible, given the government's objectives of redistributing income and providing a social safety net for all. In this view, a welfare society can flourish without the existence of a welfare state.

The Macroeconomic Context

The advent, in 1979, of a government with supply-side leanings put a tighter lid on the expansion of welfare budgets. But the slowdown in economic growth in the mid-1970s had already led the Labour government to take firm steps to bring expenditure under control. Within both the 1974–79 Labour administration and the subsequent Conservative one, there have been conflicts during the PESC annual cycle between the Treasury, seeking to contain the level of government spending, and the spending departments, in particular the DHSS, responsible for welfare expenditure. Whatever political party is in power, the rising tide of welfare expenditure demands meets the Treasury's desired ceiling for total spending and taxation: the tide is partially contained and the ceiling is raised. The size of the welfare budget both determines the overall level of government spending and taxation, while itself being constrained by the current requirements of macroeconomic policy. Policies concerned with restructuring the welfare state are invariably linked with macroeconomic concerns. For the radical Right the desire to cut government spending and taxation means looking to the welfare budget for economies. The Left's ambitious plans to expand welfare spending go hand in hand with both raising taxes and government borrowing to finance it, together with expansionary macroeconomic policies. From all perspectives, the issue of what the country can and should afford to spend on the welfare state is an essential element both of welfare policies and of more general economic policy concerns.

So far I have concentrated mainly on the role of different allocative mechanisms in securing the objectives sought from welfare policies and hence on the size and scope of the welfare state. But economic policy is not only about what combination of allocative mechanisms to use; it is also concerned with how the state production and distribution of welfare services is undertaken when the government allocative mechanism is used.

From an economic policy perspective, the main focus of interest is the way resources are allocated to the social services and how social service outputs are distributed.

RESOURCE ALLOCATION IN THE STATE SOCIAL SERVICES

The predominant economic characteristic of the state social services is that they produce mainly *non-marketed* goods. Thus resources are not allocated according to market criteria. The agencies producing the services do not decide what to produce and in what quantities on the basis of profitability. Consumers do not decide how much of a service to consume according to their willingness to pay the market price. Instead, resource allocation is determined by political and administrative means. Resource allocation in the social services covers a vast range of items, from the number of hospital beds in specific regional areas and for specific types of medical cases and the wages paid to different grades of staff, to the number of schools, the size of their pupil rolls, the number of teachers and their salary structure. How resources are actually allocated, from central government, through local bodies and finally at the service delivery point in individual hospitals, medical practices, schools and social service departments, is a vast and sketchily charted territory. All I intend to do here is outline some basic features of non-market resource allocation in the government sector.

Allocating According to 'Need'
As mentioned earlier, one of the objectives sought from the welfare state is that people's 'needs' should be met regardless of their ability to pay. The subjective and problematic nature of the concept of 'need' has also been noted. What kinds of goods and services constitute 'needed' items, of what quality and in what quantity and for which kinds of people? These are all questions that have to be answered before needs can be operationally defined. And who is to determine the answers to these questions?

When needs are provided by the market, the individual customer determines the answer to these questions as they affect him and purchases items which satisfy his needs. He is constrained in his choice by his income and the prices of goods and services. The overall distribution of income is determined by market forces and this, together with individuals' preferences, will establish answers to these questions. The problem with a pure market determination of resource allocation is that those with low incomes will be unable to satisfy all their 'needs', either as perceived by themselves or by others. One solution to this distributional problem is for the government to redistribute income in cash, as social security benefits, leaving individuals to purchase goods and services to satisfy their 'needs'. The determination of what these goods and services are is then left to individuals and households. The only administrative assessment of 'need' required from government is of the income needed by different types of household to guarantee the minimum standard of living considered acceptable.

The more government becomes involved in meeting specific needs, either in cash or in kind, as it does when producing and distributing social services, the less are these questions concerning the definition of need left to individual consumers to resolve for themselves. The electorate, the politicians, the bureaucrats employed in the social services and their customers, all have some influence in determining what and whose 'needs' are supplied by government, and how this is done.

The rational decision-making approach to allocating according to 'need' is to establish criteria of need and then to use these criteria to allocate resources. But need is a highly diffuse, malleable and imprecise concept. At a highly general level it provides a distributional justification for state production, and free or subsidised distribution of particular goods and services to specified categories of people. It is upheld as the prime criterion of state resource allocation in sectors where markets have been banished. But 'need' is a highly subjective criterion: its evaluation is influenced by the self-interest of both the suppliers and consumers of specific services.

Apart from the imprecise and subjective nature of needs, a related problem for rational resource allocation in the non-market public sector is that the whole spectrum of needs cannot be measured by a common unit of account like money. As pointed out in Chapter 8, it is difficult to measure the output of the social services, such as education or health, even in their own units of account, let alone in money terms. However some way of comparing the value of different social service outputs is necessary if priorities are to be ordered rationally, so that the best use can be made of scarce resources.

The criterion of need is easier to operationalise for a restricted range of choices specific to a particular type of service, like assessing a child's special educational needs, or the urgency with which a patient requires medical treatment or an area requires a hospital. Thus the criterion of 'need' functions as a rationing device when the demand for a specific service outstrips supply. Such a situation of excess demand is likely when services are supplied at zero price. In a free market, price would rise until demand and supply were equal; with state social services other criteria are used to allocate consumer demand to the available supply, 'need' being one of them. For instance people applying for council accommodation are awarded points according to various indicators of need, and these help to determine how quickly they are offered accommodation. NHS beds are allocated according to medical priorities; certain conditions guarantee immediate admission, others do not. There are long waiting-lists for certain conditions, because the medical profession considers them to be of relatively less inconvenience and so resources are not allocated for more beds or specialists in these areas. Much of service rationing at the point of delivery is done by professionals applying personal, intuitive criteria of need, which they may not even fully articulate to themselves. Doctors will spend differential amounts of time on different patients, as will teachers on different classes or pupils.

The more wide-ranging the allocation decisions, the less help the criterion of need offers decision-makers. Are more kidney dialysis machines needed rather than additional heart transplants? Is extra research on cot death syndrome of greater importance than more science laboratories for schools or nursery classes? To argue at this level of generality that something is 'needed' is to use emotive language in order to stake a claim on resources against competing claims.

The Power of Bureaucrats to Determine Need
Unlike personal wants which are determined by the individual, his needs are largely defined and assessed by others. At a very general level, needs which the government should provide, such as free education and health services or subsidised transport, are determined via the political system. But the detailed definition and application of needs criteria are largely in the hands of the professional bureaucrats—administrators, doctors, social workers, teachers and the like—who deliver the services to their clients. The converse of their power, is the weak position of the clients, whose needs are supposed to justify the existence of the state social services. They have restricted choice and have little option but to accept the quality and quantity of service supplied to them by the state bureaucracies. For instance, client groups complain of the hospitalised and rigid system of care given to women in childbirth, of lack of choice over state schools and over the curriculum they provide, or of the way council houses are allocated by officials. It is somewhat ironic that both socialists and libertarians are critical of the bureaucratised nature of the social services and the absence of client influence on the services delivered to them. The socialist solution is more political control by clients; the libertarian solution is more market choice for social service customers.

The power of these state sector professional groups *vis-à-vis* their customers stems from their influence in determining 'needs'. This is a manifestation of the power bureaucrats obtain from their superior access to information, which was emphasised in Chapter 8. State sector professionals, both in their capacity as individual experts and as members of their professional organisations, are closely involved in the formulation of government policy with respect to providing social services and hence satisfying 'needs'. Thus their perception of what are or should be clients' needs, or how their professional self-interest can be served by the way such needs are defined and met, is highly influential in the formulation of policy; and even stronger in implementing policy. Since customers are without the market mechanism as a means to signal their preferences with respect to social services, they have to use personal influence or political activity. This leaves the professionals in a strong position; political control of their work is weak and the sanctions of the market are absent. As experts in their fields, their perceptions of which needs and whose needs should be met and how this should be done predominate at the point of delivery.

The pre-eminent influence of the medical profession in the allocation of health service resources was noted in Chapter 8. The teaching profession dominates decisions as to how resources in the education sector should be used. Take state schools. First, parents have to make a special application to send their child to a school other than the one specified by the local authority. The curriculum, syllabus and teaching methods are determined by the education profession, in line with what they consider children's needs to be. State schools' organisation, aims and methods are very similar, especially within a given local authority. Thus parents have only a very slightly differentiated product to choose from. Similarly NHS patients have very little choice over which doctor they are assigned.

Although some clients express discontent with the state services provided to satisfy their needs, there are also many instances in which public sector trade unions and professional associations liaise with their client groups to put organised pressure on government for more resources. They thus form a policy-making community, which is often supported by representatives of their interests within government. They also campaign for public support, since the electorate's perception of the need for specific improvements in the social services influences their attitudes to political party policies on government expenditure and taxation.

Budgeting

Given the absence of market revenues or charitable donations, the social service organisations can only command resources to the extent they are allocated budgets by central and local government. The complexity of resource allocation in the social services is not only due to the multitude of allocative criteria, many of which are never clearly articulated, but is also a product of the hierarchy of agencies and budgets through which allocative decisions are filtered. This hierarchical aspect of resource allocation in the public sector was discussed in Chapter 8, using the health service as a detailed example, as well as some reference to education. A similar relationship exists between the DHSS and the local authorities with respect to personal social services and between the Department of the Environment and the local authorities with regard to housing. Over the years central government has enacted much mandatory legislation which requires local authorities to provide specific services, for instance, education for those aged between 5 and 16. Other enabling legislation makes it possible for local authorities to provide certain services if they so wish and can raise the finance. Hence local authorities vary considerably in the provision of schooling for the under-fives.

Local authorities have thus increasingly become the agents of central government policy. This puts the onus on central government to provide finance for the local authorities to help them fulfil their obligations. The centralised allocation of finance to public sector activities in the Public Expenditure Survey Committee annual cycle was described in Chapter 4. The overall budgets that the central government departments can allocate to the social services for which they are responsible are determined in the PESC round of negotiations. The two-way nature of the forces which determine budget allocations have been emphasised before. Financial allocations are not determined just at the peak of the hierarchy and transmitted outwards through the arteries. The spending agencies lower down the hierarchy send information upwards, which is used to determine budget allocations.

The information built up by PESC, which estimates the likely future expenditure given current policies, is produced by the central government spending departments, who in turn receive it from the Health Authorities, local authorities, and their other budget holders. They, in their turn, receive information from their own subdivisions. The central government departments mediate between the Treasury and the agencies supplying the social services. The DHSS, for example, has specific policies with respect to service provision that it is trying to implement: more community care for the physically and mentally handicapped, or improving the NHS in particular regions. On the basis of existing policies, with their expenditure commitments, and on the current priorities it has, the DHSS will make its case for funds to the Treasury and, if necessary, to the Cabinet. Given the budget allocation it receives, the DHSS will then make its own allocative decisions with respect to its budget holders, such as the Regional Health Authorities. If the projected increase in expenditure, based on existing policies and physical resources, exceeds the DHSS budget total, decisions have to be made as to which budgets to prune. Physical resources will have to be reduced, unless their price can be cut sufficiently. It is usually easier to cut planned investment projects than to close existing facilities, and easier to shut down physical assets than sack public sector employees. One reason for this is the political power of public sector workers, in areas unconstrained by market forces and endowed with the public esteem given to those who help the sick and handicapped and educate the young. After a decade of government expenditure restraint, the lopsided reduction in the public sector's capital expenditure at the expense of current expenditure is causing concern for the condition of the infrastructure—schools, hospitals, council housing, sewers and roads in particular.

An important aspect of the PESC system of controlling and allocating financial resources is that the Treasury seeks to control all government expenditure financed by taxation or borrowing, including that financed from local authority rates and borrowing. The extended power of the Department of the Environment over local authority spending and rate-setting since 1981 has already been noted. Central government has controlled local authority borrowing for at least 150 years. The amount of money local authorities can raise on the capital market is restricted by central government approval. In addition each local authority is set an annual limit on the amount of capital expenditure it can undertake. Prior to 1981 central government exercised detailed control over the allocation of capital spending on individual projects. This detailed scrutiny has now been to some extent dismantled and replaced by a control system which is intended to limit the overall amount that local authorities individually and in aggregate spend on capital projects.

Incrementalism is a marked feature of public sector budgeting: existing policies and existing physical resources largely determine the pattern and amount of financial allocation. In any one year there is only limited scope for reordering priorities or cutting total spending in real terms. It is easier to alter priorities when budgets are growing, and so the least favoured can be kept at a standstill or at a low growth rate, than when the total budget is constant or falling. This incrementalism slows down the reallocation of resources in response to changing circumstances and hence impedes efficiency. Vested interests make it difficult for the public sector to contract in response to reductions in demand. The decline in the birth rate since the 1960s has reduced demand for a number of social services. Teacher training places were reduced by expensive programmes of college amalgamations, absorption of staff into higher pay-scales and generous early retirement and redundancy provisions. A declining school population has not led to an equivalent cut in places or teachers. The fall in the demand for maternity services was countered by a vigorous programme to get all women to give birth in hospital. Contraction of capacity in the private sector, and even in the public corporations, is not cushioned to such an extent.

Thus a number of significant features of public sector budgeting stand out. To start with, needs-based criteria for allocating money and hence resources are extremely difficult to make operational. Not only are there inherent problems in measuring inputs and especially outputs, it is also difficult to arrive at a clear statement of priorities when competing political interests are involved. In other words, the political system fails to articulate a social welfare function which could guide resource allocation. Altering budget allocations is an incremental process; it is especially difficult to change the distribution of resources when the total budget is growing slowly or is at a standstill. Political interests in areas being squeezed resist budget cuts. Though government holds the purse-strings, its power to make decisions which affect resource allocations further down the bureaucratic hierarchy is limited, as noted here and in Chapter 8. Budgeting is a process of bargaining between central government and the budget holders, who deliver the services and who thus exercise a large measure of control of the physical resource inputs.

Efficiency in the Social Services
When welfare expenditure in real terms is growing slowly or stagnating, not only is it more difficult to change the distribution of resources, the pressures to make more efficient use of existing resources become stronger. The increased concern with public sector efficiency was noted in Chapter 8, in the context of politicians' attempts to improve the performance of bureaucrats.

In Chapter 8 it was also pointed out that these policy initiatives use efficiency concepts drawn from accountancy and management consultancy, rather than those of the economist. There are however some links between the two sets of concepts. The most satisfactory efficiency concept for economists is that of allocative efficiency. This is concerned with efficiency in consumption. It asks whether a given bundle of resources is being used to produce the combination of services most preferred by consumers. In the absence of markets in the social services, consumer preferences can only be reflected through political means or by individual action by the customer to secure services. The professional experts, the administrators and the politicians will distil their own various notions of what should be supplied to consumers. Allocative efficiency is closest to the managerial concept of policy effectiveness—the extent to which the resources devoted to a policy produce the desired outcomes. The problems of valuing the outputs of the social services make it difficult to assess either allocative efficiency or effectiveness. Some attempts are being made in the health service to assess the effectiveness of various treatments and to respond to questionnaires eliciting patients' opinions on the standard of service. In education the assessment of pupils' attainments is undertaken by the Assessment Performance Unit at the DES and the National Foundation for Educational Research. Schools are now required to publish their examination results. But the extent of such educational assessment and the publicity given to it is way behind that in the USA.

The other aspect of efficiency is *productive efficiency* or cost-effectiveness. Is a given level of service being produced as cheaply as possible? This criterion of efficiency is much easier to apply in the state social services than efficiency in consumption, since physical outputs and inputs can often be measured and cost can usually be estimated in money terms. The problem, as discussed in Chapter 8, is devising an administrative framework, with appropriate incentives and sanctions for workers, and good information and control systems.

Privatisation of the Social Services

One aspect of the Conservative government's recent drive to improve the efficiency of the social services is *privatisation*. Privatisation is advocated on the grounds that it increases competition and thereby improves efficiency, either by enhancing consumer choice or by reducing production costs. It is also advocated by those who wish to reduce the size of the public sector as an objective in its own right. It has been vigorously opposed, especially when directed at the welfare state, by socialists and trade unions, particularly those with members whose jobs have been affected.

The largest and most successful of the privatisation measures with regard to the welfare state has been the sale of council houses. The Housing Act 1980 gave council tenants of more than three years' standing the right to buy their own homes at discounts on the market price of between one third and one half, depending on length of tenure. Between 1979 and 1983, over half a million council and new town homes were sold, out of a base stock of seven million. In the years 1982–85 sales brought in around £1.5 billion a year. After scorning the policy, the Labour Party decided to stop opposing it, as it is popular amongst their actual and potential supporters.

Less successful have been measures to increase the role of private sector contractors in the NHS. Private contractors have always been employed in the NHS, but at the discretion of the health authorities. The government introduced legislation to compel health authorities to invite tenders for cleaning, catering and laundry work from outside contractors in competition with the direct labour force. Where contracts have been won by private sector firms, the existing labour force has been made redundant and often re-employed by the private contractor at lower wages or for shorter hours. The affected trade unions have orchestrated a strong campaign against these measures, claiming that private contractors provide a poor standard of service. Preference for in-house services plus the unpleasantness attached to arousing union opposition, has made many health administrators reluctant to implement the policy. Contractors have complained that health authorities have devised ways of loading tender procedures against them.[3] It was reported to MPs that the proportion of laundry services contracted out in 1984 actually fell, while that for catering and cleaning was unchanged. According to the Commons Social Service Committee only £9.4 million, out of a budget of £848 million, was saved in 1983−84; according to the DHSS annual savings were estimated to have reached £28 million a year by 1985.[4] Local authorities have similarly been compelled under the Planning and Land Act 1980 to put building and maintenance work out to tender, and encouraged to do so for refuse collection and cleaning.

However major programmes of privatisation, urged by pro-marketeers, remain on the drawing-board. One such proposal is education vouchers—a scheme which would give parents a voucher to spend on their child's education at any school of their choice. (In some schemes, this would include private schools as well as state schools.) Popular schools would be oversubscribed and would therefore expand, while unpopular schools would eventually close if they could not fill their places by improving their services. Thus the advocates of education vouchers believe that competitive pressure on state schools would spur educationalists into providing the kinds of schooling sought by parents and so improve the quality and variety of state education. Although the DES have considered education vouchers, the proposal has never surfaced as proposed policy, despite being favoured by the Prime Minister and Sir Keith Joseph, one time Secretary of State for Education. The opposition of civil servants, education administrators and teachers, claiming that the proposal is unworkable, has proved too great. Financing higher education by means of student loans has hovered nearer the brink of implementation. In 1984, Sir Keith Joseph took the first tentative step, proposing to make well-off parents pay all or part of their children's tuition fees. Outrage amongst the Conservative ranks led to the abandonment of the proposal.

The sector of education where privatisation has had most impact is vocational training. The industry training boards set up by Labour in the 1960s, to which firms had to pay a compulsory levy, were abolished. The Youth Training Scheme, operated by the Manpower Services Commission, provides programmes of vocational training for 16−17 year olds, in conjunction with colleges of further education and industry: it is jointly funded by the government and participating firms. As the aim is to provide a two-year training programme for all school-leavers, this is the most significant educational development over the last decade.

Privatisation is a very general policy of altering the balance of the mixed economy of welfare as is its opposite, *socialisation*. When applied though, it takes the form of very specific measures. The detail of its application is therefore highly varied, as is its success in meeting its objectives and the warmth or hostility of its reception. Thus some privatisation measures are likely to last beyond the tenure of the Conservatives, while others will be reversed on a change of government.

CONCLUSION

Welfare policies, which are very much the home territory of other disciplines, like social administration, are also economic policies, in that they concern the distribution and allocation of resources. Welfare policies are about which combination of three basic allocative mechanisms to use in providing welfare services; these are the market, private sector non-market methods and government. The welfare state is primarily concerned with the government's role in producing welfare services or encouraging private sector institutions to do so.

The conceptual distinction between distributional objectives and those of allocative efficiency are as useful in analysing welfare policies as in other fields. While overlapping and partly inconsistent distributional objectives dominate welfare policies, issues of allocative efficiency and of the effectiveness with which welfare policies serve particular objectives are nevertheless important. They have become increasingly so as the growth of state welfare spending has decelerated, while client demands have not.

Disenchantment with the welfare state has broken the early postwar consensus. At one extreme radical socialists look to a vast extension of state intervention to redistribute material resources and the power to control their allocation. At the other extreme, libertarians seek to dismantle the welfare state and place the provision of welfare services firmly in the private sector. Both extremes reject the current and still dominant concepts of the welfare state as an essential element of the mixed economy and of the mixed economy of welfare provision. Although the policies of both the Labour and Conservative Parties have been influenced by the radical extremes, the mixed-economy welfare state seems set to continue as the predominant framework within which welfare policies are developed.

This means that the factors discussed here which influence policy-making with respect to the welfare state will remain significant. Overall, the rational model of policy-making does not apply; there is no all-embracing system of rationally determining national priorities in the allocation and distribution of non-marketed goods. This is in part due to the practical problems of measuring the outputs of non-marketed social services and relating these to the inputs used in their production. It is also the product of the complex and extensive web of political interests who interact to determine resource allocation in this sector. The dominant pattern of decision-making is political bargaining conducted mainly between the politicians in power and the political interests who work in and benefit from the social services. Of these, the dominant element are the professional bureaucrats, often allied to public sector trade unions and professional pressure group organisers. These factors in turn contribute to the incremental nature of budgeting and resource redistribution. While policy-making is largely characterised by political bargaining, at the more disaggregated level of specific institutions and services elements of rational decision-making are apparent in the form of administrative structures and procedures for determining priorities, gathering management information and asssessing performance. The health service in particular is making a concerted attempt to strengthen this aspect of its policy-making.

This chapter has concentrated on the general characteristics of the welfare state and of welfare policies, and then considered the problems of resource allocation in the social services, taking as their key feature the production and distribution of non-marketed services. As has been pointed out, the major rationale for the welfare state is redistribution. This is largely fulfilled, to the extent that it is, by the social security system within the welfare state. This, and the overall impact of the welfare state on distribution, is the subject matter of the next chapter.

NOTES

1. Data from *Social Trends* (HMSO, London, 1984).
2. D.G. Green, 'Doctors versus workers', *Economic Affairs*, vol. 5, no. 1, 1984.
3. *Financial Times*, 2 October 1985.
4. *Financial Times*, 5 July 1985.

13 Redistribution and the Social Security System

The young, the old, the sick, the crazy
Even the shiftless and the lazy,
Eat at the common human table
Spread by the Active and the Able.
The problem is to organize
This monumental enterprise
So that—to see that all are boarded—
Both Need and Virtue get rewarded.
(Kenneth Boulding, *Economist*)[1]

This verse puts in a nutshell the problems of devising a rational welfare system—one that serves its main distributive objectives whilst ensuring that the system itself is efficient and does not impede allocative efficiency in the wider economy. The welfare state is the chief means of redistributing income. It does so by providing free or subsidised social services; by operating a social security system; and by having a progressive tax structure. The main concern of this chapter is the social security system. It examines the distributive and efficiency principles underlying the construction of a social security system and relates these to the structure of the UK system. Today's social security system evolved from the 1946 and 1948 legislation which, with modifications, enacted the 1942 Beveridge Report on Social Security.[2] Despite the Conservative government's announced intention to institute a radical overhaul, it is still appropriate to characterise the UK social security system as the Beveridge framework, amended and extended in an *ad hoc* manner. The chapter concludes by considering evidence on the overall redistributive impact of the welfare state.

THE ENACTMENT OF BEVERIDGE

The Beveridge plan for social security was based firmly on the insurance principle. Individuals should not look to state charity for income support at times when they could not earn. They should take out insurance against the contingencies of sickness, disability, unemployment and old age. Since the private sector was unable to provide adequate insurance cover, except for the better-off, and many individuals were too short-sighted to take out insurance, the solution was a comprehensive, compulsory state insurance scheme, to which all male and unmarried female workers paid the same contribution and received flat-rate insurance benefits, regardless of their income. The contributory principle was regarded as important, and continues to be officially upheld because it is claimed to have certain advantages. It requires individuals to pay for their own benefits and so instils individual responsibility. It is held that people find National Insurance contributions more acceptable than general taxation, because they appear to represent the individual's payment for benefits he or she is personally entitled to as a reward for the virtues of thrift and hard work. In addition, it removes what many feel is the stigma of means-tested benefits..

Beveridge was a firm believer in the concept of the mixed economy: the state, the individual and the market all have a role to play.

Social security must be achieved by cooperation between the State and the individual. The state should offer security for service and for contribution. The state in organising security should not stifle incentive, opportunity, responsibility; in establishing a national minimum, it should leave room and encouragement for voluntary action by each individual to provide more than a minimum for himself and his family. (Beveridge (1942), pp. 6–7)

Thus each individual should be able to claim benefits for specific contingencies as of right, because he/she has paid for them via National Insurance contributions. It was assumed that a married woman would not be attached fully, if at all, to the labour force; her right to national insurance benefits would be via her husband's contributions. If individuals wanted more than the state flat-rate benefit they should make their own provision, either themselves or through occupational schemes:

Voluntary insurance . . . is an essential part of security; scope and encouragement for it must be provided. The state can ensure this negatively, by avoiding so far as possible any test of means for its compulsory insurance benefits, and by limiting such benefits to subsistence and primary needs. The state can ensure this positively by regulation, financial assistance or by itself undertaking the organisation of voluntary insurance. (ibid., p. 143)

However, even with such a state scheme, there would be individuals without National Insurance entitlement to benefits. They would be guaranteed a minimum subsistence income, subject to rigorous tests of means and needs and 'also to any conditions as to behaviour which may seem likely to hasten the restoration of earning capacity' (ibid., p. 141). The remaining problem of poverty amongst families in work was to be tackled by giving cash allowances for the second and subsequent children. Beveridge also premised the success of his plan in eliminating poverty on the introduction of a free health service, the maintenance of full employment and the ending of distortions in the housing market, which result in households paying very different amounts for a similar standard of housing.

The Beveridge plan thus established the three types of social benefit we have today. First there are non-means-tested *contingent benefits*, paid only to those with sufficient NI contributions. They are contingent because their receipt depends on specific circumstances, like unemployment, sickness, maternity and old age, conditional on National Insurance contributions. Then there are non-means-tested, contingent benefits, like child benefit, which are non-contributory because they are paid regardless of the claimant's National Insurance record. The third category is non-contributory benefits, which are means-tested and often granted to meet specific needs. The main type of means-tested benefit is supplementary benefit[3]—the revamped form of Beveridge's national assistance.

MODIFICATIONS TO THE BEVERIDGE FRAMEWORK

In retrospect, one of the chief inadequacies of the 1940s legislation was its failure to tackle the problem of poverty amongst working families. Closely related to this problem was the less generous treatment of those in work compared to those out of work. This is not only socially inequitable but inefficient, in that it reduces the incentive to work. Several aspects of the social security system contributed to these related problems. One is that those on supplementary benefit received allowances for children and for housing costs not available to the working poor.

More Means-Tested Benefits
Successive Labour and Conservative governments have tinkered with the legislation, adding new benefits to tackle the problem of the working poor. Family Income Supplement was introduced in 1971: it makes up 50 per cent of the difference between the family's income and a set income limit and also varies with the number of children. Families in receipt of FIS are automatically entitled to other benefits in kind, such as welfare foods, free prescriptions and dental treatment. A separate housing benefit, for those qualifying on grounds of income alone, was introduced. The Rating Act 1966 brought in a national scheme of rate rebates, while the Housing Finance Act 1972 instituted a mandatory scheme of rent rebates for local

authority tenants and rent allowances for private sector tenants. These have been modified and consolidated under further legislation. By the mid-1980s one-third of all households were receiving housing benefit. This is paid by local authorities but 90 per cent financed by central government. Thus the 1940s' system was modified by a proliferation of means-tested benefits.

Universal Child Benefit

The support given for children, irrespective of income, has also been altered. The previous system of cash payments for second and subsequent children plus a child tax allowance against taxable income, was replaced in 1977 by the current flat-rate child benefit paid for all children to mothers via the Post Office. This is the major universal benefit, received in full by mothers, regardless of income since it is not taxed. This scheme of universal child benefit is justified on the grounds that it ensures that poor working families get assistance with the costs of raising children, whilst it also recognises that families with children have greater expenditure needs than childless households. In 1984—85 child benefit was paid to nearly seven million families and cost over £4 billion. Changes in social institutions have brought further modifications to the 1940s legislation, which assumed that most single parents without earned income would be widows, who would receive National Insurance benefits. To assist the rising numbers of divorced and unmarried single parents, there is now a single-parent child benefit addition and tax allowance.

The Flat-Rate Principle

The Beveridge principle of flat-rate contributions for flat-rate benefits, regardless of income, was gradually eroded. Flat-rate payments fail to secure the objective of income maintenance: the higher one's income when in work, the larger the fall in living standards when relying on flat-rate NI benefits. Flat-rate state pensions soon came to be regarded as very poor second cousins to occupational pension schemes which paid high-income earners good pensions. In 1959 a second tier of graduated state pensions was brought in to be replaced by the much more extensive and generous State Earnings-Related Pension Scheme in 1978. With income-related benefits came income-related contributions, in addition to the standard rate. Over the years the income-related element in NI contributions has been strengthened. More recently, the major reason for this development, extended in recent Budgets, is to reduce the regressivity of NI contributions. The less income-related they are, the greater the proportion of a low wage packet they take as compared to a high one. In addition, if employers pay a greater proportion of low wages than of high wages in NI contributions, low-wage labour is less attractive to employ.

The Contributory Principle

Beveridge was firmly wedded to the principle that social security should be provided by means of social insurance, not by direct transfer payments from taxpayers to beneficiaries. The risks of losing income through unemployment, ill-health and old age can all be insured against on the market. The benefits received by the individual are directly related to his or her insurance contributions, and these in turn are calculated by actuaries to reflect the risks for which the insuree is being covered. Beveridge intended that state social insurance should be based on sound actuarial principles. His reasons are contained in the extracts quoted in the previous section. Under a state insurance scheme the high risks of those with poor employment or health prospects, who would be unable to get private insurance at an affordable price, would be pooled with those in low-risk categories. It was because of this adherence to the insurance principle that the social security system was set up totally separate from the tax system. An administrative feature of this is that NI contributions are paid into a different account from other sources of government revenue, the National Insurance Fund.

Beveridge thus intended that the state pension scheme would eventually be a fully-funded scheme, one in which the individual's contributions, made by him/her and his/her employer, are accumulated over working life in the form of financial assets and then used on retirement to buy an annuity, which pays out a stream of income—i.e. the pension. The final pension thus depends directly on the value of the contributions and on the rate of return on the financial assets held by the pension fund. Beveridge had intended that the level of NI contributions should be set by actuarial principles to produce enough income to fund future insurance commitments. But if a fully-funded pension scheme is started from scratch, then it takes about 40 years until full pension rights can be paid. This is far too long a time-scale for most political objectives. Beveridge had proposed a 20-year transitional period, but the government wanted to begin paying pensions at the fully-funded rate straight away. Although the government had intended to make up the resulting deficiency to the National Insurance Fund from general taxation, this promise was swiftly abandoned for the 'pay-as-you-go' method: current contributions are used to pay current benefits. Thus the state pension scheme has always been unfunded. The only claim current contributors have to a future state pension is a political one; that when they retire the current working generation will acknowledge their past contribution to the economy and pay them a pension out of current contributions or general taxation.

The abandonment of Beveridge's flat-rate principle in favour of earnings-related pensions has placed a further wedge between individuals' contributions and their benefits. Although contributions have become more income-related, this is increasingly taking the form of a progressive tax and is not directly linked to the individual's benefits. Unemployment benefit is once more a flat-rate payment as earnings-related benefit, introduced in 1966, was abolished in 1982. Furthermore, benefits have been raised in line with prices or earnings over the years, while contributions have been raised in order to finance current benefits. The net result is that the NI benefits received in the present bear no relation to the amount of an individual's past contributions.

The problem is not that the contributions principle is inherently correct and so should be adhered to, but that there is an administrative pretence that it actually operates. In reality the National Insurance Fund is a book-keeping exercise, not an insurance fund managed on actuarial principles. National Insurance contributions are actually hypothecated taxes—that is, taxes earmarked for specific purposes, not insurance premia. Politicians and civil servants are attached to the contributory principle because of their instinctive feeling that people resent paying what they regard as insurance less than general taxation. National Insurance benefits can then be regarded by their recipients as something they have paid for rather than as state charity.

There are, however, costs to maintaining the fiction. A new bureaucratic system was set up in the 1940s to operate National Insurance contributions and National Insurance and non-contributory benefits, separate from the tax system. Though the Inland Revenue collects NI contributions it does so separately from other forms of direct taxation, with consequent administrative costs. The Inland Revenue administers income tax allowances, through which the different expenditure needs of different types of households are provided for via *tax expenditures*. An entirely separate system, operated by the DHSS, pays out cash benefits. In the late 1940s the separation of the tax system from the benefits machinery did not give rise to the later confusions and complexities, because those in receipt of benefits and those paying income tax were separate sets. But, as noted in Chapter 6, the increasing proportion of GNP taken in tax, partly to fund rising welfare expenditure, has brought low-income people into the tax net. Personal tax allowances are now below supplementary benefit. People in receipt of benefit also pay taxes. The result is unplanned anomalies, differential treatment of people in and out of work, and high marginal tax rates on low-income earning households.

A further problem that arises out of the contributions principle is that it is inherently inflexible because contributions are made in the present to cover for future contingencies. With changing social conditions, it is not possible to predict what will be the relative importance of the various causes of income insufficiency in the future. The postwar period has witnessed a marked decline in the social disapproval of divorce and of the unmarried having children. Deviations from the orthodox family pattern of a life-long marriage, in which the non-working wife and her children gained their social security via the contributions of husband and father, are no longer abnormal. Because of such social changes, social insurance, based on past contributions, has become less comprehensive with the passage of time. If the tax and benefit system is to serve people's various needs efficiently, it has to respond to social change. The problem with the current system is that when it has been adapted to reflect changing needs, this has taken the form of *ad hoc* amendments. The end-product is a complex and non-rational system which has for long been widely recognised as ripe for reform. The erstwhile reformers differ as to the respective weights they give to the objectives of redistribution and efficiency and in the means chosen to achieve these objectives. So before proceeding to examine the political and administrative problems which dog attempts at reform, I wish to consider the perceived deficiencies of the current social security system with respect to the objectives of redistribution and efficiency.

WHAT IS WRONG WITH THE SOCIAL SECURITY SYSTEM?

While the social security system has succeeded in providing a much better safety net than existed before the war, it has, over the last twenty years, been subject to mounting criticism from different perspectives: it is too costly; it is too penny-pinching and fails to redistribute income sufficiently; it fails to meet people's needs and promote social justice; it is inefficient. In the Conservative government's view 'despite mounting costs, resources have not always been directed to those most in need. . . social security is difficult to administer and at times impossible for the public to understand.'[4] These various criticisms can be grouped under the headings of distributional and efficiency failures, though in some respects these features are mutually reinforcing.

Distributional Failures
In the course of the 1960s there developed organised forms of agitation to press the view that the tax and social security systems—the tax-benefit system—had failed to eliminate poverty, to redistribute income sufficiently or promote social justice and equity adequately. The poverty lobby, consisting of various pressure groups, like the Child Poverty Action Group, the Claimants Union, Age Concern, and the National Council for One-Parent Families, have agitated for a restructuring of the tax-benefit system, together with higher public spending. The poverty lobby and the Left are dissatisfied that, since the 1950s, there has been no progress towards

greater income equality. If poverty is measured as having an income at or below supplementary benefit, there are now more poor people. High unemployment and more pensioners and single-parent families inevitably produce more people with no earning capacity. However supplementary benefit has risen in line with average earnings. In terms of absolute living standards the poor are, like the rest of us, better off than thirty years ago. However their relative position in society has undergone little change.

Beveridge's initial intention was that most claimants would rely on National Insurance benefits; only those with insufficient contributions would need means-tested supplementary benefit (or national assistance until 1966). And this was to be a subsistence income. However National Insurance benefits have always been too low relative to subsistence needs. To set them higher has been deemed too expensive. Consequently, many claimants who have paid National Insurance contributions are entitled to means-tested supplementary benefits as well as National Insurance benefits. There are also growing numbers of young and long-term unemployed and single women with children, without adequate National Insurance records, who have to rely entirely on supplementary benefit. Today 60 per cent of the unemployed and 20 per cent of pensioners claim supplementary benefit. Thus Beveridge's hope that the contributory principle would give people the right to adequate non-means-tested benefits did not materialise. Means-tested benefits fail to alleviate poverty if people do not take them up, either because they dislike the stigma and indignity of applying for them or because the rules are so complex that they are ignorant of their entitlements. The social security system is criticised on both these counts.

There is also the problem of the *poverty trap*—the situation in which a poor working household cannot increase its final income (after tax and benefits) by earning a higher original income (income before payment of tax and receipt of benefit). This problem has arisen because of the interaction of the tax system with the benefits system. A family with low earnings is entitled to housing benefit, family income supplement and other means-tested benefits. As such a family earns more, it loses its means-tested benefits and becomes liable for tax and higher National Insurance payments. The net effect is very high marginal tax rates, even exceeding 100 per cent in a few cases. In 1985, a two-child family man who increased his gross earnings from £70 a week to £115, would have been worse off by £3.23. However, only about 115,000 families had marginal tax rates of over 100 per cent. At most there were estimated to be about half a million low earners who in 1985 would have had marginal tax rates of 60 per cent or more.[5] As well as the poverty trap, which affects those in employment, there are others whose net incomes are not much improved by taking work. In 1978 around 21 per cent of working family heads would have lost no more that 10 per cent of their income if unemployed. Since then, the abolition of earnings-related unemployment pay and making unemployment benefit liable to tax, has reduced this proportion to about 3 per cent.[6] Both the poverty and the unemployment traps make it very difficult for those affected to raise their incomes by working.

Part of the complaint that the social security system does too little to redistribute income or alleviate poverty is based on the view that more should be spent on welfare benefits. Partly though, it is a criticism of the structure of the tax-benefit system, of the kinds of benefits paid, to whom they are paid and the conditions attached to their receipt. The two strands of criticism, while to some extent interconnected, are conceptually distinct. There is a strong case that within a given welfare budget, the money could be spent more effectively to achieve the aims of reducing inequality in final incomes and relieving poverty. This latter criticism is about the efficiency of the tax-benefit system in achieving its aims: an inefficient system contributes to poverty. The various facets of the inefficiency of the tax-benefit system are now examined.

Inefficiencies with Respect to the Tax-Benefit System

The one aspect of the social security system that is universally condemned is the complexity and anomalies that stem from the vast proliferation of different types of means-tested and non-means-tested benefits for different categories of claimant. There are sixty cash benefits. The supplementary benefit scheme is the main culprit in this because it endeavours to relate specific payments to individual needs, rather than pay a specific sum sufficient for living on and leaving the recipients to decide how to spend it. The supplementary benefit scheme tries to distinguish between regular weekly needs, for different categories of claimant, and special intermittent needs, such as new furnishings, household maintenance or travelling for hospital visits or in search of work. Each type of need has to be claimed for from DHSS officials who determine whether each claim is allowable under the regulations. This leads to appeals before tribunals by dissatisfied claimants and the building-up of a complex body of case law to add to the original regulations: 'The rules on single payments alone run to over 1000 lines of law: one regulation alone contains 20 separate categories of essential furniture and household equipment even before rules are set on which claimants are eligible for them.'[7] This complexity has arisen partly in response to the poverty lobby's agitation against the alternative system of letting claims be settled by administrative discretion exercised by DHSS officials. Instead it has been done by the application of rules, which by 1985 occupied 16,000 paragraphs, bound in two volumes. 81,000 staff were required to administer 16 million new claims a year and review the outstanding 20 million claims. Over the year more than 100 million giro cheques and 53 million order books were issued. In 1985 the DHSS was just starting on the full computerisation of the social security system.

The complexity of the benefits system contributes to several forms of inefficiency. One is the high administrative costs: in 1984 it cost 10 p to pay one pound's worth of supplementary benefit and 9 p in the pound for unemployment benefit, compared to 1.5 p for retirement pensions.[8] A further problem is the alienation of clients. The difficulties of understanding the system, of being subject to bureaucratic procedures, queueing, and of detailed inquiries into personal circumstances, which may even include questions on the frequency of bathing, serve to antagonise claimants. The social security system is charged with contributing to social injustice, since those not dependent on means-tested state benefits do not have to submit to such procedures. These detailed inquiries into personal means and needs have instilled opposition to any form of income-related benefit.

The structure of the existing system and the way it operates reduce its efficiency in alleviating poverty. The difficulty people have in understanding what their social security entitlements are and the personal costs of claiming benefits mean that many do not claim benefits to which they are entitled. It has been estimated that the percentage of those entitled but not receiving benefit is 65 per cent for FIS, 43 per cent for rate rebates and 31 per cent for rent rebates.[9] Universal benefits, such as the old age pension and child benefit, have very high take-up rates. From the point of view of concentrating benefits on the poor, the social security system is also inefficient because it pays benefit to those not entitled or not in need. This problem arises with respect to FIS because benefit is paid for a year on the basis of five consecutive weeks income. If income subsequently rises, the FIS benefit continues. The old age pension and child benefit are also received by the well-off. It has been estimated that only 54 per cent of the benefits paid out are strictly required to lift incomes above the supplementary benefit level.[10]

The efficiency (or lack of it) with which a tax and benefit system achieves its redistributive aims is a function of its structure and the way it is administered. A wider criterion of efficiency is concerned with the effects of the social security system on the allocation of resources in the economy as a whole. This aspect of efficiency has already been considered with regard to the tax system in Chapter 5 and that analysis applies here too. Apart from impeding the alleviation of poverty, the unemployment and poverty traps promote inefficiency in a wider sense by reducing the incentive to work. Income-related benefits produce high marginal tax rates on low earners because benefits are withdrawn as income rises. As explained in Chapter 6, high marginal tax rates reduce the attractiveness of spending time earning money relative to domestic tasks or leisure, and this substitution effect acts to reduce the supply of labour.

A further consideration with respect to allocative efficiency is the effect of state social security, especially the method of financing pensions, on the rate of accumulation and on the type of financial instruments chosen as the medium of saving. First there is the issue of whether, relative to funded contributory pension schemes, unfunded schemes reduce people's incentive to save and so diminish the rate of economic growth because a higher proportion of national resources are consumed, rather than being saved and so invested. Whatever the type of pension scheme, the payment of pensions involves a transfer of resources from the current working generation to the retired. From an efficiency point of view the only difference between schemes is whether contributory-funded schemes (those which relate an individual's pension to the amount of his or her contributions and to the rate of return on the fund's financial assets) promote a higher rate of saving and hence a higher growth rate in the economy, than a state pay-as-you-go scheme (under which pensions are determined by the amount of taxation currently devoted to paying pensions and not to the amount of saving in the form of contributions undertaken by individuals and their employers). If it is the case that 'pay-as-you-go' schemes reduce aggregate saving compared to funded contributory schemes, and that this reduces economic growth, then the former scheme is less efficient. In principle a state scheme could be funded, but the political pressures to pay high pensions relative to contributions makes this unlikely. The issue is too speculative to form firm empirically-based conclusions regarding the efficiency implications of different pension schemes. *Supply-siders* believe that state schemes, which are inevitably unfunded because of political pressures for jam today, are less efficient than private ones for the reasons just given. This argument is rejected by those who defend state pensions, usually because they favour them for distributional and political reasons.

Another implication of pension arrangements for allocative efficiency stems from the dominance of occupational pension schemes in providing higher income individuals with pensions in addition to the state scheme. Tax concessions have been biased in favour of occupational schemes, to which employers as well as employees contribute, relative to private arrangements, and saving with pension funds relative to direct share-holding by individuals. The possible implications of this for financing business investment were touched on in Chapter 5. Consequently, personal financial investment is heavily concentrated in pension funds—a highly illiquid form of asset, of which individuals have little knowledge or control. Because employers contribute to occupational schemes on their own account, rather than on behalf of the individual employee, it is difficult to distinguish the individual's personal share in the scheme. Hence employees who leave a scheme early, because they change jobs, say, usually lose pension rights. This discourages people from changing jobs, making labour less mobile, so reducing the adjustment capability of the economy.

The potential effects of the tax-benefit system on efficiency are both varied and imprecisely known. Its effects on efficiency vary from the costs of administration and its effectiveness in alleviating poverty and redistributing income, to its impact on the supply of labour and the allocation of resources to investment. Though there is a wide measure of agreement that more resources should be channelled to the poorest, there is considerable disagreement over how much to redistribute and to which classes of needy, from whom to take the resources and what means to use. Controversy reigns over the extent to which redistributive objectives can only be achieved by spending much more on benefits or whether improving the efficiency with which the system delivers its benefits is sufficient, as the Conservative government believes.

THE REFORM OF SOCIAL SECURITY

For many years now there has been consensus that the tax-benefit system needs a fundamental overhaul; at this point the consensus ends. The measures that should constitute such a reform are hotly contested. The history of attempts at reforming social security is a testimony to the power of the Pareto principle to prevent radical change. Whatever plan of reform is proposed, some groups inevitably lose out. Their protests, blended with the antagonisms of adversarial party politics, impede the conduct of a detached and rational debate over complex issues.

In 1983 the DHSS began the most thorough review of the tax-benefit system since Beveridge. A series of working parties were set up to study various aspects of the system and to make recommendations. On the basis of these deliberations the Secretary of State for Health and Social Security, Norman Fowler, initially set out his proposed reforms in a Green Paper, published in June 1985. The changes to social security are intended to serve three primary objectives: to target benefits more accurately on those who need them most; to simplify the system so that it is better understood by claimants and cheaper to administer; and to reduce the projected rate of growth of social security expenditure. The measures proposed in the Green Paper fell into two distinct categories. One was the proposed privatisation of pensions by abolishing the State Earnings-Related Pension Scheme (SERPS) and replacing it by compulsory private sector pension arrangements. The other related to the general structure of benefits—to simplifying it, removing anomalies and reducing high marginal tax rates on low-income households. This restructuring was constrained by the Treasury's insistence—backed by the Prime Minister—that the overall social security budget should not be increased.

State Earnings-Related Pension Scheme

The government's proposal to abolish SERPS was almost universally condemned, not only by the TUC and the poverty lobby, but also by the CBI and the pensions industry. SERPS had been eventually introduced in 1978 with bi-party agreement, after two decades of party wrangling over how to improve the state pension scheme for those on average incomes. It also improved the pension position of most women, who are badly provided for by private sector schemes because of their interrupted earnings record. SERPS promises to pay, on top of the standard old age pension, a pension equal to one quarter of the average of a person's best twenty years' earnings, between set qualifying limits (in 1985–86 between £35.50 and £264.50 a week.) The twenty years' qualifying earnings are revalued at the date of retirement in line with average earnings. NI contributions are earnings-related, partly in recognition that pensions will be earnings-related, but partly to make NI a less regressive tax. Those who belong to occupational schemes contract out of SERPS and they and their employers pay correspondingly lower NI contributions.

In its original form SERPS was to give much more generous pensions to average earners. It will do little to improve the pensions of low-income earners, who will find that their entitlement to SERPS disqualifies them from the supplementary benefit that they currently get. The Institute for Fiscal Studies estimates that the gross income of a retired 'average couple' will, as a result of SERPS, rise from £82 to £152 a week (in 1983 prices)—a net income on retirement which is 70 per cent of income when in work.[11] The scheme will not mature until 1998, but after then, as more retired people become eligible for SERPS, the amount of state expenditure on pensions will rise steeply. By how much is a matter of statistical controversy. The government estimates that by the year 2035 there will be 13.2 million pensioners compared to 9.3 million in 1985, while the number of NI contributors will be the same at 21.8 million; the cost of the basic state pension will have risen in 1985 prices from £15 billion to £45 billion and SERPS will add another £23 billion.[12] The Institute for Fiscal Studies estimate that, if operative today, SERPS would account for around one third of the social security budget. This sum of money could finance a 60 per cent increase in National Insurance benefits plus a reduction in the standard rate of income tax to 20 per cent.[13] This commitment by the current generation, that their children should pay them much more generous pensions than they pay their parents, at a time when there will be a higher proportion of elderly in the population, has been called by Norman Fowler 'a time-bomb ticking away as our legacy to posterity'.[14]

That SERPS, together with the swollen ranks of pensioners, will give rise to a large increase in pensions expenditure is generally acknowledged, though the government's arithmetic is challenged by those who want

SERPS to continue unchanged. The government's proposed solution to the SERPS time-bomb was to phase it out and replace it by compulsory private schemes, to which employers and employees would be compelled to contribute minimum amounts. The motive behind this is not only to reduce government expenditure in the future, but to extend privatisation. Fowler also wanted to increase labour mobility and extend direct share-ownership amongst middle-income individuals by developing portable personal pension rights. However private sector institutions cannot do this for middle-income earners because they cannot devise a funded scheme for such people that will give them as attractive pensions as SERPS. This is because private sector schemes depend on the accumulation of assets financed from the savings of contributors to the pension fund. The generosity of the pensions provided by SERPS depends on the future generation honouring the political commitment they have inherited from their forebears. The pensions industry has protested at the government's pension privatisation proposals on the grounds that it is administratively costly to invest small contributions in personal pension schemes. Using commercial criteria it is not possible under current legislation to produce SERPS pension rights at the SERPS level of contributions.

The only way the government can reduce the state's commitment of the future generation to more generous pensions for the current generation of average earners, is either by reducing the latter's pension rights or by increasing their acquisition costs. It is hardly surprising that the policy is unpopular, particularly with organisations like the TUC, which represent the main SERPS beneficiaries. It requires great political talents to sell a policy which benefits those who cannot yet vote at the expense of current voters.

Means-Tested Benefits

The furore over the proposed abolition of SERPS somewhat overshadowed the other part of the social security review, concerned with simplifying the benefits structure, targeting them more directly to those in greatest need and alleviating the poverty trap. The debate as to whether redistribution is better tackled by means-tested benefits or by some form of minimum guaranteed universal benefit, which is clawed back from the better-off in taxes, has been going on for decades. The 1970–74 Conservative government attempted to bring in a tax credit scheme. This was also intended to 'simplify and reform the whole system of personal tax collection' and 'to improve the system of income support for poor people'.[15] It proposed the abolition of PAYE and the creation of a partially integrated tax and benefits system. Only family allowances and FIS were included. National Insurance benefits and supplementary benefit were to continue as separate schemes. On the basis of family responsibilities a tax credit would be calculated. If it exceeded the individual's tax liability he or she would be paid the difference. A tax credit overcomes the problem that tax allowances do nothing to help those who earn too little to pay tax. The scheme was considered by a Select Committee of the House of Commons, which recommended universal child benefit paid to the mother through the Post Office. This amendment was accepted by the government, though it raised administrative costs. The scheme was criticised for making some groups worse off—families claiming FIS and pensioners with incomes just above supplementary benefit level; it would create anomalies between those with stable and those with fluctuating incomes; it was not sufficiently radical and did not eliminate means tests; it was administratively infeasible. Time ran out; the government lost the 1974 election and the proposal sank with it.

It is not possible to devise a system of fiscal redistribution that meets everybody's objectives. The difficult choices that have to be made are clearly evident from analysing the three basic models of fiscal redistribution. The first is the *social dividend*, which has its own pressure group to promote the idea: the Basic Income Research Group. Under this everybody would get the same minimum income from the state regardless of their condition or income, and there would be no means-tested benefits. It implies a high level of social expenditure and so has to be financed by a correspondingly high rate of income tax. A dividend as low as £20 a week would require a standard rate of income tax of 45—50 per cent.[16] More widely canvassed, especially on the Left, is the second system of fiscal redistribution. This consists of universal *contingent benefits*, given irrespective of income to those in specific categories—the old, the unemployed, families, the sick—and financed by heavier taxation of the better-off. Its advantage is that it gets rid of means tests, so improving take-up rates, and is relatively simple to administer. Though not requiring as high a level of government spending as a social dividend, for ensuring a given minimum income, it still requires more spending than restricting benefits to those on low incomes. The third solution is *negative income tax*. This aims to overcome the stigma and low take-up problems of means-tested benefits by delivering them through the tax system, rather than through a separate benefits system, which involves detailed inquiries into personal circumstances and expenditure needs. Under a negative tax system people with incomes below a prescribed threshold level are paid a social credit which is some fraction of the difference between their actual income and the threshold; they 'pay' negative income tax. Above the threshold income tax is levied in the usual way. This type of scheme involves less government expenditure than the other two.

How negative income tax works is explained by Figure 13.1. Without any fiscal intervention, a household's original income (measured along the horizontal axis) would be identical to its final income after paying tax and receiving benefits (measured on the vertical axis). Along line OY original and final income are the same. The government now introduces a negative income tax. Households with zero original income now receive OA benefit. As household income rises benefit is gradually withdrawn. The relationship between original income and final income is now given by line AB. Once original income has reached the threshold of OT income, no benefit is received; but no tax is paid either. As income rises above OT so more tax is paid. The distance between line OY and line AB is the amount of benefit received or the amount of tax paid. The marginal tax rate is given by the slope of line AB since it shows the relationship between an increase in original income and the resulting increase in final income. The less steep the slope, the higher the marginal tax rate.

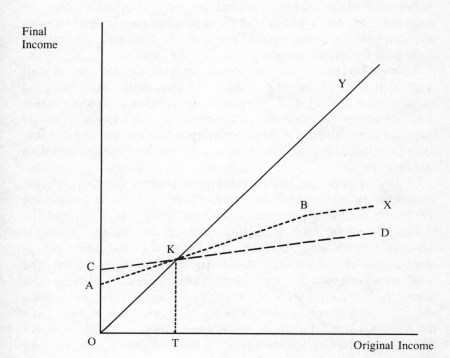

Figure 13.1: Negative income tax

The line CD shows a more redistributive tax credit scheme. The amount given to those with zero original income is higher at OC. Households with incomes below the threshold now do better, while those with incomes above OT are worse off. The marginal tax rate along line CD is correspondingly higher. The problem is that the larger the tax credits paid to those with low incomes, the higher will be the marginal tax rate experienced by those receiving the credit, as well as those with incomes above the threshold. But high marginal tax rates over the range of income earned by the majority of households are both electorally unpopular and increase the incidence of tax disincentives to work. The solution to this problem is to concentrate high marginal tax rates in income bands where there are few households: this implies the bottom end as well as the top end. If the relationship between original and final income were given by line CKBX, then those with incomes below OT would have a higher marginal tax rate than those with incomes above OT: those with the highest incomes have a higher marginal tax rate as well. The objective of minimising the disincentive effects of high marginal tax rates, required in order to redistribute income, conflicts with the notion that social justice requires that marginal tax rates should progressively increase with income throughout the income range.

The same kind of diagram illustrates the social dividend scheme as well. A social dividend of OA or OC is given to all and income in excess of the social dividend is taxed. The social dividend scheme involves higher government spending than the negative tax scheme because a flat-rate social dividend, such as OA, is paid to everybody, not just to those on zero incomes. A negative tax scheme pays out less benefit to households as their income rises.

A 'pure' negative tax scheme takes no account of people's differing circumstances, other than their income. It gives benefits to low income households regardless of the reason for their poverty or of their specific expenditure needs, such as rearing children. In contrast, contingent universal benefits give cash to people in specific categories, such as families, the old or the unemployed, regardless of their income. The disadvantage of a pure negative tax is that because everybody gets the same benefit, there is a trade-off between giving old people an adequate pension and giving the unemployed such generous benefits that there is little incentive to work for those with low earning capacity. Another disadvantage of a negative income tax is that it implies a relatively high marginal tax rate on low incomes, since benefits are withdrawn as income rises.

Non-means-tested contingent benefits avoid high marginal tax rates on low-income households, since they do not lose their benefit as they earn more. Disincentive effects can be further removed by paying pensions at a higher rate than unemployment benefit and poverty amongst low earning families alleviated by generous child benefit. By definition, universal contingent benefits are neither means-tested nor taxed. This means that the better-off, who happen to belong to a contingent category, do better out of the tax-benefit system than households with the same income but not in receipt of contingent benefits. This situation can be avoided by making benefit taxable, but this does nothing to offset the high level of government expenditure involved because benefits are paid to all qualifying by contingency, regardless of income. Though administratively simple, additional administrative costs are incurred in both the public and private sectors, because the state pays cash benefits to most households with one hand while taking them away with the other. A further disadvantage of non-means-tested contingent benefits is that they imply relatively high marginal tax rates throughout most of the income range. The attractions of negative income tax are that it implies a lower level of welfare expenditure, as it is spent only on the poor, and so avoids high marginal tax rates throughout the income scale.

In order to obtain the advantages of both income-related and contingent benefits, while avoiding the costs attendant on relying on just one of the models of fiscal redistribution, it makes sense for a tax-benefit system to use elements of both, as does the current UK system. Child benefit is a universal contingent benefit, while unemployment benefit and state pensions are contingent taxable benefits. FIS and rent allowances are income-related, contingent benefits, while rate rebates are means-tested. In designing a tax-benefit scheme, the advantages of negative income tax and contingent benefits can be combined by making the amount of tax credit depend on personal circumstances.

There is a tendency for those on the Right to prefer income-related (i.e. negative income tax)-type schemes, while the Left prefer universal contingent benefits coupled with higher taxation, especially of the better-off. The Conservative government intends to alter the balance of the current mixture of contingent and income-related benefits, with an increased element of negative income taxation for families. This does not imply a wholesale move to negative income tax, nor to the full integration of the tax-benefit system which that would necessarily imply.

In order to simplify the benefits system and reduce the complexities, indignities and administrative costs of the present extent of means testing, the government propose to replace supplementary benefit with an income support scheme. This will provide a regular weekly income, which will vary with age, marital status and client group (unemployed, single parent, disabled, retired). It gives recipients a fixed sum to spend as they please, rather than the present multitude of different payments for specific demonstrable needs. In addition there will be a social fund to which claimants may apply for money to meet exceptional expenditure needs (birth, death and other financial crises). Grants will be made at the discretion of specially trained DHSS officials, not by the application of regulations, as has now largely become the practice. The government's intention to do away with an appeals mechanism, which it argues would require the current complex legalistic rules and procedures, has aroused considerable opposition.

For those in work, FIS will be replaced by a new family credit. The objective here is to remove both the unemployment and poverty traps and to give more help in cash rather than in kind. Thus the scheme should ensure that net income in work is above income support payments. Some move towards integration of the tax and benefit systems is proposed, as family credit will be paid through the tax system operated by employers and the Inland Revenue. However the integration is only partial. The DHSS and not the Inland Revenue will, on application, estimate how much family credit an employee is entitled to. The employer will then be informed and will deduct the family credit from the employee's tax liability. Some will get reduced tax payments, while those whose credit exceeds their tax liability will receive an additional payment. As family credit will be assessed on net income, including housing benefit, rather than on gross income as is FIS, it will not be possible for a household to be taxed in excess of 100 per cent. Although the worst aspect of the poverty trap will be removed, there will be an estimated increase from 250,000 to 700,000 in the numbers of low-income earners taxed at a marginal rate of more than 80 per cent. This is the consequence of more families being entitled to family credit than to FIS and because of the rate at which benefits are withdrawn as income rises. A slower tapering off of benefits would increase the cost of the scheme to taxpayers.

Another reason for a relatively high rate at which benefits are lost as income rises is the retention of housing benefit as a separate benefit. Housing benefit is calculated with respect to the difference between a household's income and its 'needs allowance', which is determined by officials with reference to household circumstances, such as the number of children. Under the current scheme recipients of supplementary benefit have all their housing costs met in full, but those in work are assessed differently. This means that working households, whose income is around supplementary benefit level, may well get less help with their housing costs than those on supplementary or unemployment benefit. The government proposes to simplify housing benefit by having a common set of criteria for both income support and housing benefit.

Housing benefit also has implications for local authority expenditure and revenue policies. As poor households pay no rates, they have every incentive to vote for councillors promising high spending on local services.

Furthermore, a local authority only loses 10 per cent of its subsidised rates, as it receives 90 per cent back from central government. The Conservative government has been locked in battle with high-spending Labour authorities to make them reduce their expenditure. High rates place little constraint on such authorities, when large numbers of their supporters pay no rates. Hence the government propose that all households should pay at least 20 per cent of their rates. A further consideration is that areas with large numbers of poor households living in council accommodation are usually Labour-controlled. Such councils can raise rents on estates occupied by low-income households, knowing that they will mainly be paid by central government. The government therefore proposes unspecified measures to ensure that local authorities have 'a greater incentive to monitor and control costs, [in] the interests of the tax and ratepayer'.[17]

THE PROCESS OF POLICY-MAKING

Fowler's social security reforms illustrate the consultative method of policy-making. The final proposals appeared in the White Paper, *Reform of Social Security*, published after two years of consultation. It records that nineteen public sessions were held with 62 organisations and individuals giving oral evidence. Over 40,000 consultation documents were issued and nearly 450,000 pieces of written evidence received. The original proposals were set out in a Green Paper. This is often an important stage in the policy-making process. The government's proposed course of action is presented in public in a semi-crystallised form, which can be reset in the light of external reactions without great loss of face.

The Role of Political Interests
With a realm of policy so explicitly about distribution and affecting the whole population, there is bound to be intense activity amongst a whole host of political interests; especially when it is not possible to restructure a complex tax-benefit system without some interests losing out. The Fowler proposals for improving the efficiency of the tax-benefit system are linked to the objective of reducing government expenditure. As detailed in Chapter 12, welfare expenditure has for long grown more rapidly than overall government spending; within the welfare budget, the social security expenditure programme is large and growing relatively fast, and promises to continue doing so. It is therefore a prime target for pruning by the radical Right, both within government, but most vociferously from outside. Given the government's overall desire not to increase its spending, the restructuring of social security has been constrained by the limitations of its

existing budget allocations. Hence to improve the lot of those the government favours—poor families and the disabled—means reducing the entitlements of other categories, in particular those of the single young unemployed. Also, there will be more pensioners who will be worse off because of the cut in housing benefit than the number who will be made better off. It is estimated that the restructuring will make 1.4 million social security recipients better off and 1.7 million worse off compared with the current system.

Pressure from diverse political interests has been applied both within government, as well as more obviously and stridently from without. As far as the poverty lobby is concerned, the government's restructuring of social security is motivated entirely by its desire to reduce expenditure and so every aspect of the proposals is condemned. Within the government itself there have been conflicts over the relative weights that should be given to the objectives of expenditure reduction and improved efficiency. The Treasury has sought expenditure reductions from the social security review, in the near as well as distant future; while the DHSS has been more concerned with improving the effectiveness of the system in targeting benefits at those it considers most in need.

In addition there are vital electoral considerations at stake. Mrs Thatcher is reported to have vetoed any tampering with untaxed child benefits as this would lose electoral support from the better-off, especially as it would, in general, be men who paid the tax while their wives collected the benefit.[18] Both the Treasury and the DHSS saw advantages in abolishing universal child benefit—the Treasury to secure a reduction in expenditure, the DHSS in order to target a given social security budget more effectively on the poor. In the event the government favoured the retention of universal child benefit, ostensibly on moral grounds: 'It is right that families at all income levels should receive some recognition for the additional costs of bringing up children.'[19] Fowler is reported as having wanted to drop the proposal to make everyone pay at least 20 per cent of their rates, but was unable to overcome Mrs Thatcher's insistence that it should remain, despite the unfavourable electoral reaction from pensioners.

Outside government the various political interests have been particularly vociferous in the period following the publication of the Green Paper which, as is standard practice, is the time when the government encourages comments on its proposals as part of a consultative process. The interested parties make representations to the government and also seek publicity for their views. The government takes these into account in deciding whether or not to proceed with the proposals and, if so, how to revise them. The Social Security Green Paper elicited 7000 written responses, most of them critical. The abolition of SERPS was almost universally criticised. The poverty pressure groups have objected to the proposal to cash limit the

Social Fund and for claimants to have no right of appeal; to the payment of family credit to fathers through their pay packets and not to mothers, who currently receive FIS; and to the cut in housing benefit and the failure to raise the social security budget so that fewer beneficiaries are made worse off by the changes. TUC and Labour Party criticisms are similar.

In response to the reactions to the Green Paper, the DHSS modified its final proposals, as published in a rather delayed White Paper. The major retreat was the retention of SERPS. It will be modified to reduce the entitlements of those who will start claiming pensions in the 21st century and thus diminish its cost. Various inducements are being made to encourage individuals to take out personal and hence portable pension schemes. Other modifications made in response to pressure group lobbying include dropping the minimum residence period for entitlement to Social Fund benefits, which had raised an outcry from the ethnic minorities. Also the Green Paper had proposed lower income support for all under 25s; this is now limited to the single and childless. The final product has not been the fundamental restructuring of the benefit system which the Secretary of State had proclaimed.

The task of restructuring taxes and benefits so as to achieve specific aims is technically complex. The full implications for distribution of any given set of measures are not easy to discover. Ministers, officials, politicians and the professional experts representing the various political interests, have conducted a war of statistical claim and counterclaim. As is often the case in public debates over policy, the waters are muddied by the intermingling of several related issues. The context in which the government has conducted the social security review has bound the issue of the level of social security spending and the extent of redistribution, which arouses great political heat, more closely to that of improving the efficiency with which the tax-benefit system attains specific objectives. The latter issue is amenable to dispassionate and rational analysis. However, the emotions aroused over the perceived threat to the relative living standards of the lower income groups has made it more difficult to reach a consensus on the appropriate structure of the tax-benefit system as an issue separate from setting benefit rates. These measures involve considerable administrative costs to implement and affect the decisions people need to make with respect to a long time-horizon, such as pensions provision. If they do not command a reasonable degree of consensus, there will be continual costly readjustments when the reins of government change hands.

Because it is difficult, if not impossible, to ascertain the full implications of such proposals, the mass of the electorate are not in a position to make informed judgements. Apart from some awareness of the impact of benefits and taxes on personal pockets, public opinion responds to the effectiveness with which the policy protagonists present their arguments. A propaganda war is not the best setting for conducting a rational debate on complex issues.

The Role of Government Bureaucracies

The institutional structures and practices of government bureaucracies constrain the extent to which rational policy solutions can be devised, let alone implemented. The problem of the haphazard interaction of the tax and benefits system in the UK has already been alluded to. It can be traced back to a period when people who received benefits did not at the same time pay taxes. The separate administration of taxes and benefits has made it extremely difficult to devise a plan of reform which would fully integrate the two systems. Both the 1972 and 1985 proposals involved only limited integration. The 1985 Social Security Review was conducted by the DHSS and deliberated over by Cabinet and Cabinet committees. Meanwhile the Treasury was preparing a separate Green Paper on the reform of personal income tax. Both the DHSS benefits system and Inland Revenue tax collection are at last on the road to becoming fully computerised, after this was postponed in the 1970s in order to allow time for integration. Two separate computer systems are being installed.

The Inland Revenue has not been closely involved in the Social Security Review, nor is it evident that they have been eager to cooperate with new schemes which would involve them in administrative changes. For instance, the professional actuarial bodies have pointed out that the feasibility of the DHSS proposals for personal pensions, depends on changes in the rules operated by the Inland Revenue's Superannuation Funds Office which grants tax approval to private pension schemes and supervises them.[20] The Green Paper proposes the cumbersome administrative procedure whereby the DHSS works out an employee's Family Credit, which is then delivered via the tax system operated by the Inland Revenue. The Inland Revenue have claimed that they cannot work out Family Credit because they no longer collect data on children.[21] This is another example of how political interests manifest themselves as the sectional interests of particular bureaucracies within government and influence policy-making, often to the detriment of devising efficient means of securing specific policy objectives.

CONCLUSIONS ON THE PROCESS OF REFORM

The objectives of various political interests, different moral and social values and the rational application of policy instruments to achieve specific ends, have all been involved in the design and modification of the social security system. From the perspective of rational policy analysis the tax-benefit system we have is non-rational, as it is not the most effective way of achieving specific redistributional goals for a given amount of expenditure. As with the tax system itself, the advocates of rational reforms are in for a long wait. Those with patient resignation at the workings of a pluralist political system applaud any move in the direction of a more rational tax-benefit system. The Institute for Fiscal Studies, which aims to promote rational policy-making, saw the social security Green Paper 'as a first step to the goal of an integrated and coherent tax and benefit system'.[22]

There are those who see virtue in pluralist policy-making, because there is sufficient involvement of diverse political interests to ensure that the resulting compromise is acceptable. From the pluralist perspective, policy is judged more by the process through which it is made and implemented and less by how well the instruments that thereby emerge attain specific objectives. This contrasts with the rational perspective on policy which judges it in terms of its outcome—and not in terms of the decision-making process that produced the outcome—and assesses the outcome in relation to how efficiently specific objectives are achieved.

One can discern both pluralist and rational elements in policy-making with respect to social security. There is some endeavour to design policy instruments which secure specific objectives efficiently. But the choice of which objectives to pursue and with what priority, emerges from the political interaction of sectional interests, who have different preferences with respect to objectives. Nor is the distinction between objectives and instruments as clear-cut as it is in economic analysis. What economists regard as the means to securing objectives, are often for others objectives in their own right. For some, policy instruments have ethical attributes or their use is in the interests of those operating them. Even within government there is rarely a complete agreement on the priority to give to conflicting objectives, as in the case of the social security review. What emerges is the result of a compromise between what the various government departments want, what is judged electorally sensible and what the government assesses can be successfully implemented, given the reactions of those involved in operating the policy and experiencing its effects. The ensuing concoction is likely to be found inefficient when judged from a rational perspective, since it did not emerge from a rational decision-making process. The basic features of policy-making with respect to social security, namely the intermingling of distributional and efficiency issues and the impact of the political process of policy-making on the ensuing policy output, is replicated in many other spheres of economic policy.

THE DISTRIBUTIONAL IMPACT OF THE WELFARE STATE

As the overriding rationale for the welfare state is the attainment of various distributive objectives, the chapter concludes with a brief examination of some evidence on its redistributive impact. Governments redistribute real income by taking income away through taxation and by giving it back by means of cash transfers and benefits in kind, such as health services and education. Other aspects of economic policy also have redistributional aims, as has regional policy for example. This has endeavoured to offset geographic inequalities in regional income levels by promoting industrial development and employment opportunities in the less affluent regions through subsidies to firms locating there. There is now diminished confidence in the efficacy of such policies, especially under the Conservative government, which has reduced regional development grants. Agricultural policy, examined in the next chapter, is another set of measures aimed primarily at redistributing income—in this case, to a specific class of producers. All economic policies inevitably have some distributional consequences, even when their primary objective is not redistribution. The full impact of government economic policies on the distribution of income and wealth is not known. To arrive at any such estimate would require an enormous amount of quantitative information as well as the use of specific and, inevitably, arguable assumptions about the impact of policies relative to their absence.

An estimate of the impact of taxation and government expenditure on the distribution of income is produced annually by the Central Statistical Office. These estimates are based on the Family Expenditure Survey, which asks a sample of about 10,000 households to detail their expenditure and incomes over a two-week period. The CSO manage to allocate 60 per cent of government revenue and 49 per cent of government spending to households. The original income of a household is what it would receive prior to any government intervention. This is shown in the first row of Table 13.1 which ranks households into five groups, or quintiles, according to original income. The average person in the bottom fifth of households had, in 1985, an original income of £75; just over 1 per cent of the average income per head in the top quintile on households. The bottom rows of the table indicate the main reason why the bottom quintile have such low original incomes: each bottom quintile household on average contains only 10 per cent of an economically active person, compared to 2.2 per household for the top quintile. Between 60 and 70 per cent of the bottom quintile are retired households; about 10 per cent single adults, including students living away from home; and almost 20 per cent are families with children, largely unemployed or single parents.

The second row shows the average amount of cash benefits received per person in each group of households. It reveals the strong redistributive impact of the social security system. Lower income households get a significantly larger amount of cash benefit per person. The third row gives the average amount paid in income tax and national insurance contributions—almost negligible for the poorest fifth. However, indirect taxes, given in the fourth row, do not have a redistributive effect. The fifth row gives an estimate of the value of state benefits received in kind. These include health services, welfare food, housing subsidy (excluding mortgage interest relief which appears as a reduction in income tax), travel subsidy and education. The inclusion of students living away from home in the bottom quintile, increases the value of benefits in kind from education attributed to this group of households. Though the size of benefits in kind does decline with income, their redistributive impact is very slight. Final income is original income plus benefits and minus taxes.

Table 13.1: Redistributive effects of taxes and benefits (1985)

	Quintile groups of households ranked by original income					
Average per person ª (£)	Bottom	2nd	3rd	4th	Top	Average
Original income	75	1432	3242	4765	7443	3943
Plus cash benefits	2038	1353	500	304	223	739
Less income tax and NICs	6	−189	−608	−985	−1767	−839
Less indirect taxes	−494	−747	−854	−1015	−1280	−935
Plus benefits in kind	856	737	600	573	530	635
Final income	2481	2586	2880	3642	5149	3543
Average per household (no.)						
Adults	1.4	1.7	2.0	2.2	2.7	2.0
Children	0.4	0.4	0.8	0.8	0.6	0.6
Economically active	0.1	0.6	1.3	1.8	2.2	1.2
Retired people	0.8	0.8	0.2	0.1	0.1	0.4

Source: *Economic Trends*, November 1986.
Note: a. Children counted as half an adult.

Table 13.2: Percentage shares of households in total personal income, 1985

Quintile group	Original income 1975	Final income 1975	Original income 1985	Final income 1985
Bottom	0.8	7.1	0.3	6.7
2nd	10	13	6	12
3rd	19	18	17	17
4th	26	24	27	24
Top	44	38	49	40

Source: *Economic Trends*, November 1986.

By comparing original income with final income it can be seen that the redistributive impact of the total system of state benefits and tax is quite marked. Individuals in the bottom quintile have their original incomes increased 33 times, whereas those in the top group have their original incomes decreased by almost a third. The top quintile start with 99 times the original income of the bottom quintile and end up with just over twice as much final income. One measure of the redistributive effect of the tax and benefit system is given in Table 13.2. It shows the share of total national income going to households which is received by each quintile. The tax and benefit system increases the share of the two bottom groups and reduces that of the two top groups.

As already indicated, cash benefits are the most important way this redistribution is effected. Table 13.3 shows the proportion of final income that is received from various sources and taken away in tax. The bottom quintile receive 82 per cent of their final income in cash benefits, compared to 21 per cent for the average household and 4 per cent for the top fifth. Benefits in kind have a much smaller role in redistributing income, though their importance in relation to final income declines as income rises. Income tax and National Insurance contributions are quite progressive; the bottom group receives a small income tax rebate from mortgage option schemes and life insurance tax relief while the proportion of income tax rises with income. Indirect taxes are very slightly progressive up to the third quintile and then fall as a proportion of final income.

Table 13.3: Original income, taxes and benefits as a percentage of final income per person, 1985

Average per person [a] (£)	Quintile groups of households ranked by original income					
	Bottom	2nd	3rd	4th	Top	Average
Original income	3.0	55.3	112.4	131.0	144.5	111.4
Cash benefits	82.3	52.2	17.3	8.4	4.3	20.9
Income tax and NICs	0.3	−7.3	−21.1	−27.1	−34.3	−23.7
Indirect taxes	−19.9	−28.9	−29.6	−27.9	−24.9	−26.4
Benefits in kind	34.6	28.5	20.8	15.8	10.3	17.9

Source: *Economic Trends*, November 1986.
Note: a. Children counted as half an adult.

The CSO data also indicate how the impact of the tax-benefit system changes over time. One aspect of such changes is indicated in Table 13.2. The distribution of original income has become more unequal since 1975. This has been largely offset by the tax-benefit system so that the increased inequality in final income is considerably less. Since 1975 the lowest quintile group has come to rely more heavily on cash benefits: while the second quintile has doubled its reliance on cash benefits, from 24 to 49 per cent of gross income (original income plus cash benefits). This is because of the higher proportion of retired households in the second quintile, having been pushed out of the bottom group by the rising numbers of unemployed. There are now more claimants than ever before. Between 1979−80 and 1984−85 the number in receipt of state pensions and widow's benefit has risen by over half a million to 9.7 million, while the number unemployed has risen by around 2 million.

While these data are the most comprehensive published, they are subject to a considerable range of estimating error. Different assumptions about how to classify households and which benefits to include and how to allocate benefits and taxes would produce different results. What they do give is an indication of the relative redistributive impact of the various taxes and benefits and of the overall system. Other researchers [23] have argued that benefits in kind have failed totally to have any redistributive impact, arriving at estimates which show that the higher socio-economic groups receive more state expenditure on health, education and travel subsidies per capita than the lower groups. For education the reason is pretty obvious; the higher the socio-economic group the larger the proportion of children entering more expensive post-sixteen education. For health spending the reasons are less obvious. Partly it is due to the geographical distribution of resources. Other possible reasons are the easier access to doctors through better transport facilities and paid time off work, as well as better consumer information and ability to press for better treatment.

Thus the unequal distribution of resources prevails, though the market has been banished. Even a government committed to a more equal distribution of resources by area or class cannot achieve significant redistribution because the available resources are only partially in its control. The professional and other workers in the social services have a large influence on resource allocation, especially of existing physical resources, which in themselves commit the government to predetermined patterns of financial allocation. The clients too influence resource allocation by the demands they place on the suppliers, not in the form of cash payments, but by personally seeking services or combining to form interest groups. Some are inevitably better at this than others.

After forty years of the welfare state there is now a greater appreciation of the limits to which redistribution can go, especially in a slow-growing and painfully adjusting economy. The main instruments of redistribution are the tax system and social security. The provision of free universal welfare services ensures a possibly acceptable minimum standard for all, rather than counter-vailing the advantages of the affluent. How much redistribution is done, to whom, from whom and by what methods is the outcome of an accommodation between the welfare state policy communities formed of alliances between bureaucrats and client pressure groups on the one hand, and those interests that pay for it through the tax system, on the other. The full complexity of the policy-making process and the impact of the policies that emerge on economic efficiency and distribution are only partially understood.

328   *Economic Policy-Making*

NOTES

1. Kenneth E. Boulding, *The Principles of Economic Policy* (Staples Press, London, 1959), p. 233.
2. W. Beveridge, *Social Insurance and Allied Services*, Cmnd 6404 (HMSO, London, 1942).
3. To be called income support from 1988.
4. *Reform of Social Security*, vol. 2, Cmnd 9518 (HMSO, London, 1985), p. 1.
5. A.W. Dilnot and G. Stark, 'The poverty trap, tax cuts and social security', *Fiscal Studies*, vol. 7, no. 1, 1986.
6. A.W. Dilnot, J.A. Kay and C.N. Morris, *The Reform of Social Security* (Oxford University Press, Oxford, 1984), p. 59.
7. *Reform of Social Security*, op. cit., p. 18.
8. *Financial Times*, 26 May 1985.
9. Dilnot *et al.*, op. cit., p. 50.
10. Ibid., p. 50.
11. Ibid.
12. *Reform of Social Security*, vol. 2, p. 4.
13. Dilnot *et al.*, op. cit., p. 60.
14. *Financial Times*, 9 October 1985.
15. *Proposals for a Tax Credit System*, Cmnd 5116 (HMSO, London, 1972).
16. *Financial Times*, 28 May 1985.
17. M. Beenstock and M. Parker, 'Abolish the poverty trap', *Economic Affairs*, vol. 6, no. 1, 1985.
18. *Financial Times*, 15 April 1985.
19. *The Reform of Social Security*, vol. 2, p. 48.
20. *Financial Times*, 4 June 1985.
21. E.H. Davis, A.W. Dilnot and J.A. Kay, 'The Social Security Green Paper', *Fiscal Studies*, vol. 6, no. 3, 1985.
22. Ibid.
23. J. LeGrand, *The Strategy of Equality* (George Allen and Unwin, London, 1982).

14 Agricultural Policy

The Common Agricultural Policy shall have as its objectives:

(a) to increase agricultural productivity by promoting technical progress and by ensuring the rational development of agricultural production and the optimum utilisation of the factors of production, in particular, labour;
(b) thus to ensure a fair standard of living for the agricultural community, in particular by increasing the individual earnings of persons engaged in agriculture;
(c) to stabilise markets;
(d) to assure the availability of supplies;
(e) to ensure that supplies reach consumers at reasonable prices.

(Article 39 of the Treaty of Rome (1957), establishing the European Economic Community)

The aims of the Ministry of Agriculture, Fisheries and Food in negotiating Common Agricultural Policy measures within the Community and in operating those parts of the programme which are partly or wholly within its control are

(i) to foster an efficient and competitive agriculture industry;
(ii) to encourage improvements in the Common Agriculture Policy which will lead to greater economic rationality and full recognition of UK interests. . .

(*The Government's Expenditure Plans 1986–87 to 1988–89*, Cmnd 9702-II (1986) pp. 68–9)

One sixth of milk output is already surplus to requirements, while consumption of milk products is declining. We shall not be able to persuade Europe's taxpayers and consumers to support that indefinitely. We cannot expect importers and other exporters of milk outside Europe to relieve us of that burden, even though we can dispose of some part outside the Community.
(Roy Jenkins, President of the European Commission, 1977–81, *European Community*, September 1978)

It would be grossly unfair to disregard the triumph of British agriculture in expanding production . . .Yet it has been essentially a technical achievement: science and technology have been applied to agriculture and the results have been triumphant. Sadly, it has been done at a very high cost; and the cost is shameful. (Richard Body (farmer and Tory MP), *Agriculture: the Triumph and the Shame* (London, Temple Smith, 1982, p. 2)

At present no accounting is undertaken by the Community which in any way measures the economic costs imposed by the CAP, the way in which these costs are distributed, or which assesses these costs against the benefits which result. It follows that if costs are not measured they can be neither monitored nor controlled, and we see little evidence that they have been. When government agencies are able to transfer the costs of their policies to the private sector without these costs appearing as explicit items of public expenditure, the scope for fiscal irresponsibility is particularly great. (Institute For Fiscal Studies)[1]

The question of the recent EEC dairy farmers' settlement has infuriated much of the local farming community. . ... Some normally loyal Tory farmers are not only threatening to abstain. They are saying that they will vote for the dreaded Liberal-SDP Alliance as a protest at the reduction in milk quotas. . ... The seriousness with which the threat is taken was apparent last week when Mrs Margaret Thatcher doggedly tramped the muck at Banbury cattle market dealing with complaints from irate local dairy farmers. (*Financial Times*, 4 June 1984)

The CAP is at a crossroads. Left unreformed it could break down. If this were to happen the committee fears that the existence of the EEC itself would be put in jeopardy. (*Reform of the CAP*, 17th Report of the House of Lords European Committee, HL 237, 1985)

The President of the Court of Auditors, appearing before a Council of Finance Ministers, said that if the EEC accounts for 1984 were those of a private company, he would be unable to approve them. (*Financial Times*, 11 March 1986)

The prices of most food items in the European Community are determined not by market forces but by government. Consequently, cereals, milk products, meat and sugar are between 1½ to more than 2 times their prices outside the EC on world markets. The effect of this on family budgets can only be guessed at: the House of Lords Report, quoted above, reckoned that the Common Agricultural Policy (CAP) added about £6 a week in 1984 to the food bill of a family of four. High food prices are maintained by protecting Community agriculture from foreign competition through import tariffs and a system of intervention buying, whereby government agencies purchase any surplus produce from EC farmers at guaranteed prices. As a consequence of this policy, intervention food stocks have been mounting, as has state expenditure on agricultural support, with CAP accounting for about 70 per cent of the European Community's budget. Efforts to reform the CAP have stemmed not so much from consumer unrest as from a budgetary crisis: the EC has experienced increasing difficulty in securing the revenues to pay for the CAP, let alone for the other programmes it wishes to expand.

Apart from its financing difficulties, agricultural policy is widely criticised for failing to promote either allocative efficiency or social equity. This chapter examines these issues by first outlining the agricultural measures adopted and then considering the resulting distribution of costs and benefits to different countries and to different interests within the EC. The role of organised farming interests is crucial in promoting and sustaining the established framework of the CAP and in resisting proposals for reform.

SETTING UP THE CAP

When the six original members (Belgium, France, Italy, West Germany, Netherlands and Luxembourg) formed the EC, they had already developed their own national agricultural policies, as had Britain with the Agriculture Act 1947. In fact, governments in all developed market economies support farming to some degree with special measures. Agricultural support policies are a manifestation of the welfare state: the case underlying them is that leaving the agricultural sector to the free play of market forces subjects farmers to low and unstable incomes.

Economic development has involved the movement of people away from the land to the industrial and service sectors. As national incomes rise, the demand for food does not rise proportionately. Unless the total population is growing rapidly, this means that agricultural markets grow more slowly than the economy as a whole. Farm incomes can only rise in line with those in other sectors of the economy if agricultural productivity increases sufficiently, and this involves a continual contraction in the number of agricultural workers. Left to market forces, this process works by low farm incomes inducing people to leave the land to earn more elsewhere. Furthermore, farmer incomes are unstable in a free market since output, and hence prices, can change erratically because of diseases, pests and unpredictable weather.

These are the standard arguments for government intervention in agriculture and underlie the objectives of the CAP, set out above. They were of great political importance for the European states in the 1950s because of the size and backwardness of their agricultural sectors. In the 1950s 18 million people—over 26 per cent of the workforce—were engaged in agriculture, producing 11 per cent of GDP. Farms were uneconomically small. Over three million (nearly a half) were less than four hectares.[2] The UK was quite different; less than 5 per cent of the labour force were employed in agriculture and there were proportionately fewer small farms. Thus the political strength of the farming interests was greater in Europe; and though West Germany is highly industrialised, farming interests there have considerable influence because of their key role in the balance of party political power.

In the aftermath of World War II, during which food imports were severely disrupted, the CAP's fourth aim—to secure domestic food supplies—was widely accepted as being in the national interest. The first four aims of the CAP are all clearly in the interests of the farming community and contribute to the maintenance and enhancement of their real incomes; while the fifth aim, of reasonable prices for consumers, conflicts with that of higher farm incomes from agricultural earnings.

The founders of the EC wanted the objectives of the CAP to be pursued in ways which were consistent with their aspirations for European economic and political integration. Economic integration involves establishing a common market, or customs union, in which goods, services, labour and capital are traded freely between member states, who all operate a common set of trade barriers with respect to non-members. The economic argument in favour of the establishment of a customs union is that the consequent increase in competition will promote allocative efficiency. The road to political integration was begun by establishing the legislative, consultative, executive and judicial institutions of the EC. Integration would be hampered by the continuance of diverse national agricultural policies. If the member states continued to operate different subsidies and price regimes, free trade in agricultural produce within the EC would not be possible. Hence the five primary objectives of the CAP had to be pursued by establishing a uniform price support policy with a common system of market organisation, determined at Community level and jointly financed by the Community as a whole. Hence the significance of the common element of the agricultural policy. So when the UK joined the EC in 1973 it had to abandon its former agricultural support methods and adhere to the CAP, which had been moulded to reflect the interests of the original members, as well as their aspirations for European integration.

THE STRUCTURE AND OPERATION OF THE CAP

The Treaty of Rome set out only the objectives for a common agricultural policy not the means to attain them. After much painful negotiation between 1961 and 1964, agreement was reached on the form of agricultural support policy to be used and how to finance it. This was first implemented with respect to cereals in 1967 and similar arrangements were subsequently extended to 90 per cent of EC agricultural produce.

CAP Market Support Arrangements

Under the marketing arrangements for cereals the Community sets a target price every year for each type of cereal. To prevent domestic farmers being undercut by non-EC producers a levy is charged on imports. This import levy is the difference between the external, or world, price of the imported product and its EC target price. If domestic EC demand for, say, wheat is less than the amount produced within the EC, then government agencies will buy and store the excess supply at a predetermined intervention price, which is only slightly below the target price. Alternatively, EC traders may export wheat and receive an export restitution from the EC to cover the difference between the price it is sold for abroad and the EC intervention price.

Dairy products and wine have very similar regimes in that, until recently, governments would buy at the guaranteed intervention price any output that could not be marketed, and store it. Other products—sugar, poultry, eggs and pigmeat—are supported mainly by import levies alone. Part of the complexity of the CAP is that slightly different arrangements exist for each product. In part these reflect the differing political clout of the various farming sectors, with the large cereal growers being articulate and well organised, while the numerous small family farmers are concentrated in livestock and dairying. The interests of northern farmers have always been more strongly represented than those of the south.

Table 14.1: Agricultural prices in the EC as a percentage of world prices for selected years

	1967−68	1975−76	1980−81
Soft wheat	185	124	146
Hard wheat	200	145	138
Rice	117	137	100
Barley	160	117	134
Maize	160	128	147
Sugar	438	109	85
Beef	175	196	190
Pork	147	113	135
Butter	397	320	286
Olive oil	166	207	214
Oil seeds	200	127	168

Source: B. Hill, *The CAP; Past, present and future* (London, Methuen, 1984).

The aim of enhancing farmers' incomes has been pursued by ensuring high prices for their output. For most products in most years the EC price has been considerably in excess of the world price, as indicated in Table 14.1. As elementary demand and supply analysis predicts, raising the price of agricultural produce has induced farmers to increase output. Aided by technological and scientific advances, EC farmers have invested in capital-intensive farming methods, using large quantities of fertiliser, pesticides and improved plant and livestock strains. Agricultural labour productivity in the EC rose by an average annual rate of 6.3 per cent between 1968 and 1973 and by 4.5 per cent from 1973 to 1981. Between 1960 and 1980 yields per hectare rose by 86 per cent for wheat, 74 per cent for maize, 44 per cent for potatoes, while the milk yield per cow rose 38 per cent.[3] Helped by increased yields, total EC agricultural output has risen on average by about 2.5 per cent a year, while the demand for food in the EC has risen at just over 1 per cent a year,[4] and has even fallen slightly in the UK. Consequently the ratio of food output to consumption—the self-sufficiency ratio—has risen over the years, as shown in Table 14.2.

Table 14.2: EC self-sufficiency ratios, major agricultural products (ratio of output to domestic consumption)

	Wheat	Barley	Milk powder	Sugar	Potatoes	Wine	Butter	Beef	Pork	Eggs
1973/74	104	106	208	91	101	99	101	89	101	100
1982/83	125	117	410	144	102	111	123	104	101	103

Source: Commission of the European Communities, *The Agricultural Situation in the Community* (1984).

As self-sufficiency considerably exceeds 100 per cent in cereals, sugar, milk, butter and wine, replacing imports has not provided a sufficient outlet for these products. Various means of disposing of these surpluses are used. One way is to sell them at lower prices to distinct domestic markets—hospitals, prisons, student hostels and pensioners get cheap intervention butter—or to sell the surplus for animal feed, suitably contaminated to prevent resale to humans. The ultimate in recycling is feeding calves with milk powder. Alternatively, the surplus can be exported, sometimes at very low prices, as in deals with the USSR or used for famine relief. The Community ensures that EC producers still obtain the higher EC price by paying export restitutions. International hostility towards the dumping of subsidised foodstuffs on world markets inhibits the EC from expanding its food exports even further. As all output cannot be disposed of, intervention stocks have mounted, as shown in Table 14.3. In 1985 the UK stocked enough cereals to feed the nation for 61 days, butter for 177 days and skimmed milk powder to last 343 days.[5]

Structural Policies

CAP price support measures have succeeded in ensuring security of food supplies and reducing price fluctuations. But they only contribute to the aim of higher real incomes in agriculture by paying farmers to produce more. However if farm profit margins are low then farmers' incomes will also be low, unless a very large output can be produced per farm worker. Farming conditions in the EC are highly diverse, even within a single country. Britain, for example, contains very fertile land in East Anglia, but 53 per cent of agricultural land consists of less favoured hill and upland areas, where yields are lower. Economies of scale are such in agriculture that average production costs are lower on large farms than small ones, which predominate in the upland areas. Small family farms tend to be high-cost producers: prices have to be high if these farmers are to get a modest return for their labours.

Table 14.3: Intervention stocks, EC and UK (000s tonnes) (main commodities only)

		1975	1980	1983	1985
Wheat	EC	1799	4914	6857	11,580
	UK	0	91	189	2971
Barley	EC	523	1086	1102	2152
	UK	0	529	648	976
Beef	EC	252	302	372	606
	UK	1	26	17	50
Butter	EC	117	128	692	879
	UK	12	19	108	134
Skimmed	EC	1112	230	983	489
milk powder	UK	28	3	190	51

Source: National Audit Office *The Achievements and Costs of the CAP in the UK* (1985).
Note: * For 1985 as at Feb/March.

Under free market conditions, inefficient farmers are induced to leave the land by their inability to make a sufficient return in competition with low cost farmers at home and abroad. As farms are amalgamated and lower cost farming methods are introduced by those remaining in the industry, yields and labour productivity rise; so, consequently, do farm real incomes in these areas. However the process is painful as it works through the pressures of penury. It changes the social structure of rural communities as family farms disappear and the remoter areas are depopulated—developments which governments have generally accepted as being undesirable.

As declared in the Treaty of Rome, governments have wished to promote increased agricultural efficiency, especially in the backward areas but, at the same time, to do so without the undesirable social consequences of relying on market adjustment. There is a problem though: removing the painful side-effects of market adjustment tends to impede adjustment as well. By raising agricultural prices the CAP induced farmers to remain on the land and produce more, when they would otherwise have quit because of low relative living standards and moved into other occupations. Mansholt, a Dutch Agriculture Minister who went on to become the first European Commissioner for Agriculture, foresaw these problems very early on. In a speech in 1958 he declared

> Since it has recently become apparent that excessive support for prices easily leads to overproduction, it is easy to see the limitations of price as a means of underpinning incomes. . . .. The first rule for a market policy within the framework of a common agriculture policy must be to try and create an organic equilibrium between production and a market for the products.[6]

As the actual CAP that emerged from political haggling ignored these considerations, Mansholt put forward a plan to restructure agriculture by encouraging an exodus of five million farmers between 1960 and 1970. He proposed lower prices, coupled with monetary inducements, for farmers to retire, retrain, enter new rural industries, amalgamate landholdings and invest. Five million hectares of land should be taken out of agriculture, mainly for afforestation. The Mansholt Plan was badly received by the farming organisations who have successfully opposed lower prices. However it did lead to the adoption of various structural measures, called guidance policies, on the lines suggested by Mansholt. But the guidance measures have always been overshadowed in importance by the price support (or guarantee) policies. These take up well over 90 per cent of CAP expenditure—96 per cent in 1983.

There is, in addition, a proliferation of national structural measures paid for out of national Exchequers. The UK government pays enhanced capital grants and livestock allowances in areas designated under CAP as less favoured. It also finances agricultural research, the Agricultural Development and Advisory Service, which is free to farmers, animal health programmes, land drainage and flood protection. To put the relative expenditures in perspective, the UK government in 1984−85 spent £1378 million on CAP measures: of this only £31 million was for structural policies. In addition it spent £15 million on national support measures (mainly for wool and potatoes) and a further £859 million on non-support initiatives of its own, including £332 million for what are officially termed structural measures, such as capital grants for specific purposes and hill livestock allowances. Altogether, the EC states spend as much again as the CAP on their national agricultural policies.[7]

Uncommon Prices

The discussion of structural measures has revealed one significant aspect of the CAP: it is not really common. The European ideal of a uniform agricultural policy, applying to all member states, has not fully materialised. Hence the potential efficiency gains from setting up a common market have not been fully realised. When national governments give agriculture—or any other industry for that matter—differential subsidies, then output continues to be produced by less efficient resources which could not compete profitably without such protection. In general the EC has sought to stop governments giving preferential treatment to their own country's industries, as such action is incompatible with establishing a common market in order to promote greater allocative efficiency. In fact, some of the state agricultural aids are against Community rules: in 1980 the Commission listed 51 illegal aids, 39 of them in France.

The failure of the CAP to be fully common goes beyond the persistence of diverse, nationally-funded agricultural policies. Common prices for agricultural produce throughout the EC have yet to be established. So Britain, for example, has lower food prices than Germany. This state of affairs has arisen because of the way agricultural prices are set at Community and then at national level. The Community prices for agricultural commodities are negotiated annually by the Agriculture Ministers of the member states. The price of each commodity is expressed in a common currency, the European currency unit (ecu). Its value is a weighted average of the individual member state currencies. Prices are first set in terms of ecus. For example, in 1983 1 tonne of wheat cost 350 ecu. But its price in sterling depends on the rate of exchange between sterling and the ecu. In 1983 £1 was worth 1.7 ecu, so the sterling price of wheat was around £205. However if sterling appreciated to £1 = 2 ecu a tonne of wheat would have cost only £175. Conversely, a depreciation of a country's currency in relation to the ecu will raise its food prices.

When the CAP was being formulated in the 1960s the world was on a fixed exchange system and so the problem of national food prices varying as exchange rates fluctuated was not fully anticipated. In the late 1960s Germany revalued the DM but because of the political importance of its farmers, did not want to lower its agricultural prices immediately. France devalued the franc, but did not want its consumers to face higher prices immediately. Hence it was agreed as a temporary measure, which matured into permanency, that for agricultural prices the rate between individual currencies and the ecu could be different from the market exchange rate determined daily in the foreign exchange markets. The agricultural rate of exchange is popularly known as the 'green rate'. Furthermore each member has been able to vary its own green rate. In Britain, where consumer interests are more important than in Germany, lower food prices have been maintained.

The complications could not end here, though. If goods were cheaper in France than in Germany in terms of francs and Deutsche marks, then traders would buy grain from French farmers to sell in Germany at a profit, thus taking markets away from German farmers who would either have to agree to lower prices or sell their enlarged surplus into intervention stores. To prevent this the EC established border levies. Thus, if wheat is exported from France to Germany, a border tax is levied which is the difference between the German and French prices. If Germany exports wheat to France then a payment is made to the French to compensate them for buying at a higher price than the one that prevails in France. These border payments are called *monetary compensatory amounts*. A country which maintains a green rate above its market exchange rate thereby keeps its food prices lower than if the two rates were equal, and receives positive compensatory amounts from the EC on food imported from EC countries with higher prices. This was the UK's practice in the 1970s. In 1984 the Community agreed to eliminate monetary compensatory amounts by 1987–88.

Financing the CAP

It would be entirely practicable for each country to pay directly for its own CAP expenditure. However, the joint funding of the CAP is an expression of aspirations for European political unity. The CAP is financed by the European Agricultural Guarantee and Guidance Fund (EAGGF). The guarantee section finances market support measures: it pays for expenditure on buying intervention stocks and storing them, as well as for export restitutions when the stocks are sold off at below intervention prices. The other items of guarantee expenditure are the monetary compensatory amounts. The member states actually operate the market support policies and initially incur the related expenditure but are reimbursed from the EAGGF. Similarly the much smaller amounts spent on CAP structural measures are financed by the guidance section of the EAGGF. On the revenue side of the budget, the Community has its 'own resources'. Each member state contributes to the EC budget its import levies on agricultural products from outside the Community plus a fixed percentage of VAT, which in 1986 was raised from 1 to 1.4 per cent to provide additional revenue to meet EC expenditure commitments.

Common financing was agreed in order to give expression to the political objective of European integration. Without a Community budget the existence of the Community as a distinct political entity, separate from the member states, would be much more nebulous. As the EAGGF is the major element in the Community's budget, accounting for nearly 70 per cent of it, the common financing of CAP fulfils a political objective quite distinct from the aims of agricultural policy *per se*. Common financing is a sacrosanct principle for the European Commission and its officials: it provides them with a *raison d'être* and enhances their functions, influence and prestige.

With common financing the amount spent on EC programmes in any one country is not directly related to the amount that country contributes to financing overall Community expenditure. Because Britain has a relatively small agricultural sector, and was traditionally much more reliant on cheap food imports from outside Europe, it is a net loser from the CAP. Conversely, EC members who are net exporters of agricultural goods gain from CAP, as they collect little in import levies for the EC budget and receive export restitutions from it. Also the larger the proportion of agricultural output in national output, the more a country will gain from CAP expenditure. The budgetary transfers arising from the CAP in 1982 are given in Table 14.4. Overall, the UK's net payments to the EC are less than its net budgetary transfers due to CAP, because it receives refunds for expenditure on other Community programmes as well as budgetary rebates to offset its otherwise high net contributions relative to its national income. The rebates were negotiated with much accompanying rancour in 1980 and 1984.

Table 14.4: Budgetary transfers arising out of CAP by country, 1982 (billions)

	Gross EAGGF expenditure	All levies	VAT-based contribution to EAGGF	EAGGF balance*
West Germany	2.75	0.44	3.24	−0.93
France	3.37	0.35	2.67	0.35
Italy	2.41	0.33	1.46	0.62
Netherlands	1.43	0.26	0.58	0.59
Belgium/Luxembourg	0.61	0.21	0.46	−0.6
United Kingdom	1.14	0.67	2.46	−1.99
Ireland	0.46	0.03	0.08	0.35
Denmark	1.08	0.07	0.22	0.79
Greece	0.62	0.18	0.18	0.26

Source: Buckwell (1985).
Note: EAGGF balance is gross EAGGF expenditure minus levies minus VAT payments.

The ever-rising agricultural output stimulated by the CAP's high level of price support has led to steadily increasing spending on EAGGF, which in turn has been reflected in overall EC budget expenditure. Expenditure on the CAP rose 20-fold in money terms between 1967 and 1983, from 0.1 per cent of Community GDP to 0.6 per cent. A further problem with guarantee expenditure is that its level is difficult to predict and cannot be cash-limited. Even if production quotas were set, expenditure on export restitutions rises when world prices fall. This can happen either because of an increase in world agricultural output or due to exchange rate changes. For example, it was estimated that the fall in the value of the dollar would add 1.5 billion to CAP expenditure in 1986 and cause Community expenditure to outstrip its revenues. The pressure to reform the CAP has come from the increasing difficulty experienced in financing it, given a general unwillingness to raise revenues. By acceding to Britain's demands that its EC budget contributions should be reduced on grounds of equity, the need to curtail CAP spending became all the more pressing.

THE COSTS AND BENEFITS OF THE CAP

The expenditure and revenue flows associated with the CAP, and other national agricultural measures, constitute only the most visible part of a complex distribution of costs and benefits. Who benefits by the CAP and who loses depends on their economic function as farmer, landowner, producer of intermediate goods for agriculture, civil servant or taxpayer and also on their nationality, both within and outside the EC. It is notable that the officials who operate the CAP at both national and EC level are not interested in undertaking any wider assessment of its distributional implications.[8]

Academic economists have somewhat greater incentives to undertake such research and it is on this that I shall primarily rely. All such efforts are somewhat speculative by their very nature. One reason is the need to postulate some alternative policy to compare with CAP in order to assess how much better or worse off various groups are as a consequence of CAP. One popular assumption is the alternative of free trade at world prices. The standard analysis of the effects of introducing an import tariff is explained with the help of Figure 14.1 which depicts the demand (DD) for a commodity in a single country, say Britain, and the supply curve of domestic producers (SS). The world price of the commodity is P^w. With no import tariff, consumers will buy OB of the commodity, on which they spend an amount equal to rectangle OP^wHB. Domestic producers are willing to supply OA of the commodity. The rest, AB, is imported at the world price. An import tariff is now imposed, which raises the price in the British market to P^d. Consumers now buy less and cut their purchases to OD. Now that the price is higher, domestic producers can expand production by bringing higher cost capacity into use. They now supply OC to the domestic market and imports are cut to CD. The gain to domestic producers is area P^wEFP^d; this represents the additional revenues over and above their production costs received as a consequence of the higher price. The government gains because it collects import tax revenues on CD imports; the import dues are worth FGIJ. (However, given the EC budget arrangements, the British government does not receive these levies as they are paid to the EC.)

The losers in all this are the consumers. Their losses derive from two sources: first, there is the extra they pay for the amount OD of the commodity they are still buying. This is equal to rectangle P^wIGP^d. Second, consumers suffer an additional loss because they no longer buy quantity DB. The value of this loss is given by triangle GHI. It represents the extent to which consumers valued units DB of the commodity in excess of the amount they had to pay, which was IHBD. The total welfare losses to consumers is therefore rectangle P^wIGP^d plus triangle GHI.

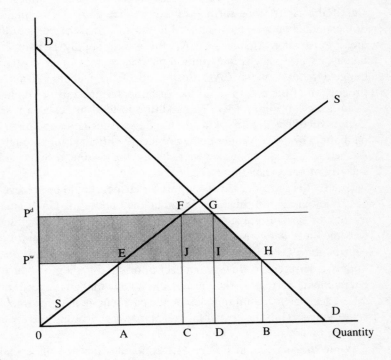

Gainers
producers: P^wEFP^d
government: FGIJ

Losers
consumers: P^wHGP^d

Net social costs
FJE + GHI

Figure 14.1: Costs and benefits of an import tariff on agricultural produce

If one is prepared to make the value judgement that £1 gives everyone the same amount of social welfare, then the net social cost of the import tariff is assessed as the sum of the losses minus the sum of the gains. Consumers' loss is area P^wHGP^d; the gain to producers and government is area P^wEFP^d + FGIJ. Subtracting gains from losses gives a net social loss of FJE + GHI. It is this demonstration that import tariffs result in a net social cost that leads to the conclusion that these policies are allocatively inefficient. Higher-cost domestic production replaces cheaper foreign output and hence there is a misallocation of resources.

In Figure 14.1 the domestic price with the tariff is still low enough to permit some imports, since domestic demand exceeds domestic output. But if the tariff were further raised so that domestic output exceeded domestic demand, as has occurred in the EC, then the costs of the policy are even greater. Under the CAP the excess supply is paid for by the taxpayer who finances intervention purchases and storage costs. Thus the budgetary costs of the CAP are the tip of the iceberg. A much higher proportion of the costs is paid by consumers in the form of higher prices, as indicated in Figure 14.1. The addition to food prices as a result of the CAP is, in effect, a form of taxation, and so is termed an *implicit tax*. It is paid direct by the consumer to the producer, without going through the state Exchequer and so being registered as a tax on the revenue side and a subsidy on the expenditure side.

Exactly the same degree of support for farmers could be achieved by way of explicit taxes and subsidies as is obtained under the CAP. This was the method of agricultural support used in the UK prior to joining the EC and was known as deficiency payments. The price of agricultural produce was kept at the world level for consumers who benefited from cheap food imports. Farmers were guaranteed a price for their produce by the government; if the market price fell below the guaranteed price, the difference was made up in a deficiency payment by the government out of tax revenues. Thus the cost of farm support was borne entirely by taxpayers and not by consumers of food.

While the analysis in Figure 14.1 concludes that the net social cost of import tariffs will be positive, this need not be the case for an individual Community state because of the common financing of the CAP. A country which is a net exporter of farm produce to other countries, both in the EC and outside it, will end up a net beneficiary because it receives tax revenues collected in other member states. Thus for Britain the net costs of the CAP are greater than suggested by Figure 14.1; its reimbursements for CAP expenditure are less than its revenue contributions to the common financing of the CAP.

There have been several attempts by economists to estimate the costs and benefits of the CAP to the UK, using the kind of analysis displayed in

Table 14.5: The costs and benefits of the CAP, 1978 (£ million)

	Consumer loss	Producer gain	Taxpayer loss	Net loss or gain	Consumer and tax loss per capita	Producer gain per capita (approx.)	Loss or gain as % GDP
Germany	4598	4035	1177	−1740	93.4	2400	−0.53
France	3167	3624	761	−286	74.5	1800	−0.12
Italy	3413	2257	386	−1541	68.1	700	−1.26
Nlands	892	1403	305	+206	87.4	4900	+0.31
Belgium	725	680	226	−259	93.2	5100	−0.50
UK	1787	1148	731	−1370	45.0	1700	−0.86
Ireland	175	408	32	+201	66.8	1700	+3.24
Denmark	291	713	117	+324	81.6	3200	+1.15
EC-9	15,041	14,286	3357	−4112	71.2	1700	−0.41

Source: C.N. Morris 'The Common Agricultural Policy', *Fiscal Studies*, March 1980.
Note: Not all EC subsidies have been allocated to individual countries.

Figure 14.1. One quite widely quoted estimate, which the researcher stresses is tentative, is presented in Table 14.5. Producers obviously gain at the expense of taxpayers and consumers throughout the EC. However the Netherlands, Ireland and Denmark end up as net gainers at the expense of other members, particularly Germany, Italy and Britain.[9] The net cost in current prices for the UK was estimated at around £1.4 billion in 1978 and £2.4 billion in 1980. In a subsequent study[10] an attempt was made to estimate how much the CAP had raised retail food prices in 1978 and hence what implicit tax rates it imposed on various food items. The highest tax rate was 34.5 per cent on milk and dairy products, followed by 19.6 per cent on animal feed, 13.1 per cent on meat and 5.8 per cent on bread and grain. The average CAP implicit tax rate on food was estimated to be 4.5 per cent. But as low-income households spend a higher proportion of their income on food the tax is regressive; it was estimated as 6 per cent for households with less than £2000 a year compared to 2.9 per cent for households earning over £10,000. As can be seen from Table 14.5, the loss per individual consumer-cum-taxpayer from the CAP is quite small compared to the very considerable gains accruing to the average agricultural producer. The total transfers from consumers and taxpayers in the UK now exceed the net income of the farming sector.[11]

Have Farmers Gained From the CAP?

It might well be thought after reading this evidence that farmers are cheering all the way to the bank. But this is not so. And, to do them justice, this not due to insatiable greed. For, despite all these measures, farm incomes on average in the EC remained well below those earned in other sectors of the economy, and the relative incomes of farmers have not in general improved since the 1950s. Only in Britain and Ireland are average farm incomes on a par with those earned elsewhere in the economy. In Britain, as in a number of other EC countries, real farm incomes have tended to fall since the mid-1970s. This is indicated in Figure 14.2, which depicts indices of net value added per person employed in agriculture and in the whole economy. (Net value added is the difference between the revenues obtained from agriculture and the costs of capital and intermediate goods. This difference is the reward received by labour.) Because of this decline in value added per unit of labour, real net farm income per full-time UK farmer in the early 1980s was roughly the same as twenty years previously, at around £6000 in 1980 prices.[12]

How do the facts of high farm prices and rising agricultural output per worker square with declining real incomes in farming? The first thing to appreciate is that agricultural prices have been high relative to what they would have been without such a protectionist farm policy. Relative to manufactured goods and services farm prices have fallen. In the EC countries agricultural prices in real terms fell between 25 and 40 per cent in the twenty years since 1960. They only fell by 9 and 5 per cent over the period in Ireland and Britain respectively, as they experienced substantial increases on entry to the EC in 1973.[13] This fall in relative prices is entirely explicable when, over the long run, world food production has been rising faster than consumption. The only way it could have been prevented was by a slower rise in agricultural output. And for that to be accompanied by a rise in real per capita farm income, the number of agricultural workers would have had to contract by even more than the 33 per cent decline that occurred between 1970 and 1982.[14]

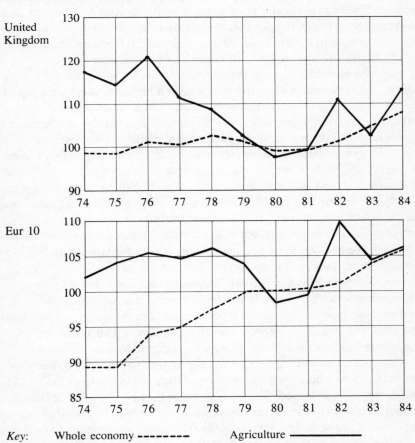

Key: Whole economy -------   Agriculture ————————

Source: Commission of the European Communities, *Proposals on the Fixing of Prices for Agricultural Products and Related Measures* (1985/86) COM(85) 50/1 final.

Figure 14.2: Net value added per person employed in agriculture and the whole economy: the EC and the UK (1979 = 100)

The second point to appreciate is that the price farmers receive for their output is only one side of the income equation. The other is costs. If costs rise when prices rise, then the profit per acre is not improved. Hence to measure efficiency in terms of output per worker or per hectare, as is so widely done in proclaiming the efficiency gains of agriculture, is quite misleading since it ignores the other factors of production: land, capital equipment, fuel oil, fertiliser and pesticides. Higher prices have induced farmers to work land more intensively, applying more capital and intermediate goods, as well as using them to replace labour as it became relatively more expensive. They have also brought into use land which prior to CAP was too costly to cultivate. Moorlands have been turned into pasture, and grazing land put under the plough. In 1980 there was the same amount of land in Britain under tillage—around 12.3 million acres—as in 1953, despite the loss of 1.5 million acres to development.[15]

Thus the *marginal costs* of the agricultural sector as a whole rise with output: extra output can only be produced at a higher cost per unit. Since farmers are individually price-takers (an individual farmer cannot influence price), then the marginal cost curve traces out the supply curve, as depicted in Figure 14.1. If the government guarantees domestic farmers price P^d, considerably above the world price, P^w, then farmers are induced to supply OC units of output—AC more than if the domestic market were not protected and imports came in at price P^w. The additional cost of producing AC units of output is given by the area under the marginal cost curve, which is area AEFC. In other words, resources to the value of AEFC are attracted into farming. Land of low fertility, which might otherwise be afforested or be open moor and marshland, is used for farming and its use induces more farmers to stay on the land. Another source of increased output is raising yields on all intramarginal land by investing in mechanisation and applying fertilisers and pesticides. Marginal costs thus rise because more inputs are used per hectare. The extra land, capital and intermediate production goods are all resources which could be used elsewhere in the economy and so have an opportunity cost.

Whatever the amount of agricultural output there will always be marginal farmers—those whose marginal costs equal the price of output, whether OA or OC output is produced. Thus they make no profits. They stay in farming because their earnings in alternative occupations are low or because they attach considerable value to their rural lifestyle. Their incomes are bound to be low if derived only from their revenue from farm produce. And, over time, given that the demand for food rises more slowly than supply, their existence exacerbates the problem because their additional output depresses world prices. Under CAP guarantee measures the impact of this growth in output on domestic farm prices can only be resisted by spending ever-increasing amounts on intervention stocks and export restitutions.

It might well seem that the non-marginal farmers, working fertile land, who could produce profitably without protectionist policies, gain considerably from the extra profits. Given the intensity with which farmers lobby for these policies it is evident that they see them as operating in their interests. Referring to Figure 14.1, you can see that the area OP^dF represents the excess of price over marginal cost and thus gives the total profit on OC agricultural output. As the result of protection it has been increased by area P^wP^dFE over what it would otherwise be. However, before jumping to the conclusion that farmers as a class are better off as a consequence of these profits, we need to take into account the effect of farm profits on the price of land. The rent on land is not included in marginal costs as it is a fixed cost—it does not change as farmers produce more output.

When farm profits rise due to the introduction of agricultural support policies, existing owners of land can sell it at an enhanced price. Purchasers are willing to pay a higher price for farm land, the greater the potential profits to be earned on it. There is very little scope for increasing the quantity of land available, and so the price of existing land will be bid up until it fully reflects the rise in profits from its use. So for somebody entering farming, either by buying or renting land, the amount they are willing to pay for land will rise until the rate of profit, taking account of the cost of land, is equivalent to that obtainable from investment in other sectors. The demand for land has also been increased because it became an even more attractive investment for wealthy people wishing to avoid capital transfer tax. The government responded to special pleading from the farming interests to accord tax privileges to the transfer of agricultural land ownership. In line with the predictions of economic theory, land prices since World War II have risen around 15-fold in real terms; land prices in upland areas, with additional structural subsidies, have gone up even more. One would also expect the increased demand for intermediate production goods used in agriculture to raise their prices as well. Table 14.6 shows how the effect on farm incomes of rising nominal output prices has been offset by even greater increases in the prices of farm inputs.

If land prices and hence farm rents rise to reflect fully any increased gap between agricultural output prices and the marginal costs of production, then new entrants to farming are no better off in terms of net income (i.e. revenues minus cost of all inputs except labour) than they would have been without government price support. The people who have gained are those that owned farmland prior to the introduction of government price support. This *capitalisation* of the state subsidy to farming into higher land prices is just one example of this phenomenon. Similarly, the mortgage interest subsidy on housing also gets capitalised into higher house prices. In both cases the people who gain are those who owned the fixed assets prior to the introduction of the subsidy. New entrants do not benefit relative to the pre-subsidy situation. However now that they have bought their house or land at a price which includes the capitalised subsidy, any reduction in the subsidy would cause the value of the fixed assets to fall and inflict a capital loss on their owners. So farmers who bought their land at high prices and incurred heavy mortgage payments would have higher costs than new entrants acquiring land at lower prices. So, even though it is doubtful that agricultural protection improves farm incomes in the long term, it is always going to be an attractive policy for farmers. Newly instituted, it gives them capital gains; once in place its removal inflicts capital losses and bankruptcies.

Table 14.6: Farm output and input prices and incomes in the UK (1970 = 100)

Year	Farm product prices	Farming income	Land values	Fuel	Farm machinery	Farm labour	Retail price index
1964/65 to							
1965/66	90	75	76	78	81	65	78
1970	100	100	100	100	100	100	100
1971	106	113	111	103	108	109	109
1972	112	120	183	107	118	122	117
1973	147	168	264	122	131	150	132
1974	166	142	225	179	159	195	154
1975	206	177	193	216	200	245	191
1976	265	228	263	266	235	293	222
1977	275	224	334	320	291	318	258
1978	294	221	450	328	339	365	279
1979	313	201	604	393	377	425	317
1980	331	179	629	515	435	516	374
1981	366	232	604	623	470	570	418
1982 (provisional)	392	318	627	702	507	623	452

Source: R.W. Howarth, *Farming for the Farmers?* (1985).

Which Farmers Benefit Most?

Farm interests are themselves differentiated. CAP has affected farmers differently, depending on the type of agriculture they practise and on the size of their farm. CAP has worked to the particular advantage of cereal growers, who also tend to operate large farms. The small, family farmers, who are the focus of social concern about rural poverty and depopulation, have individually received less help. The small family farms in less favoured areas are primarily suited to livestock farming. As cereals are used as animal feed, livestock farmers' costs were increased by the high cereals prices upheld by the CAP. Milk prices have had to be correspondingly high to protect dairying, with the consequent depressing effect on demand. As consumption fell, dairymen have produced rising quantities of surplus milk to maintain their real incomes. Cereals, beef and milk (until 1984) have been favoured with unlimited intervention stocks. Sugar has always been subject to quotas; other products, such as poultry and pigmeat, have not been supported by intervention.

So the CAP has been inequitable in its distributional effects within farming. First, because price support—the major component of CAP—inevitably favours large producers who have higher incomes. Second, because it has favoured cereal growers over livestock farmers, who must use cereals as an input, and who predominate in small family farming. Third, because the common financing of CAP benefits farmers in countries with large agricultural surpluses. Table 14.4 suggests that the producer gain per person in agriculture is larger in the richer countries—Belgium, Netherlands, Denmark and Germany—and least in the poorest countries—Italy, Ireland and the UK. Fourth, because the additional profits from protection have been capitalised to the benefit of those who owned farmland prior to CAP: landless farm workers and new landowners gain little in comparison.

Environmental Costs

One of the arguments in favour of agricultural support policies is broadly environmental; to preserve rural communities in their rural pursuits and so help to maintain our traditional rural landscapes. However agricultural support policies have affected the environment in ways many find displeasing. The extension of arable farming has denuded the landscape of hedges and thickets, while weedkillers have destroyed wild flowers and pesticides have harmed bird and insect life. Nitrates in fertilisers and the effluent from intensive, indoor livestock rearing pollutes rivers. Moors and marshland have been turned into farmland, disturbing natural habitats and diminishing the open countryside. All these effects are external costs about which the environmental movement has protested with increasing vigour. Farmers have seized some advantage from this agitation and can now claim state compensation for undertaking conservation measures.

International Effects

The expected trade diversion effects of creating a customs union have occurred with respect to the EC. Between 1960 and 1980 agricultural trade within the EC trebled; its food imports fell by 5 per cent, while its food exports to the rest of the world more than doubled. The EC has become the world's second largest exporter of temperate foodstuff, after the USA.[16] The CAP has thus had a decisive impact on world trade; by closing EC food markets to outsiders and dumping subsidised exports on world markets, the CAP has harmed farmers in other parts of the world. Traditional agricultural exporters, like the USA, Australia, New Zealand, Argentina and Brazil, have been forced to accept lower prices and cut production due to lack of market outlets. EC surpluses have reduced returns to domestic agricultural producers in developing countries, who have to compete against lower priced imports, and have thereby contributed to their inadequate domestic food supplies. The CAP is inconsistent with the EC's postwar commitment to liberalising international trade under the auspices of GATT (General Agreement on Tariffs and Trade). EC tariffs on most industrial goods are below 10 per cent, but are around 100 per cent on agricultural products.

Even in the absence of any altruistic concern for the welfare of these countries, the costs to the EC are heightened tensions in their world trading relations. Retaliation against the EC takes the form of threats to counter with export dumping or import tariffs on foodstuffs, or with action against EC industrial exports, such as the USA's quotas on EC steel products and retaliatory action on certain agricultural products. Thus the EC's agricultural interests conflict with those of other sectors wishing to promote their overseas markets.

POLITICAL INTERESTS IN AGRICULTURE

It is evident that agricultural policy, as practised, promotes neither efficiency nor equity. How this state of affairs has arisen is partly explained by the role of political interests in the formation and implementation of the policy.

Creating the Common Agricultural Policy

The initial decision to use price support as the primary instrument of the CAP was taken at the Stresa Conference in 1958, to which agricultural interests were invited. Subsequently, considerable difficulty was experienced in getting the members to participate in a common policy. The German farmers under their umbrella organisation, Deutscher Bauernverband, resisted it as they felt they did better under their national policies. The European Commission, anxious to consolidate its role by establishing a common policy, formed an alliance with the French cereals farming organisation, which urged its own government to negotiate a favourable CAP regime for grains. For political reasons the German government wanted to promote European unity but, to placate its farmers, bargained for a wheat price 11 per cent higher than that in France. To avoid electoral losses from alienating their farmers, the French government agreed to this rise in prices. The wheat agreement then set the tone for the subsequent arrangements on other products.

The Organisations Involved in the CAP

The main institutional framework for operating the CAP is common to all aspects of EC policy-making. For each policy area, such as agriculture, there is a Council of Ministers made up of the individual ministers from each member state. It meets regularly and is the main law-making institution. The European Commission is a permanent body of officials, appointed from all the nationalities of the EC. Its job is to propose legislative measures to the Council of Ministers and to implement the decisions of the Council. Each year the Agriculture Directorate of the Commission puts to the Council of Agriculture Ministers proposals for operating the CAP in the forthcoming marketing year. These proposals include target and intervention prices for the various products, and the conditions with respect to quantity and quality under which these prices are paid.

Prior to submitting these proposals, the Commission has extensive and formal consultation with national farming experts employed by member governments and with the farming interests. The formal framework for these consultations is provided by the Special Committee on Agriculture which is made up of national officials, such as civil servants from the Ministry of Agriculture, Fisheries and Food (MAFF), representatives of farm organisations, trade unions and consumers. The work of the special committee on agriculture is channelled through a set of management committees for each type of product. The agricultural interests are strongly represented on these committees, both through civil servants from agricultural ministries and the Commission's Agriculture Directorate, and via farmers' organisations. Thus the Commission's original proposals are often considerably modified by these committees before they reach the Council, and have been already agreed by majority voting of the representatives of the affected interests, who are dominated by farming interests.

The Farming Organisations

The Commission consults extensively with the Comité des Organisations Professionelles Agricoles (COPA). This is a 'peak' organisation, made up of the main farm organisations of the member states, such as National Farmers Union (NFU). COPA was founded in 1958 at the Stresa Conference at the instigation of the Commission. From the start, the Commission made it clear that it will only officially consult interests organised at European level and not give direct access to national interest groups. The Commission instituted this practice to strengthen its political position *vis-à-vis* national governments by giving it direct access to the organised interests of member states. These organised interests are known as Eurogroups and form the mainstay of the Brussels lobby. One of the most effective is COPA, which is well-funded and has a well-staffed secretariat. It has continuous and extensive contacts with the Commission. It nominates members of the management committees; its executive board members meet high-ranking Commission officials and its secretariat is in close contact with middle-ranking Commission officials.

COPA is dominated by large cereals farmers—as is the NFU—because they have more time and money to devote to such activities. Both COPA and national farm organisations, like the NFU, face the problem of maintaining unity amongst disparate farming interests. Their strength lies in their ability to present a united front to government. A peak organisation, like COPA, is useful to a government department, because it performs the task of aggregating the interests of its constituents through its own process of reaching compromise. Because it is useful to government it is granted direct and easy access to the decision-makers, and this power in turn enhances its ability to retain its members. Dissatisfaction amongst small farmers with the policies of COPA, which favours price support as against structural policies, led to the formation of a rival Eurogroup, COMEPRA (European Committee for Agricultural Progress). This is somewhat critical of the CAP and is not granted by the Commission the status of a fully legitimate organised interest.

COPA is strongly in favour of the CAP and has been highly resistant to the Commission's reform proposals in the 1980s. As it reiterated in 1985, 'COPA cannot accept the general policy approach put forward by the Commission of continued and reinforced pressure on prices combined with direct income aid'.[17] It has successfully watered down the Commission's proposals for real price cuts and quotas. COPA has successfully capitalised on the Commission's fear that if the CAP fails to deliver sufficiently to all member states' farming interests then agricultural policy will be 'renationalised', by member governments making their own arrangements for farm support. Such moves would threaten the Commission's political importance, as the CAP remains the prime common European programme that has as yet materialised. Its fear of agricultural policy being renationalised weakens the Commission's ability to resist COPA's demands.

For a national farm organisation there are two main channels of influence on CAP. One is via COPA and the European Commission; the other is via its national government, influencing both the civil servants who participate in the Special Committee on Agriculture, and the Agriculture Ministers who take the final decisions in the Council of Ministers. In the UK the National Farmers Union, to which 80 per cent of farmers belong, has the reputation of being one of the most effective lobbies. It achieved close liaison with government during World War II. The Agriculture Act 1947 gave farmers' representatives a statutory right to be consulted by government in the annual review of farming. The right of representation is jealously guarded by the NFU who maintain a strong secretariat of experts, some of whom are ex-civil servants. The NFU are in almost daily contact with MAFF and are involved in the earliest stages of policy-making. They also employ a full-time parliamentary lobbyist and brief MPs for questions and speeches.

Agriculture is a good example of how a sectional interest encompasses not only the organised pressure groups outside government but also the state bureaucracy which concerns itself with that sector. MAFF and its agencies, such as the Intervention Board for Agricultural Support, The Meat and Livestock Commission and the Home Grown Cereals Authority, the British Wool Marketing Board, and the proliferation of similar agencies in the other EC countries, all have a vested interest in the continuation of agricultural support policies. It was the pre-CAP existence of agricultural intervention agencies in the member states that ensured that the CAP would be operated by national, not European, agencies. The officials in the national agencies are not unhappy with the failure of a truly European agricultural policy to emerge. The complex institutional and regulatory system gives them considerable control over their country's agricultural policy and an influential position in relation to their clientele. As one observer has noted:[18]

Closely related to a civil servant's job satisfaction is his relationship with the ministry's clientele, because it places him in authority with regard to groups and individuals dealing with the ministry and thereby contributes to his position of power and prestige. Moreover, clientele relations may generate constituencies which would oppose the reduction of functions of individual organisations or their complete liquidation.

Apart from the officials, ministers also take on the role of advocate for the interests represented by their department. An extreme example of this is François Guillaume, the French farmers' union leader, who became France's Minister for Agriculture in 1986. British Ministers of Agriculture have often had some farming interests of their own. Farmers in the UK still wield more political influence than their dwindling numerical strength, now at 2 per cent of the electorate suggests.[19] Some 9 per cent of MPs have agricultural interests, as did ten members of the 1984 Cabinet. The farm vote is more significant in other EC states, and particularly so in the new entrants: Greece, Spain and Portugal. The UK has complained most vociferously about the CAP, especially in the context of claiming budget restitutions. However, it is still the UK Minister of Agriculture who negotiates directly with his opposite numbers in the Council of Ministers over CAP measures. He represents agricultural interests more strongly than consumer, taxpayer, environmental or trade interests.

The Council of Agricultural Ministers has further watered down the CAP reform measures proposed by the Commission in their attempts to contain CAP expenditure. Not only do the ministers represent agricultural interests; they have been constrained by the Luxembourg Accord to reach unanimous agreement. This has enabled a single country to hold out for a higher price for a particular product, in order to placate domestic farm interests.

Other Interests and Agriculture

Interests which are harmed by the CAP are more diffuse and less well organised. Food and drink manufacturers and consumers are organised as officially recognised Eurogroups. The former represent too many diverse interests to be effective in constraining the CAP. The peak consumer organisation, Le Bureau Européen des Unions Consommateurs, can present a united front in favour of removing price support and using direct income maintenance for poor farmers and regions. They articulate their views on official EC committees but have been relatively ineffective. One reason is that a complete restructuring of the CAP is not (as yet) on the political agenda. It is not under consideration by the Commission and has not even been proposed by the UK, the member which loses most.

The greatest restraint on the CAP has come via the taxpayers, as represented in Europe by the Finance Ministers and Heads of State. In response to Britain's demand for a reduction in its EC budget contribution, the European Council of Heads of State in 1980 mandated the Commission to put forward proposals for restraining the growth of CAP expenditure within the basic framework of the existing policy. Since 1981 the Commission has proposed reductions in agricultural prices in real terms and limitations on the quantity of output for which intervention prices are paid. These proposals have been repeatedly watered down by the Council of Agriculture Ministers. Finally, in 1984, the heads of state agreed that in conjunction with a reduction in the UK's budgetary contribution and a raising of the VAT contribution to revenues to 1.4 per cent, CAP spending should grow more slowly than EC budget revenues.

Against the background of increasing financial constraints and mounting intervention stocks and surpluses, there has been some cutback on agricultural support. In 1984 milk quotas were imposed and prices for a number of products fell in real terms. With budget expenditure threatening to outstrip revenue in 1986, the pressures for changes in the CAP mounted. The Commission has favoured reductions in prices rather than quotas, which are less efficient and difficult to implement, but is still firmly wedded to the basic framework of the CAP. However farming interests, especially on the Continent, are still resistant to such proposals. The NFU are prepared to accept gradual price cuts if compensated by additional structural measures and further import restrictions.[20] In the 1986 price-setting negotiations, the Agriculture Ministers watered down the Commission's proposals. After a five-day negotiating marathon, culminating in an all-night session, they agreed to some small decreases in intervention prices, as well as a one per cent a year cut in milk quotas. Nevertheless, the agriculture budget was still overspent by 1.5 million ecu, and so breached the financial discipline guidelines agreed by the Finance Ministers. In the negotiations for 1987, further cuts in prices and quotas were agreed.

The Effectiveness of Pressure Groups

The effectiveness of the agricultural lobby against the interests of the far more numerous taxpayers and consumers is readily explained by the economic theory of pressure groups, outlined in Chapter 9. Individual farmers have much more to gain from agricultural policies than individual consumers and taxpayers have to lose, as can be seen from columns 5 and 6 of Table 14.5. Thus the return from pressure group activity is much greater per individual for farmers, and for the firms who manufacture farm equipment and chemicals. A smaller number can be more efficiently organised; the number of internal conflicts of interest is likely to be less. A further problem for a pressure group is preventing free-riding. One effective way of minimising this is to provide members with services as does the NFU. It provides insurance schemes and help to its members in dealing with the multitude of government regulations that affect them— including assistance in securing the money from the state agricultural support programmes for which they lobby. Thus the success of the farm organisations in getting state transfers for their members reinforces their ability to defend their interests. It is notable that large arable farmers have done better from agricultural support policies than small farmers. They are wealthier, better educated and more articulate; they employ staff and arable farming does not require daily all-year attendance, so they can leave their farms more easily to engage in political activity. There are fewer of them to organise. In comparison, livestock farmers are in general poorer, cannot leave their farms easily and are much more numerous.

CONCLUSION

Agricultural policy provides an excellent case-study for deploying the main themes of this book. The effects of the policy can be assessed against the criteria of efficiency and distribution. There are several dimensions in which agricultural policy has increased allocative inefficiency. It has replaced cheaper food from outside the EC with increased output of more costly food in the EC. Because of the failure to achieve a truly common price system, the CAP has not even promoted a more efficient allocation of agricultural resources within the EC. Furthermore it has distorted the allocation of farming resources in relation to the product mix by favouring arable farming over livestock. It has also incurred external costs by transforming the landscape in ways many find displeasing.

The distributional transfers due to agricultural policy have favoured farmers over taxpayers, consumers and conservationists, and have harmed farmers outside the EC by displacing and disrupting their markets. The policy has also been inequitable in that it has given greater benefits to the better-off farmers and regions. Over the long run, it has not succeeded in increasing the real average incomes of farmers relative to the rest of the population. Because the additional profits due to agricultural protection are capitalised in higher land prices, the main beneficiaries are those who owned land prior to the introduction of agricultural support policies.

The general nature of the effects of the CAP were predictable using the basic principles of economic analysis—in particular, the theory of demand and supply. The objectives of the CAP listed at the beginning of the chapter are not mutually consistent. Protecting farm incomes by means of price support is not consistent with increasing efficiency and securing reasonable prices for consumers.

The policy was adopted because of political pressures from farm interests together with general aspirations for social equity. It was further fashioned and sustained as a vehicle for political aspirations for European unity, exploited by farming interests for their sectional benefit. The influence of farm interests, both within government bureaucracy and without as an organised pressure group, illustrates many of the features of the general theory of pressure group behaviour and collective choice. For example, there are larger returns to producers from lobbying than to consumers and taxpayers; organised pressure groups counteract the free-rider problem by providing members with services from which non-members can be excluded; the operation of policy programmes serves the self-interests of the bureaucrats involved.

From a rational perspective agricultural policy has promoted neither efficiency nor equity: in principle, alternative policy instruments would be more effective in achieving such aims. For instance direct income maintenance would be more effective than price support in preventing rural depopulation and poverty. However this ignores psychological and social aspects. It seems that people prefer to be paid by the government for producing unwanted goods and wasting resources rather than getting a direct income subsidy for doing nothing except belong to an officially deserving category. Implicit taxes also conceal the cost of the subsidy programme from those who ultimately finance it. Under such conditions, the political system fails to give the electorate an explicit policy choice, since most voters remain even more unaware of what are the policy's distributive costs and benefits than if explicit taxes and subsidies were used.

NOTES

1. C.N. Morris, 'The CAP', *Fiscal Studies* (March 1980).
2. J. Marsh and P. Swanney, *Agriculture and the European Community*, (George Allen and Unwin, London, 1980).
3. B. Hill, *The CAP, Past, Present and Future* (Methuen, London, 1984).
4. Commission of the EC, *The Agricultural Situation in the Community, 1984 Report*.
5. *The Government's Expenditure Plans 1986–87 to 1988–89*, Cmnd 9702-II (HMSO, London, 1986).
6. F. Duchene, E. Szczepanik and W. Legg, *New Limits on Agriculture* (Croom Helm, London, 1985), p. 26.
7. R. Howarth, *Farming for Farmers?* (Institute of Economic Affairs, London, 1985).
8. National Audit Office, *The Achievements and Cost of the CAP in the UK* (HMSO, London, 1985).
9. A.E. Buckwell, 'The costs of the CAP', in A.M. El-Agraa, *The Economics of the EC* (Philip Allan, Deddington, 1985).
10. A.W. Dilnot and C.N. Morris, 'The distributional effects of the CAP', *Fiscal Studies*, vol. 3, no. 2, July 1982.
11. Howarth, op. cit.
12. Ibid.
13. Duchene, op. cit., p. 14.
14. C. Caspari, *The CAP: The Direction of Change*, Special Report No. 159 (Economic Intelligence Unit, London, 1983).
15. R. Body, *Agriculture: The Triumph and the Shame* (Temple Smith, London, 1982).
16. Duchene, op. cit., p. 31.
17. COPA, *Reactions to the Green Paper of the Commission concerning 'Perspectives for the CAP'* (Brussels, 3 October 1985).
18. W.S. Fel, 'Implementation of the EC's CAP: expectations, fears, failures', *International Organisation*, Summer 1979, p. 37.
19. Howarth, op. cit.
20. National Farmers' Union, *The Way Forward: new directions for agricultural policy* (NFU, London, December 1984).

15 Can Economic Policy-Making be Done Better?

The main aim of this book is to convey an understanding of how economic policy is made in a representative democracy, in the context of British political institutions and policies. Apart from satisfying one's curiosity as to how economic policy-making is undertaken in Britain, the natural question that then arises is whether British economic policy-making could be done better. There must be very few who, in view of Britain's generally acknowledged poor economic performance, do not feel that economic policy-making could be better conducted. There is no shortage of advice on how current economic policies could be changed for the better, or how the institutions and procedures which govern the making of policy could be modified in order to produce better policies. Given such a plethora of conflicting advice, it is not my intention in this short concluding piece to offer any further definitive opinions on the matter. Rather I wish to consider briefly what can be meant by 'better economic policy-making', and place into broad categories the remedies on offer, relating these categories to the main characteristics of economic policy-making that I have described and analysed in the previous pages.

Any economist, if asked to define better economic policy, would say it was one which was more effective in achieving the objectives desired of it, bearing in mind the trade-offs between the objectives that can be chosen given the economic constraints. To some extent this accords with the gut feelings of the electorate, that better economic policies would improve living standards by promoting a faster rate of economic growth, would lower unemployment and keep down inflation; others would emphasise redistribution without the prior requirement of growth.

One can distinguish three fundamental reasons why government has not been able to deliver better economic performance. The first is that government has limited control of the behaviour of all the economic agents in an economy whose interactions largely determine the amount and composition of national output. The socialist solution to this problem is for

358

the government to take on more control of the economy. However this has become a less viable solution as economies have become more integrated into a world economy and hence much more affected by factors beyond the control of a national government. For those who favour enhanced government economic power there are two responses to the problem of international interdependence. One is autarky—reducing the economy's links with the outside world by means of trade and exchange controls, as do the Eastern bloc countries. The other is to promote international governmental links by means of international agencies, like the IMF, or by joint agreements to coordinate economic policies.

Nowadays economists are less confident than in the Keynesian heyday of the extent to which governments in mixed economies can control private sector economic agents by altering market signals through changing taxes, interest rates or exchange rates, for instance. It is not that government has no effect by operating on these policy instruments; the problem is that the effects are not sufficiently predictable, which they have to be if government is to make economic agents behave in ways that achieve the policy's intentions. In recent years the importance of expectations in influencing economic agents' behaviour has been more fully appreciated. When expectations change, agents change their behaviour. If the government cannot gauge how agents' expectations will change it cannot successfully manipulate that behaviour. It is essentially this argument that is used by those economists who are highly dubious of the effectiveness of economic management policies. This argument is based on the view that economic agents have rational expectations because they base their anticipations of what will happen in the future on all the relevant information currently available. Part of this information concerns the activities of government. So if the government changes its policies, economic agents consequently change their expectations and hence their behaviour. Their behaviour is then different from that anticipated by government when it made its policy change. As a result the policy does not have the effects the government intended. It is notable that over the years both the simple policy rules of Keynesians and then of monetarists have not worked out as expected by their advocates.

The limited ability of governments to control economic behaviour is closely related to the second reason for their inability to deliver more successful economic policies. This is the absence of a tried and accepted body of knowledge concerning how mixed market economies, linked to others through international trade and finance, actually work. A realistic and modest assessment is that economics as a discipline offers some valid insights into the workings of the economy, and produces forecasts that are an improvement on simple trend extrapolation and intuition. Individual economists feel they have a rough outline knowledge of how economies function, but have to accept that this knowledge is not soundly based on scientific verification. It is evident from the ideological cleavages amongst economists and their adherence to different schools of thought, that there are many issues on which reasonable and rational practitioners can differ because the empirical evidence, based on statistically observed past behaviour, cannot clearly distinguish between rival theories. In the absence of soundly-based scientific evidence on economic relationships, then plausible reasoning, the subjective interpretation of observed behaviour, and political credos all affect economists' conception of the economic knowledge at their disposal when designing economic policies. That the discipline of economics is in this unsatisfactory state and always has been, is much more apparent in the last ten years than in the 1950s and 1960s when a much greater degree of consensus prevailed.

The third reason for inadequate economic policy-making is the failure to apply the economic knowledge we do possess to attain the desired objectives. This failure can be laid not only at the door of economists as policy advisers, but is also—and in economists' eyes almost entirely— attributable to the politicians, bureaucrats and interest groups who have failed to take the appropriate rational decisions. The catalogue of complaints is quite extensive. Voters and politicians have ignored evidence on the economic constraints and pursued infeasible objectives, such as too rapid a rate of growth or too low a rate of unemployment. They have been unwilling to make the unpleasant choices involved in trading off one objective against another, such as welfare state expenditure versus private consumption, and so have pursued inconsistent objectives. Policy objectives and policy measures have been chopped and changed as different political parties took office. Short-term political expedients have dominated policy-making at the expense of more considered and effective long-term strategies. Governments have allowed policies to be moulded by the need to accommodate powerful political interests and have failed to take a more detached view of the overall implications of their measures on the economy, on a broad spectrum of interests and over the longer term.

So far I have dealt with the causes of unsatisfactory economic policy-making entirely within the perspective of the rational decision-making model. Policies are judged in accordance with their efficiency in achieving given ends. So a valid critique from the rational perspective is that objectives have not been clearly specified nor the trade-offs necessary between competing objectives realistically faced and explicitly selected prior to deciding which policy instruments would best achieve the desired ends. This approach takes for granted that a government conducts itself as a unitary decision-maker and so is capable of specifying its priorities in relation to its policy objectives and then acting in accordance with them.

However an alternative characterisation of economic policy-making is not as a rational procedure but as a political bargaining game. Many instances of this have been documented in the book—government expenditure and taxation-setting, resource allocation in the welfare state, running the public corporations and protecting agriculture, for instance. So if one adheres to the rational model as the way good policy ought to be made then the scope for bargaining between influential political interests should be reduced and the role of rationally-minded economic planners increased.

But this still leaves unresolved the problem of choosing the objectives and priorities for economic policy; that is, determining the social welfare function. I have earlier argued that the welfare economist's solution of by-passing political institutions and directly eliciting evidence on citizens' preferences by their willingness to pay has won very limited acceptance. This is because its ethical basis is neither widely understood nor accepted. Furthermore, the difficulties of quantifying social benefits and costs makes these measurements somewhat arbitrary and hence controvertible.

The political system of representative democracy does not aggregate the diverse preferences of individual citizens into a form which could be characterised as a social welfare function representing the agreed preference rankings of society as a whole. In the political bargaining mode of policy-making the divergent preferences of different interest groups are brought to bear as the parties negotiate policy amongst themselves. The policy outcomes that finally emerge reveal which and whose preferences have been satisfied. So another dimension of inadequate policy-making is the complaint that it has not enabled certain or sufficient political interests to participate. From the perspective of such a pluralist-type critique it is the policy-making process itself which needs improvement, to broaden its legitimacy, quite independently of its outcomes.

More extensive and purposive economic intervention by government is a crucial element of socialist economic policy; it may be accompanied by an emphasis on rational economic planning by which a political and bureaucratic elite establish policy objectives after winning some form of popular mandate for them. However the desire for more direct democratic accountability by government agencies for their actions has grown over the years amongst a wide spectrum of political positions. The desire to combine government economic planning with greater democratic participation boils down to the belief that the rational mode of policy-making can be grafted onto the political bargaining mode to arrive at the best of all worlds. I find this an unrealistic proposition. Economic planning requires a policy-making elite who can determine a stable and enduring ordering of society's preferences and make their policy choices on that basis. If a high degree of participation and involvement of society's diverse interests in policy-making is desired then there is little hope of reaching a stable and consistent set of resource allocation choices for the whole economy. In the absence of consensus, a high degree of political participation would stultify policy-making, unless the extent of government intervention is limited either by decentralisation or by narrowing its scope in the overall economy.

So I conclude that in advocating 'better' economic policy-making, there is, as always in economics, a trade-off. Here, the trade-off is between the desire for greater rationality and hence efficiency in achieving given ends, and the objective of more extensive participation in the determination of both ends and means. There is only a limit to which greater participation can improve the efficiency of policy-making by rendering its outcomes more acceptable. Once that limit has been reached, the merits of rational policy-making have to be traded off against those of political bargaining as a policy-making process. As befits an economist, my preference is for rational policy-making; but one has to recognise its limitations when applied within the actual organisations where collective decision-making in its many forms takes place.

Bibliography

Alt, J.E. and Chrystal, K.A. *Political Economics* (Wheatsheaf, Brighton, 1983).

Arrow, K.J. *Social Choice and Individual Values* (Wiley, New York, 1951).

Ball, R.J. *Report of Committee on Policy Optimisation* (HMSO, London, 1978).

Barnett, J. *Inside the Treasury* (André Deutsch, London, 1982).

Beenstock, M. and Parker, M. 'Abolish the poverty trap', *Economic Affairs*, vol. 6, No. 1, 1985.

Beesley, M.E. and Kettle, P. 'The Leitch Committee's recommendations and the management of the road programme', *Regional Studies*, vol. 13, pp. 513–29.

Bentley, A.J. *The Process of Government* (Principia Press, Evanston Ill. 1949).

Beveridge, W. *Social Insurance and Allied Services*, Cmnd 6404 (HMSO, London, 1942).

Body, R. *Agriculture: The Triumph and the Shame* (Temple Smith, London, 1982).

Boulding, K.E. *The Principles of Economic Policy* (Staples Press, London, 1959).

Breton, A. *The Economic Theory of Representative Government* (Aldine, Chicago, 1974).

Buckwell, A.E. 'The costs of the CAP', in El-Agraa, A.M. *The Economics of the EC* (Philip Allan, Deddington, Oxford, 1985).

Caspari, C. *The CAP: The Direction of Change*, Special Report no. 159 (Economic Intelligence Unit, London, 1983).

Castle, B. *The Castle Diaries 1974–76* (Weidenfeld and Nicolson, London, 1980).

Clarke, R. *Public Expenditure, Management and Control* (Macmillan, London, 1978).

Coates, R.D. *Teachers Unions and Interest Group Politics* (Cambridge University Press, Cambridge, 1972).

Commission of the EC, *The Agricultural Situation in the Community, 1984 Report*.

Crossman, R. *The Diaries of a Cabinet Minister* (Hamish Hamilton, London, 1975).

Davis, E.H., Dilnot, A.W. and Kay, J.A. 'The social security green paper', *Fiscal Studies*, vol. 6, no. 3, 1985.

D.E.S. *Better Schools*, Cmnd 9469 (HMSO, London, 1985).

DHSS, *Reform of Social Security*, vol. 2, Cmnd 9518 (HMSO, London, 1985).

Dilnot, A.W., Kay, J.A. and Morris, C.N. (1984) *The Reform of Social Security* (Oxford University Press, Oxford).

Dilnot, A.W. and Stark, G. 'The poverty trap, tax cuts and social security', *Fiscal Studies*, vol. 7, no. 1, 1986.

Dilnot, A.W. and Morris, C.N. 'The distributional effects of the CAP', *Fiscal Studies*, vol. 3, no. 2, July 1982.

Downs, A. *An Economic Theory of Democracy* (Harper and Row, New York, 1957).

Duchene, F., Szczepanik, E. and Legg, W. *New Limits on Agriculture* (Croom Helm, London, 1985).

Fel, W.S. 'Implementation of the EC's CAP: expectations, fears, failures', *International Organisation* (Summer 1979).

Glynn, A. *The Economic Case Against Pit Closures* (NUM, Sheffield, 1984).

Ham, C. *Health Policy in Britain* (Macmillan, London, 1985).

Hayek, F. *The Road to Serfdom* (Routledge and Kegan Paul, London, 1944).

Hayek, F. *Individualism and Economic Order* (Routledge and Kegan Paul, London, 1949).

Heath, A.C., Jowell, R. and Curtis, J. *How Britain Votes* (Pergamon Press, Oxford, 1985).

Heclo, H. and Wildavsky, A. *The Private Government of Public Money* (Macmillan, London, 1981).

Henderson, D. *Innocence and Design* (Basil Blackwell, Oxford, 1986).

Hill, B. *The CAP, Past, Present and Future* (Methuen, London, 1984).

Homer, A. and Burrows, R. *Tolley's Tax Guide* (Tolley Publishing Co., Croydon, 1984).

Howarth, R. *Farming for Farmers?* (Institute of Economic Affairs, London, 1985).

Kay, J.A. and M.A. King, *The British Tax System* (Oxford University Press, Oxford, 1983).

Kay, J.A. *The Economy and the 1985 Budget* (Basil Blackwell, Oxford, 1985).

Keynes, J.M. *The General Theory of Employment, Interest and Money* (Macmillan, London, 1936).

King, A. (ed.), *The British Prime Minister* (Macmillan, London, 1985).

Kogan, M. *The Politics of Education* (Penguin, London, 1971).

Jackson, P.M. *The Political Economy of Bureaucracy* (Philip Allan, Deddington, Oxford, 1982).

Lange, Oskar and Taylor, F.M. *On the Economic Theory of Socialism*

(Minneapolis, 1938).

LeGrand, J. *The Strategy of Equality* (Allen and Unwin, London, 1982).

Leitch, G. *Report of the Advisory Committee on Trunk Road Assessment* (HMSO, London, 1978).

Marglin, S. *Public Investment Criteria* (Allen and Unwin, London, 1967).

Marsh, J. and Swanney, P. *Agriculture and the European Community* (Allen and Unwin, London, 1980).

Marsh, R. *Off the Rails* (Weidenfeld and Nicolson, London, 1978).

Maude, A. *et al.*, *The Right Approach to the Economy* (Conservative Central Office, London, 1977).

Mayston, D. and Terry, F. *Public Domain, A Yearbook for the Public Sector* (Public Finance Foundation, London, 1986).

Meade Committee, *The Structure and Reform of Direct Taxation* (Allen and Unwin, London, 1978).

Mishan, E. *Introduction to Political Economy* (Hutchinson, London, 1982).

Morris, C.N. 'The CAP', *Fiscal Studies* (March, 1980).

Morrison, H. *Socialization and Transport* (Constable, London, 1933).

Mosley, P. *The Making of Economic Policy*, (Wheatsheaf, Brighton, 1984).

National Audit Office, *The Achievements and Cost of the CAP in the UK* (HMSO, London, 1985).

National Audit Office, *The Rayner Scrutiny Programmes, 1979 to 1983* (HMSO, London, 1986).

National Farmers' Union, *The Way Forward: New Directions for Agricultural Policy* (NFU, London, December, 1984).

Niskanen, W. *Bureaucracy and Representative Government* (Aldine, Chicago, 1971).

Olson, M. *The Logic of Collective Action* (Harvard University Press, Cambridge, Mass., 1965).

Olson, M. *The Rise and Decline of Nations* (Yale University Press, New Haven, Conn., 1982).

Pliatsky, L. *Getting and Spending* (Basil Blackwell, Oxford, 1982).

Plowden Report, *Controlling Public Expenditure*, Cmnd 1432 (HMSO, London, 1961).

Robinson, A. and Sandford, C.T. *Tax Policy-Making in the U.K.* (Heinemann, London, 1983).

Sandford, C.T. *Hidden Costs of Taxation* (Institute of Fiscal Studies, London, 1973).

Self, P. *Econocrats and the Policy Process*, (Macmillan, London, 1975).

Shipley, P. *Directory of Pressure Groups* (Bowker, Essex, 1979).

Stibbard, P. 'Measuring public expenditure', *Economic Trends*, August (HMSO, London, 1985).

Stockman, D.A. *The Triumph of Politics* (The Bodley Head, London, 1986).

Treasury, 'Making a budget', *Economic Progress Report*, no. 153, January (Treasury, London, 1983).

Wootton, G. *Pressure Politics in Contemporary Britain* (D.C. Heath, Lexington, Mass., 1978).

Index

National Health Service 133, 161,
175-82, 186, 187, 192, 199, 238,
274-6, 284, 285, 296
National Insurance 81, **82**, 88,
102, 283, 284, **301**-6, 307, 312,
313, 325, 326
National Union of Farmers 197,
351, 352, **353**, **355**
National Union of Mineworkers
40, 46, 48, 53
nationalisation/nationalised
industry 13, 24, 40, 42-3, **125**,
132, 154, 174, 240, 247, **248-9**,
250-65
need **131**, 176, 274, **279-80**, 284,
289-92, 294, 302, 306, 308,
316, 317-18
negative income tax **314**-17
neoclassical economics **128**, 284
non-market allocation/goods 21,
22, 135, 165, 169, 171, 172, 183,
184-5, 188, 248, 273, 283, 287,
289-97, 298
normative economics (*see also*
welfare economics) **36**, **216**,
217, 233

objectives (of economic policy)
4, 30, 36, 144, 156, 175, 179,
180, 182, 183, 188, 199, 203,
209, 215, 216, 217, 235-36, 237,
238, 239, 240, 242, 252-5,
258-62, 270, 277-82, 321, 323,
329, 332, 358, 359
Office of Fair Trading **126**
opportunity cost **49**, 53, 54, 114,
124, 170, 179, 225, 227, 259
optimal, optimality **219-20**,
221-2, 236-7, 259, 261

Pareto efficiency **57**, 59, **115-16**,
137, 146, **222-3**
Parliament 15, 26, 28-9, 70, 74,

76, 100, 101, 103, 104, 178, 179,
191, 197-8, 229, 236, 248, 257
pensions 95, 281, 283, 287, 303,
304, 309, 310-13, 317, 321, 322,
327
performance indicators (NHS)
182, 185
planning 12, 33, **43**-6, 55, 75,
128, 176, 182, 204, 215, 221,
223-5, 239, 251, 264, 361
pluralism 38, 133, 136, 178,
208-9, 238, 278, 323, 361
plurality **146-7**, 158, 162
political bargaining 3, 5, 6, 73-5,
136, 144, 186, 188, 192, **203-8**,
210, 215, 237, 238, 239, 243,
267, 271, 278, 298, 361, 362
political business cycle **153-4**
political interests 3, **31**, 37, 73,
74, 78, 104, 108, 118, 125, 128,
130, **135**, 143, 161, 188, **191**,
192-212, 228-31, 233, 237, 240,
243, 251, 256, 261, 264-5, 267,
277, 295, 298, 319-22, 323,
333, 350-5, 360-1
politicians 26-7, 152-9, 167, 169,
172, 178-9, 186, 187, 189, 195,
210, 211, 221, 233, 237, 243,
270, 290, 360
politician's surplus **157-9**
politics-economic theory of
153-61, 211-12
positive economics 4, **36**, **216**
poverty trap **94**, **307-8**, 309,
318
preferences 6, 26-7, 113, 115, 129,
132-3, 142-3, 144, 145, 149-50,
151, 152, 156-7, 158, 160, 161,
162, 166, 172, 174, 178, 186,
187, 189, 203, 211, **217-22**, 226,
237, 239, 243, 289, 295, 361;
see also time preference
present value **226**-7, 232